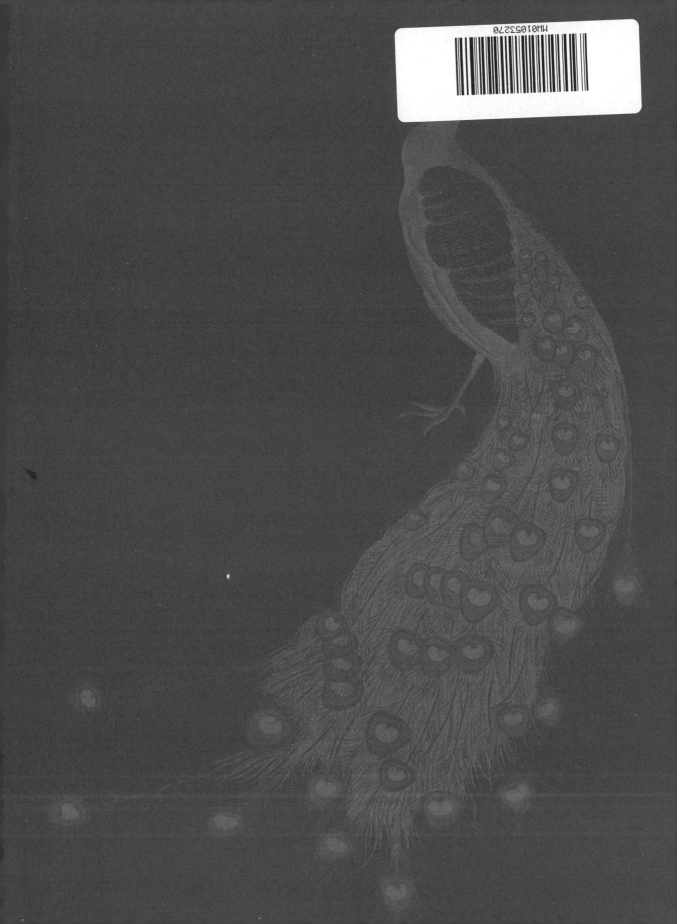

MW010532270

ADELE NOZEDAR

The Secret Language of Birds

A Treasury of Myths, Folklore
& Inspirational True Stories

HARPER
element

For Adam

For all those who understand the World Without Words

And for all the birds
(especially Saskia and Willa)

He who understands has wings

(Rig Veda)

HarperElement
An Imprint of HarperCollins*Publishers*
77–85 Fulham Palace Road
Hammersmith, London W6 8JB

The website address is www.thorsonselement.com

and *HarperElement* are registered trademarks of
HarperCollins Publishers Ltd

First published by HarperElement 2006

1 3 5 7 9 10 8 6 4 2

Copyright © Adele Nozedar 2006

Adele Nozedar asserts the moral right to be
identified as the author of this work

Illustrations copyright © Finlay Cowan 2006

A catalogue record for this book is
available from the British Library

ISBN-13 978-0-00-721904-9
ISBN-10 0-00-721904-0

Printed and bound in
Thailand by Imago

All rights reserved. No part of this publication may be
reproduced, stored in a retrieval system, or transmitted,
in any form or by any means, electronic, mechanical,
photocopying, recording or otherwise, without the prior
permission of the publishers.

We wish we could fly,
We wish we could hear the tiniest of sounds
And swoop gracefully and swiftly
To the most definite of conclusions.

The wind and wing's secret is this;

We do fly,
We do hear the tiniest of sounds.
We do arc and swoop, with ultimate grace
To the most definite of conclusions.

Jont, Mexico City, August 2005

"In a country the colour of a pigeon's breast I acclaimed the flight of 1,000,000 doves. I saw them invade the forests, black with desires, and the walls and seas without end ... I saw a pale, white dove, flower of the desert. She refused to understand. Along the length of a cloud a superb man and woman danced the carmagnole of love. The Dove closed herself in her wings and swallowed the key forever."

Max Ernst

Contents

How it Started:
The attainable border of birds

"The Language of Birds is very ancient, and like other ancient modes of speech, very elliptical: little is said, but much is meant and understood."

Gilbert White

Where I live, in Wales, could be perceived by many to be remote. I am 2,500 feet up in the foothills of Pen y Fan, the highest mountain in South Wales. The bird life here is rich and varied, and despite reports to the contrary all the birds seem to live together with a great degree of harmony, from the peregrine falcons (fastest creatures on the planet) to the tiny wrens (who seem to have some sort of time-share agreement with the house martins whose empty nests they occupy during the winter months!)

For me, though, the idea of birds as messengers gradually came to be more than a theory but an actual reality.

I suppose I should try to explain.

It probably sounds a bit strange, and I didn't tell anyone what was happening for a while. After all, what would you'd have done?

However, certain birds seemed to be more prominent than others on some days, and it got to the point where I couldn't really ignore them any longer … so, just as a sort of experiment, I started to ascribe the characteristics of certain friends to the birds I'd notice, and it got to the point where if

I spotted an owl, for example, I would know that a particular person would make contact that day or would need me to call them. This might sound strange, but you should try it – you seriously should – just make sure your associations are consistent and you'll hopefully see what I mean.

Then I started noticing that on some days the birds behaved slightly differently. Just little things. There might be a buzzard sitting silently on the ground, for example, not moving as I passed by, which they don't usually do, or a robin and a wren sitting on a branch together (again, unusual behaviour since both are pretty territorial). How to interpret what the messages were was the tricky bit though, and as to explaining it to anyone …

One day, however, I mentioned the idea to a friend and was encouraged to find that he thought the idea was not only feasible but also entirely possible.

As my friend was talking we were sitting by the stream in my garden and a kingfisher flew past his shoulder, the bird almost invisible except for a blur of iridescent blue. This bird has many of the qualities of my friend, coincidentally – moves fast, hard to catch hold of, likes fish – I was inspired to continue with my research, and found encouragement in lots of places and with lots of people.

Then the most amazing thing happened.

I found that what I'd thought to be my own personal discovery, my own invention, was in fact part of a very ancient belief system, which has been largely ignored in recent years.

I have to tell you, this was something of a shock. But it was reassuring, as you might imagine, to know that I wasn't going crazy, and that what I was experiencing was a continuation of a very, very old belief, which I'd had not a single clue about.

I hasten to add that I am no expert ornithologist, either, beyond recogniz-ing all the usual birds that everyone knows, and I still don't have any really good binoculars!

I started doing some more serious research. Part of this involved asking people what sort of bird they'd like to be and why, and, as an afterthought, their birth sign. I got some funny answers, some inspiring answers and some unexpected answers. Some of these answers, from all around the world, are in this book.

People often ask me which bird 'belongs' to me. Well, although we all have a little bit of every bird inside us, since we are connected to one another and to the greater universe, there is one particular bird I resonate to, really by default. This is a small hawk called a merlin, and there's a specific reason for this – I wouldn't have chosen this bird for myself. (If asked I would probably choose the seagull, for its flying power, its adaptability and its anonymity – and its ability to get away with quite a lot, such as stealing ice creams from small children!) I do have another, secret, bird, too.

Here's the story of how the merlin came into my life. It all started with a life-threatening illness, which is often the catalyst for a life-changing experience.

It was a depressing, rain-lashed November day about seven years ago. It was a Saturday afternoon and I was sprawled on the sofa downstairs. I couldn't get the fire going, everything was wet (and in any case fire-starting is something I'm completely useless at) so I was trying to keep warm primarily by shivering, since I was recovering after an operation that had left me in a great deal of pain, weak and barely able to walk. Truly, I had to have a walking stick and everything, and I'm not an old lady! In any case, I was alone in the house and feeling thoroughly sorry for myself. Just thinking about it now makes me want to put my hand to my brow and sigh loudly. You know that kind of mood.

Then there was a thump at the window next to where I was malingering.

I looked out to see a bird perched on the ledge looking back at me. We studied one another for a short while. I hadn't ever seen a bird like this before. It didn't seem to be going anywhere and after a while I thought it might be a good idea to go outside to see if I could see what it was, as it (no doubt) flew away.

It was with some effort that I managed to drag myself up, negotiate my way outside and around the back of the house, holding on to the walls for support and getting pretty sodden in the process. I seem to remember I was barefoot, too – big mistake.

I looked up into the rain-soaked sky; no bird was visible. But lo and behold it was still there on the ledge. I lurched right up to it. It was a small kind of falcon with speckled markings and a very direct stare. It let me stroke it freely without flinching away or showing any kind of fear, and I thought at the time that it might have stunned itself against the window. For some reason the presence of this small bird was very reassuring. It was a nice bird. I liked it a lot.

Back inside the house I was too exhausted to find the bird book that would tell me what kind of bird it was. Instead I fell into a deep, dream-ridden sleep. There were birds in my dream, too, but that's another story.

To my astonishment the bird was still there the next day and again let me touch it. In all, she was there for three weeks and assisted my recovery greatly (since I was pretty keen to get myself up and outside to visit her) until I was strong enough to walk unsupported, albeit slowly. I even picked up and handled the bird, and again she showed no fear whatsoever.

The bird was a merlin. I didn't know then that you're not meant to handle wild birds in this way; however, the bird still appears from time to time, often around about the same time of year, and always seems to lead me to where I'm going, both on a physical and spiritual level. It's an odd thing, but I can be with other people and they don't see the bird; once she flew right over the heads of myself and three friends, so low that I could have almost touched her, but no one else noticed. If someone had told me this before my interest began I probably wouldn't have believed them, but I know now that there is more to these creatures than meets the eye.

I still wonder sometimes; was this bird 'sent' to me? If so, was it an emissary of 'angels', or did it have some kind of sense that I needed it there? I can't answer these questions; what I do know is that its presence had a profound effect on me, for good.

There is of course another fact about birds that we must be aware of, which is that many of them are diminishing in numbers and species are even dying out. The sparrow population in the UK is down to 62 per cent of what it used to be just 25 years ago, for example. Intensive farming methods, manicured, too-tidy gardens, pesticides, herbicides and the chemicals we use to 'organize' our planet are all contributory factors. Did you know, for example, that slug pellets are partly responsible for the decline in the population of the song thrush? The slug eats the pellet, the bird eats the slug, and the result is a dead bird. We often fail to see the link; we can fail to see the bigger picture.

In starting to remember what the Ancients knew – that there is dimension to birds beyond them simply being ornamental creatures – I hope we'll also begin to see the whole world in a different way. More than anything I hope that you'll start to understand for yourself the secrets of the birds around you, and that you'll start to learn something of their language.

Adele Nozedar
Torpantau, Wales
September 2005

The Secrets of the Birds

> "How do you know but every bird that cuts the airy way Is an immense world of delight, closed by your senses five?"

William Blake, *The Marriage of Heaven and Hell*

Bird Watching

Do you ever watch birds?

They're fascinating creatures. In fact, just about every single country in the world has its birdwatchers, some mere hobbyists, others more serious ornithologists. You can take a bird-watching holiday anywhere you choose on this planet, and wherever you decide to go, you will meet with experts in birds from all walks of life. In fact, the interest in birds is so huge that two of the major organizations I have spoken to, the Royal Society for the Protection of Birds (RSPB) in the UK and the Audubon Society in the USA, both say that it is impossible to count the numbers of people with more than a passing interest in birds.

The fact that there are over one million members of the RSPB in Britain is testimony to the popularity of our avian friends, but did you also know that the bird-watching industry is worth £200 million per year? Or that travel costs within the UK alone for 'twitching' purposes amount to some £25 million? In the USA, the Audubon Society continues to flourish more than a hundred years after its inception.

Put into this context, then, the fascination with birds seems obvious.

However, there's a partially forgotten aspect of man's fascination with winged creatures that goes far beyond the desire to seek out rarities or mark

scorecards or travel the world in search of unusual birds. It is that birds have played an important role in the material and spiritual world of mankind for thousands of years. The cave paintings at Lascaux, for example, which were discovered in 1940, include a prominent scene which has been named 'Death of the Bird Man' and which indicates that there was probably some sort of a bird cult as far back as Upper Palaeolithic times. There are plenty of other historical examples, from all over the world, which give proof of the importance of our bird friends.

OMENS AND WEATHER LORE

In Paulo Coelho's *The Alchemist*, the main character, Santiago, makes his decisions by watching omens carefully, especially those given by birds; eventually Santiago wins love, glory and riches; indeed, Paulo Coelho operates much of his own life by observing the signs and omens around him.

For thousands of years, and in cultures all over the world, birds were used as a divinatory tool. Divination by watching birds is known as orthomancy. Their flight patterns were observed, the type of bird was taken into account and their calls and cries were analysed; sometimes this divination took the form of an analysis of bird's or animal's entrails! (This method was known as 'haruspicy', origin of the word 'auspices' — admittedly, not great news for the creature who had to be sacrificed.)

In the Qur'an, the word for 'bird' is synonymous with that for 'fate'.

Indeed, the old practice, which is still carried out of course, of snapping the breastbone of the chicken, turkey or goose with someone else to see who gets the longest part, and hence who gets the 'wish', has its origins in a different form of divination. The bone of a duck would be examined to determine what the weather was likely to do, with the tradition being that a dark-coloured bone would denote a severe winter, and a lighter coloured one would show the opposite to be true; in the same way the breastbone of the goose would be dried and then carefully examined to forecast the weather. This information was then used by (amongst others) the Teutonic knights to decide on their two annual military campaigns during Summer and Winter.

As modern methods of forecasting the weather are becoming more and more accurate, it is easy to forget how such information would have been crucial at a time when the planting or harvesting of crops had to be decided by other means. A more gruesome version of interpreting the future from a part of a bird is the Vietnamese practice of boiling the foot of a cock, which is seen as a symbol of the universe, and using the foot in fortune-telling practises.

In some parts of the world, there is still the belief that birds can foretell electrical storms and earthquakes. In particular, the hoopoe has this skill; indeed, at one point in the Old World it was the chief of the birds, because it was said to be able to detect 'the electrical God in the Earth'. The name 'hoopoe' actually takes the meaning of its name from the Greek 'to see' and this could indicate the bird's ability to 'see' the electrical charge given off by storms. This ability of the hoopoe to detect piezoelectrical charges is currently being investigated by Japanese and American scientists. It's wonderful that new scientific knowledge is able to give veracity to what are often thought of as old wives' tales or simple superstitions!

Augury

There are more reminders in our language that bring us back to the importance of the messages from birds.

The Latin word 'augury', which is taken to mean an omen or portent (or in Roman times signified one who was able to interpret natural signs in order to see into the future, i.e. the 'augur'), has its root in the meaning of the word 'bird', according to Ogilvie and Annandale's *The Students English Dictionary*, published by Blackie and Son in 1913:

> **Augur** – (Latin 'augur' and French 'avis', a bird, and root of gusto, to taste; or akin to augeo, I increase, whence augment). One who among the ancients foretold future events by observing the flight of birds, and their chattering and motions, and by other omens; a soothsayer.

The augurs, i.e. those who had the necessary skills to carry out auguries, formed such an important part in Roman society that they travelled with the armies and kept cages of chickens with them, from which they would extract the relevant information about the likely outcomes of battles. These birds were looked after by an official called the Pullarius. If the chickens ate their food then all was going to be well, but if they refused their feed or showed signs of querulousness then the signs were not so good.

However, not everyone paid such close attention to the birds. One Roman general, in response to his augur's report that the chickens were not feeding and therefore the fleet should not commence battle, got very annoyed that his plans were seemingly being thwarted by a cage full of chickens. His response was simply: 'Let them drink instead', and he threw the birds overboard …

Understanding the Language of Birds

Why should this be? Why should birds have had such an important part to play in the lives of the ancient Greeks, the Romans, Native American Indians, the ancient Mexicans, the Celts, the Egyptians, the Mayans, the Indians and just about every other society and spiritual belief system you care to mention? I think I have part of an answer.

THE UNINVENTED WORD

Cast your self back to a time before language existed, before words were spoken or needed to be spoken … Cast yourself back to a time when thoughts were shapes and symbols rather than words.

It is often difficult to even see stars in built-up cityscapes, let alone see what they're telling us, yet we still read our newspaper horoscopes – often with little or no contact with the actual origins of that information. The meanings hidden in the flight patterns of the birds are, for many of us, even further away than that.

Everything starts out with an idea: every invention starts as a need for something; the need is recognized and the 'object' given a shape before it is given a word. Every solid object or philosophical concept starts out from a formless void and is brought into the 'real' world by means of sheer force of will and effort. We are conditioned to think in the words we have invented. As human beings, we have lived with language and words for such a long time that it is very difficult for us to go back to that still space inside ourselves where there are no words. To find that space inside is a skill that some can enhance through meditation; the mechanics of sport or exercise can help attain that state of being for others.

For early man, the survival of the species relied on a form of communication that went beyond the ability to speak out loud. It was a more primitive, animalistic means of getting a message across. If you have pets or keep animals you will know how they communicate with one another in ways that don't involve making a sound. We still have these skills, all of us, but we don't think we need to use them, and we are often taken by surprise when they come into play unexpectedly. The following may seem a little academic, but bear with me for a short while.

INTUITION

The Naskapi Indians on the Labrador Peninsula lived in heavily wooded areas, and they lived by hunting. They hunted in small nomadic bands and their survival relied on them being able to locate the right places to hunt – this was of course a life-or-death matter. They didn't often see one another, and in order to be guided to the correct place to hunt they relied on something called 'Mista Peo', which means 'my friend' or 'the voice inside'. This instinct was sometimes backed up with divination from the burned bones of birds and animals. Because the Naskapi rarely saw one another they had no need for an organized religion or society. The 'voice inside' worked in complete harmony with, and as a part of, the Universe. The Naskapi had no need to externalize their God. For them, hunting was a spiritual occupation and respect for the animal was a prerequisite.

As man's society developed, he started to look for signs outside himself to tell him that he was on the right track. He extrapolated information from water, he cast stones or bones, he watched cloud formations, and he watched the flight of birds and the types of birds that appeared. Then humans decided that they needed to communicate these messages to each other, and language and writing was born.

THE INVENTED WORD

Legend has it that Mercury, the Messenger of the Gods, the great communicator, actually invented the alphabet by watching the flight patterns of birds – those of cranes in particular. If you get a chance to watch cranes in flight, their wings form peculiarly hypnotic zigzag patterns that flow like sparkling lines of darkness against the sky; it's easy to understand how this belief came about. Robert Graves in *The White Goddess* tells us that the secret symbols of the alphabet were kept in a crane-skin bag, which makes perfect sense, given that the Alaskans also used to use the skins of cranes, swans and eagles as bags since these skins are very strong. Early alphabets were often carved into wood or rock and the easiest way to do this is to create sharp lines rather than curves. In this context, we can understand the link with the patterns made in the air by the wings of the crane, which is one of the oldest birds in existence, as we will see.

Lecterns often bear an eagle, which was the symbol of St John, the 'bearer of the word'.

The letters of the alphabet carried great power. They were not just letters, but calendars, calculators, symbols and concepts of divinity, and the ability to be able to use these symbols, to be able to read and write, was a sacred art reserved for the privileged few.

Rossetti's Chaffinch

Dante Gabriel Rossetti, whose beloved wife Elizabeth Siddal died of a laudanum overdose, believed that her spirit visited him in the form of a chaffinch, and he told his doctor that he had seen her every day for two years. His famous painting 'Bella Beatrix', which was painted after her death and now hangs in London's Tate Gallery, shows Lizzie, head thrown back in spiritual ecstasy, holding her hands cupped to receive something; nearby is a red bird carrying a white poppy – symbols of sleep (the flower) and death (the red bird).

WINGED MESSENGERS

With birds and their language, and the secrets they hold for us, it is worth remembering that these creatures have existed on the planet for far longer than mankind. Birds have been here for 150 million years; in William Fiennes' book *The Snow Geese* he describes the aforementioned (sandhill) crane as 'the oldest species of bird in existence, known to have lived in Nebraska in the Miocene, nine million years ago'. There is further evidence of the extreme age of the sacred ibis, whose fossil records go back 60 million years, and we have evidence of records of this bird and its part in human history which goes back 5,000 years.

Homo sapiens is a relative newcomer, and has been on this earth for approximately 35,000 years. There is little wonder, then, that these winged creatures, which the ancient Mexicans believed belonged in the fourth dimension – the dimension of fire – and which can also exist under water, on the water and in the air, would have some wisdom to impart to us; and indeed, that the Gods had sent the birds here for the purpose of giving us messages.

Is it any coincidence, then, that the feather or quill was/is a popular means of communicating the written word? And that the French phrase *nom de plume*, taken to mean 'pen name', actually means 'name of the feather'?

UNEXPECT THE EXPECTED

The William Blake quote at the beginning of this chapter strikes a particular resonance with me, because I discovered it by accident at about the same time that I started really to understand about the nature of birds as messengers and watch them closely to see if I could discern what they were saying. The quote tells us to expect the unexpected, to look at things in a new way, to ask questions of the things around us which may often be taken for granted, to assume nothing.

Over recent years we may have had to put our telepathic or psychic skills on the back burner while we developed different talents and means of communication as our survival mechanisms changed. The Naskapi's hunting grounds, for example, no longer exist in the way they did, since mining and the building of 20 hydroelectric dams on the Labrador Peninsula altered the landscape conclusively and the people have had to adapt their lifestyles to fit in with a modern world. With telephones, the Internet and satellite communication we are able to transmit and receive information in an extraordinarily efficient way. But communication isn't just about facts and figures; it's about instinctive feelings and the hidden 'other' world. The world without words.

We still, however, have these earlier skills, like those of the Naskapi, born of a need to survive out in the wild. Often we do not realize how powerful these latent talents are until we find we need to call on them; a mother suddenly realizing her child is in danger, for example, or close friends knowing when one or other has some important news.

It is still possible to tap into our often-dormant psychic abilities. I believe that by taking notice of the messages given to us by birds we can rediscover our hidden selves and start to reawaken our telepathic and intuitive powers. It's like exercising a muscle.

All we have to do is watch, listen and understand.

The secret language of the birds is available to everyone.

The Messages of the Birds:
'A little bird told me ...'

"**B**irds are such adept communicators that 'the language of the birds' is symbolic of the special rapport between animals and humankind. Being conversant with that language implies the possession of insightful wisdom about nature and often includes the ability to predict the future."

Elizabeth Atwood Lawrence, *Hunting the Wren*

Although we seem largely to have forgotten about the nature of birds as messengers, once we start accepting the possibility, the next thing to do is to look for evidence. And evidence there is in abundance. This chapter takes a brief look at just a few of the aspects we'll be looking at in closer detail later in this book.

I have to tell you, as I'm sitting here writing, I am listening to my first cuckoo of the year, and actually hearing it is a wonderful reminder that all nations, everywhere, view the call of the cuckoo as a harbinger of Spring and of better times ahead!

How do Birds Speak to Us?

The answer to this question is simple: birds speak to us in many ways, some simple, some more complex.

First we'll investigate the symbolism of birds, taking the premise that what was true for 'ancient' man is relevant for us today. Birds move through time and space and carry their stories and messages with them; they have no need to count the days and years in the way man does so assiduously. When we start to investigate the historical symbolic meanings attached to birds we find that nothing at all has changed from thousands of years ago to the present day. Myth and legend also gives us clues. Similar themes occur all around the world. You'll see the word 'ancient' used almost by default. The myths of the Greeks and the Romans, to name just two cultures, tell us an awful lot about why certain associations are linked to specific birds, and this knowledge is all part of understanding the messages these creatures have for us. Superstitions and old wives' tales occasionally have their origins in fact, although the scientific background for these folk beliefs may sometimes still be elusive. It is only recently, for example, that we have known for sure that some birds' senses are more advanced than those of humans; for instance, condors can physically see the thermals that carry them effortlessly up into the sky.

Our personal experiences with birds can give us information, too, and can help us access a wider understanding of the world.

It's surprising just how many people have stories about how birds have touched them personally. Often the incidents may have been half-forgotten, but a chance reminder can trigger the memory. Recently I met someone who has had relationships with hawks for most of his life, having been given his first bird as a child. He spoke about the inherent freedom within the relationship and the dilemma of 'training' a wild creature up to a certain point while allowing it to retain its nature. He described how, every time he watches his bird fly away he knows that she may not return.

Birds have long been symbols of human properties and feelings and personality types. But, a language of birds? It's not so far-fetched as it might seem. Historically there have been certain human beings who were able to understand what the birds were telling them, among them Apollonius of Tyana, Anaximander (both of whom were also reputed to have been magicians) and St Francis of Assisi.

The Ancients

In Greek, the actual word for 'bird' could also be used as a synonym for a forewarning, or omen, or indeed a message from Heaven, so the idea is certainly nothing new. As early as 414 BC, the Greek play-wright Aristophanes wrote a play called *The Birds*, in which the birds form their own kingdom in the sky in order to intercede between the Gods and Humans.

A bird flying into a house foretells an important message.

> We are your oracles too … Whatever you are going to do, whether it's a matter of trade, of feeding the family, or getting married, you always consult the birds. Why, you even use the word bird for anything that brings good luck or bad luck; whether it's a chance remark, or a sneeze, an unexpected meeting, a noise, a servant or a donkey, you call it a bird! So you see, we really are the oracle you depend on most!

It may well be that we have turned our birds into angels, using the wings and feathers as a symbol of a celestial creature who lives somewhere between Heaven and Earth.

The Old Testament

> The birds of the air will carry your voice,
> or some winged creature will tell the matter
> *Ecclesiastes 10:20*

Among the Jewish people, too, birds were considered to have supernatural knowledge, probably again because of the fact that they lived in the air, and there are lots of references to this. In the Psalms there is a direct comparison of the soul of man being like a bird:

> Flee as a bird to your mountain
> *Psalm 11:1*

The Jews believed that the souls of man were kept in a huge cage, called a 'Columbarium' – the word 'Columba' also means 'dove' – and even now the image of a cage full of birds represents souls. Indeed, one of the symbols of the dove is of a pure and righteous spirit. It is still an old custom in some parts of the world that if someone dies, the windows are opened so that their spirit can fly free.

The 'Green Language'

Delving in another direction, there is a lot of evidence about a secret language, called the Language of the Birds, or 'the Green Language'.

> The reader ... needs to understand the Language of the Birds, to understand the word games of the phonetic Cabala, and to know how to read the Stars. He must question the Tarot and the Zodiac to discover the secret of Arcadia.
>
> **Jean Pierre Deloux and Jacques Bretigny,** *Rennes le Chateau, Capital Secret de l'Histoire de France*

The Language of the Birds is a sort of code, relying on wordplay, puns, coded messages and double meanings, which would appear to give the key to many hidden secrets and mysteries. Bird imagery forms a large part of this code, which appears in astrology, alchemy, the Kabbalah, the tarot – everywhere. A good example of this comes in Robert Graves's *The White Goddess*, a fascinating book that investigates, among other things, the Gods and Goddesses, myths and fables and their origins, folklore and the origin of magical symbols. Apparently, one poet asking the other 'When shall we meet again?' could receive the reply, 'When the brown-plumaged rook perches on the fir below the fortress of Seolae.' The letters would spell out the word CRAS, which is the Latin for 'tomorrow'. A somewhat cryptic method, admittedly, but there may have been a time when this kind of information needed to be kept secret!

The ancient art of alchemy, which people popularly perceive to be the attempt by man to turn base metal into gold but which is in fact about both material and spiritual transmutation, is rich in bird and animal symbolism. These symbols were used not only because they accurately described the processes which were going on, but also because they formed a sort of code which would be understood only by initiates into the ancient arts, which understandably had to be kept secret.

Another sect rich in secret symbolism were the Knights Templars. The subject of the Templars is vast and there are many books dealing with the subject. In short, the Templars held arcane knowledge and information, and part of what they were involved in included the design and construction of sacred buildings, particularly Cathedrals. The last Grand Master of the Templars was burnt at the stake (they were declared a heretical sect) and after this happened the rest of the Templars scattered to the four winds, taking their secrets with them.

Tarot expert Jean-Claude Flornoy, in a fascinating essay entitled 'The Language of the Birds', tells how he stumbled on one of the secrets:

> At the Romanesque-Byzantine abbey built by Eleanor d'Aquitaine at Souillac, the capital [top] of the 8th ambulatory pillar depicts doves putting their beaks into an owl's ear. This is Athena's owl of course, and represents access to knowledge … During one of my visits to Souillac I calmly pursued my labyrinth while paying special attention to the different images sculpted on the capitals in the choir. Coming to the 8th pillar and not understanding the image, I put my back against it and closed my eyes, creating as much stillness as I could, and waited. I was not disappointed. After some minutes of meditative idling, my ears were ripped apart by a terrible noise. Emerging from my torpor with a powerful shock and opening my eyes, I found that I was alone except for a tourist who was standing at the entrance in the process of putting a postcard into an envelope!
>
> It was this infinitesimal sound which had, from sixty meters away, blown my head away … I understood that this was the sound's second harmonic, audible only from that specific spot. That is why the birds unstop the owl's ears and offer you access to what the ancients call the 'third ear' …

I love this direct, practical and astonishing example of how a symbol, that of the doves whispering something to the owl, has a hidden message and a surprise. The symbols also kept a secret of a hidden vibrational frequency, created by the skills of the craftsmen.

THE ANCIENT MEXICANS

> The Ancient Mexicans believed that nine or thirteen different heavens existed … The fourth and fifth were the sphere of fire, and birds belonged to the God of Fire … All species of birds belonged in the fourth heaven, and from there they came to Earth.
>
> **Professor Emeritus Rafael del Campo**

There's an important text in the Jewish faith, called the Baruch Apocalypse, which has the birds belonging in the fourth heaven; this was also the belief of the ancient Mexicans. The fourth and fifth dimensions are also said to be the areas of true non-verbal communication, of telepathy, of intuitive leaps and of psychic powers.

The Mexicans had an extensive knowledge of the birds around them and Montezuma's zoo in Tenochtitlán included the first ever-known aviary, where many birds were kept in captivity. Birds were a vital source of inspiration for the Mexicans, and their feathers formed a valuable part of their artistic pieces. The feathers of certain birds were great status symbols, and certain colours and types held symbolic significance.

Some villages and towns still bear the names of birds, for example, Tecolutla, meaning 'where owls abound'.

BIRDS AS SYMBOLS OF TRANSCENDENCE – SHAMANISM AND BIRDS

> The bird is the most fitting symbol of transcendence. It represents the peculiar nature of intuition working through a 'medium', that is, an individual who is capable of obtaining knowledge of distant events – or facts of which he consciously knows nothing – by going into a trance-like state.
> Joseph L. Henderson

It seems obvious that a creature with wings should symbolize the soul taking flight from the body; the spiritual leaving behind the material. However, it is important that spirit and matter connect, and the shaman's ability to do this is remarkable. Every nation has its shaman/priest character, and their habits of accessing arcane and instinctive knowledge are similar the world over. Shamans are often believed to have been conceived by a bird, and wear feathered costumes representing birds. Even in the prehistoric cave paintings at Lascaux there is an image of a shaman wearing the mask of a bird, with a bird perched on a staff beside him (this symbol represents the coming together of spirit and matter).

Feathers themselves form an important part in our understanding of the Language of the Birds. In themselves they represent truth, lightness, the heavens, flight to other realms and the soul. When shamans don costumes, they are said to take on the attributes of the animal from whose skin the costume is fashioned. When the shaman puts on a feathered bird costume, then, he assumes the power or spirit of the bird, including their instinctive knowledge and their magical powers, and thus he can enter the realms of the birds to bring back information, knowledge and messages.

A Magical Connection

Early chocolate moulds were made in the shape of birds, because chocolate is a magical food which helps to connect us to the Gods, and birds also serve as an interface between mankind and the heavenly realms.

In other words, feathers are totem objects, and concentrating on their meanings is part of the mechanism of 'connection' that help the shaman enter into the other world.

Recently, I had correspondence from Anand Yogendra, whose spiritual quest involved taking a journey to the Amazon jungle to take part in a shamanic ritual, which included the controlled ingestion of a magical herb called the ayahusca vine. The quest involves the individual focusing on what they want from the experience, and Anand asked 'to be delivered from ignorance into wisdom' and 'to eradicate all fear from my being'.

During the ceremony, which took place over five days, the shaman appeared to Anand in what is considered to be his true form:

> His spirit is a huge, luminous, bird-type being, in every colour of gold, from white to the purest yellow colour, each feather giving off its own light … I saw him standing, taller than the trees, taller than the jungle, and I knew I loved this man.

In the Celtic tradition, feathered cloaks represent the journey to the other world from whence knowledge comes. In Scandinavia, the Goddess Freyja wore a feathered cloak that enabled her to fly through the air.

Gods and Goddesses across all cultures have strong associations with birds. We'll look into this further and show which birds belong to which deities later on.

St Francis and His Sermon to The Birds

Examples keep cropping up of renowned figures in history who are reputed to have understood the Language of the Birds. Among these we have to include St Francis of Assisi. Whatever your religious or spiritual persuasions, there are certain truths – and bird language is one of these truths – which transcend these barriers.

St Francis is reputed to have had birds and wild animals come close to him; they had no fear of him at all. Apparently he did not eat the flesh of animals, either. There's a lovely story about an incident that is said to have happened in Italy. Francis saw a large variety of birds all together, and walked towards them, expecting them to fly away. They didn't. He asked the birds instead if they'd be interested in hearing the Word of God. The birds stayed, and seemed to be listening, so Francis delivered a short sermon.

> My little sisters, the birds, much bounded are ye unto God, your creator, and always in every place ye ought to praise him, for that he hath given you liberty to fly about everywhere, and hath also given you double and triple rainment; moreover he preserved your seed in the ark of Noah, that your race might not perish out of the world; still more are ye beholden to him for the element of air which he hath appointed for you; beyond all this, ye sow not, neither do you reap; and God feedeth you, and giveth you the streams and fountains for your drink; the mountains and valleys for your refuge and the high trees whereon to make your nests; and because ye know not how to spin or sew, God clotheth you, you and your children; wherefore your creator loveth you very much, seeing that he hath bestowed on you so many benefits; and therefore, my little sisters, beware of the sin of ingratitude, and always to give praises unto God.

The birds listened intently, stretching their wings and ruffling their feathers. Francis moved among them, touching them with his cloak, but they didn't fly away. Francis gave them a blessing and made the sign of the cross over them, and only then did they take to the air. From then on, Francis would always include the birds and animals when he asked people to give thanks to the Creator.

APOLLONIUS OF TYANA

By all accounts, the philosophy and actions of Apollonius of Tyana, who lived sometime in the first century AD, are very similar to those of Jesus Christ. He was reputed to be able to raise the dead, heal people, deal with demons and make predictions. In addition, his life was guided by dreams, and he interpreted dreams for others. He was widely travelled and spoke many languages, including, it is said, the Language of the Birds.

Apollonius refused to eat animal flesh, and believed that it was his healthiness and pure life that gave him the ability to understand so much and to divine things. There's a story about how, at Ephesus, he was strolling along a covered walkway talking to his friends about how things should be shared among people. Nearby, there was a tree full of sparrows. As they walked past, a new sparrow flew up to the tree, chattered to the others for a short while, and then suddenly all the birds left the tree.

Auguries were a regular occurrence at this time and the onlookers believed the sudden flight of the sparrows portended some important event. But Apollonius simply said that they'd been invited to join a banquet. And this indeed was the case. Some people ran off to see if what Apollonius had said was true. They found that some grain had been spilled a little way away and the birds were all enjoying this unexpected bonus!

Apollonius had a message about this, which is still very relevant:

Ye see what care the sparrows take of one another, and how happy they are to share their goods. And yet we men do not approve, nay; if we see a man sharing his goods with other men, we call it wastefulness, extravagance, and by such names, and dub the men to whom he gives a share, fawners and parasites. What then is left to us except to shut us up at home like fattening birds, and gorge our bellies in the dark until we burst with fat?

AN IMPORTANT MESSAGE FROM A BIRD

And Solomon was David's heir. And he said, 'Oh mankind, lo! We have been taught the Language of the Birds and have been given abundance in all things.'
The Qur'an

Another prominent historical character who was able to understand the Language of the Birds was Solomon. There's an interesting story about this, which is found in the Qur'an. The bird in question is sometimes given as a lapwing and sometimes as a hoopoe. In any case, Solomon had an army of birds who kept him informed of all sorts of matters that were going on all over the world – useful allies for anyone to have!

(Coincidentally, the lapwing has a secret name, which actually means 'hide the secret'. This is probably because of the bird's habit of hiding her eggs in grassy mounds in the earth, rather than in a tree.)

Legend has it that in his daily conversations with his army of birds, Solomon noticed that the lapwing was missing, and at first was quite annoyed about this. But when the bird eventually returned she was able to tell Solomon about an incredibly beautiful, wealthy Queen, a heathen Sun worshipper, who lived in a land called Saba. The bird explained to the King that it would be well worth his meeting such an intriguing woman. Accordingly, Solomon built an incredible palace for this mystery woman, without yet having met her. The Queen was of course the Queen of Sheba – a good day's work for the lapwing!

Messages From Birds – the Modern World

I hope that you now have a better understanding of the nature of the many ways we can understand what the birds are telling us. However, birds can carry messages in a practical way, as well as in a more esoteric sense.

THE PIGEON POST

Everyone has heard the term 'pigeon post', but few of us realize exactly what this meant for the thousands of pigeons who have been employed at various times, in different parts of the world, to carry messages.

My great-great-grandfather was a champion pigeon breeder in Scotland and ended up looking after the pigeons during the First World War. The pigeon coops were based in the gardens at Buckingham Palace – a safe place for all those top-secret messages coming in and out. Apparently, King George was something of a pigeon man himself so he used to sit in the coops with my grandaddy of an evening to smoke, chat and check out the incoming mail.

Tyler, San Ginesio

Because pigeons have an unerring ability to return directly home after long flights, they're often referred to as 'homing pigeons', and these birds have been bred for hundreds of years to do just that. A healthy pigeon can fly stretches of up to 1,000 kilometres, or 600 miles.

Usually, the message to be sent is rolled tightly into a plastic capsule, which is then fastened to the leg of the pigeon. Because pigeons are particularly susceptible to being caught by birds of prey, two birds will be sent out with the same message.

Pigeons were used during the early Olympic games in Greece to carry news of victories to competitors' cities, where citizens waited in eager anticipation for news of their heroes. In Iraq and Syria in the twelfth century, pigeons were extensively used to carry news. According to records, the first instance of an actual pigeon post was in 1146. At this time the Caliph of Baghdad used a fleet of pigeons to carry mail throughout his territory. More recently, the news of Napoleon's defeat in the Battle of Waterloo was carried to England by pigeons belonging to the Rothschild family. The pigeons managed to get the message back to England four days faster than the best teams of couriers travelling by horseback and by water.

In the state of Orissa, in India, the pigeon post is still a regular part of the mail service. There are three categories of training for these amazing birds: Static, where the birds are taken to one particular far-off part of the territory in order to communicate with HQ; Mobile, where (as the name suggests) the pigeons are taken to various different places; and Boomerang, in which the pigeons are trained to come back with a return message. All pigeons are trained in all three of these categories, which is quite a long and expensive procedure, but the nature of the territory pretty much precludes any more 'normal' form of communication.

In 1954, during the celebrations for the centenary of the pigeon post in Orissa, the message containing the news of the election of the Indian president was carried by pigeon all the way to the UK!

Perhaps the most famous use of pigeons to carry messages was during the two World Wars.

The birds formed an essential part of wartime strategy for both sides during both wars. For example, the German forces took possession of more than a million Belgian racing pigeons, and there's a memorial in Lille to the 20,000-plus birds that lost their lives in military action. However, many of the birds did survive and lived very long lives – 20 years or more. One particular bird, a German pigeon known as the 'Kaiser', lived to be 32 years old after he was taken 'prisoner' and relocated to the United States.

Although you'd think that there would be a high fatality rate for the pigeons, both from enemy fire and from other birds, a reputed 95 per cent of pigeons returned safely with their messages. Even airships and warplanes were accompanied by their military pigeons. One pigeon in particular, named Cher Ami, saved the lives of 194 men.

Freddy Dyke, who was involved with the National Pigeon Service during the Second World War, comments that there were 200,000 pigeons involved in Allied war work, this figure being made up from the combined service records from the National Pigeon Service, the Army Pigeon Service, the RAF Pigeon Service, the Middle East Pigeon Service, the Australian Army Signal Corps and the Signal Corps United States Army. According to Freddy, the parachute drops with pigeons were only accomplished under cover of darkness, and were extremely risky. Sometimes the birds would be captured by the enemy and sent back with a small explosive charge contained in the message capsule – this tactic was apparently spotted pretty quickly before too much harm was done.

During the Second World War, Allied pigeons held the rank of Captain and would be buried with full military honours.

The courage of some of these birds was incredible. Whether or not they were just following instinct is a debatable point, but I like to think that as sentient beings they would have had a sense of the crucial nature of the missions they were sent on. Many of these birds would have had to fly in extremely difficult conditions – in the dark, in strange territory, and often surrounded by hails of bullets. A pigeon called Snow White, for example, had to fly through Berlin during heavy bombardments, and was awarded the Military Cross. There was even a special medal for bravery among these valuable birds, called the Dicken Medal, which was awarded to around 30 birds.

THE SECRET GARDEN

One of the loveliest examples in literature of a bird carrying a message comes in Frances Hodgson Burnett's *The Secret Garden*.

Mary Lennox is a lonely little girl who has been shipped back home from India to Yorkshire. Left to her own devices, and bored, in a big, empty old house, she discovers that there is a mysterious secret garden in the grounds of the house, which she longs to find. But how? It is a well-known fact that the key has been buried years ago, for reasons Mary will discover later. It seems as though she'll never find the garden – until, that is, she finds an unusual ally in a robin.

> … there, on the top of the wall, perched Ben Weatherstaff's robin redbreast, tilting forward to look at her with his small head on one side.
>
> 'Oh!' she cried out. 'Is it you – is it you?' And it did not seem at all queer to her that she spoke to him as if she were sure that he would understand and answer her.
>
> He did answer. He twittered and chirped and hopped along the wall as though he were telling her all sorts of things. It seemed to Mistress Mary as if she understood him, too, though he was not speaking in words.

Later, the robin not only shows Mary where the lost key is buried; in a moment of timelessness, he shows her the lost doorway into the Secret Garden:

> There, lo and behold, was the robin … He had followed her, and greeted her with a chirp …
>
> 'You showed me where the key was yesterday,' she said. 'You ought to show me the door today; but I don't believe you know!'
>
> The robin flew from his swinging spray of ivy on to the top of the wall and he opened his beak and sang a loud, lovely trill, merely to show off. Nothing in the world is quite as adorably lovely as a robin when he shows off – and they are nearly always doing it.
>
> Mary Lennox had heard a great deal about Magic in her Ayah's stories, and she always said that what happened almost at that moment was Magic.

A gust of wind picks up the thick curtain of ivy covering the wall, revealing a doorknob; this is undoubtedly the way into the Secret Garden.

Mary's heart began to thump and her hands shake a little in her delight and excitement. The robin kept singing and twittering away and tilting his head on one side, as if he were as excited as she was.

If you want to know what happens next – read the book!

All around the world, we find bird stories with recurring themes. Again and again we see these archetypal tales, a challenge to find the King of the Birds, for example, or stories about a white bird being turned black as a punishment. One of the most important of these stories concerns the creation of the world, in which the bird always has a major part to play.

Here's a latter-day creation myth, about the time before words existed.

Haunted by Feathers

Once upon a time, before there was nothing, even, there was a bird.

She was the only bird, fluttering about it the dark nothingness that was space; and she knew that the feeling she was experiencing was isolation, only there was no word for it; indeed, there were no words for anything at all.

She knew that the only way she could change things was to invent things in her own head, for that was the only place that was real.

What to invent was the difficulty, because thoughts are powerful things; wishes can be violent, or violet, and both can be hard to deal with.

What she wanted more than anything was a place, a space, with just the right amount of everything, and she thought as she fluttered in the nothingness of how it should be.

There were only five things necessary for an interesting life, she decided wordlessly; fire, air, waters, earth, and ether, this last being vital, containing the living essence of things and the independent spirit which would add unruly fascination to the others.

Once the thought had crystallized the elements came into being.

BANG! went the fire, in the form of a huge ball, so bright that the bird was blinded for a while by the unaccustomed light, which was far brighter than she had imagined.

CRASH! went the earth, another huge ball, floating in a parallel dimension to the fire, and borne of it.

SLOOSH! went the water, as the condensation between the hard cold earth and the soft hot sun created something called science, and the waters started to invent themselves as seas, and eddies, and whirlpools, and rains.

WHEE! went the air, and the movement caused movement upon movement, and the collective life of everything brought about the ether, the indefinable, the magic ...

Then the bird, head spinning at what she had done, decided that she needed a rest and the time to contemplate things, wordlessly for a little while; and what was that, there on the earth, created from the five elements independently?

A tree ... somewhere to perch upon for the first time ever, and, head under the wing for the first time, to sleep ...

Far below, in old-fashioned black and white photography, stood a man newly invented in a field, surrounded by a flurry of white feathers, and he just stood there and let them be, wondering about other wordless things, and looking as though he'd just invented it all.

And the bird saw this and it made her smile. She thought he looked quite nice, but about her, he would never know the beginning or the end.

There's nothing like a mystery.

Be careful what you wish for. Some of it can be very good.

Elene Kurtesz, 2003

Bird Brain?

During the course of researching this book I have asked myself time and time again why it is that the term 'birdbrain' or 'featherhead' should be used in a derogatory sense, to mean that someone has very little intelligence.

Putting myths and legends to one side, I have amassed some evidence to show that we humans are very likely to be mistaken in assuming that this is the case – in fact the opposite is true. If anyone were to call me a 'birdbrain' (and a few have, I can tell you) I'd now take it as the highest compliment. Here's a look at just a few examples of avian intelligence.

Dr Louis Lefebvre, who is an animal behaviourist at McGill University in Montreal, Canada, has compiled the world's only comprehensive avian IQ index. He did this by studying 2,000 reports of feeding innovations presented in ornithological papers over the last 70 years, and judging bird intelligence by how innovative the bird proves itself to be. The Corvids came top of the list, with hawks and falcons, herons and woodpeckers not far behind.

The Einsteins of The Bird World

THE CORVID FAMILY

The birds of the Corvid family, which include jackdaws, jays, magpies, crows and ravens, are considered to be the most intelligent of all the birds; in the section about the raven (page 60) there is a description of their tool-making and -using capabilities that puts them on a par with primates. And cunning crows have been known to steal fish from fishermen by pulling up the lines when the fishermen were looking in the opposite direction!

Proportionately, ravens have exactly the same brain-to-body ratio as dolphins, and almost the same as that of humans. If crows were human, their average intelligence quotient would be 135. The average IQ for human beings is 100.

Makes you think, doesn't it?

If men had wings and bore black feathers, few of them would be clever enough to be crows.
Henry Ward Beecher

Ravens have a brain the same size as that of a chimpanzee; fascinatingly, although chimps can be taught by humans how to fashion and use simple tools, no chimp has as yet been seen to think for itself and make a tool on its own, unlike some birds. Jays will wedge a nut between the branches of a tree to make it easier to crack, and others have been seen opening nuts by pounding them with rocks.

It's generally accepted that the more social an animal is, the more intelligent. The Corvids tend to work together either in very large flocks in order to defend territory, or in smaller groups to get food. There is a story of a dog on a tether who has a bowl of food within his reach; one raven taunted the dog by hopping about just beyond the range of the tether while another bird stole the food.

Another of the reports compiled by Dr Lefebvre relates a story about how Japanese carrion crows had been seen waiting for cars to stop at red traffic lights. When they did, the crows would place a nut under the wheel of a waiting car, which would then conveniently crack the nut as it drove off!

On the Pacific island of New Caledonia, crows have been observed not only using sticks to prise grubs from holes in tree trunks, but also making tools for the job; they will fashion hooks from twigs, or make serrated rakes from stiff leaves. These tools will be carried from one job to the next.

OTHER BIRDS' USE OF TOOLS

It's not only the Corvid family that use tools. The Woodpecker Finch of the Galapagos Islands will snap off a twig from a tree and, after trimming it to the correct size, will employ its new tool to tease insects out from underneath bark. A Cactus Finch in captivity watched the Woodpecker Finch and learned the same skill, and the Woodpecker Finch kindly passed the captive bird a cactus spine to use as a prising tool.

Another woodpecker story: the Gila Woodpecker, from Mexico and the south western part of the USA, makes a scoop out of tree bark so that it can carry honey home to its chicks.

Herons will often use bait to help them to fish. They will drop small insects and the like on to the surface of the water in order to lure the fish towards them.

The bowerbird, who builds elaborately decorate nests, has devised a method of actually painting his home. He uses fibrous material for his nest, which will absorb the 'paint' pigment he creates from fruits such as cherries. In this way he sets about improving his nest by adding colour.

LANGUAGE AND COMMUNICATION

Language skills are another area in which it is possible to make a judge of intelligence. These skills are not simply about calls and the like, but about body language too. According to Theodore Xenophon Barber, in his book *The Human Nature of Birds*, scientists have distinguished over 300 different kinds of crow calls, although they have not been able to decipher very many of them. However, it's also recognized that crows have different dialects according to where they come from!

Hand-reared ravens, taught to do certain tricks, will teach other, wild ravens to do the same.

When microphones were placed secretly in places where crows rested and ate, it was discovered that the birds made many more, often whispered sounds, than had been suspected. The researcher in this case made a note that 'they hold conversations … as if they were reviewing the days events'. Ravens and crows will also share information about the whereabouts of food, such as large carcasses; one bird might discover the meal and will let the others know its whereabouts.

PARROTS

Although parrots are our best-known language birds, they were not considered to be particularly intelligent but merely very good, if mindless, mimics. However, Dr Irene Pepperberg has challenged this opinion quite dramatically. In particular, her work with an African grey parrot called Alex has proved that the parrot has the ability to recognize words and to use them correctly. Alex has a vocabulary of over 100 words, which he uses meaningfully, and he also has the ability to put these words together in phrases. Alex has been taught colour and shape recognition and the difference between 'yes' and 'no', and is able to make requests, such as for particular food treats, or to be taken to certain places (since his wings are clipped Alex is unable to fly). Alex can also count up to six.

Aside from Alex, there are many parrot owners who will tell you the same thing; that, contrary to what they are 'supposed' to be able to do, parrots can recognize words and use them correctly for themselves.

Hawks and Birds of Prey

In a similar way to the Corvids, hawks will use tools to crack open hard-shelled eggs and the like; in fact eagles have been known to drop tortoises from a height in order to crack their shells. In what must be one of the most unfortunate and unlikely accidents, Aeschylus, the famous Greek playwright who lived from c.525–c.456 BC, was reputedly killed when a tortoise dropped by an eagle hit him on the head at some velocity.

In India, the Black Kites there are called 'fire hawks' because of their practice of stealing smouldering sticks from fires and then dropping these burning twigs on to dry ground. This causes a fire which drives out small mammals from the undergrowth, making them easy prey for the fire hawk. Again, an inventive use of available tools.

Bald Eagles in the USA know that small fish such as minnows can be frozen just below the surface of icy lakes. In order to access the fish, the eagles will chip small chinks in the ice and then jump up and down on the surface so that the minnows are pushed up through the holes.

The Avian Brain Nomenclature Consortium

In order to persuade people to rethink how bird intelligence is perceived, and in the hopes of doing away with the derogatory 'birdbrain' notion, the Avian Brain Nomenclature Consortium has been established by 29 neuroscientists from all around the world.

Professor Erich D. Jarvis, of the Department of Neurobiology at Duke University Medical Center in Durham, North Carolina, kindly explained to me precisely what the organization's aims are:

The aim of my research is to understand how the brain produces learned behavior. To accomplish this, we analyze bird species that have the ability of vocal learning, which is a substrate of spoken language. We believe that knowledge gained from studying these bird species will give us a better appreciation of brain function specifically and animal intellect generally.

The Special Senses and 'Superhuman' Capabilities of Birds

Birds have specialized senses which mankind does not have access to – increased faculties that enable them to operate in an extra dimension. Some of these senses have been contributory factors in many myths, legends and 'old wives' tales'; here is a closer look at some of the more intriguing ones.

NAVIGATIONAL SKILLS

How do pigeons travel such long distances, delivering messages around the world? How do migratory birds return to the same places, year after year, after flying halfway round the globe? How do they find 'home', every time, without fail?

There have been numerous experiments carried out to try to disorientate birds in order to understand more about their navigational abilities. For example, sparrows were displaced to Maryland and Louisiana and still managed to find their way back to their home base, where their nests and chicks awaited them, and Laysan albatrosses managed to find their way home to a small island in the middle of the Pacific after they were displaced to the West Coast of America.

We used to believe that these skills were simply a matter of reflex; this isn't the case. Birds have been found to be able to gain information from the subtle clues provided by the natural world, such as the stars, the position of the planets, landmarks visible from above and the movements of the sun and moon, which they are able to use like a compass.

In addition to these skills, birds are also able to analyse barometric pressure.

MAGNETIC PRESSURE

You know how some people have an unerring instinct about what direction they're facing, even when there are no visible clues? This is because some of us have an innate sensitivity to the earth's subtle magnetic fields, although we don't need to use this sense very often. Birds have a much more developed awareness of these fields – another tool in their remarkable ability to navigate.

STORM DETECTION

Many birds are believed by human beings to have the ability to predict the weather. This is not mere folklore but has its basis in scientific fact. It is a relatively recent discovery that the hoopoe, for example, is able to detect piezo-electrical charges in the atmosphere, which can presage lightning storms, and the bird's behaviour alters as a result of them. So the hoopoe really can be used as a reliable indicator of harsh weather to come.

HEARING ABILITIES

Birds have a larger range of audible frequencies than humans, too. We don't have access to the higher or lower frequencies available to birds, so there are aspects of their songs and calls that we are unable to hear. Birds are also more able to separate out different sounds, and can do this with great speed; the time resolution of birds has been estimated as being ten times more efficient than that of humans, therefore what we hear as one sound could actually be ten different sounds for the bird. This explains in part the astounding ability of certain birds, such as the Mynah bird, to be able to mimic sounds. We already know that birds communicate with one another by their songs and calls, but the greater subtleties are something we're unlikely to be ever able to fully comprehend.

Baby Zebra Finches learn their songs in their sleep.

Nancy Saves the Day

Eighty-two-year-old Miss Rachel Flynn, of Cape Cod, was taking a walk on her own when she fell over a 30-foot cliff on to a lonely beach. She was shocked and too hurt to move and her first thought was that she would have to stay there until she died. However, she noticed a seagull hovering over her as she lay trapped between two huge boulders. Although seagulls to us look pretty much of a muchness, Rachel thought it could possibly be the one which she and her sister, June, were used to feeding, and which they had named Nancy. She remembers saying, 'For God's sake, Nancy, get help.'

The gull then flew off to Rachel's home a mile away where it irritated June by repeatedly tapping on the window and flapping its wings frantically. June tried to shoo it away, but the bird just would not go. After 15 minutes June decided that, however unlikely it might seem, the seagull might be trying to tell her something … The bird flew ahead and led June to the edge of the cliff where she looked over to see her sister lying below, and rescue for Rachel followed soon after. 'It was simply incredible the way she came to the window and caused all that racket,' June told reporters later.

Dennis Barden, Psychic Animals

VISION

Surprise, surprise! The bird's visual ability is much more advanced than that of human beings too, and again we find many folk tales that involve using the eyes of the bird to imbue us with keener sight. This acute vision means that the eagle, for example, has access to a three-mile vista and his sight is sharp enough to be able to spot a small rodent within this vast landscape as he flies above it.

Birds can see a greater range of the colour spectrum. The iridescence of feathers, which looks gorgeous to us, must look spectacular from the bird's eye point of view; the raven, which appears to be black to us, would for example appear to be almost silver to another bird.

Some birds can 'see' thermals. The vulture has this ability and so is able to ride these currents easily and soar effortlessly for great distances.

I hope that this chapter has made you think again about the intellectual capacity of birds, and that once and for all we can do away with the notion that a 'birdbrain' could mean stupid!

Organized Columbiform Crime?

'I was walking in one of the busiest avenues of Athens, along the national gardens. Outside the entrance of the gardens there are these mini shops that you can only find in certain Mediterranean countries, where they sell everything from shampoos to DVDs. They also have ice-cream refrigerators and lots of seeds (to buy and feed the birds in the garden or enjoy on your own!).

'It was winter though and no one wants to eat an ice cream in the winter so the guy who owned the shop had put all the seeds and popcorn on top of the fridges. As I walked by the shop, I saw a pigeon on the fridge pushing along bags of sunflower seeds with its beak. It was trying to get them to the edge of the fridge and push them down. When I looked down, there was another pigeon opening the seed bags and eating ... There was organized crime taking place right in front of my eyes!

'Of course, I said nothing to the owner of the shop. It was the funniest thing!!'
Yolante, Athens

One World, One Tribe, One Bird:

Birds of myth and legend

"They had changed their throats and had the throats of birds."

W. B. Yeats, *Cuchulain Comforted*

If you can consider for a moment that language is a sort of territory, in that it puts up boundaries and restrictions, and if you can imagine again a world without such a construct, then we can start to understand just why so many myths and legends appear all around the planet in varying guises, but all usually recognizable as having the same conceptual origins.

Despite the apparent differences in the societies and cultures around the world, some things are inherent in the nature of mankind, and one of these is the universal desire to explain how we come to be here, and how the world was created, how the sun, the stars and the planets work, how the seasonal variations in the astral bodies affect the fortunes of mankind. These concepts are beyond language, beyond religion and beyond race; they are part of the common territory of mankind.

Myth provides a way for us to explain the nature of the Universe. Just as in Classical mythology the Gods and Goddesses of Greece have their counterparts in the Roman world, in the 'bird world' there are many legendary birds that have their counterparts around the globe. In the descriptions below, it becomes apparent that although many of the birds have different names, their symbolic meanings and stories are very similar, even though they may exist at opposite sides of the planet.

Birds are not governed by our linear interpretation of time. They move according to the flow of the seasons. Birds, unique within the animal kingdom, have the power to fly and to transcend barriers, both physical and metaphorical. Because of their migratory routes, birds traverse the world, carrying their stories and legends with them as they go.

Whether some of these mythological birds have their origins in truth or not, the legends are fascinating; let's take a look at some of them.

The Alicanto

From Chile, the Alicanto is a nocturnal bird that has a predilection for eating either gold or silver from veins in the ground. This peculiar diet means that it is too heavy to fly. Although its wings are perfectly normal, its crop becomes so engorged with precious metals that the bird is simply too heavy to take off.

As might be expected, the variety of Alicanto which feeds on gold can be identified by a golden glow which emanates from its wings at it runs along the ground with them open, and the silver-eating bird can be similarly identified by a silvery glow. When it is hungry the Alicanto can actually run fast; when it has just eaten, however, it can hardly crawl along the ground.

Naturally, because of its metallic diet and its need to find food, the Alicanto is popular among mining prospectors in Chile; however, if the bird realizes it is being followed, it will close its wings and simply slip away in the dark. Alternatively, the Alicanto might decide to suddenly change its path and cause its followers to fall into a ravine, and it has therefore been blamed for many mysterious deaths.

The habits of the Alicanto – its hunger for gold and silver and hence its inability to take off – could be a reminder that material possessions and greed may be responsible for the neglect of a more spiritual path and the ability to 'fly' in the metaphorical sense of the word.

The Anka

This Arabic bird has some similarities to the Phoenix, in that it lives for a long time (1,700 years has been quoted) and renews itself by fire. It also has similarities to the Roc, since it seems to have acquired the habit of carrying away elephants.

Alerion or Avalerion

A bird of India, again with some of the qualities of the Phoenix. There is only ever one pair in the world, and the bird is as large as an eagle and coloured red and gold. Every 60 years the female lays two eggs, and when after 60 days they have hatched, the parents, followed by a retinue of other birds, go off to drown themselves in the sea. The young birds are cared for by the birds of the retinue until they are old enough to fly.

Ba

From Egypt, the Ba has the body of a bird and the head of a human being, and represents the part of a man that continues after death. The Ba has been likened to a psychic force, represented in bird form. It is often depicted hovering over tombs and the like.

Bagucks

A Chippewa bird, the Bagucks is extremely stubborn to the point of starving itself – which is why it appears in a spooky skeletal form, no doubt.

The Bar Yokni

Mentioned several times in the Talmud, the Bar Yokni is another extrapolation of the giant bird that often appear in legends, such as the Ziz. The name comes from the fact that the bird was considered to be ostrich-like, and, like the mother ostrich, the Bar Yokni doesn't sit upon her eggs but just lets them lie in the nest. The name Bar Yokni means 'Son of the Nest'.

The Benu

> I go in like the hawk, and I come forth like the Benu, the Morning Star of Ra; I am the Benu which is in Heliopolis.
> **The Egyptian Book of The Dead**

This Egyptian bird has so many similarities with the Phoenix that some believe it is the forerunner for this bird. However, it is unsurprising that there should be similar interpretations of a magical bird which renews itself by fire – this is of course a way of explaining how the sun works.

Initially represented as a yellow wagtail, the Benu is more popularly represented as a heron, because the heron would perch on the high grounds by the Nile. The Benu is dedicated to the Sun God, Ra. In fact the Benu was said to be the 'ba' of Ra, that is, it represented the undying aspect of the God. The name 'Benu' means 'to shine'.

The Benu is the symbol of Heliopolis, which was built at the point where the sun appeared to rise from the Nile. The sun symbolism doesn't end there. The bird is said, like the Phoenix, to have the ability to renew itself, and sits at the top of the Persea tree in Heliopolis, from where it reincarnates itself.

The symbol of the Benu would be depicted on amulets, particularly on those used in funerals, and represented the anticipated rebirth of the dead person in the next world.

The Caladrius

It is unclear as to the origin of the European bird on which the Caladrius is based, but it is generally believed that it would have been a pure white water bird. The Caladrius is obviously a useful bird to have around since it is said to be able to tell at a glance whether someone is going to live or die. If the former, the Caladrius is happy to face the patient; this noble bird would then take the illness, fly away into the Sun and disperse the disease. If however the diagnosis is death, the bird apparently turns away.

> The diagnostic value of the Caladrius caused it to be a troublesome commodity for the bird-seller. The ailing purchaser had only to enter a bird-shop, ask to see a Caladrius, note whether it looked at him or away from him, and then, making some excuse about the purchase price, he could go away with all he wanted to know, without buying the Caladrius. The result was that few dealers were willing to display their goods without cash down; a fact which may account for the difficulty in identifying this particular bird.
>
> T.H. White, *The Book Of Beasts,* Jonathan Cape, 1956

The Chamrosh

The Chamrosh is a Persian bird, said to be the protector of all the birds on the Earth. It is also believed to protect its country from 'pillagers'.

Cinomolgus

Another Arabian bird with some similarities to the Phoenix, in that it makes it nest out of cinnamon and lives high in the treetops. It is an unfortunate bird, in that people would throw rocks and sticks in order to dislodge the nest and get the cinnamon!

Comulatz

The Comulatz is one of the trio of Mayan birds who taught a rather telling lesson to the first men after they showed disrespect to the Gods. It tore their heads off.

The Cu Bird

The Cu bird comes from Mexico, and apparently he used to be not very pretty to look at. He decided to ask all the other birds if they could each spare him a feather. They agreed, on condition that Cu became their messenger. This he agreed. Because of the incredible collection of feathers he started to wear, the Cu very quickly became the most beautiful bird instead of one of the ugliest. As a consequence he got very proud and rather overbearing, and eventually all the other birds become annoyed and stripped him of his feathers, flinging them into the air – which is how the rainbow was made!

The Feng Huang

The Feng Huang is, in effect, the Chinese version of the Phoenix. Unlike the Phoenix, however, the Feng Huang comprises two birds, male and female, who live together as a pair. Because of this, in China the symbol of these birds is often seen in wedding decorations. The bird also symbolizes the union of female and male, or yin and yang.

The bird lives to the east of China, in a place called the Kingdom of the Wise. Its body contains all the five basic colours – black, white, red, yellow and green – and it seems to be a combination of parts of different birds and animals. Sometimes it carries scrolls or a box, which is said to contain sacred books. The Feng Huang can also be depicted with a fireball.

The entire body of this fantastic bird represents the celestial bodies: the head is the sky, the eyes are the Sun, the Moon is its back, its wings are the wind, its feet are the Earth and the tail represents the planets.

The Feng Huang is a peaceable creature and during troubled times it hides itself away. The bird is said to have originated in the Sun.

The Gansas

This is reputed to be a large migratory bird, a little like a swan, with only one foot that has one talon, like an eagle. Their migratory route is a little odd too; once a year the birds return to the Moon.

There is a seventeenth-century story called 'The Man In The Moone', written in 1638 by the Bishop of Hereford, which possibly influenced the story of Baron von Munchhausen. In the story the hero, Domingo Gonzales, finds himself trapped on an island. He manages to tame some of the Gansas birds that, conveniently, are living there, and devises a contraption by which means he can be carried by the birds to the Moon.

The Garuda

The Garuda, whose name originates in Sanskrit, is possibly one of the most ancient of the mythological birds, and has some similarities to the Roc – again, it is a case of archetypes. Like the Roc, the Garuda is said to be able to pick up elephants in its talons, and is so big that its flying body would obscure the Sun. Similarities with the Phoenix are there too; the Garuda is believed to be a form of the Fire God because it is a bright, shining sort of a bird. In Malaya, the Garuda is often taken to be the equivalent of the Phoenix. In Hindu stories, when the Garuda was born there was such a bright light that the word got around that the new arrival was the Fire God and angels came to pay homage.

The Garuda was hatched from the cosmic egg that also held the eight elephants said to hold up the Universe, in Hindu mythology. Another aspect of the Garuda in the Hindu world is that the Kumbh Mela, a huge religious festival held on the banks of the Ganges every 12 years, is held at one of the four places where this incredible bird is reputed to have rested during a battle with demons. The battle took place during the Garuda's search for the divine nectar of immortality, and his fight lasted 12 days (or, in mortal time, 12 years), which is why the Kumbh Mela is held every 12 years.

It is good evidence of the influence of Indian cultures that the Garuda has taken flight in so many other areas of the Eastern world. There is a posture in yoga known as the Garuda, which also means Eagle, and indeed the Garuda is a Hindu and Buddhist deity in both India and Japan. The bird is easy to identify, having a white face, red wings in the shape of eagle's wings, and the body of a man. However, in Buddhism, the Garuda has the head of a bird and the body of a lion. In Hindu literature and folklore, the God Vishnu is seen riding on the back of a Garuda.

The Garuda has an impressive pedigree; it is well known in Tibet, where it takes the name of Cha Khyung and protects the world, and in Japan it is known as the Karura. In Thailand, the Garuda is the King of the Birds and is a symbol of the Thai monarchy, appearing on the official seal of the government. The Garuda, or Karura, is a popular decoration in temples in South East Asia, from Angkor to Java. The bird is said to be the enemy of the dragon and snakes, and according to some accounts it is alleged to feed upon dragons. Apparently the dragon can only escape the Garuda if it has converted to Buddhism and carries a special talisman with it at all times.

My favourite Garuda story is one that seems to exemplify the idea of fate, or karma, or destiny; however much we may attempt to direct a course of events, there's a higher force at work, which is ultimately in control.

Once, the Garuda was perched on Mount Kailish, guarding the gates of Shiva's palace, where he saw a very tiny, beautiful bird. The Garuda watched the little bird for a while, marvelling at its loveliness. Garuda commented, 'How wonderful, to think that the God who made this mountain also made this tiny, beautiful bird! They're completely different yet equally wonderful!'

At this point Yama, the God of Death, came along for a meeting with Shiva, riding his customary black buffalo. Garuda noticed that Yama's gaze fell upon the tiny bird; this meant that the bird would die. Garuda thought he might be able to avert this, so he carried the little bird gently into a deep forest, where he placed it close to water and in a comfortable place. Then Garuda returned to his usual position, guarding Shiva's gate.

Shortly after, the God of Death came out of the gate, and said hello to Garuda. Garuda asked Yama about the bird.

'I saw you look at the bird, and you looked thoughtful …why was that?'

Yama replied, 'I knew when I looked at it that the lovely little bird would meet death by being eaten by a python. I was puzzled because there are no pythons high on Mount Kailash. The nearest pythons are far away, deep in the forests …'

It's an unfortunate ending for the bird, but a story that shows the inevitability of fate.

The Halcyon

The Halcyon is a Greek bird, closely identified with the kingfisher. Ceyx and Halcyone were husband and wife, the King and Queen of Trachis. Unfortunately, despite the warnings of Halcyone, Ceyx went out to sea one day and was drowned. Halcyone was told of this event in a dream, when the God of Sleep, Morpheus, came to her. Grief-stricken, Halcyone threw herself into the sea and was transformed into a kingfisher, along with her husband. Legend has it that the Halcyon bird nests upon the water during a time when the sea is calm and the winds are tranquil. In Greece, there really are Halcyon Days, a period just after the Winter Solstice when the waters are calm and the weather gives a promise of Spring, and we use the term to denote a period of calm happiness and security in our lives.

The Hameh

A bit of a spooky one, this. The Hameh is an Arabian bird that comes to life from the blood of a murdered man. Its cry, 'Iskoonee', which means 'Let me drink', never stops until the bird drinks the blood of the murderer. If you believed in the existence of the Hameh and happened to kill someone, for whatever reason, your belief would in all likelihood drive you insane!

The Hamsa

In Hindu stories, this celestial bird is depicted as a goose or a swan. As the Kalahamsa, the bird represents Brahma, and is the bird that laid the egg from which the Universe hatched; the name means something like 'the swan in space and time'. According to the Upanishads, the Hamsa is in fact two birds, Ham and Sa, 'dwelling in the mind of the Great, who subsist entirely on the honey of the blooming lotus of knowledge'.

Heloka and Melatha

In Native American stories, Heloka and Melatha are the birds who represent thunder and lightning. Heloka, the female, seems to have had a lackadaisical approach to motherhood. Whenever it was time for her to lay an egg she would simply alight upon the nearest cloud and let the egg drop to the ground! As the egg dropped it would naturally crash and bump into clouds, and this was heard as thunder. Melatha, the male, at this point would have his work cut out; possessed of great speed, he'd zip hither and thither across the skies trying to catch the dropped eggs. He'd fly so fast that sparks would come from his feathers – lightning. In addition, he'd also crash headlong into various objects, dislodging rocks, felling trees and the like.

If everyone – particularly children – imagined these silly birds up in the sky every time there was a thunderstorm, there would be no need for any fear of storms!

The Ho-Ho or Ho-Oo

This is the Japanese version of the Phoenix, and has similarities to the Chinese Feng Huang in that it symbolizes two birds, male and female, representing harmony and union, and by doing good wherever it goes. Its appearance signifies the dawn of a new era. This bird is also the symbol of the Empress of Japan.

The Hol

The Hol appears in Jewish mythology as the bird who nests in the Tree of Knowledge. When Eve has been persuaded by the serpent to eat the apple, she of course tries to entice every other living creature to taste the fruit, and on the whole, they all do. But the Hol bird refuses. As a reward, God says that the bird should live forever; every thousand years the bird will burn, but be renewed from its own ashes – another Phoenix legend.

Homa

A Persian bird, the Homa is a noble creature and brings glory and good fortune. It brings back blessings from Heaven, since it can fly there. The Homa prefers to feed on pieces of unwanted bone, in order not to take any food away from anyone else.

Hugin and Munin

In Norse mythology, Hugin and Munin are ravens that belong to Odin. The birds serve as advisors and informants to the God. They set out at dawn to travel the world to see what's new, returning every evening to sit on Odin's shoulders and whisper secrets into his ears. Hugin means 'thought' and Munin means 'memory'. It's because of Hugin and Munin that Odin is known as the Raven God.

The Hyrcinian Bird

This is a massive bird from Germany, whose feathers are said to light up!

The Imdugud

In ancient Sumeria, the Imdugud was a giant eagle, with the head of a lion, whose roaring was said to be thunder: an extrapolation of the Thunderbird myth.

The Kalavinka

In Buddhist legend, the Kalavinka is a very special bird. Originally believed to have been based on either a cuckoo or a sparrow-like bird which lived in the snowy Himalayan mountains, in the 'pure land', the Kalavinka is the 'sweet-voiced bird of immortality', a magical bird, which appeared when the Buddha attained enlightenment. The Kalavinka is said to sing even before it has hatched from its egg.

The Kalavinka is often depicted holding a musical instrument. It is said to be possible to hear the voice of the Kalavinka bird at a certain stage of spiritual and intellectual development in the practice of yoga.

The Karshipta

In Persian mythology, the Karshipta is a bird with the power of speech who is said to have brought the word of God to mankind.

Kinnara

In Hindu myth, the Kinnara is a half-man, half-bird creature, often portrayed playing the zither.

The Krut or Pha Krut

In Thailand, the name for the Garuda.

Kwa'Toko

In the myths of the Hopi Indians, Kwa'Toko is a huge monster eagle, of quite a malicious nature. He was said to have a heart of stone:

> Kwa'Toko was a great eagle, as high as a man and the spread of his wings was as wide as a large house. He swooped down and carried off men, women, children …

If you ever do see a Kwa'Toko darken the skies, my advice would be to get indoors immediately.

The Ndadzi

In South African folklore, the thunder and lightning bird. It is meant to fly on the 'wings of thunder', and its eyes flash lightning. It holds the rain in its beak, and when it lays an egg, if the egg drops to the foot of a tree then the tree will be destroyed by fire. All in all the Ndadzi has some similarities both to the Thunderbird of Native America lore, and to Heloko and Melatha, the Native American thunder and lightning birds.

Pegais

These are Scythian birds with the heads of horses, and of course are the origin of Pegasus, the winged horse.

Pheng

Another one of the giant birds, Japanese this time, who can not only eclipse the sun because of its size but is also said to eat camels!

The Phoenix – The Immortal Bird

> Now I will believe
> That there are unicorns, that in Arabia
> There is one tree, the phoenix' throne, one phoenix
> At this hour reigning there
> **William Shakespeare**, *The Tempest*

The Phoenix is a bird of great beauty and the incredible power to give birth to itself. Although the classic Phoenix myth originates in Arabia, birds with similar characteristics – primarily, the ability to renew itself, to create itself without the need for parents, and its great longevity – appear in folk tales all over the world, and is possibly the best-known of all the 'mythological' birds.

(I insert quotation marks because, after all we never know, and there's no smoke without fire, particularly where the Phoenix is concerned!)

This bird has appeared in imagery, literature and the cinema, and is a popular symbol for large corporations and the like. Who could forget Fauks, Professor Dumbledore's pet Phoenix in the *Harry Potter* books, or fail to be entranced by E. Nesbit's story *The Phoenix And The Carpet*, about four children living in Edwardian London who give a home to both a newly hatched Phoenix and a magic flying carpet?

In the 'real world', the Phoenix is an astronomical symbol for a cyclic period in China, Egypt, India and Persia. A new Phoenix period was said to have begun in AD 139.

The word 'phoenix' is Greek, although the Greeks adopted the earlier Egyptian form of the bird, the Benu, and the name changed to Phoenix, which translates as the colour red/purple or crimson.

This amazing bird lives either in Arabia or in Ethiopia, near a cool well of water, and its dawn song is so incredibly beautiful that even the Sun God would stop what he was doing to listen to it. There's a story that the sparks from the chariot of the Sun God started the conflagration that caused the first ever Phoenix to burn.

The Phoenix doesn't eat 'normal' food, so doesn't need to kill anything. It lives on dew and the smoke from rare incenses. Ovid's *Metamorphoses* tell us:

> The Phoenix of Assyria … feeds not upon seeds or verdure but the oils of balsam and the tears of Frankincense.

This quality, of not harming anything in order to eat, means that the Phoenix is a popular symbol in Chinese and Indian Buddhist belief systems. In the same way, the bird has become popular in Christian literature and art as a symbol of resurrection and of life after death.

There can only exist one Phoenix at a time, and its lifespan is reputedly anywhere between 500 and 1,461 years. When the time comes for the Phoenix to renew itself, we have a splendid account, again from Ovid:

> When it has lived 500 years, it builds itself a nest in the branches of an oak, or on the top of a palm tree. In this it collects cinnamon, and spikenard, and myrrh, and of these materials builds a pile on which it deposits itself, and dying, breathing out its last breath amidst odours. From the body of the parent bird, a young Phoenix issues forth,

destined to live as long a life as its predecessor. When this has grown up and gained sufficient strength, it lifts its nest from the tree (its own cradle and its parent's sepulchre) and carries it to the city of Heliopolis in Egypt, and deposits it in the temple of the Sun.

There may well be a basis in fact for the Phoenix myth, since there is a specific bird species in East Africa that makes its nests on salt flats, which are too hot for the eggs or chicks to survive. So the bird makes a mound several inches high and lays the egg on top of the mound, which affords just enough of a drop in temperature. But the hot air vapour rising up around the mound looks a little like a flame.

Although many cultures seem to have adopted the story of the Phoenix, there's an account by an Indian sage called Larkhas, from the first century AD, who says:

> The Phoinix … visits Aigypto every five hundred years, but the rest of that time it flies about in India; and it is unique in that it gives out rays of sunlight and shines with gold, in size and appearance like an eagle; and it sits upon the nest, which is made by it at the springs of the Nile out of spices. The story of the Aigyptoi about it, that it comes to Aigyptos, is testified to by the Indians also, but the latter add this touch to the story, that the Phoinix which is being consumed in its nest sings funeral strains for itself. And this is also done by the swans according to the account of those who have the wit to hear them.

Despite this story that the Phoenix spent most of its time in India, there's another account that tells us that the bird's real home is in Paradise. However, immortality must be a heavy burden, and when the time comes for the Phoenix to die, it has to fly into the mortal world, taking a journey across the jungles of Burma, across India and on to Arabia. Here the bird collects the herbs and aromatic spices it needs, then it flies on to Phoenicia in Syria, finds a tall palm tree, and then constructs its funeral pyre; as the next day dawns the bird rises again, like the sun rises every day.

> He knows his time is out! and doth provide
> New principles of life; herbs he brings dried
> From the hot hills, and with rich spices frames
> A pile shall burn, and Hatch him with his flames.

On this the weakling sits; salutes the Sun
With pleasant noise, and prays and begs for some
Of his own fire, that quickly may restore
The youth and vigour, which he had before.

Whom soon as Phoebus spies, stopping his rays
He makes a stand, and thus allays his pains …
He shakes his locks, and from his golden head
Shoots one bright beam, which smites with vital fire

The willing bird; to burn is his desire
That he may live again; he's proud in death
And goes in haste to gain a better breath.
The spice heap fired with celestial rays
Doth burn the aged phoenix, when straight stays

The chariot of the amazed Moon; the pole
Resists the wheeling, swift orbs, and the whole
Fabric of Nature at a stand remains.
Till the old bird anew, young begins again
Claudian, *The Phoenix*

The Phoung

In Vietnamese mythology, this is the same bird as the Feng Huang. It has a similarly composite body, and also carries scrolls or a box of sacred books.

The Piasa

In some branches of Native American mythology, the Piasa is a giant man-eating bird.

The Pou Kai

Another one to avoid … the Pou Kai is a Polynesian bird that delights in devouring human beings.

In Maori myth, the same bird is called the Poua-Kai, and becomes a giant as well as a man-eater!

The Roc or Rukh

All feathered things yet ever known to men,
From the huge Rucke, to the little Wren:
From Forrests, Fields, from Rivers and from Ponds,
All that have webs, or cloven-footed ones;
To the Grande Arke, together friendly came,
Whose severall species were too long to name.
Michael Drayton, *Noah's Flood*

There are legends and stories all over the world about the Roc, or Rukh, an incredible gigantic bird that was said to be big enough to carry several people at a time. The Roc could also carry up to three elephants (like the Anka).

The Roc is either Arabian or Chinese, and is written about both in the *Arabian Nights* and in *The Travels of Marco Polo*, which the explorer wrote while in prison in Genoa in 1298. Marco Polo has the Roc living in Madagascar, although it's possible that he may have meant a different giant bird, one which was 'real' although probably now extinct, which definitely existed in Madagascar and is the possible origin of the Roc legend.

The quote at the beginning of this section, which includes the Roc among the animals that went into the Ark, shows that belief in this giant bird was very prevalent. Indeed, in the sixteenth century European seamen returned from the Indian Ocean with huge eggs which they had taken as souvenirs. These eggs were said to have a fluid capacity of almost two gallons (nine litres), which is equivalent to 200 chicken eggs, and three times the size of dinosaur eggs.

The bird that laid these eggs could well have been the Roc, but it came to be known as the Elephant Bird (*Aepyornis Maximus*). It was 10 feet (3 metres) tall and was the largest bird that ever lived on Earth. It couldn't fly, but its sheer size meant that it had no predators. Prior to the Elephant Bird, we have fossil evidence that giant birds did exist prior to man's appearance on the planet. The extinction of the Elephant Bird on Madagascar was probably as a result of the taking of eggs and the deforestation of the island. In 1658 the Governor of Madagascar wrote, 'So that the people of these places may not catch it [the Vouron Patra, or Elephant Bird], it seeks the loneliest places.'

In the *Arabian Nights*, Sindbad the Sailor is accidentally marooned on an island after falling asleep in the sunshine after a heavy lunch. Realizing he is stranded, Sindbad panics for a while, and then his resourcefulness gets the better of him and he decides to climb a tall tree to think about what to do next. From the top of the tree he spies a huge white dome over on one side of the island, so he goes to investigate, thinking it might be a large building and that there might be some human habitation. As he's investigating

> The air grew suddenly dark, as if obscured by a thick cloud … I perceived it to be occasioned by a bird of a most extraordinary size, which was flying towards me. I recollected having heard sailors speak of a roc; and I conceived that the great white ball which had drawn my attention must be the egg of this bird.

The ever-resourceful Sindbad manages to tie himself to the claw of the Roc without the bird noticing anything at all, and is carried away from the island to a place where the valleys are encrusted with diamonds – but that's another story!

The Safat

The Safat is said never to land; she flies constantly and never comes to rest, a little like the swift is popularly supposed to do. This means of course that she lays her eggs while in the air. They hatch mid-fall and the young Safat flies away. If the fallen eggshells happen to be eaten by an animal, the animal is said to go mad.

The Sarimanok

From the Philippines, the Sarimanok bird plays an important part in the creation myth of those islands.

Flying across the Pacific, which is, of course, a vast tract of water, the Sarimanok needed to take shelter, and alighted on top of a lone bamboo shoot on one of the Islands. The Sarimanok, being hungry, pecked at the shoot, and was alarmed when the shoot started to split into two halves. The bird flew away and was never seen again (hence the difficulty in finding a description of it!) but from the two halves of the bamboo emerged a handsome man (named Malakas, meaning 'strong') and a beautiful woman, Maganda, meaning 'beautiful' – the first Filipino people.

The Shang Yang

The Shang Yang is a fabled bird in China. It is the Rainbird. She draws up water from rivers and sprays it out again as rain.

The Shu Jaku

In Japanese stories, the Shu Jaku bird represents the Sun, or the South, and the colour red.

The Simurgh

> We have a King; beyond Kaf's mountain peak
> The Simurgh lives, the sovereign whom you seek,
> And He is always near to us, though we
> Live far from His transcendent majesty.
> **Farid Ud-Din Attar,** *The Conference of The Birds*

A Persian bird, the Simurgh is another bird of profound longevity, having lived so long that it has seen the world end three times so far. With the head of a dog and four wings, the Simurgh resides in the Tree of Knowledge, which is laden with seeds from all the plants in the world, with the result that when the bird flies from the tree these seeds are scattered in all directions. The Simurgh seems to be a kind bird and is willing to foster children; indeed, there's a story that the bird fosters an unwanted child called Zal, who turns out to be Persia's greatest hero. According to another story, the Simurgh attended upon the Queen of Sheba.

The Simurgh was the king of all the birds in Persia, and the name actually translates as 'Thirty (Si) Birds (Murgh)'. At one time all the birds decided that they would try to find the Simurgh, having found out that he dwelled in the Mountains of Kaf. There is a superb book, called *The Conference of The Birds*, written by Farid Ud-Din Attar in Persia in the twelfth century. The book describes the journey of the birds to meet their King, the Simurgh, and is seen as one of the most significant works of Persian literature.

At the end of the journey, the thirty birds who manage to stay the course under the direction of the Hoopoe realize that they, collectively, are the Simurgh — they are the God they have been seeking:

> ... close at hand, the Sun's rays flashed upon them and filled their souls with light. Then these thirty birds, the earthly Si Morgh, gazed upon the spiritual Simurgh in the light reflected from their own faces. Busily they gazed at the Simurgh until they realized that he was none other than Si Morgh, that is to say that they were themselves the Godhead. Thus the mystic only achieves union with the Godhead when the own self is annihilated.

The Stymphalian Birds

From Greece, the Stymphalian birds are giant cranes, with long, lance-shaped beaks that are strong enough to pierce armour. Their feathers are similarly sharp and can be used as arrows, which they occasionally shoot at people, and to add to the weaponry, the Stymphalian birds also have brass claws which they use to full effect where necessary, so a useful bird to have on the side of your army! They are said to live by Lake Stymphalus in Arcadia, whence they had fled to escape wolves. However, the birds were allegedly all killed by Hercules as part of his labours. If there were any left after they were all shot with arrows after being beaten into the air with huge bronze clappers, then they understandably never returned to Greece.

Tecumbalam

Another bird best left alone. In Mayan mythology, the Tecumbalam broke the bones and muscles of the first men, since they were disrespectful to the Gods.

Thunderbird

In Native American mythology, the Thunderbird is of immense importance. Again, like many of the mythological birds in other cultures, the Thunderbird is a giant, able to eclipse the sun. An important part of the Thunderbird myth is its association, of course, with thunderstorms. In general, among all the different Native American tribes, the Thunderbird is seen to be a benign creature, a nature spirit, and not to be confused with less benevolent giant birds of prey.

It's easy to imagine how the story of the Thunderbird could have started, after all the domain of the birds is in the sky, the origin of thunder and lightning, and some lightning fork shapes could be said to assume the shapes of giant birds. The Thunderbird's colossal wings flapping cause the sound of thunder, while lightning bolts issue from its beak. Moving shadows cast upon the ground were from these huge birds flying overhead.

Actual descriptions of the Thunderbird, beyond the characteristics already mentioned, are few and far between, since the bird would generally be obscured by dark, rolling clouds. Its symbolism is popular, though – it is a brand of alcohol, for one thing; there's a Thunderbird automobile, and the United States Airforce has a squadron called the Thunderbirds.

In deference to a story about how the Thunderbird grabbed a whale out of the sea and ate it, Indian fishermen off Vancouver Island painted effigies of the Thunderbird on the sides of their bodies and homes in the hopes that the bird would protect them. There is also a Quillayute Indian story that shows the benevolent nature of the Thunderbird.

The tribe were having a terrible time. There had been hail and rain, which had destroyed their crops, and indeed many of their people had been killed by the severe weather. The Quillayute were starving and desperate, and eventually the Chief decided to call upon the Great Spirit to help them.

The people waited and waited, growing more and more desperate. Suddenly, everything went dark. There was a sound of huge flapping wings, and flashes of lightning cut through the gloom. Everyone gazed up at the sky to see a huge bird-like creature flying towards them. The bird was so massive that in its claws it held a whale, which it deposited before them. Then the bird turned away, back to the Great Spirit who had sent it to rescue the tribe.

It could well be that the Thunderbird legend has its roots in truth. Just as the Elephant Bird of Madagascar was a real bird, there's evidence to suggest that there were huge birds in the Americas until relatively recently. There have been fairly regular sightings of giant birds in the USA, and the most recent was on September 25th, 2001, when a witness claimed to have seen a giant bird flying over Route 119 in Greensburg, Pennsylvania. The witness reported a sound 'like flags flapping in a thunderstorm'.

She saw a bird whose wingspan appeared to be approximately 10–15 feet (3–5 metres) long, with a head about three feet (90 cm) long. The witness further reported, 'I wouldn't say it was flapping its wings gracefully, but almost horrifically; it was flapping its wings very slowly, then gliding above the big passing rig trucks.'

Apparently the giant bird landed on a dead tree, which practically broke under its weight.

What's even spookier is that there were several sightings of a giant bird in the same area in June and July of the same year. On June 13th a resident of Greenville saw what she thought was a grey-black coloured small aircraft, before realizing that the object was a bird; she saw the feathered body and, again, estimated its size at between 10 and 15 feet (3–5 metres) long. And it happened again on July 6th in Erie County – the same description.

As a comparison, the largest 'real' bird we have records of is the Wandering Albatross, with a wingspan of around 12 feet (4 metres), and the Andean Condor, with a 10-foot (3-metre) wingspan.

I find it quite inspiring to think that there's a possibility that somewhere in the world exists a giant bird which has managed, against all the odds, to hide itself away all this time.

Tla'Nuwa

A large mythical hawk of the Cherokee, the Tla'Nuwa was said to be about the size of a turkey and smoky blue-grey in colour. It has a habit of following flocks of wild pigeons, which it attacks and eats while on the wing.

Xecotcovach

Alongside the Tecumbalam and Comulatz in Mayan mythology, this bird assisted in the destruction of the first men, by tearing their eyes out – just be careful what you say!

Ziz

A biblical bird, the Ziz was considered the king or ruler of all the birds in the same way that the Leviathan was the king of the fish (incidentally, both birds and fish were said to have been created on the fifth day).

The Ziz is a gigantic size; its feet are on the earth and its head is in the sky. There's a story about sailors in a boat who come across the Ziz; they could see that its ankles were coming out of the water, so they assume it is safe to get it out of the boat – the water can't be that deep. However, as they're about to disembark they hear a beautiful voice warning them

> Alight not here! A carpenter dropped his axe here once, and it took him seven years to touch the bottom of the ocean.

When the Ziz opened its wings they were large enough to darken the sun. The advantage of the wings of the Ziz, however, is that they also protect against wind. However, the unfortunate inhabitants of 60 cities were drowned at one time when the Ziz dropped an egg and the contents caused an almighty flood!

I hope you've enjoyed this brief exploration into some of our so-called mythological birds, and that the similarities of some of them have set you wondering.

Feathers and Forecasts:
Divination by birds

" As the years pass,
The generations of birds pass too.
But you must watch carefully.
The same towhees and jays
Seem to have been in the same places
To thousands of generations of men."

Kenneth Rexroth

The Nature of Time and the Mantic Arts

Mankind has always had a fascination with trying to predict what will happen in the 'future'. However, in attempting to do this, we come to a very sticky area.

Since the dawn of time, man has attempted to have foreknowledge of what lies ahead, and has employed many and varied ways of doing so; in fact there are thousands of methods, ranging from the seemingly ridiculous (Tiromancy – the art of divination from analysing the holes in a piece of

cheese) to the sublime (Phyllorhodomancy – divining the future by slapping a rose petal between the hands of the querant, or asker, to ascertain a simple 'yes/no' answer). All these methods can be grouped under one name, and since the methods often end in 'mancy', such as 'ornithomancy', they are called, collectively, the Mantic Arts.

The problem comes when we come to consider the nature of 'time'.

Without leaping into the realms of quantum physics, about which I know very little and could explain even less, we have to question the very nature of everything that man has invented as a convenient way of charting or measuring things, such as time. The Sandhill Crane has no clock or watch, yet Greek fishermen know exactly when to put out to sea each year because they watch the migratory patterns of the birds. The birds do not know what time it is, yet they herald the start of a new day via their Dawn Chorus; simple man seems quite backward in comparison with his use of alarm clocks and the like.

We cannot castigate ourselves for our lifestyles. We cannot run our lives according to the amount of light in the sky anymore, because everything we have become precludes this. Some of us need to black out our bedrooms by drawing curtains and blinds, since we have decided to run our lives according to a very different kind of clock to that of the Sandhill Crane, a clock which often pays no attention to the hours of daylight, especially in our 'civilized' lives in the Northern Hemisphere.

To understand that we exist in the midst of a timeless space can be a rather frightening concept for some: no more of the linear 'blocks' of seconds, minutes, hours and days with which we have lived for several generations. If philosophers are correct, and there is a set pattern to the Universe, then everything we do or experience is meant to be. All we really need to 'do' is slot into the timeless zone in order to know that all is well, but this still leaves me with a deep suspicion of 'knowing' or attempting to 'foresee' what lies in the future.

I hope that we have all experienced periods of what Jung called 'synchronicity'; this is the word he invented to describe those series of 'meaningful coincidences' that permeate our lives constantly: sometimes we are in a better state to receive the messages than at others. It is this feeling of interconnectedness, of 'timelessness', and the realization that we are not simply physical beings, which gives us personal responsibility for our lives, the present moment and ultimately, our 'future'.

It is worth bearing in mind that this 'magic', this synchronicity, is there regardless of our differing states of sensitivity to it, which can alter at various times in our lives. It is the awareness of it happening regardless that is key.

WHAT ABOUT BIRDS AND DIVINATION?

Reading Aristophanes' play *The Birds*, which was written in 414 BC, is probably something I would never have considered before I realized the truth about birds. But this incredible play is a good indicator of the timelessness of human concerns. The issues that occupied ancient Athens, or Rome, or Egypt, or anywhere else for that matter, are really very little changed from our issues and worries today. However, when a writer or artist, a musician, a philosopher, a mathematician or scientist, anyone hits a stream of truth, then this carries with it a certain timelessness which transcends our human concerns: ego, mortality, retention of consciousness after death.

With any form of 'prediction', the very most we can hope for is that to be forewarned is to be forearmed, which is also the major strength in astrology. Look at the tendencies, and concentrate on improving the 'bad' parts, and leave the good to their own devices; this for me is how we should be able to improve ourselves as individuals and, in so doing, help towards making this beautiful world we live in a better place. Put yourself beyond 'time' and nothing hurts quite so much.

DREAMS AND TIMELESSNESS

It is generally accepted that the dream state allows us to move in and out of time in a way that our waking consciousness often precludes. The 'dream state' is not necessarily one involving sleep; it can involve a deep state of concentration which allows us to bypass certain parts of our mind, such as when playing music, or painting; some people can achieve this timeless state through meditation.

There are many instances of birds carrying messages in dreams, both in mythology and folklore, and in real life, in all times and in all cultures.

The information in this book should help you to analyse any bird-dreams you might have, given that our subconscious mind often speaks to us via symbols rather than in 'real' words.

Divination By Bird

Taking into consideration everything I've just said, it might be fun to have a look at some of the various forms of divination involving birds, before we delve into Auguries, which, as I will point out, is a different matter entirely! Some methods of observing birds in order to divine the future were pretty random, such as the Italian practice of charging a small fee to have a parakeet choose from among several slips of paper; the slip would hopefully bear the answer which the querent wanted to hear. Other methods were a little more organized.

Alectryomancy or Theriomancy

In general, this was the art of divining the future by means of observing the behaviour of animals, although there are some specific methods that involved birds.

The Etruscans used the following method. First, a circle was drawn on the ground, and around it was scratched or otherwise inscribed the 20 letters of the Etruscan alphabet. A kernel of grain would be placed next to each letter.

Then a cockerel or hen – possibly chosen because of the bird's habit of crowing or calling as the sun rose and so foretelling the birth of the day – was put into the circle, and would then, of course, begin to nibble at the grain. You've guessed the rest – the order in which the bird ate the letters would provide the answer to the question.

In India there was a form of Alectromancy called 'Pakshi Shastra'; a parrot was used to select fortune-telling cards from a deck. There was something very similar in Italy, too, using a parakeet to select slips of paper.

ORNITHOMANCY

Generally, the art of prophesy by observing the flight patterns of birds. This is something we shall look at in greater depth in the following chapter, entitled 'Of Rainbows and Ravens – The Modern Augur'.

TASSEOGRAPHY

Although not just to do with birds, tasseography is the art of reading tea leaves left in a cup. There are, however, certain symbolic meanings attached to the types of birds that might be discerned in the patterns of the leaves.

A bird in general would be taken as good news. What the bird might be occupied with indicates more precise information; for example, if the bird is perched or featured with a telephone or letter, the querant is waiting for news. If the bird is flying, then news is on its way; in a cage, then something is trapped in the life of the querant.

The types of birds featured all have their meanings, too. A crow signifies a puzzling person, whereas a dove means love. A duck stands for gossip; a parrot is a show-off; a penguin, someone who is dapper and groomed but possibly egotistical (this latter quality also applies to the turkey). A vulture represents someone who is corrupt.

Finally, as an example of birds being able to detect something inaccessible to humans, this story comes from Narasinham in India, where the tsunami of 2004 devastated millions of homes and lives:

> I am in the habit of leaving some food on the balcony of our second-storey flat at Chennai everyday around 5 a.m. and it used to be picked up by the sparrows and other small birds, usually they'd be there waiting for it and it would be gone very quickly.
>
> On the day the tsunami struck our place, on December 26th, 2004, we rushed out around 6.45 a.m. and it was only after 8.30 that I noticed that the sparrows had come back to my flat to take the food I had left at 5 a.m.
>
> These birds were obviously more 'grounded' than we humans and had a forewarning or an instinct, and it seemed as though their return again was evidence that they knew that it was safe again at 8.30 a.m.

Of Ravens and Rainbows:
The modern augur

"Among the Romans not a bird
Without a prophecy was heard.
Fortunes of an empire often hung
On the magician magpie's tongue,
And every crow was to the state
A sure interpreter of fate."

Winston Churchill

"Not a whit we defy augury; there's a special providence in the fall of a sparrow. If it be now, 'tis not to come; if it be not to come, it will be now; if it be not now, yet it will come: the readiness is all."

William Shakespeare, *Hamlet*

In ancient times, the role of the augur was to interpret signs from nature, particularly from birds, in order to determine the will of the gods. Today, we sometimes need external agents to remind us that we are on the right path, and the impersonal nature of good divinatory tools ensures that the augur, or seer, is detached enough from the signs to be able to read them correctly and in as unegotistical a way as possible. Nowadays, the word augury can apply to almost any form of divination, but in this chapter we're going to concentrate on auguries in the true sense of the word – understanding messages from birds.

> *Auspicium* q. *Avispicium*, was taken from the flight of birds, either on the right hand or on the left; and hence is the proverb *avi sinistra*, good luck, because in giving or going, the right hand is opposite to the receivers left.
>
> **The Augur**, *No. II, October 1791*

What is Meant By Augury?

… to express the unknown, awoken in certain persons by the sight of a bird flying or an animal passing, and of spiritual concentration after its disappearance. It is a faculty of the soul which through the intellect, prompts a swift grasp of things seen or heard, which provides the substance of a forewarning. It is a faculty which assumes a strong and vivid imagination.

Toufic Fahn, *La Naissance du monde selon l'Islam*

The beauty and simplicity of augury is that it is distinctly separate from 'fortune telling'. Whereas the fortune teller will attempt to look into the future by various means and methods (crystal-ball gazing, the tarot, palmistry, etc.), augury is about being 'in the moment' and looking for the signs which tell us that all is well and that we are on the right track. This is possibly more important than any attempt to see the future – after all, if we knew precisely what the future held then it could be a little like being in a cage …

This is why it is said to be well-nigh impossible to tell one's own future. We simply know too much about ourselves and our desires and dreams!

How Did It All Begin?

It is worth pointing out that, although we are going to concentrate most specifically on the Roman and Greek forms of augury, the skill was practised extensively not only by these people, but also by the Chaldeans, Etruscans, Celts, Indians, Tibetans, Jews, and others.

THE BYA-ROG-GISKAD-BRTAG-PAR-BYA-BA

Yes, you did read that correctly – that is, as long as I spelled it right. This is the name that the Tibetans gave to their methods of divination from the flight patterns and calls of birds. They relied mainly on the crow as the most significant bird. In fact, this name actually translates as 'investigating the cries of crows'. There was a specific interest taken in the habits of each individual crow, since they are all quite different to the practised observer. Also to be taken into account was the angle between the observer and the crow, and the direction of the flight of the bird or of its call.

The time of day also factored into the equation. For example, the day was divided up into three-hour chunks, starting at 6 a.m., so we find that if a crow approached from the south east during the first watch between 6 a.m. and 9 a.m., then this would signify the approach of an enemy; whereas a crow appearing from a northerly direction between the hours of the third watch, between 12 noon and 3 p.m., would signify the arrival of a good friend.

THE CELTS

In Britain, the Celts had their own methods of divination by interpreting the flight paths, calls and species of birds, but since prophesy and soothsaying was one of the skills of the Druid priests they had no need for a formalized body of augurs.

The birds favoured by the Celts were the eagle, the wren, the raven or crow and the woodpecker. Swans were also important.

THE FIRST ROMAN AUGURS

In Rome, there was a College of Augurs, so important was the role considered to be. It is no exaggeration to say that absolutely no important matters of state were carried out in Roman times without first consulting the birds.

The first mention we have of augury in any form comes in Homer's Greek epic the *Iliad*, from around 700 BC. The very first record of the Roman form of augury is from about 600 BC, with the story of a swineherd, Attus Navius.

The story goes that Attus lost one of his pigs. He made a promise to the Gods that if the pig was found, then he would give them the very best bunch of grapes that he could find in his vineyard. The next day the missing pig reappeared; accordingly, Attus decided to employ scientific means to locate the best bunch of grapes.

His vineyard being quite large, Attus used his staff to divide it into four quarters, and as he was about to start looking, he noticed that the birds favoured one particular quarter. He headed for this section of the vineyard and again divided it into quarters. Then he did the same again, and eventually discovered a huge, beautiful bunch of grapes, simply by watching where the birds were telling him to go.

News of Attus's discovery spread like wildfire; his neighbours began to consult him, and soon his fame was such that the King of Rome, Tarquinius Priscus, employed Attus as his Augur.

There's another story related by the Jewish historian, Josephus. An owl flew down to sit on a branch of a tree which Agrippa, a grandson of Herod the Great, was leaning against while he was being held prisoner in Rome. A fellow prisoner predicted that because of this Agrippa would become King, but that if the bird reappeared then Agrippa would die. (Agrippa is better known from the Acts of the Apostles, erroneously, as Herod Agrippa.)

Roman auguries were carried out in public whenever there were important decisions to be made which could affect society as a whole; indeed, the word 'inauguration', still used for presidents and high-ranking officials, shares the same root. There were private ceremonies of augury, too, which would generally be carried out by the senior male householder.

How Did The Ancients Carry Out Their Auguries?

It is important to bear in mind, and worth repeating again, that the *raison d'etre* of the augur was not to look into the future but to ensure that the will of the Gods was being carried out – that the right thing was being done and that the correct course of action was taking place. After all, whatever lies in the 'future' is a difficult thing to master, and being in the present, doing the right thing, is the most essential purpose we can have for our lives.

Looking into the practices of the Ancients, there are some things on which there seem to be accord, and the best records of augury are the ones we find in the Roman tradition.

First, the augur would find a high point geographically from which to carry out the divination. There is a story that relates how, in Rome, Romulus consulted an augur on the Palatine Hill about where the city should be founded. In addition, Remus took similar advice on the Aventine Hill. Later, the official place of augury, the Auguraculum, was sited on a spot now known as the Capitoline Hill. Although Remus also took auguries, Romulus received more of the favourable auspices of vultures, and this is why Romulus is regarded as the founder of Rome. In fact, under the name of Quirinius, Romulus also became Rome's first augur.

Generally, the first thing to be done was the establishment of an area for the auguries to be carried out. This was known as a 'templum', and at an established Auguraculum the templum was a permanent feature.

To make the templum, first a line called the 'cardo' was marked out, running from East to West in accord with the spot on the horizon where the sun would rise and set. The next thing to do would be to mark out the 'decumanus', a line running from North to South, determined by the Pole Star. No calculations were made. Both of these key lines would be judged accurate by following the signs given by nature. As you can imagine, these lines would also change according to the seasons. Once the key lines were established, two sets of parallel lines would be drawn to establish a rectangle of a 6:5 ratio, and then a tent, known as a 'tabernaculum', would be erected, with its entrance facing South.

Overseeing these proceedings would be a magistrate known as the Auspex, who would usually sit somewhere high above the tabernaculum and observe the proceedings. It was the role of the Auspex to ensure objectivity, to act as a kind of check and balance, and the job of the tabernaculum was to provide the 'field of play' for whatever signs were about to happen. Anything occurring outside this area would not be included.

Often flute players would play during the ceremony; this would probably be to draw in the birds, although it could also have been so that the augur, who would be blindfolded, would not be distracted by external sounds. The actions of the birds would be described to the augur so that he remained completely impartial; the rules of augury were kept a tight secret, and the role of the augur was, politically, of vital importance.

In birds of prey, the female bird is usually larger than the male.

Once all this was set up, the magistrate would use his staff to outline another templum in the sky. The staff was called the 'lituus' and was only used during augury. It was a long straight piece of (usually) ash or hazel, with a curve at one end. (Interestingly, the lituus still survives today; it became the crosier, the hooked staff carried as part of ritual by the bishops in Anglican and Catholic churches.) The sky templum would be delineated by various points on the ground such as trees, boulders and the like.

In the same way that the swineherd Attus divided his vineyard into quarters, then divided it up again, the celestial and earthly templa were similarly split into 16 sections. Each section was assigned to a particular divinity. Then various prayers were said, and the analysis would begin.

In Roman augury, birds were distinguished as either 'oscines' (talkers) or as 'alites' (flyers). The flight patterns of certain birds were the key feature. The main birds were vultures and eagles (of which Pliny tells us there were six kinds). In addition, the calls of certain birds were also examined.

DIRECTION

The direction from which the birds arrived was important. From the South and East was considered favourable, but from the West or from behind (North) was seen as unfavourable. But these signs would be altered according to whether the birds were considered good omens or bad omens, and could also be dependent on the body language of the birds, too. As well as being intuitive, the augur would also have had to be familiar with the habits of birds in a particular area, so he would be something of a naturalist too.

For the Greeks, in general, birds arriving from the left signalled an unfavourable omen, whilst the right was good; the Romans believed the opposite. There was an attempt to create a 'standard' for augury in Ephesus in the sixth century BC; only fragments of the 'rule book' exist today, however:

Line of flight from right to left. If the bird disappeared from sight the omen was favourable; but if it raised its left wing and then soared and disappeared the omen is ill.

Line of flight from left to right. If it disappeared on a straight course it is an ill omen; but if it raised its right wing and then soared and disappeared the omen is good.

As if this were not enough, remember how the area of the templum had been divided into 16 sections, with each section being dedicated to a deity? Each bird was dedicated to a deity too, so if, for example, the dove (dedicated to Venus) arrived in the section designated as Venus's quarter, then this would be heralded as particularly favourable. There would be some ground rules set out at the outset though. There would be a specific purpose for taking the auspices, and certain signs ('imperativa') would be particularly looked for and other signs ('oblativa'), while still relevant, could be regarded as omens but need not be a part of the augury itself.

Greek Versus Roman Methods of Augury

There are two kinds of divination, of which one is a matter of art, the other a matter of nature.

For the Romans, their methods of augury fell into the former category; for the Greeks, the latter was true. The quote above is from Cicero, who was one of the early members of the College of Augurs and who wrote an essay about auguries. In it, he discusses the practicalities and the theories pertaining to the practice. Here is an extract from the introductory passage:

There is an ancient belief, handed down to us even from mythical times and firmly established by the general agreement of Roman people and of all nations that divination of some kind exists among men; this the Greeks call foresight and knowledge of future events. A really splendid and helpful thing it is – if only such a faculty exists – since by its means men may approach very near to the power of the Gods. And, just as we Romans have done many things better than the Greeks, so we have excelled them in giving to this most extraordinary gift a name, which we have derived from 'divi', a word meaning 'gods', whereas, according to Plato's interpretation, they have derived it from 'furor', a word meaning 'frenzy'.

Fighting talk indeed! It seems amusing now that there should be such a sense of competition between the Romans and the Greeks over this matter. Then again, if we look a little more closely into the methods of each, we can see that they relied on quite different approaches to divine the messages from the birds.

The Romans favoured a very formalized approach, relying on set patterns and meanings; the augurs were appointed officials who worked to a rigid set of rules and guidelines.

The Greek word for augur was 'oionopolos', which translates as 'expert in bird omens'. The major source of any information we have regarding these oionopolos is from Homer, and the large birds of prey commonly used by the Greeks for augury, raptors, were of prime importance, probably reflecting the predatory nature of Greek society at the time. The ancient Greeks had an almost universal faith in the power of omens, and signs from birds were regarded as a reliable indicator of what the Gods held in store.

As opposed to the very rigid Roman ways of doing things, the Greeks favoured a much more free-form approach, which sounds to me as though it has similarities with the way in which shamans work. The Greeks believed that the will of the Gods would be revealed by a heightening of consciousness in man, which might involve fasting or taking hallucinatory drugs or psychotropic herbs in order to 'free the mind'.

It's likely that both ways were equally valid.

Birds and Other Signs

Augurs and understood relations have
By maggot-pies and choughs and rooks brought forth
The secret'st man of blood.
William Shakespeare, *Macbeth*

A writer called Psellus, living in the tenth century AD, wrote a treatise on auguries entitled 'Divination from Shoulder Blades and Birds'. In it he outlined some guidelines, including the 'Rule of 4'.

THE RULE OF 4

The Romans had four features of augury. These were signs in the weather, the flight patterns of birds, the calls of birds and the appearance of certain animals. Following the same pattern, each feature again divides into four:

1. **Ex Caelo –**
    Cloud forms – nimbus, cirrus, stratus, cumulus
    Precipitation – snow, sleet, hail, rain
    Lightning – sheet or forked, and thunder – rolling or a clap
    Light – rainbows, occulation of the sun, moon or stars, shooting stars or comets
2. **Ex Avibus Alites (flight)**
    Eagle and/or vulture
    Hawk
    Crow
    Woodpecker
3. **Ex Avibus Oscines (calls)**
    Raven and/or crow
    Owl
    Woodpecker
    Hen
4. **Ex Quadrupedibus**
    Wolf
    Fox
    Dog
    Horse

Another factor to be brought into the equation would be how long the auguries should take place. This time would be designated at the start, but once the magistrate had left his seat then the ceremony would be ended.

How the Questions Were Asked

In any form of divination, knowing what question needs to be asked is of paramount importance.

The questions asked of the Gods in augury required straightforward 'yes' or 'no' answers. Favourable signs were called 'nuntiato', and unfavourable 'obnuntiato'. In announcing the results to the public, if the signs were favourable the cry would be 'Aves Admittunt!' ('the birds allow it'). If unfavourable, the call would be 'Alio Die', meaning 'another day', and the drawn-out process of reading the messages of the birds in the context of other signs of nature would be repeated on another day.

How to Interpret These Methods for Our Own Augury

The first thing to remember is that you don't need to be an expert ornithologist! Augurs differ very much from ornithologists. You don't have to be a bird expert in order to be an augur, although it's likely you'll become more interested in the types of birds and their behaviour almost by default.

As we've seen, the methods of the Romans seem to be pretty complex, but then the needs of that society were different to ours, and the emphasis placed on such portents as birds, cloud formations and the like were taken more seriously than they would be today by most government officials. However, the knowledge that we are doing the right thing, at the right time, for the right reasons – that that we are following our path, however difficult various aspects of it may seem at the time – is as relevant now as it ever was, and the messages that birds give us are equally valid, if only we recognize how they work and how to use them.

The Romans used the birds prevalent in their environment from which to extrapolate signs and portents. Similarly, we should do the same thing. If we were waiting around for eagles or vultures to tell us what's going on, some of us might have a very long wait indeed!

A Bird Diary

I keep a record of the birds I have seen and the events that coincided with their appearance. For example, several times when I have seen three snipe one after the other there has been something wrong somewhere, some kind of discrepancy. Certain birds, for me, represent certain people in my life, and the appearance of different kinds of bird together gives me a sort of instinctive idea of what is going on somewhere. The easiest way to develop this sense is to give each bird you see its own page, and then record what events coincide with the bird's appearance. You need to be rigorously objective and consistent about this. You may find that some birds 'speak' to you at certain times more than at others, either literally or metaphorically. The method you use could be different but whatever way you choose to analyse the secrets of the birds in your life, it's important to keep a record of how they appear and what any subsequent events might be.

Be Aware of the Birds Around You

You may live in an area which may not appear to have much bird life. However, bear in mind that you are more likely these days to see sparrows and pigeons if you live in a high-rise block than if you live in the country, and keep your eyes peeled – peregrine falcons nest quite happily on tall buildings as well as on cliff faces. You will find that a walk down a busy city street will reveal jays, crows and jackdaws, all members of the highly intelligent and adaptable Corvid family, and you're there too; doesn't that tell you something?

> There are fewer people on the planet than there are chickens.

Once we become aware of something, life has a way of seeming to push that thing into our path wherever possible. When I was researching this book, part of my investigations included asking people what kind of bird they would be if they could choose. Since they chose, several people have told me that 'their' bird seemed to be more prevalent than before, more obvious, more 'on their path'.

DREAMING

You may find that you dream of certain birds, or perhaps you may dream that you are flying; this is not a book about dream analysis, but to dream about flying is said to be about transcendence of the soul, rising above our earthly ties. In addition, to dream that we are flying can signify a way of solving problems by rising above them and seeing those difficulties as a part of the bigger picture.

Keep a dream diary. Once you start doing this, to paraphrase Jung, it's almost as if your subconscious mind comes out to play, and your dreams will start to become more and more meaningful. In the modern Western world we often forget our dreams, but there is a part of us, often not so very deep inside, which is described as 'primitive' and is in better accord with our inner world than our rational, conscious selves. You may find, in that waking moment between sleep and 'reality', that you remember far more than you had anticipated – the birds you need to hear from or speak to can be pretty insistent.

The dream state enables us to move in and out of linear 'time' as we know it, and you may find that your dreams are simply ones of prophecy. (For instance, I had a lucid dream about a dark swan on the lake behind my house, which had travelled from the North. A few weeks later I was visited by a beautiful dark-haired woman, at that time a stranger, called Swan, who had travelled down from Scotland.) Or you might find that the birds you dream of can be interpreted as symbols – the at-a-glance guide to the symbolism of birds on page 482 will help you with this.

SEEING

The next step is to really start to observe the birds around you, and to give them meanings that apply to you personally. You could use the list in this book (page 482), which shows some of the traditional meanings associated with various birds – though where possible it would be good to personalize your analysis. You may find, as I did, that certain birds represent people in your life; you may associate particular events with birds. It doesn't really matter so long as you extract your own meaning from the signs you are being given and keep them consistent.

HEARING

You don't need to be able to recognize every single different bird call, but you may find that you notice bird song in a new way once you become aware of the different sounds – amidst the background of bird song when you're in wide open spaces at certain times of the year, a particular call or cry may stand out from the others. Try to find out which bird is making this sound; watch out for it and be aware of the events surrounding it in your own life. The call of the cuckoo is the traditional sign that Spring is coming; therefore this sound has a universality about it. Similarly, you will start to find that the sounds of certain birds will become associated with particular events, people or places.

IMAGINING

At the next possible opportunity you have, get out into some wide-open spaces and watch birds in flight. It almost doesn't matter what kind of bird you might find to watch: housemartins or swallows on summer evenings are spectacular, almost like fish as they swoop and dive and weave about; you may be lucky enough to see a flock of red kites close to one of the feeding stations dotted around the UK, or in the USA you may be able to see eagles and vultures circling. Lie back in the grass if you can and simply watch the birds; imagine that you are at one with them, and imagine what it feels like to fly. Close your eyes and picture what the landscape looks like from their angle: see how the tops of the trees look from above; see more of a river than you have ever seen before; see the patchwork patterns of fields and the shadows cast by trees and hedgerows – see the world from a new dimension.

Your Own Way of Augury

What you need to do now is to decide how you want to conduct your augury.

Initially, it's probably a good idea to keep it very simple; decide on your own experimental rules and stick to them, keeping a record of what happens. You might simply decide that a bird flying from the left to right signifies a yes, and the opposite is a no. Or you might decide to meditate in an open space, tune into nature and simply 'free form' as you develop the ability to move out of time. This is more akin to the Greek method of augury.

Absolute objectivity is the key. It is very important to remain unattached to the outcome; everything that happens, happens for the best possible reason, even if we don't always see it at the time.

However, ritual is also important, and you may choose to emulate the traditions of the ancient Romans. Described here is a way of following their methods.

First, you will need to find the correct location. The Romans would have found a high place, a hill or mountain. We need to be practical. Not everyone has access to a mountain, and it is more important for you to find a spot which 'feels' right and which is geographically convenient.

As the Romans would have marked the cardo (the line running from East to West in line with where the sun rises and sets on the horizon) you can easily do the same thing. You could use small stones as markers, or stick twigs into the ground. Similarly, the Romans would mark out the decumanus (the line running from North to South) by observing the Pole Star. Unfortunately, with light pollution these days, it's not always possible to find the Pole Star, and in the spirit of the Roman way of doing this, equipment was not really meant to be used; however there's no reason why you shouldn't use a compass!

FANCY BUILDING A TEMPLE?

In Umbria in Italy, the word 'angla' meant the birds that were used for omens and signs. The root of the word is from the Latin, 'angulus', meaning 'corner'; and this is because the place where a flight of birds would suddenly do an about-turn was of great significance to the augur. More words: the Umbrian word for 'temple' is 'verfale' and the root of this word is the Latin for 'to turn'; the place where birds turned was believed to be the correct place for a temple to be built.

This is all relevant information for the next step.

Once the cardo and the decumanus are established it is a simple matter to mark out your templum.

If the area you are going to use for your auguries is to be a permanent one you might want to consider planting saplings at each of the four corners of the templum. If the area is not to be permanent then you could use the natural materials you find around and about, such as rocks or pieces of wood.

The next step for the Romans would be to mark out, in the sky, a similar templum, to demarcate the part of the sky to be observed for birds, cloud formations and the like. We have seen that the Romans used a staff of ash or hazel, with a curve at one end, called a lituus. You may choose to fashion your own lituus using the same kind of wood, or you could simply point out the area using your index finger.

ASKING THE QUESTION

We now come to the most important part of this ritual – the asking of the question.

Remember that the Romans kept this very simple, and made sure that the question could be answered with a simple 'yes' or 'no'. It is crucial that you are asking the correct question and that you remain 'unattached' to the answer. Often we get caught up in our own issues and we apply our will to our vision: we alter or bend an outcome according to what we would like it to be rather than facing the facts as they are. This is why it may be easier to perform auguries on behalf of another person, so that you can be objective about the outcome.

Once the question had been honed, the Romans would send a message to the Gods; the essence of their prayer would be 'if it is the right thing, send the signs which will indicate the answer'. Keep in mind at all times the fact that performing auguries is not about seeing into the future but about making sure that we are 'in the moment' and doing the right thing at the right time.

Now all that remains to do is to decide how long you are going to devote to this particular session, and to find a way of also marking out the time. You could use an hourglass, perhaps, or if the visibility is good you could decide to stop when the sun reaches a certain point in the sky.

Finally, simply wait ... and then interpret the signs you will be given according to your own observations.

Remember the signs you need to watch out for. You need to observe which kind of birds or combinations of birds are in the sky; from which direction they are flying and to which direction they are flying; what calls or sounds they make; and their flight patterns. For the Romans, shifts in the weather and the cloud formations were also important, and you should factor these into your equation too.

Good luck. Remember that not all your auguries may work. There is a possibility that there will be no birds whatsoever, and you'll need to try again another day. This was an occupational hazard for the Roman augur too, so stay philosophical if nothing goes right!

One for Sorrow

'When I was 17 I was living on Dartmoor for a few months with my parents.

A boyfriend came to visit. We had a very magical relationship – always ending up in faerie rings or enchanted woods. It was lovely for a while but I knew the relationship was over (it wouldn't work) and didn't know how to tell him.

We lay down in a field close to the house and I felt sad. Suddenly a Magpie flew down and landed on me, cocking its head and making funny little squawks. He jumped and hopped around us and came back to me a second time and looked me straight in the eye. David looked at me and somehow knew what I wanted to tell him – as if the Magpie told him telepathically.

"That's what this means! You want to end the relationship ..."

At that point we both cried and the magpie flew away.'

Helen, Morocco

Communication from Birds:
Some examples of augury

> " My heart lifted up with the great grasses;
> The weeds believed me, and the nesting birds."

Theodore Roethke, *A Field of Light*

Historically, there are numerous instances where messages from birds have been analysed correctly, and unsurprisingly, given the importance of augury to the ancient Greeks and Romans, many of these examples are to be found in classical literature. I have also included some more recent examples.

The Chicken

Yes, the chicken! Caged chickens were kept specifically so that their behaviour could be analysed. This was usually a very simple matter; if they ate their food as normal, then the signs were good. If they failed to eat, then the prognosis was generally bad.

The Eagle

The eagle was one of the key birds in the auguries of the Greeks, the Romans and the Persians. There are countless episodes, but here are just a few.

In the *Iliad*, Priam, King of Troy, asks Zeus to send a favourable omen, and accordingly, Zeus sends his own bird, the eagle:

> And straightaway he sent an eagle, most ominous of birds, the dark hunter, whom they also call the 'black eagle'. Wide as the doors with bars that fit tight in a rich man's high vaulted hall, so wide stretched its wings on either side. It swooped through the city on the right and those watching rejoiced and their hearts cheered within their breasts.

There are plenty of examples of the eagle as omen in the *Odyssey*, too:

> Just as the eagle there descended from the mountain, where it was born and reared ... so shall Odysseus return home after long trials and wanderings and wreak vengeance.

There's an episode recorded by Xenophon about the armies of Cyrus coming to help Cyaxares, the King of Medea, in his battles with the Assyrians. An eagle flew over the Persian troops, which was taken as a favourable omen, and must have encouraged the troops significantly.

Mexico City was founded in the place where the living evidence of a formerly mythical legend took place: the Mexica knew from their folkloric history that a mighty civilization would be founded in a place where an eagle would be found perched on a stump; the stump would be coming out of marshy ground. This sign was seen and acted upon, and the marsh ground, with a river next to it, proved an ideal place for the new city to flourish because the waterway was useful for trading purposes.

The Heron

The *Iliad* tells how Odysseus and Diomedes set out to raid the Trojan camp, and were sent a heron as a sign, reputedly by the Goddess Athena. The heron was sent from a favourable direction – from the right – and although it was dark so that Odysseus couldn't actually see it, fortuitously, it called, and, we are told, 'Odysseus rejoiced at the bird of omen and gave thanks to Athena.'

The Owl

Although we shall see later in this book that there is some ambivalence about the owl, with it being regarded as a 'dark' bird while also associated with wisdom, it is an important bird for the purposes of augury. The Greeks in particular held the bird in great esteem as a symbol of Athena, and in one instance the leader of an army, Agathocles, 'cheated' by releasing owls among his troops to encourage them; not a true augury, perhaps, but a good indicator of the importance of the bird since Agathocles knew the sight of the owls would have a profound morale-boosting effect.

The Raven

Alone amongst the important birds of augury, the raven was believed to be able to understand the information and messages it carried. There are plenty of instances, however, of the raven being considered the bearer of dark news.

Ravens are reputed to have led Alexander the Great to the oracle of Ammon Ra in Egypt: the journey was several days' march into the desert, hence the party must have been greatly relieved to have had the assistance of the birds:

> And when the landmarks became confused and the travellers wandered about and were scattered in bewilderment, ravens appeared and assumed the role of guides, flying swiftly in front for them to follow and waiting for them when they marched slowly or lagged behind.
> *Plutarch,* **Life of Alexander**

But, Plutarch reports, they also prophesied his death:

> He observed many ravens flying about and striking one another, some of which fell dead at his feet.

The Stork

During the battle for Aquileia, in AD 451, the Roman city was under siege from Attila the Hun, although it seemed to be holding out bravely. However, Attila noticed that the storks were leaving their nests with their babies and took this as a sign that the city would soon give up if he kept up the attack. This he did, and indeed, the storks were correct with their information.

The Swallow

There's an account by Plutarch which relates how swallows nested in Cleopatra's flagship; unfortunately the birds were attacked by bigger ones, chased from the ship and their nests destroyed. This was taken as a bad omen, and indeed the Egyptian army lost the battle of Actium shortly afterwards, when Octavian defeated Cleopatra and Antony's combined forces.

There are other instances of swallows carrying messages. Alexander the Great was taking a rest in his tent during the siege of Halicarnassus. A swallow came into the tent, and despite Alexander trying to swot it away so he could get some sleep, the bird kept settling on his head, so he decided to consult an augur, Aristander of Telmissus, whose analysis of the swallow's behaviour was that Alexander had a disloyal 'friend', but that the betrayal would soon come to light. This proved to be the case.

The Vulture

To the ancient augurs, the vulture was an incredibly important bird of omen. Because its flight pattern was steeped in messages, the bird was dedicated to Apollo.

It's worth bearing in mind that Rome, one of the world's major cities, was founded in the spot chosen by Romulus; he in turn was given this privilege over his brother Remus simply because, during an augury, Romulus was favoured with the approval of 12 vultures whereas his brother had only 6 vultures on his side.

The Woodpecker

The woodpecker was 'much esteemed by the Druides for divination...' The bird was also revered by the Romans because it had been responsible, with the wolf, for raising Romulus and Remus.

A woodpecker had a key role to play in an incident in Rome, when an unfortunate counsellor, Aelius Tubero, was giving judgment at the Forum when a woodpecker landed on his head. The bird appeared to be so tame that Aelius was even able to hold it in his hand. Accordingly, the augurs were consulted; they decided that, if the bird were released, disaster would befall the state, but if it were killed then disaster would be restricted merely to Aelius. Courageously, Aelius cast aside any personal feelings and ripped the bird to pieces; shortly afterwards he apparently met a terrible end, although we're not sure precisely what nature this took.

The Wren

The wren is believed to have been domesticated in order to give omens, and is one of the birds who were believed to have their own language; we are told by Walter Gill, in his *Second Manx Scrapbook*, dated 1932, that this language was part of a tradition which existed 'in most parts of the world, and which appears in many a legend and fairy tale'.

The Roman writer Suetonius tells us that it was the wren who predicted the death of Julius Caesar when he was stabbed on the Ides of March; it was attacked and killed by other birds as it flew towards its nest with a laurel leaf in its beak. Caesar, of course, wore a crown of laurel leaves. The wren was also one of the most important birds of augury for the Druids, who considered it to be their 'King of the Birds'.

As in all auguries, the direction that the wren was coming from and flying towards had great relevance; here's a short extract from *Prognostications from the Raven and the Wren*, by Eriu, dated 1916:

> If the little bright-headed one call to you from the East, pious men are journeying towards you ... Should the wren call from the south-east, it is proud jesters that are coming ... If it calls from the North, dear to you is he that is coming ...

As recently as 1927, the wren was able to decide the fortune of a French village called Mazan. A wren was captured alive and brought into the church. If the bird flew to the high altar or perched on a statue the fortunes of the village and its inhabitants would be good. But if the bird flew up into the roof, then the prognostication was not so good.

Tree of Knowledge

'I used to have a recurrent dream that I was a bird, sitting in the uppermost branches of a very tall tree at the top of a mountain. Sometimes the dream is different but it always starts this way. Down below are branches bearing gold and silver fruit. I can see the fruit but it seems unimportant. Below the branches with the fruit are clouds and mist because I am so high up. Then one day, in real life, I had a sort of waking dream; I was lying on my back, relaxing, after a yoga class, and I suddenly felt a weight in either hand. I could feel that I had an apple in one hand, and a pear in the other, and I knew that I had been given a great gift, the gift of information or knowledge, and that I should share this knowledge.'

Serena, Spain

A Telling Dream

'Years ago, at the end of an unhappy affair, I had a vivid dream. In the dream, a weeping woman stood in the foreground, with one hand covering her face in grief so that her features were hidden. From the other hand, which was extended, love letters in her grasp "leaked" words into the air. And behind her, among the branches of the leafy trees, sat birds. But all of their beaks had been tied shut.'

Judy, UK

Elizabeth's Story

The following is a very moving story; it also has elements of augury about it, but Elizabeth would have had no awareness of this at the time. She was simply seeking a straightforward answer to a question.

I have recently been planting a memorial oak tree for my parents, and I believe that a bird helped me to know where my father's ashes were buried – over 35 years ago. My mother's ashes were no problem, but I really wanted this to be a tree for both parents, for myself and to spiritually reunite them.

When father died I went to the funeral but not the crematorium, women did not go as much then. I had a fairly hysterical mother (who didn't believe in graves, funerals, etc.) and a six-week-old baby – there was never time for me to grieve or think about my role in the bereavement. I think I must have drawn a veil over it all in my mind, I cannot think now why I waited 35 years to visit.

Going there was very hard, I didn't know where he had been placed, even when the records told me it was the Gorse Garden there was no way of knowing the exact spot. It was November, and there were only wintering plants, few leaves to speak of. As I wandered about the corner, one bed produced a beautiful little rose bush, full of blooms – it stood out like a beacon, but it felt important not to jump to conclusions just because it was pretty. I went to other areas and felt absolutely nothing.

I decided at this point that I couldn't do this by myself. I can clearly remember the words of my thoughts – 'OK, I could really use some help round here' – and I turned towards the original bed with the roses. As I approached, but still some way off, just to the side of the rose there was a little gorse bush with something under it – then I realized it was a bird. As I did so another bird flew from behind me almost skimming my shoulder to the extent it made me jump. It joined the other bird and there they sat as I got closer.

I went fairly close, but not wanting to alarm the birds, and stood there for a long time, thinking my thoughts, very still, very moved. I had decided that this was as close to unravelling an unsolvable question as I would ever get. I was perhaps 15 minutes just standing there. The birds left in time, but when I was ready to move I walked the small distance left towards the bed, my next thoughts being, 'I know this is perhaps asking just too much, but if there could be anything you could do to really help me to believe I have found the right place I would be very grateful.' When I stood in front of the gorse bush I realized there was something resting on the top, I had to put on my glasses to see. When I did there was a large white bird feather (a seagull-type size – not the little ones of the birds I had seen) sticking up out of the centre of the bush just like a feather in an Indian headdress.

I cut some of the twigs from the bush and buried them, together with the feather, under the oak tree, alongside my mother's ashes. I feel inside me that it really is their tree now.

Did these birds help me?

The margins between a real happening, imagination and fanciful thought are probably very slender – but I'm not sure I care. This occasion was very precious to me.

The Ravens

In a dead tree, split in two by lightning, were perched three huge, black birds, too big for crows. I had never seen anything like them before.

'Ravens,' said Charles.

We stood stock-still, watching them. One of them hopped clumsily to the end of a branch, which squeaked and bobbed under its weight and sent it squawking into the air. The other two followed, with a battery of flaps. They sailed over the meadow in a triangle formation, three dark shadows on the grass.

Charles laughed. 'Three of them for three of us. That's an augury, I bet.'

'An omen.'

'Of what ?' I said.

'Don't know,' said Charles. 'Henry's the ornithomantist. The bird-diviner.'

'He's such an old Roman. He'd know.'

Donna Tartt, The Secret History

Starlings and star signs, parrots and planets:
Birds and astrology

Did you know that in India there's a form of astrology, featuring birds, known as the Pancha Pakshi Shastra? Based on ancient Tamil literature from Southern India, Pancha means 'five' and Pakshi means 'bird'. It should not be confused with another Indian method of divination with the help of birds, called simply Pakshi Shastra; this is where a parrot is used to select fortune-telling cards from a deck!

How Pancha Pakshi Shastra works is that the five elements (earth, water, fire, air and ether) are extrapolated as the natures of particular birds, and these birds influence the actions of human beings. Added to this, each part of the day or night is signified by one of the five birds and the whole cycle is governed by the phases of the Moon.

The five birds are the vulture, the owl, the crow, the rooster and the peacock, and they can engage in one of five activities at any time; these activities are to rule, to eat, to walk, to sleep and to die. In addition, the five birds also rule the days of the week, as well as times of day, and elaborate charts are drawn up and used in pretty much the same way as our Western astrological charts are with their forecasts and interpretations.

In the run-up to the Bush/Gore elections in the USA in 2000, an Indian astrologer called Vinod Kumar Gupta analysed the chances of each candidate being elected President, and the method told him that Gore would have hurdles put in the way of his being President, whereas Bush, in combination with the horoscope of his father, would be more favoured. History revealed Vinod to be a pretty astute astrologer!

In the course of researching this book, I surveyed many people, asking them what kind of bird they would be if they could choose, and also what star

sign they were. What had started out as a piece of fun suddenly became incredibly interesting. The resemblances started to become uncanny; for example, so many Leo people chose Eagles that if someone chose the Eagle who was *not* a Leo, we'd do a little digging and as often as not discover that the rising sign of that person would be Leo.

That so many Leos chose the Eagle is not unsurprising. After all, this is the bird of the Sun (the ruling star of the Leo) and in Egyptian mythology two Eagles are said to hold up the rising Sun. The bird is also the symbol of empires and emperors, kings, queens and the mighty; it is a powerful bird, majestic and proud, and has many qualities of the Lion.

Similarly, looking at the traits attributed to the 12 signs of the Zodiac, and the characteristics and idiosyncrasies of the birds, parallels can be drawn between bird-type and star signs. Remember, these birds were chosen from the answers given by several hundred people – I simply took the most popular bird for each sign and then intuited the rest.

Further, I found that the bird/character types bore some relationship to the four elements used in conventional Western astrology, namely fire, air, earth and water, so I grouped the types according to this rule.

If your bird type doesn't seem to fit, then it might be worth bearing in mind other factors. For example, your ascending sign – the sign which was coming on to the horizon at the time you were born – also has a strong impact upon your personality, as does the influence of the other planets. There are plenty of informative books about astrology and so I will not even attempt to emulate anything like the level of information here which is available elsewhere. However, see if your personality type, or those of your friends, matches the following information. Better still, see if you can guess the star sign of the person by seeing which description they believe best fits them.

The poetry in this astrology section is by kind permission of the author, Elene Kurtesz.

The Birds of the Element of Earth

In Western astrology, the signs that share the common element of Earth are Taurus, Virgo and Capricorn. Earth can be many things. It could be the soil in our gardens, or it could be the shifting sands at the shoreline; it could be a peat bog, or it could be bed rock. It could be a mountain, or it could be a valley …

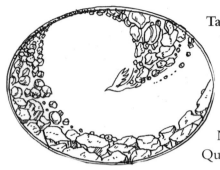

Taurus – The Bullfinch: tenacity; courage; security
Virgo – The Dove: nobility; honesty; guilelessness
Capricorn – The Wren: diplomacy; wisdom; kindness

Other Earth element birds you may feel an affinity for include the Chickadee, the Magpie, the Nightingale, the Nightjar, the Ostrich, the Partridge, the Pheasant, the Quail, the Sparrow, the Turkey and the Wagtail.

Taurus: 21st April–22nd May

THE BULLFINCH

You remember me every year;
and you laugh with delight as I talk to you;
You do not know what I am saying
This makes me laugh too
Elene Kurtesz

People born under the sign of Taurus, ruled by the planet Venus, have a close affinity with the bullfinch. The time when the Sun is in the sign of Taurus equates to the time that the popular little bullfinch is singing beautifully in late spring gardens. Chaucer, using the old English name of the Alpe, talks about 'the sweetness of hir melodye' which fills the May morning.

Taurus is ruled by the planet Venus, the Goddess of Love, and the bullfinch is a much-loved bird, being a herald of the Spring and of better times to come. In accordance with the Earth element, bullfinches seem to spend quite a lot of time quite close to the ground. They are exceptionally fond of fruits of all kinds and can often be seen in small flocks systematically and patiently stripping a tree or bush of its tasty delights!

The quality of patience extends to other areas of the bullfinch's life, too. It will be happy to work away steadily at many aspects of its life, often for several years; it is sometimes possible for the bullfinch to get a little stuck in a rut and it would be as well for this bird to realize this tendency and remember to shake up their lives every so often.

Bullfinch people are often regarded as being one of the most attractive birds, and will retain their good looks as they age, often appearing to be much younger than they look; but this bird is so charming that it is unlikely to attract jealousy. The bullfinch has a tendency to be shy, and prospective friends would do well to realize this, because the friendship of a bullfinch is a valuable commodity indeed; these birds are loyal, kind, diplomatic and generous and have a wonderful tendency to see the best in everyone.

Music is important to the bullfinch, and these birds will often have lovely voices or a musical talent. If this is the case, learning an instrument even as a hobby would be a highly enjoyable and fulfilling thing to do. As well as music, bullfinches have a great appreciation of other arts. They will often gravitate towards delicate, time-consuming hobbies such as tapestry, stained glass making or mosaic work; all these pastimes can be highly enjoyable to the bullfinch, and it may be likely that these pursuits could form the basis of a career, given encouragement.

The Bullfinch's Nest

The nest of the bullfinch will often be in a state of near-completion for several years, as the house is improved upon little by little. The bullfinch is perfectly happy with this, so long as a part of the home is relatively dust-free; when finally completed, the home will be lacking in none of the creature comforts, and will often be full of nooks and crannies and lovely places to sit and read a book or enjoy the view from the window. The bullfinch is a domesticated bird and enjoys the delights of the home; frequently the kitchen will be the focal point and will often be full of friends and family chatting while the busy bullfinch does everything to ensure that the guests are comfortable and looked after.

Work

Financial security is important for the bullfinch; this, combined with the bird's quality of patience, means that they may find themselves involved in jobs which combine attention to detail with long-term aims. Bullfinches make good researchers, for example, or teachers; the latter is an area where the renowned patience of this bird would prove invaluable, and would also provide a great sense of achievement. Lecturing would also be a good choice; bullfinches have marvellous powers of communication and once they get over a natural diffidence they can make good public speakers.

Bullfinches have an innate ability to generate money, both for themselves and others, so it is possible that financial areas of work could prove successful for this bird.

The bullfinch is happy to leave work behind when he or she finishes the day; it is unlikely that this bird will fret after hours, although the perfectionist side of the nature of this bird means that it will be more than happy to work overtime to ensure that everything is exactly as it should be. The bullfinch hates to be unprepared and will put in as much time as necessary to make sure it has all the information it needs to hand.

Bullfinches generally get on with anyone and everyone and are likely to make close friends through work. These friendships will carry on outside the workspace, and even if one or both parties have changed jobs.

Relationships

The bullfinch is a charming and handsome bird, and will have no trouble physically attracting people. However, the bullfinch has a lot of depth too, and is more likely, for themselves, to be interested in the intellectual qualities of a potential partner; a sense of humour will also be close to the top of the list. If the bullfinch decides that someone will be a suitable mate, they will be prepared to wait a long time if necessary for that person to be 'ready' for them.

Bullfinches prefer to mate for life, but tend to be a little jealous and possessive, which can be off-putting. It may simply be a sign of a deep-rooted insecurity, which it would be as well for this bird to be aware of, since it is unlikely to make the mistake of choosing a partner who would be unfaithful. Bullfinches are affectionate, loving birds, and need to have these qualities reciprocated; more sensual and tactile than most, these birds are very 'touchy-feely' and gain reassurance from lots of hugs and the like.

There is also another aspect to the bullfinch's nature which he or she needs to be aware of: there can be a slight tendency to want to control the partner. Bossiness can start to come to the fore once the bird feels secure in the relationship, and this should be curbed!

Children are important to the bullfinch, and any prospective partner should of course feel the same way. The bullfinch's ideal would be to have lots of children running around the garden swinging from the apple trees.

Forewarned . . .

An innate sense of insecurity may cause the bullfinch to be a little bossy once this bird is sure of his or her partner; this is unnecessary, because the bullfinch is wise enough to make a good choice. Relax a little!

Virgo: 22nd August–22nd September

The Dove

I am softness itself;
my feathers are soft, my song is soft, my heart is soft.
I am the mother; therefore my soul is strong
and my wings are comforting
Elene Kurtesz

Ruled by Mercury and being of the element of Earth, Virgo people have a great affinity with the dove.

The dove was one of the sacred birds of Aphrodite, the Goddess of Love, and the symbolism of the dove is used the world over to represent love, purity and simplicity. It also represents the soul, and the word 'dove' is often used in literature to mean 'woman'; the dove is the epitome of femininity.

Despite appearances to the contrary, the dove is often a busy bird. Although its graceful demeanour and soft beauty make it appear as though the bird isn't doing very much, there's often hidden activity, as anyone who has ever seen a dove or pigeon suddenly take flight will testify.

Dove people have an air of unruffled calm and serenity, which belies the bustle of activity which is constantly stirring around them. Doves are able to get an awful lot done with seemingly little effort, and will often start out the day with a vast range of tasks on their 'to-do' lists. Although doves always seem to be busy, it is sometimes the case that a little extra planning or organization might make for a more efficient use of time.

Doves can be shy, and some tend to be 'backward at coming forward'; while this isn't a problem in itself, it can mean that sometimes the dove might feel him or herself to be under appreciated, and this could express itself in something approaching petulance; the dove occasionally needs to see herself as others see her in order to understand that she appears to do anything she turns her hand to with such seeming ease – despite the invisible hard work underlying the effort – and could do well, sometimes, to let people know about the hard work involved.

Doves are fantastic in emergencies; they have the ability to rise above any disaster quickly and take control. This aspect of the dove's character would surprise many people but it is an incredibly useful quality to have.

The Dove's Nest

The dove's nest will be tidy and organized, with 'a place for everything and everything in its place'. This bird doesn't like to see the home messy or dirty, and could be the type to be worried about muddy boots; once visitors have left, the dove will heave a sigh of relief and waste no time in straightening things out again.

The dove will be happy to make do and mend things and has a natural abhorrence of waste or indulgence of any kind. The dove has modest needs and will never take more than she really requires, and will ensure that other people's needs are put first. This tendency should be watched, because sometimes it can turn into self-sacrifice, and that is not such a constructive trait.

Doves have a very natural sense of the aesthetic, which reflects itself not only in the bird's domestic surroundings but also in its appearance. Dove people always appear well-groomed no matter what the circumstances, and they are the type who emerge from a tent in the pouring rain looking as though they'd spent the night in a luxury five-star hotel!

Work

Doves have a very strong sense of duty and will often be the ones who could forego weekends or evenings in favour of getting a job done; doves are relentless perfectionists and if there's a tiny detail that isn't quite correct then this can be quite upsetting to them. Others, understanding this trait, could possibly play upon it unfairly, so the dove could sometimes be taken advantage of.

Doves have a wide interest in a range of different subjects, and often pursue many and varied hobbies in the company of close friends. It is guaranteed, though, that whatever pursuit appeals to the dove, it will be done to perfection, with the result that some of the original enjoyment could be removed from the activity – this is something to be aware of.

As the dove is often critical of herself, this tendency could also spill over towards other people, and what is a genuine desire to advise or help the other person to improve something in the work environment could come across in the wrong way; the dove may often find herself thinking 'what did I say?' Again, it's a simple matter of being wise to the way we come across to other people to make sure that this doesn't happen.

Doves love to help other people, and will often be found working very hard in a background role. With their grace, beauty and serenity they can make good 'behind the scenes' workers, and the heart of any large organization will often reveal a fair number of doves working industriously and harmoniously to ensure the smooth running of the endeavour.

The dove can have a tendency to be self-critical; this is because, in her efforts to please others and take care of their needs, she can neglect her own wants. The dove should be aware of this, and should also be more willing to accept help. Bear in mind that sometimes it's fun when people tackle a job together, and be willing to relinquish a little control!

Relationships

Although it may take time for the dove to find the right partner, one who will understand and appreciate the deeper inner workings of this bird, once the dove decides that the partner is right then they will usually have a long and happy partnership. Couples you sometimes read about, who have met and married very early and live to celebrate 50 or more years of wedded bliss, are more likely to be doves than any other kind of bird.

Doves are naturally modest despite their beauty; they can often be surprised to be found attractive by the opposite sex. This modesty can in itself be an extremely attractive attribute, although sometimes doves would do well to have a greater sense of self-esteem, despite their natural shyness and diffidence.

Despite the fact that the dove is a great friend to have, and will put huge efforts into maintaining true friendships, it is worth bearing in mind that family will always come first. The dove tends to shy away from large gatherings, preferring to have just a few friends around the table than a huge crowd.

Forewarned ...

A tendency towards self-sacrifice should be kept in check; it's not comfortable for others, as well as being an unnecessary trait!

Capricorn: December 22nd–January 20th

The Wren

My humility is not a mask;
my benevolence is the truth.
In reality, I fear nothing;
we are all the same.
Not everyone is ready for my kindness.
Elene Kurtesz

Wrens make prey where eagles dare not perch
William Shakespeare, *Richard III*

People born under the Earth sign of Capricorn, which is ruled by the planet Saturn, have a close affinity with the wren.

Wrens tend to build their nests in bushes and shrubs which are close to the ground, and can be seen flying about at ground level in woods and scrubland, reflecting the Earth element of the Capricorn. Wren people are also, literally, 'down-to-earth' souls and tend to have wonderfully practical natures; they are often able to fix anything at all and indeed will take great delight in 'make do and mend'.

The wren is one of the wisest and most diplomatic of birds. Indeed, in many cultures the wren is the king of the birds. However, this unassuming little bird will often bide its time before revealing its true feathers.

The wren will often have a wide range of acquaintances and is very popular; however, the wren usually has quite a small circle of what it would call close friends, and these it may take some time to cultivate, since the bird is naturally cautious. Although the wren can appear to be gregarious, it has a rich inner world and a hidden reserve. Sometimes the wren may have a fleeting regret that it might have missed its moment, however, this is never the case: everything at the right time.

There is something the wren would do well to be aware of, and that is a tendency to let a fear of failure prevent it from doing things. There can also be a sense of inadequacy. These fears should be put aside and the wren should realize that its intelligence, knowledge and intuition are very valuable qualities, which should be shared, leaving aside the self-conscious shyness that can often take the place of modesty.

Thrifty by nature, while also being incredibly generous, the wren will put a huge amount of consideration into the comforts and pleasures of others; this is not self-denial, because the wren takes genuine delight in making others happy. The wren has an intuitive ability to know what people need, producing the precise thing at the right moment almost like magic; this level of intuition and concern for others is indeed a magical power, and the wren person often seems to be surrounded by fairy-dust, as though they are from another world.

The wren has great aesthetic sense and generally can appear to make something out of nothing. The wren does not like to see waste and will invent innovative ways of recycling or re-using discarded items. The wren will never force knowledge or information on anyone, but shows by example its wisdom, intuition, kindness, grace and humility.

The wren has a very unusual sense of humour, which is often based around puns and word play. This bird also has an uncanny ability to say out loud just what everyone else is thinking. The wren will make subtle points in a diplomatic way, and they are persuasive birds; they can find ways of gently altering an awkward situation to everyone's advantage, or will be able to talk round a cantankerous or awkward person without the person realizing this.

The Wren's Nest

The nest of the wren will be cosy and occasionally cluttered-looking, because this bird has so many interests; but despite the clutter the home will be tidy and clean, apart from maybe the odd cobweb. Wrens have an innate sense of beauty and enjoy being surrounded by beautiful things; often these objects will be the result of carefully scouring thrift stores or junk shops, reflecting again the wren's dislike of waste and its delight in spotting a bargain or recognizing beauty or quality in something that other people have missed. The wren is a sensuous bird and this passion will be reflected in its surroundings, as well as in its love of gorgeous fabrics and textures.

The wren is also a keen gardener and can make things grow beautifully just about anywhere; it is the most green-fingered of all the birds.

Work

Wrens are wonderful to work with, being diplomatic, kind and funny, and tend to be happy in almost any job so long as the people are nice to work with. The wren will not be at all interested in working just for money, but what money there is will often be saved up for a long-term plan. Such plans will generally come to fruition, although the wren will not make a great song and dance about it, but will just get on quietly with its life!

While the wren would prefer to be at the top of their chosen profession, this will be attained by subtlety and hard work; there is absolutely nothing cut-throat or ruthless about the wren's nature. If wrens are encouraged to have freedom of expression in their work, they will tend to work much better than if they are kept under close observation. Wrens are ultimately reliable and trustworthy; if they say they are going to get a certain task done, then you can count on them to do it.

Occasionally the wren will suffer from a crisis of confidence and there are some areas of responsibility that make it feel uncomfortable. Because this is such a reliable bird, it will put great effort in getting a thing right and this trait can occasionally be taken advantage of by others. This is a fact the wren may be only too aware of, but this bird is usually too nice to do anything about it except to heave a deep sigh and get on with the job.

Relationships

Naturally cautious and often a little shy, the wren will take some time before deciding on its partner, but once the decision is made it will generally mate for life; if something does go awry, it's likely that the wren will remain friends with any significant exes. Wrens will generally work very hard at keeping relationships alive and interesting, and will be happy to share interests with their partner. However, they should be careful lest their own desires be sublimated.

Sometimes the natural reserve of the wren can seem to be an obstacle to deepening a relationship, and any prospective partner must be aware of this. By the same token, the wren should be aware of this tendency and relax a little! The wren is a patient bird, and will view with humour and compassion some of the seemingly more awkward foibles of a partner.

Once the wren has awakened it is a passionate bird, and it loves sensual delights.

Forewarned . . .

The wren should be aware of its natural diffidence; *do it anyway!*

The Birds of the Element of Water

In Western astrology, the signs that are gathered together under the element of Water are Cancer, Scorpio and Pisces. Again, there are many aspects to water; it could be a cascading waterfall, or it could be a still lake (or 'sky mirror' as it's known to the Native Americans). It could be a calm or troubled sea, or a bubbling stream.

Cancer – The Swan: sensitivity; humanity; calmness
Scorpio – The Raven: intuition; intelligence; healing
Pisces – The Owl: spirituality; wisdom; imagination

Other water element birds you may feel an affinity towards include the Blackbird, the Crow, the Duck, the Heron, the Lapwing, the Loon, the Nightingale, the Pelican and the Stork.

Cancer: June 22nd–July 22nd

THE SWAN

Cutting across with no ripple
My wake is silent, invisible, grace uncountenanced;
at home in the elements am I
curve upon curve furled close
Elene Kurtesz

Ruled by the Moon and being of the element of Water, Cancerian people have a great affinity with the Swan. The spirals, which are the symbol of Cancer, are akin to the spirals created in the water by this beautiful bird.

At home both in the air and in water, swan people tend to be very fond of travel, and while they would rather 'go somewhere and do something', and may often be the type to work outside their home country, it's likely that the swan will be happy simply to visit exotic destinations as part of a holiday.

Swans seem to make everything effortless, but the grace and ease which appears on the surface can often belie the frantic activity beneath the waters;

and when the swan decides to move fast, then this bird can really shift, as anyone who has ever seen a swan make a sudden decision to cross a lake will testify.

Swans are sensitive and thin-skinned. They have a soft centre and can easily be hurt, but hate to show it; friends and partners need to be aware of this. Swans have fantastic powers of imagination, and few people realize that this bird will often have its own fantasy world; if this propensity is given free rein, it could manifest in stories or books, especially for children.

The swan can also dwell in the past rather too much, especially reliving past hurts or injuries; if you are a swan and this applies to you, it is important that you learn to let go of these incidents and not to define yourself by the negative rather than the positive. The easiest way to do this is simply to alter your perception and see the benefits that seemingly painful or difficult situations can bring in their wake. We can change the world by a simple shift in our consciousness, by changing our minds …

The Swan's Nest

The home of the swan is often centred around the kitchen, which will be warm, welcoming and cosily cluttered, and often filled with other people's children as well as the bird's own brood. Swans have excellent memories and a great interest in historical fact; this, combined with their interest in collecting things, will often be reflected in their bookshelves and display cases, for the swan loves to be surrounded by 'things' and often this bird is a keen shopper – retail therapy is possibly more important to the swan than to any other bird.

The swan has a natural need to protect and to nurture; this bird is the type to keep an eye on people whether they are aware of it or not. This nurturing is part of a strong maternal instinct, which also expresses itself in a love of cooking or baking; feeding people gives the swan a great deal of pleasure and fulfilment.

Work

The swan has a propensity to worry, and because some of these worries can be of a financial nature, whatever career the swan chooses, the financial side is likely to be a strong factor. Financial security is probably more important to the swan than to most other birds. Consequently, the swan is unlikely to follow a purely vocational course unless he or she knows that financial rewards will follow at some point.

This tendency to worry also means that the swan is unlikely to 'switch off' after work; this bird should be aware of this trait and ensure that whatever career is chosen, it is one which can be left behind after hours as far as possible. The swan is a giving bird, and takes great pleasure in helping others; any career that encompasses this could give a great deal of satisfaction.

The swan also has a desire to help on a wider basis, and may often become involved with charitable organizations or community-based schemes and projects, in particular those which involve children. Swans are more than happy to work as a volunteer so long as their own financial needs do not suffer.

Whatever their chosen career, swans work well with other people and will be meticulous and hard working. They will prepare everything beautifully and hate to be seen lacking in any area; swans do their homework well, and generally will be very knowledgeable about their chosen subject, and will have all up-to-date information to hand.

Relationships

Swans prefer to mate for life; this means that they will not rush into relationships quickly, and it's very rare to find a promiscuous swan. This bird will weigh up all the positive and negative aspects of someone they feel an attraction for before making a commitment; but once the commitment is made, that's hopefully it, for life. When first approached by a prospective partner, the swan could possibly send out the wrong signals; a natural defensiveness and shyness can kick in, and the suitor who wishes to pierce this protective armour must be both patient and persistent.

The concepts of family and home are very important to swans; these birds are very fond of children and it's important that this aspect of the swan character is shared by their partner.

The swan can worry unduly about people who are close. This bird must be careful that this natural tendency to worry does not manifest itself as nagging. The very worst aspect of this quality is the likelihood that this anxiety could appear to be some sort of a control mechanism, something which makes people feel guilty; the swan should relax a little more, and often simply being aware of a tendency is enough to fix it.

The swan can also be moody, for no apparent reason. If their partner is not to be exasperated or confused by these sudden mood swings, the swan would do well to reassure them that this is simply a part of its make-up and not to be taken personally. It would also be wise to realize that, when one of these moods takes over, the swan can be unnecessarily cutting and could cause hurt; again, being aware of this trait can often be enough to fix it.

Forewarned . . .

A propensity to dwell on past hurts as though they happened yesterday; let it go!

Scorpio: October 24th–November 22nd

THE RAVEN

I have my eye on you;
I know you inside out, all your secrets,
the jewels you hide within are my delight.
You think that I am black; look again with new eyes
In truth, I am a silver bird
Elene Kurtesz

Scorpio people, ruled by the planets Pluto and Mars and the element of Water, have a close affinity with the raven.

The Corvid family includes ravens and crows, and these are by far the cleverest of birds. Their native intelligence has resulted in the bird being known, in several mythologies, as the Trickster, but this could be seen to be unfair since the term simply refers to the abilities of this extraordinary bird. It does mean, however, that the raven may be prone to secrecy, and might hide its true nature. Intrigue and secrecy are important aspects of the raven's nature, and people close to the bird should be aware of this.

The time when the Sun is in the sign of Scorpio includes Samhain, or Halloween, the old New Year and the time when the veil between the world of the living and that of the spirits is thinnest; ravens are a favoured form for witches and wizards to shape shift into.

As well as being the bird of intelligence, the raven is also the bird of psychic abilities, clairvoyance and the supernatural. The raven may be considering developing these abilities or may already be on that path; bear in mind that the energy can be used for either good or evil, and use it wisely and well. The future cannot be forced and the raven should endeavour to be patient enough to let events unfold. As long as the raven knows in its innermost heart that it is doing the right thing to the best of its abilities, then all will be well. The raven is also the 'Doctor' bird, and raven people may show a propensity for healing of some description.

Ravens can have an innate suspicion of authority figures but will be too clever to make this obvious. The raven will always make up its own mind and is a revolutionary thinker. The raven has a great sense of personal destiny, and a sense of purpose, but exactly what this is can sometimes seem to be elusive. However, the answers can come to the raven in unexpected ways, such as in 'waking visions' or dreams; the raven would be advised to make a note of these experiences and observe how they unfold.

The raven brings messages from the Sun gods and has been known as the fire stealer; a most beautiful bird, the raven turns to silver in the sunshine and spreads happiness and joy to those around it.

The Raven's Nest

The raven has great aesthetic sense and can usually be found wherever there are beautiful objects, especially crystals, old glass, jewels or silver. These items need not be valuable; the raven will take as much delight in a beautiful pebble from the seashore as in a priceless diamond. The raven home will often be quite theatrical and dramatic; the love of beauty means that the raven has an innate ability to place objects well, and has impeccable taste although is not 'fussy' about the home being used as intended. Although the raven loves to have beautiful things around, this bird is not attached to them and will often give away valuable pieces, knowing that things are ephemeral.

Work

There is a profound responsibility for the raven to make the most of its extraordinary talents, and never to doubt that the way forward will be revealed in the fullness of time.

Ravens like to be challenged; they need to be stretched and any role that is not demanding enough will mean that the bird will get bored. Ravens are likely to become immersed in their work and will not see a dividing line between their career and the rest of their life, and will be happy to take work on holiday with them. It's likely that the raven will find a way to make a hobby or passion into a means of making a living, so this bird is able to combine the best of both worlds.

The aesthetic sensibilities of the raven means that some involvement in design could be likely – the raven has a precise sense of small detail and notices things which other people would generally miss

Usually, although the raven likes to have money, this will not be the over-riding factor in any career path. And when money is there, the raven is the type of bird who will be likely to have cash earmarked for bigger, more ambitious projects.

Relationships

The raven has a playful character, as befits all intelligent creatures, and needs a mate with similar characteristics. It is inspired by language, word play, double meanings, ideas and concepts; these latter are often more of a turn-on than more conventional sexual characteristics, and combined with physical attraction can make for a devastating combination.

The raven would, however, do better to have no partner at all than to make do with second best, because this will only waste time and cause problems in the long term. Once the raven's true partner is found the combination is so powerful that the pair feel like they could move rocks or levitate; it is important that the ravens understand this power and realize that they can use it for the greater good of mankind at many levels; it's as well for the raven to be aware that this is possible and wait for the right person to come along.

The raven's love of intrigue means that he or she might be more likely than other birds to have affairs while in a long-term relationship. However, these affairs are generally just about sexual expression and will be unlikely to endanger the 'real' relationship, so long as the raven's partner is able to deal with this.

Forewarned ...

The raven has a propensity for jealousy; although this bird could itself stray from time to time, the thought of their partner doing the same is anathema. This jealousy can also rear its head in friendships, and the raven may feel excluded if a couple of friends seem to be geting along too well with each other. But this trait need not be a problem if the raven is aware of it; forewarned is forearmed.

Pisces: 19th February–20th March

THE OWL

I am sleepless again;
the night is wild in its silver moon mood
and I must seek restlessly my fortune.
Destiny hides in strange places;
I will find mine before the dawn, and yours too
If you ask me
Elene Kurtesz

People born under the sign of Pisces, whose ruling planet is Neptune (before Neptune was discovered the sign's ruling planet was Jupiter) and whose element is that of Water, have a close affinity with the owl.

Owl people are often well read but without being bookish; they are interested in a wide variety of subjects and like to keep well informed about as many things as possible. The owl will have a predilection for writing, too. This bird has a strong sense of the poetic, and is often able to call to mind verses and to quote them appropriately.

There is a dichotomy about the owl. Whereas it is associated with darkness, witches and evil afoot simply because it is a nocturnal bird, the owl is symbolic of wisdom and sagacity and was also the bird of Athena, the Goddess of Wisdom.

Owl people are indeed often nocturnal, and may have more than a casual interest in occult matters; this is something they are unlikely to tell the world about. The owl is also wise; he or she notices things which other people miss, and can make intuitive leaps about many things – people's personalities, for example; there's not much that escapes the notice of this observant bird.

The dual nature of the owl means that they can inadvertently create a degree of chaos around themselves from time to time. This is not intentional, but the owl does often have a mischievous side to its nature and the wicked part of this bird can sometimes enjoy seeing other people a little confused about what's meant to be going on!

The owl can be prone to asthma or other difficulties with the lungs; that cold night air sometimes isn't very healthy for this bird.

The owl has a vivid imagination, which is, of course, a wonderful gift; as with many aspects of the owl's character, though, there's another side to the coin, and this bird may also have a tendency to invent stories, which can occasionally get out of hand. It's my betting that Walter Mitty would have been an owl! The owl should be aware of this trait; being aware of something is usually enough to enable a person to adjust their behaviour accordingly.

Because the owl is able to see more than most, this perception also extends to people, and the owl will have a wide circle of friends. Some of the characters surrounding the owl will be looked at askance by others close to this bird, but the owl is able to see the good in everyone and doesn't care about other people's opinions. The owl will be a loyal and supportive friend and it takes a lot for this bird to lose a friend. However, if the owl is let down this sensitive bird will find it hard to forgive the hurt.

The Owl's Nest

The most noticeable thing about the home of the owl will be the prevalence of books. There will probably be books in every room and on every available surface. The home is liable to be a little messy, but welcoming; the owl will often have friends over, and it's likely that they will talk into the early hours of the morning.

Work

The owl has tremendous creative powers, which will be used no matter what field of work they choose. Whatever they decide to do they will bring a deal of flair and imagination to the table, which will put others to shame. The owl is an extremely versatile bird, and will often know just as much as other individuals within an organization, and could probably do their jobs too; however, the owl will be careful not to make people aware of this.

Owls do not fit easily into any particular category of career; they are so versatile that they could probably make a good job of anything they decided to tackle. Owls, like ravens, are likely to be able to turn a passion into a way of making a living, and they also like to be able to get on with their work without any interference. There are likely to be a high proportion of owl people who are self-employed, and this bird is more prepared than most to take huge risks, although financial security is important and the owl can be devastatingly clever at business; the ability to see more than most can be an invaluable characteristic in this area.

The owl should be aware of a tendency to sacrifice a huge deal for work-related matters, and should bear in mind its own well-being and that of its family and children. The owl could be the type to suffer from nervous exhaustion from over-work. In addition, the creative potential of the owl must be satisfied in whatever career path it chooses. If this vital part of the owl's personality is ignored, then the owl could suffer from depression. In any case, this aspect of the bird's personality is so strong that using it will greatly benefit both the owl and other people in the workplace!

Relationships

Owls fall in love easily; they often have an idealized notion of what a relationship should be, though, and may have impossibly high standards for their partners – again, this is a trait the owl should be aware of. The owl is a sensitive and emotional bird and will wear its heart on its sleeve very often; the owl will make its feelings plain, and often early on in a relationship, which could perhaps be a little alarming for the opposite party.

The owl is an intuitive, instinctive bird, and is unlikely to make logical decisions regarding potential mates. However, these leaps of faith have a tendency to work out in the long run.

The owl is more likely than many other birds to make sacrifices for its partner; this is a kind characteristic in itself but could result in some frustrations for this bird in the long term; it is important to keep a clear idea of your own goals and objectives within the context of the relationship rather than sublimate the self for the significant other. It is important for the owl's self-esteem that it retains a sense of its own identity.

Forewarned...

Unless the creative aspect of the owl's personality is given free rein, this bird is liable to become frustrated.

The Birds of the Element of Air

In Western astrology, the signs ruled by the element of Air are Gemini, Libra and Aquarius. The quality of air has many and varied aspects; it can be a light breeze or a strong wind; it could be mountain air or the ozone rush of the sea which our birds relate to.

Gemini – The Woodpecker: versatility; enthusiasm; scepticism
Libra – The Condor: balance; effortlessness; generosity
Aquarius – The Seagull: inventiveness; inspiration; navigation

Other air birds that you may feel an affinity towards include the Albatross, the Bluebird, the Crane, the Goose, the Jay, the Kite, the Lark, the Oriole, the Song Thrush and the Vulture.

Gemini: May 22nd–June 21st

THE WOODPECKER

The woods hold many secrets;
most of them I have found.
I can usually guess at the rest
and the others don't matter at all.
You call me beautiful; examine my mind
For truth is the real beauty.
Elene Kurtesz

Gemini, ruled by the planet Mercury and the sign of the twins, is an Air sign, and has a strong affinity with the Woodpecker.

Romulus and Remus's mother was a vestal virgin, Rhea Silvia, who was seduced by the God Mars. The twins were ordered to be drowned, but fate intervened and the babies were washed up on the banks of the River Tiber, where they were suckled by a wolf and fed by a woodpecker until rescued by a shepherd. Since that time the woodpecker has had an association with twins, and if we examine some of the characteristics of the bird we'll see just how closely the star sign and the bird are related.

The woodpecker is a versatile bird; as befits being ruled by the planet Mercury, the woodpecker doesn't let the grass grow under its feet and will often be involved in many different endeavours. Woodpeckers are fantastic communicators and particularly charming; they have a way of making everyone feel comfortable around them and this charisma extends to animals and children, who love to bask in the warm glow of the woodpecker's personality.

Although the woodpecker can be an emotional bird, the rational mind tends to be stronger, and often these emotions will not be entirely trusted. Woodpeckers prefer an analytical approach and there will often be a deep distrust of 'alternative' therapies and lifestyles, albeit running alongside a tremendous curiosity and a desire to explain the inexplicable. Woodpeckers will test everything before making their minds up about anything, which makes this bird a marketing man's nightmare – they cannot be 'sold' to but prefer to make their own minds up.

Outspoken and challenging, if the woodpecker is bored he or she will often, in a very naughty but funny way, provoke a discussion knowing that some sort of argument could ensue. The woodpecker will then sit back and enjoy the fun, boredom alleviated for the time being! If there's one thing that the woodpecker cannot tolerate, it's boredom; the prospect of an hour or so in some tedious pursuit is enough to make the woodpecker fly for several miles in the opposite direction.

To be around a woodpecker is a continual source of fun and delight; they have a mischievous quality, and an infectious laugh – the sort of laugh which makes everyone else around them burst into fits of giggles without exactly knowing why. The woodpecker can also be flirtatious and sexy and will attract members of both sexes who frequently become close friends. Woodpeckers are often slender and young looking and will be fortunate enough to keep their good looks for their entire lives, becoming beautiful old ladies with many stories to tell or dapper old gentlemen with a real twinkle in the eye.

There's also a secretive side to the woodpecker; these birds will often have whole areas of their lives or work in which they could be incredibly successful and innovative but which they will keep to themselves or reveal only to certain friends on a 'need-to-know' basis. This isn't a deliberate deception but simply a result of an innate modesty, which makes showing off anathema.

The Woodpecker's Nest

Woodpeckers keep beautiful nests; they prefer natural materials and like to keep things as open-plan and as spacious as possible. These birds have impeccable taste. The woodpecker of both sexes is very fond of flowers but would prefer to be given a bunch of wildflowers in a jar over a florist's hothouse bouquet any day.

Because of their fear of boredom, woodpeckers will ensure that there is a string of activities to keep them occupied and lots of people coming and going through the house; lesser mortals will wonder just how they manage to pack so much into one day. The result can be that the woodpecker sometimes exhausts him or herself and can occasionally need time to recuperate. The woodpecker usually recognizes this and will simply take off and go to bed early, waking refreshed and raring to go the next morning.

Work

Woodpeckers have an infectious enthusiasm and will tackle a variety of jobs or situations with verve and inspiration. They will often carry people along in the wake of this liveliness and so prove inspiring leaders who attract great loyalty among the people with whom they work.

Woodpeckers have a fantastic sense of humour and are very funny. They love puns and word play in particular, however sometimes their witty asides can be missed because they're often just too fast for anyone else. This ability with language, both written and spoken, might provide material for a career.

Woodpeckers work well in teams with other people because they are gregarious and charming, and their innate intelligence will enable this bird to get the best out of any environment or situation.

Relationships

Patience is not the strongest virtue of the woodpecker; this bird likes to get straight to the point and get on with things. Accordingly, their direct nature could frighten off potential suitors. This won't phase the woodpecker; their analytical side will kick in and quite rightly this bird will know that any future partner will need to be able to cope with this directness. Woodpeckers are likely to have quite a few 'relationships', and once the sexual side is over they are likely to remain good friends. However, once the woodpecker has found his or her equal there will be an instant recognition, and this bird is likely to find a partner for life.

As a parent, the woodpecker is imaginative and fun. It is likely that a woodpecker home will be full of other people's children having far more fun than they would in their own homes.

Woodpeckers have astute instincts and decide very quickly about people; they won't waste time with anyone not of a like mind and have the ability to recognize a potential friend almost immediately, even among a room full of strangers. These friends are likely to come from all age groups and all spectra of society; the woodpecker is not a snobbish bird and will accept just about anything on face value. Although the woodpecker can be naturally sceptical, once again the strong logical part of the mind will kick in and this bird will give anything at all a chance to prove itself either way.

Forewarned ...

The woodpecker is likely to exhaust itself looking after the needs of others; let someone tend to your needs for a change!

Libra: September 23rd–October 23rd

THE CONDOR

> Cast aside care for a moment;
> imagine you were I.
> The freedom of the skies is mine;
> I want for nothing, I need nothing, I own it all –
> This privilege is mine.
> **Elene Kurtesz**

Librans, ruled by the planet Venus and belonging to the element of Air, have a close association with the Condor.

Condors can fly for ten miles without even flapping their wings; they can visibly detect the thermals, which they are then able to ride with the greatest of ease. Similarly, Librans are unflappable people who are able to achieve a great deal without seeming to try. Indeed, very often the condor doesn't need to make an effort, because this bird has a natural lucky streak and an instinctive knowledge of what will work and what won't that give it a distinct advantage over others who may not have the long-range vision of this clever and talented bird.

The condor's ability to ride the thermals requires a great deal of balance – mental and physical. This aspect is shared by Librans, whose astrological symbol is the scales, which also represent justice.

Because the condor finds everything so effortless there may be accusations of laziness, but the condor can't help its nature; it does tend to find things easy in areas where other birds might struggle. Perhaps some of the accusations of laziness are not unfounded; if the condor were to occasionally try to put in a little effort, this bird could find itself soaring at very great heights indeed. This is the bird of emperors and kings, but generally this bird is not ambitious and is happy to crest those thermals and take time out to enjoy the view!

As befits a bird ruled by the element of air, condors will take an especial delight in aerial displays of fireworks; the evanescent nature of rockets and the like satisfies the aesthetic sensibility of this bird more than most. This sense of beauty is especially marked in the condor and a love of music and art will be prevalent; it's possible that this bird could be involved in these fields in some way.

Condors are generous to a fault, and love to entertain; even if they are exhausted, the prospect of a party or a gathering of some kind will perk them up immediately. They do not suffer fools gladly, but rather than endure a difficult or boring person, they will simply walk away; this bird cannot bear to be bored in any way.

A strong humanitarian streak will mean that the condor could find itself getting involved, almost by default, with fighting some of the injustices of the world. The condor is the type to give to charities without anyone ever realizing it. Condors hate waste and will usually be keen to recycle and re-use wherever possible.

The Condor's Nest

The preferred home of the condor is likely to be as open-plan and as spacious as possible. This bird has great taste, and the interior of the home will be beautiful without being imposing; he or she tends to like unusual pieces of artwork and would rather invest in a couple of sensational pieces than lots of 'bits'. The condor home will often have quite a theatrical or dramatic element to it; this bird loves open fires wherever possible, large windows with uninterrupted views and natural materials. Lighting and colour are particularly important to the condor, and this bird will spend time and money on getting these aspects of their abode exactly right.

Work

Condors cannot stand to see injustices and will often be the first to defend the underdog; this can sometimes lead to the choice of career for this bird.

In common with other birds of the element of air, condors need to have a great deal of freedom in any chosen profession; they work much better if they are simply left to get on with the task in hand. Condors are likely to be self-employed or at the top of a company. They make good bosses because they choose their staff well, relying on intuition and being able to fit the person to the job on the basis of personal talent and ability rather than simply relying on paper qualifications; the condor will often be the first to give a chance to a keen younger person who needs work experience, and this bird will prove a fantastic and patient mentor, and will gain lots of loyalty from anyone under their employ.

The condor is an eloquent and entertaining speaker. Although these skills will not necessarily form the cornerstone of a career, they are useful attributes and will be used to advantage by this bird.

Relationships

The condor is usually in love all the time – not just with people but with animals, a fabulous painting, even a beautiful cloud formation. Before the condor settles down, he or she will usually have a series of relationships, some serious, some not, but nearly all pleasurable. However, when the significant one arrives on the scene the condor, with its innate intuition, recognizes it quickly and 'knows' that their life partner has arrived; without either party mentioning it there will be a lovely feeling of inevitability that a wedding will take place.

This long-lasting, monogamous relationship will form the absolute cornerstone of the life of the condor. It will give the condor a huge amount of inner strength and will really help the individual to become rounded and fulfilled; the arrival of children will further aid the deep contentment, happiness and balance which is the ultimate desire of every condor type. The knowledge that he or she is secure in any relationship enables this bird to fly even higher. The partner will be cherished, and the early romance of this bird will be kept very much alive, possibly more so than by other birds. In later life the condor will find itself surrounded by a loving family in a beautiful home, and will appreciate every minute of this.

As a friend, the condor is invaluable. Once the condor has decided that you are its friend, the friendship will last for life, and any small arguments or pettinesses will be forgotten immediately. It's not that the condor is a particularly forgiving bird, but simply that it doesn't recognize that there is anything to forgive; this bird has a deep understanding of people and is very accepting.

Forewarned . . .

Because the condor is the type of bird that finds everything easy and can accomplish things without trying, there's a possibility that it's potential is not always achieved.

Aquarius: January 21st–February 18th

THE SEAGULL

> I fly;
> I soar;
> I leave you behind –
> and yet I come back for you, willingly.
> **Elene Kurtesz**

Aquarian people, who ruled by the planet Uranus (and prior to that planet's discovery, Saturn), belong to the element of Air, and have a close affinity with the Seagull. This is the bird of the inventor, the inspirer, the infinitely adaptable and the navigator.

The seagull travels far and wide and can be found in every country on the planet. A beautiful bird that flies effortlessly, cresting thermals and soaring gracefully against the blue sky, the seagull carries the very essence of freedom and adventure. The seagull is the bird of the map or chart reader, and of the sailor, and will often have an interest in sailing, the sea, ships or travel.

Yet the seagull appears to be so common that it can be anonymous and invisible. Although this bird inspires, it can do so in such a modest way that often it receives no acknowledgement for the effect it has on others – they simply don't notice – and sometimes the seagull can feel a little hurt or over-looked, or that its efforts are unappreciated.

As a friend, the seagull is wonderful; this bird will go out of its way to make people feel at ease, and it loves to help people. However, if a friendship is betrayed the seagull can take a long time to get over the hurt and it's likely that he or she will never quite trust that person ever again.

The seagull is infinitely resourceful and has an innate sense of mechanics and how things work. Higher physics, music and the workings of the Universe intrigue the seagull and will often be grasped intuitively by this bird. The seagull will be able to invent solutions for all sorts of problems and takes great delight in doing so.

The seagull needs to be free to travel and can feel hemmed in by domesticity. In that case the freedom that is necessary for its survival will cause this bird to seek comfort in the freedom of the mind, and it could turn to outside stimulants such as drugs or alcohol to expand its horizons. The seagull must be careful not to abuse these methods.

The seagull is a deep thinker and may have a tendency to be hurt by unintentional slights; this is a sensitive bird, and any partner must be aware of this and take extra care to show the seagull that it is loved. The seagull's moods can be affected strongly by climate and the weather so it must be aware that the reason for mood changes could be external rather than internal, and be warned against being blown about by the weather, physically and metaphorically – who hasn't seen a lone seagull blown off course? Occasionally, the seagull may look around and wonder how it got to a certain place in its life – almost like awakening from a dream.

This bird has a great understanding of humanity yet a detachment from it; this neutrality is a fine and rare quality and the seagull should endeavour to remember this.

The Seagull's Nest

The seagull is more likely to be concerned with what surrounds the home than what is inside it; this bird has a pragmatic approach to its nest, and while it will enjoy lovely surroundings, seagulls are unlikely to get too involved with actually creating them. However, because of its love of the outdoors, the seagull will take a keen interest in the garden and land surrounding its home, and enjoys an environment out in the open country or by the sea, where distant horizons are clearly visible.

Work

The seagull is quite likely to find a routine sort of job very frustrating; this bird thrives in wide open spaces and needs as much freedom as possible, so it's likely that self-employment is the answer. Money, while a handy means to an end, is rarely a motivation for the seagull; given the choice of spending time in lucrative tedium or making very little money doing something really enjoyable, the seagull will go for the latter option without a second thought. Quite rightly, this bird recognizes that time is a much more important commodity than money.

Being an original thinker, the seagull will thrive in any area where they are required to provide solutions to peculiar problems. Being inventive and having great concern for humanity, it's likely that the seagull will come up with some innovation to make the world a better place. It's also likely that the 'mad professor' type will turn out to be a seagull person!

Seagull people have great powers of concentration and can get through a colossal amount of work in a relatively short space of time, often making co-workers wonder what they've been doing with their own time.

Relationships

Any prospective partner must bear in mind that the seagull needs his or her personal freedom. This does not mean that the partner need worry about the seagull's fidelity, because once committed the seagull is not likely to stray.

The seagull does have areas of self-doubt, and it could be that occasionally this bird worries about whether he or she is stimulating enough for any partner. It is important that both seagull and partner bring fresh experiences into their relationship, otherwise there could be a tendency for things to stagnate a little as the seagull can be preoccupied with its own thoughts and inventions.

The seagull is a romantic bird, and will continue to court the partner although they may have been together for many years. This is a delightful quality, and more than makes up for the occasional bouts of this bird being 'away with the fairies'.

Forewarned ...

The seagull has the ability to see the good in every situation, yet conversely, if it is not allowed the freedom it needs, it can become jaded or unhappy. This is something to be aware of. The seagull has the power to make its thoughts become a reality – the power of eidetic vision – so it must be careful to guard against negativity and the desire to be right. The seagull will learn a great lesson if it appreciates that there are no 'mistakes', only opportunities for learning, otherwise this bird could become depressed. Its confidence can be knocked easily and rather than say anything, the seagull will often opt to suffer in silence.

The Birds of the Element of Fire

In conventional Western astrology the three fire signs are Aries, Leo and Sagittarius. Although we may tend to think of fire as dangerous – hot hot flames lapping into the air – there are many aspects to this element which bears relation to the birds chosen. There is no smoke without fire, don't forget, and no fire without smoke …

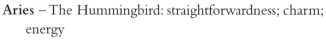

Aries – The Hummingbird: straightforwardness; charm; energy
Leo – The Eagle: intuition; inspiration; complexity
Sagittarius – The Hawk: charisma; positivity; freedom

Other fire birds that you may feel an affinity towards include the Cardinal, the Falcon, the Hoopoe, the Macaw, the Mockingbird, the Parrot, the Peacock, the Robin, the Rooster and the Swallow. And, of course, the Phoenix!

Aries: 21st March–20th April

THE HUMMINGBIRD

A candid bird
The hummingbird
says
'look at me ! I bring delight
in what
the fire of the Sun
has made my own'
Elene Kurtesz

Ruled by the planet Mars, and belonging to the element of Fire, people born under the sign of Aries have a great affinity with the Hummingbird.

Hummingbird people tend to be very straightforward. They know what they want, generally, and also know how to get it, and they'll generally achieve their aims in a charming and direct manner. They are also truthful to the point of bluntness; the hummingbird husband for example will not be the type to be tactful about the partner's choice of dress. If hummingbirds are asked an opinion they will give it as honestly as possible, and their candour can sometimes cause people to laugh out loud, but their innate charm will sweeten any pill.

Hummingbirds have a very uncomplicated attitude to life, and because of this tend to be good problem-solvers; they can see a direct line from the problem to the solution that might elude others with cloudier, or less straightforward, minds. These birds like to move fast and tend to be more biased towards action than contemplative thought; navel-gazing isn't for the hummingbird.

Because hummingbirds like action, office jobs and all the constraints imposed by a regular routine will certainly not be attractive, although they can do it at a push. Whatever the hummingbird does, this bird really, really likes to win, and can be quite competitive, even if this tendency is hidden, and the hummingbird will often be hard on itself if the bird feels that it has not been able to offer its very best effort.

Ruled by Mars, hummingbirds can be impatient and do not suffer fools gladly. Because they often have an excess of energy, it's as well to channel this vigour into physical activity in case it stagnates into frustrated aggression –

remember that the Aztec warrior-god Huitzilpochtli took the form of a hummingbird.

Hummingbirds need to have a purpose in life otherwise they can get very frustrated. They can be impetuous, generous and true friends; friends in trouble or in need of comfort will never be let down by the hummingbird, who will put aside its own needs in order to help in any way it can.

Hummingbird people are fortunate in that they tend to be slim, and will retain their youthful looks and aura as they get older. Often people are genuinely surprised to learn the true age of older hummingbirds, and their youthful attitude and invigorating energy will be largely responsible for this.

The Hummingbirds' Nest

Hummingbirds can be quite territorial and like the world to know 'their patch'. In spite of this, the hummingbird is not particularly worried about domestic appearances. Often the house will be messily comfortable, but the hummingbird is not the type to fret about this. They have the attitude that a slightly scruffy house with lots of activity going on is a far healthier and happier place to live than a sterile environment, and as a result hummingbirds often have lots of friends around who enjoy this relaxed attitude.

However, the hummingbird does seem to enjoy building and adding to the home in this way. The bird enjoys doing as much of this sort of work as it can itself, and it's another way of using up some of that fantastic, enviable, excess energy!

Work

Hummingbirds tackle any task with a great deal of enthusiasm and energy and can get a huge amount done in a relatively short space of time, and people around hummingbirds will sometimes feel that they are underachieving in comparison. Often the hummingbird will have several interesting changes of career, but the downside to this is that they may have a tendency to leave lots of tasks half-finished as their attention is attracted elsewhere.

Hummingbirds are instinctive, impetuous and risk-taking types; these risks can be physical as well as career-related. To the outside, many of the decisions made by hummingbird people may appear to be insane; these risks, however, are normally backed up by sound common sense and the hummingbird will usually succeed in anything it decides to do. The hummingbird is

forward-thinking and resourceful and will never waste time musing over what might have been, or 'what if' scenarios; the hummingbird lives very much in the present and is able to be 'in the moment', and because of this attracts a great deal of luck. The 'glass half empty/half full' issue is completely irrelevant to the hummingbird – after all, even if the glass appears to be half empty it's still half full of air!

Hummingbirds cannot stand to be bored or trammelled in any way. Rather than stoically continue with a task that starts to wane in interest, the hummingbird will do something else. Similarly, if cornered at a party or some similar event by someone who appears to be dull and uninteresting, the hummingbird will often walk away abruptly. This may appear to be rude but, quite frankly, if it gets the hummingbird away from a potentially boring moment, it won't care at all.

Relationships

When hummingbirds fall in love, they tend to go head-over-heels very quickly, and the inexperienced hummingbird could often be disappointed that this impetuous passion is not always reciprocated, simply because the other party may not be ready for such an impulsive relationship. Hummingbirds can also tend to show off rather a lot in an attempt to attract a potential mate; the advice here would be to *cool it*! However, once the hummingbird has realized that this approach can frighten away potential lovers, the passionate nature of this bird will ensure that it is an interesting and exciting partner.

As a friend, the hummingbird is fun to be with – enthusiastic, funny and great company to be around. This enthusiasm can be infectious, and the hummingbird's all-embracing attitude to life is an incredibly inspiring aspect of their character. The hummingbird can help people realize that, with effort, energy and focus, truly anything is possible.

Forewarned...

The main thing that hummingbirds need to be aware of is that their straightforward approach, and their ability to simply go out and get what they want, can make them appear to be rather selfish. It's not selfishness, just honesty, but if the hummingbird is aware of this tendency then potential problems can be avoided.

Leo: 23rd July–22nd August

The Eagle

I am fire;
I scorch the surface of the sun with my wings.
Look at me closely;
I am not what I appear to be
Elene Kurtesz

People born under the sign of Leo, whose ruling star is the Sun, and whose element is Fire, have a great affinity with the Eagle.

The Eagle is one of the highest-flying of the birds, and has keen eyesight, being able to spot prey across open terrain across a distance of three miles or more. This perception is not just physical for the Eagle person but extends to the psychic field, too, and the eagle may often find that he or she is able to make leaps of deduction, which point to an extremely intuitive nature.

Eagles have an inherent belief that they are superior to most birds; this is understandable, because after all, the eagle is born under a star, not a planet. However, sometimes in younger birds this can come across as arrogance, although as the eagle matures it will find it easier to relax and let go of this egoism. At this point the eagle can be an inspiring leader, especially with younger people and children, since the eagle will talk to everyone as an equal and will find friends in all walks of life and social strata.

The Eagle is a tricky bird to understand because there are some dichotomies; a seemingly open and transparent nature often hides an incredibly complex inner world, which can bear no relation to the outside appearance of this bird.

The Eagle's Nest

The eagle likes to nest in remote, rocky places of altitude, and eagle people similarly prefer wide-open spaces where they can spread their wings. The home of the eagle can be a dramatic affair, with rich colours and a love of the theatrical, as befits such an important bird whose folklore is rich in symbolism and extremes.

Eagles are generous birds, and this generosity extends far and wide. As a result of this tendency, the home of the eagle will often be full of people, with the result that the eagle may sometimes feel crowded out – the eagle would do as well to be as kind to itself as it is to other people.

Eagles tend to prefer to be outdoors rather than inside; where this is not possible, this bird will take off to wide open spaces, the mountains or the sea, as often as possible. More than most birds, the eagle will suffer from grey winter months and will prefer if possible to follow the Sun at these times.

Work

The eagle can soar with apparent effortlessness, and needs challenges; it would be all too easy to relax to the point of torpor as the bird simply soars aloft with everyday concerns far below. The Eagle pays close attention to detail, which is usually combined with an ability to see the 'bigger picture', and eagles will often be found working in the visual arts.

Eagles can have ideas that others might judge to be insane or ridiculous, or possibly even grandiose; however, as we have already seen, this bird is a visionary, and will often as not find a way to make these ideas become realities. These visionary ideas will often find their way into the working environment, and the prospect of being self-employed will appeal to the eagle more than most.

Although eagles can be very well organized, in the working environment they hate to feel trammelled in any way and will often shy away from any sort of long-term contractual obligation. Also, there's a strange dichotomy in the eagle personality in that there is a need to shine or excel, along with a natural, often hidden, lack of self-confidence. Therefore the eagle will often find a way to do something which no one else can do, so that there simply is no competition; alternatively, the eagle may simply only bother doing the things it knows that it is good at.

The eagle tends to relish the thought of big, important, unique projects. Often it may be some years before the correct 'mission' is embarked upon, but once the path has been found the eagle will make a huge success of whatever is chosen.

Relationships

When they fall in love, which is not very often, eagles can fall very, very hard indeed and often the prospective partner can be put off by the fervour of the eagle's passion. Eagles tend to make the running in any partnership, and commit everything at a quite early stage if they feel that all the signs are right; they are also loyal and faithful to the point of self-denigration. The eagle will challenge the partner to find new ways of doing things since they have a huge fear of getting into any kind of a rut.

The eagle who is aware of this propensity for stagnation will fight it tooth and nail and will often find colossal challenges for itself. However, if the bird is aware of this tendency and the partner does not understand or is unwilling to be a part of the journey, sometimes the partnership will be sacrificed rather than the eagle being prepared to endure a state of boredom.

Eagles, while being sociable and gregarious, are also very happy to be left alone. In fact most eagles have to have some quality time with themselves at least once a day or they start to feel crowded. This need to find their 'own space' should not be taken as a personal slight to friends or partners, but simply as a part of the make-up and psyche of this particular bird.

Despite their appearance to the contrary, eagle people often wear their heart on their sleeve and can be incredibly sensitive and easily hurt; fortunately the eagle will usually find a way to turn a seeming disappointment into an advantageous learning opportunity, and the bird's optimism and ability to see a different angle on things will generally kick in before very long. Because of their sensitivity, eagles need plenty of encouragement in creative and artistic endeavours. To outsiders, the bird appears to be all confidence and bravado, but eagles can suffer from incredible self-doubt and insecurity.

Eagle fathers are fantastic with their children but will sometimes look at their life and wonder how it happened. Eagle mothers are involved parents but are not too sorry when the time comes for the children to leave, and because of this attitude they will often find that they have better relationships with their grown-up children than do other birds.

Eagles will have a very wide range of acquaintances who love to bask in the warm, sociable glow of this bird, but what the eagle would call true friends are few and far between. Once the eagle has decided that a particular person falls into this category, however, they will support them and stick by them through thick and thin.

Forewarned . . .

The exterior of the eagle often belies a fragile interior. People may not always realize this, so don't take things too personally!

Sagittarius: 23rd November–21st December

The Hawk

Like an arrow will I fly
Straight to the point; my truth
Will scud across cloudburst, through rainbow
into Winter Sunlight
Elene Kurtesz

The Fire sign of Sagittarius, ruled by the planet Jupiter, has a close affinity with the Hawk.

Hawks fly close to the Sun and are a solar symbol, reflecting the fire-element of Sagittarius. The time when the Sun is in this sign is a time of winter, when people's attention turns to hunting; the hawk is indeed a skilled hunting bird, and has been used by men as such since time immemorial. The hawk likes the challenge of a chase of any kind, and will find clever ways to get what it wants without hurting anyone else.

The hawk revels in discovering its own weak points or limitations, and will endeavour to overcome them. This bird seeks constant personal improvement and will often have an interest in self-help books, or might possibly become interested in some aspect of the healing arts. Hawks have a very positive attitude towards life and delight in finding solutions to difficult problems, either for themselves or for others.

The Jupiter element means that the hawk has a great deal of charisma and charm, and, in general, a happy manner. The hawk is a fortunate bird in that it retains its youthful good looks and usually has a good level of fitness; provided the bird does not give in to the occasional tendency to overindulge then it's not unlikely that the hawk will take up tai chi, for example, at the age of 90!

The hawk is a lively, friendly bird, and will have a wide circle of friends. It is the sort of bird others will turn to if they're feeling low, and the hawk will be able to help people to look on the bright side and face their difficulties with a lighter heart. However, the hawk does not like to dwell on its own problems, choosing to tackle them alone; it would be as well to remember that the sharing of a problem can lead to its resolution, and that it's not necessary to be quite so stoic.

Hawks have strong opinions about important matters, and are persuasive talkers. They despise racism or bigotry of any kind, and will be outspoken on such matters where necessary.

The Hawk's Nest

The preferred home of the hawk will be a spacious, airy place, with large windows showing an uninterrupted vista, and wide doorways, which will be thrown open as often as possible. The home will often reflect the bird's hunting abilities by containing many items tracked down in antique shops or flea markets. Although the hawk prefers spaciousness, this bird also has many and varied interests and hobbies, and it may be that the space appears cluttered because of the paraphernalia associated with these interests. The hawk is a sociable bird and will have an open-door policy towards friends, and its home is likely to be the scene of lively evenings with intelligent debate over the delicious food prepared by the bird – cooking can be a major interest and the hawk will delight in finding obscure ingredients and unusual recipes.

Work

The hawk has a wide range of interests and enthusiasms, and can become bored doing just one thing; this bird needs a vocation or career that will provide constant stimulation. The hawk does not welcome being told what to do, so if this bird isn't the boss, whoever is should understand that the hawk will get on much better if left to its own devices. Indeed, the hawk will relish the chance to work at his or her own pace and will usually do a much better job if allowed to work in freedom.

Hawks have a great ability to see the 'bigger picture' and can visualize the end result, but will not generally like to get bogged down by small details. If the bird finds itself in a dull job for a time, then it is vital to find some other outlet for its creativity – a sport or absorbing hobby, or further education, will tide the hawk over until such a time as things prove more stimulating. The hawk will not mind working for relatively little money so long as it's a means to an end.

The hawk will often have a flair for languages and this, combined with the bird's love of travel and an interest in people, could point to certain career options. The hawk is also a good entertainer and is naturally gregarious; this could point towards some other career options. Regardless of the choice, it is essential that the bird finds constant satisfaction and stimulation in whatever it chooses.

Relationships

The hawk needs to find a partner who understands its need to 'fly'; the hawk cannot stand to be restricted or held in, and because possessiveness is simply not a part of its nature the hawk can find this aspect of some personalities a little difficult to understand. Because the hawk does not like to be tied down, this bird may seem reluctant to settle for a long-term commitment until later on in life. Indeed, there may be a tendency for the hawk to have more than one lover at a time if it feels that either relationship is not 'the one'; also, the aspect of secrecy can be exciting for the bird. The downside to this aspect of the hawk personality is that the bird may miss out on the satisfaction of a long-term relationship and all that this entails.

Like the eagle, the hawk has an almost pathological fear of boredom, and this fear extends to the partner. The partners of hawks need to have their own interests, to bring something new and challenging into the relationship to make sure that it does not stagnate. The hawk is not a jealous bird and will encourage the partner to have varied interests and friends; nor will it mind if the partner would rather travel or holiday alone, for example – anything to keep the relationship exciting and alive. The prospect of any kind of 'routine' in any aspect of its life is likely to make the hawk feel claustrophobic, so the partner needs to be aware of this and should act accordingly. By the same token, no one should attempt to try to 'tame' the hawk; it won't work, at least not for very long, and it's as well to revel in the glorious freedom that is such a vital part of this bird's make-up.

Forewarned ...

A tendency to bottle up problems while being a counsellor for others; ask for help when it's needed!

Charms, Murders, exhaltations:

The collective nouns of birds

All those group names we often wonder about – some of these are truly inspired! Who could fail to be enchanted by the idea of the Charm of Finches, or chilled by the thought of a Murder of Crows? And a Paddling of Ducks is so apt! It's unlikely that we will ever find out just how these collective nouns came about, but the following is a collection from all over the World. The terms are fascinating and intriguing and contain a poetry all of their own.

- A Badelynge of Ducks
- A Band of Jays
- A Bank of Swans
- A Bazaar of Guillemots
- A Bevy of Quails
- A Bouquet of Pheasants
- A Brood of Hens
- A Building of Rooks
- A Cast of Falcons (or Hawks)
- A Charm of Finches (or Hummingbirds)
- A Chattering of Coughs
- A Chevron of Geese
- A Chime of Wrens
- A Cloud of Seagulls
- A Colony of Gulls (or Penguins)
- A Commotion of Coots
- A Company of Parrots (or Wigeons)
- A Congregation of Plovers
- A Conspiracy of Ravens
- A Convocation of Eagles
- A Covey of Grouse (or Partridges)
- A Crowd of Redwing
- A Deceit of Lapwings
- A Descent of Woodpeckers
- A Dole of Doves

A Dopping of Shelducks
An Exaltation of Larks
An Exultation of Nightingales
A Fall of Woodcocks
A Flight of Swallows (or
Cormorants, or Goshawks)
A Fling of Dunlins
A Flock of Pigeons
A Gaggle of Geese
A Head of Curlews
A Herd of Cranes
A Host of Sparrows
A Kettle of Hawks
A Knob of Pochards
A Leach of Merlins
A Mischief of Magpies
A Murder of Crows
A Murmuration of Starlings
A Muster of Storks (or Peacocks)
A Mutation of Thrushes
A Nye of Pheasants
An Ostentation of Peacocks
A Pack of Partridges
A Paddling of Ducks

A Parcel of Oystercatchers
A Parliament of Owls
A Party of Jays
A Peep of Chickens
A Plump of Wildfowl
A Pride of Peafowl
A Puddling of Mallards
A Pitying of Turtledoves
A Rafter of Turkeys
A Run of Poultry
A Sedge of Bitterns
A Siege of Herons
A Skein of Geese (or Flamingos)
A Sord of Mallards
A Spring of Teal
A Tok of Capercaillies
A Train of Jackdaws
A Trip of Dotterels (or Plovers,
or Waders)
An Unkindness of Ravens
A Walk of Snipe
A Watch of Nightingales
A Wedge of Geese (or Swans)
A Wisp of Snipe

Which came First?
The mythology and symbolism of the egg

It would be almost impossible to look into the Secret Language of the Birds without also looking at the mythological beliefs and mysteries surrounding the Egg. Not surprisingly, there are many creation myths that have the universe being created from a form of Celestial or Cosmic Egg.

The egg is symbolic of completeness, wholeness, totality. The possibility of perfection, of perfect creation, of promise and potential, are all contained within … and this in itself is a mystery. The egg represents the principle of life, resurrection and hope. It also represents magic, medicine, food and omens. These meanings can be found across the world – in Egypt, India, China, Phoenicia, Greece, Fiji, Finland, Central America and Europe. In short, every nation seems to hold the egg in reverence as the ultimate symbol of creation. It is no accident that the principal symbol at Easter, the time of Spring and new beginnings, is the egg.

Which came first … the bird, or the egg? I'm afraid I can't offer any definite answer either!

Africa

The Dogon tribes of Africa (who knew that there were two moons around Sirius way before our modern astronomical equipment was powerful enough to spot them), believe that the Creator made the 'egg of the world', or 'aduna tal'. This egg goes on forever, containing fire, water, air and a kind of metal called 'sagala'. However, the egg is small and incredibly heavy, containing as it does the essence of all the iron and seeds found on the Earth. Also inside the egg are male and female twins, who mature inside the egg; when they reach maturity they are androgynous.

The ostrich lays the largest eggs of any bird.

China

In China, ancient texts called the Sanwu Lichi relate that Heaven and Earth were mixed together in a chicken's egg. Inside the egg was a being, called P'an Ku. The egg was rent in two after 18,000 years, with the light and bright parts (the yolk) becoming Heaven, and the dark and heavy part (the albumen) gravitating downwards towards Earth. Between Heaven and Earth lived P'an Ku. After another 18,000 years the Earth had increased in thickness by 10 feet, and Heaven had increased 10 feet in height. This meant that after another 18,000 years, legend has it that Heaven and Earth were separated by 30,000 miles.

Greece

The creation myth of Greece tells of a bird with black wings, which lays a golden egg. It was forecast that the God of Love would come from within the egg. When the egg broke, one half of the shell became the Heavens, and the other became the Earth.

India

In Hindu belief, the entire Solar System is called the Egg of Brahma. This 'Cosmic Egg' was laid by a divine bird on the first waters. When the egg broke Brahma emerged from it, and the two halves of the egg then formed Heaven and Earth. The Egg of Brahma hangs in the darkness. If it were possible to view this from a great distance, the observer would see, hanging in the blackness, a huge egg-shaped body of light, a nebula. The egg contains everything and is divided into three parts: the realm of the senses, the Heavens, and the formless world.

The heart of the egg is the Sun, and the Egg of Brahma is said to consist of concentric spheres centred in the Sun itself.

Buddhism

Buddhist doctrine tells us that the eggshell is the 'shell of ignorance', and that to be able to break through it is symbolic of our second birth – our awakening or enlightenment – which must be a continuous process.

Egypt

In Ancient Egypt, the Sun, Ra, was hatched from the Cosmic Egg. This egg had been laid by the Nile Goose, which could be the origin of the 'goose that laid the golden egg' in fairy tales. The Cosmic Egg was created by the God Ptah at his potter's wheel, and Ptah is known as the Great Creator. He also made Sun and Moon eggs, too.

Pre-Christian Belief

Among the ancient Pagans, the Egg was associated with the coming of Spring and the rebirth of Creation. Winter was ending and the earth was awakening again and starting to burst with life, just as the egg burst with new life.

Christian Beliefs

As Christianity replaced the older spiritual beliefs of Europe, the egg came to symbolize the rebirth of man rather than the rebirth of nature. The Egg symbol has such universal cachet, though, that it could be almost anything, and it was also taken to depict Christ's rising from the tomb. It can represent the Virgin Birth, too. The Easter Egg, of course, is a rather more recent extrapolation of the egg symbol, and a fine excuse to eat quantities of chocolate – a good idea at any time of the year!

The Ukraine

In Ukrainian folklore, birds are considered messengers of God, and would fly back to Heaven during the Winter. In the Spring the birds would return, bringing eggs, new life and blessings from God with them. To symbolize this, there is a very old Ukrainian tradition of decorating eggs with beautiful, colourful patterns using a technique of melting beeswax on shells and then using paint. These eggs are called Pysanka, and the symbols render the eggs even more powerful as talismans. These pysanka have their superstitious and ritual usage, too. There was a special motif painted on an egg to ward off lightning, with the egg then being placed in the attic, presumably as the place closest to the source of a possible strike. There's another design that, if the pysanka is placed in a beehive, will ensure a good crop of honey. Pysanka would be placed in the coffins of children, and also in the coffins of adults, but only during Easter time.

The eye of an ostrich is bigger than its brain.

Downy Plumes:
The story of feathers

"Feathers ... are a way of receiving affirmation and acknowledgement that Spirit is not a figment of the imagination. Feathers are a physical manifestation of the Spirit that connects us all."

Starfeather, *Sacred Feathers*

The Symbolism of the Feather

Fragile and beautiful, multicoloured or plain, human beings always seem to have had a fascination with feathers.

Recently, I was given an amazing gift. I've got it here in front of me. It was brought all the way to Wales from California, from some Native American friends, and it's a very old raven feather. The base of it beautifully beaded and decorated. The feather is wrapped in red cloth with white ribbons, and there's a sprinkle of deliciously chocolate-scented wild tobacco with it. This is because tobacco aids flight into the Otherworld, as does the feather.

The care that has been taken with this feather marks it out as a magical item, something to be treasured as an exquisite object in its own right, let alone for any mystical powers it might have. Because of its function and association, the feather is a very powerful symbol of the ascent to Heaven, or whatever we choose to call that seemingly unattainable 'higher place', and indeed is used as a tool to gain passage there.

As a representation of the ability to defy gravity, and subsequently as a symbol of the element of Air and of wind, the feather is supreme. Light,

strong and beautiful, and unique to birds, there's a real magic about feathers, which is primal to human beings, transcending barriers of race, religious belief, language and time. Feathers, or representations of feathers, are used on awnings held over spiritual leaders such as the Pope; the Egyptian Gods and Goddesses often had plumes of feathers in their headdresses; in Medieval Britain and Europe feathers were used by knights and warriors as an indicator of rank and status. Taoist priests, who are known as 'feather scholars' or the 'feather guests', have feathers as an attribute, again symbolic of communion with 'higher' or heavenly realms. The ascent to Heaven is described thus:

By means of feathers he was transformed and ascended as an immortal.

The feather, because of its lightness, symbolizes truth. The Egyptian Goddess Maat is depicted with an ostrich feather, which is particularly symbolic of justice because the feather is perfectly balanced on both sides; Maat's feather is weighed against the hearts of men at the time of reckoning.

And of course, to 'put a feather in your cap' is to give yourself well-deserved praise!

Feathers are associated with the powers of second sight and divination, again because of their contact with the Otherworld. They are used in shamanic practices the world over, although we can use the term 'shamanic' fairly loosely, knowing that we are encompassing, for example, Wicca and Druidry as well as Native American practices. The Norse Goddess Freyja wears a cloak of feathers, which makes it possible for her to fly. Maori chiefs use feather-decked sticks to help the souls of the dead rise to the heavens.

Feathers are used as totem items, which help the bearer or wearer get in touch with the other, heavenly realms. Druids would wear cloaks made of swan's feathers; the swan is associated with poetry, a major art of the ancient Celts. The feather of the eagle is particularly significant for American Indian tribes; as highly valued as a horse, the feather of the adolescent eagle is black and white and represents male and female, day and night, light and darkness, war and peace, life and death.

As well as their association with heavenly realms and the spirit world, feathers are linked with the growth of plants and vegetation. In their Great Feather Dance, the Iroquois give thanks to everything, using feathers as a part of the ritual – the stars, the plants, the waters, animals, fruits, the sunshine and the moonlight.

Feathers as Decoration

Because of their ability to help us connect with the world of the Spirit, it's no surprise that feathers have been used since time immemorial by holy men all over the world. But there's a purely decorative aspect to the use of feathers, too.

Ostrich and peacock feathers in particular have adorned hats and clothes. Marie Antoinette was nicknamed 'Featherhead' by her brother because of her habit of wearing plumes in her hair; the peacock and ostrich feathers she wore one evening sparked a great demand for these items. In the late nineteenth century, the fashion for feathers as ornamentation was reaching another peak, and it was not just feathers but wings, and even entire small birds, that were sported by fashionable ladies in something approaching shamanic imitation. Obviously, this was not great news for the birds: by 1900, conservationists guessed that as many as 200 million birds were destroyed for their feathers on an annual basis, and some species were even put under threat of extinction because of this fashion. In 1884, *Forest and Stream* Magazine reported that 'the destruction of American wild birds for millinery purposes has assumed stupendous proportions'.

Concerned conservationists formed the American Ornithological Union and the Audubon Society, and by 1916 had successfully lobbied to stop the trade in feathers that had done so much damage to the bird population.

The Anatomy of Feathers

A feather is made up of hundreds of small filaments, which are generally held together with tiny barbs in order that the separate components can come together as a strong whole; in fact, feathers started out as scales. Birds generally carry four different types of feathers. There are contour feathers on the wings, the tail and the body, which are shaped to help the bird's aerodynamic function; down feathers insulate the bird and help to regulate its temperature (down feathers have no barbs and are fluffy); the semiplume feathers are a combination of barbed feathers and down feathers (these feathers will

> The Secretary Bird is so-called because of its crest of long plumes, which resembles the assortment of quills belonging to an old-fashioned lawyer's clerk or secretary.

usually have barbs towards the tip and down towards the base); and finally there are the filoplume feathers, which are very small and delicate and send messages to the bird to tell it when to adjust the contour feathers.

There are other feathers that are not common to all birds, which are used to protect the bird in some way. For example, a woodpecker will have bristle feathers to keep wood dust out of its nostrils; and some birds have powder-down feathers, which break down into a fine dust in order to help the bird remove dirt.

Colours

Feathers come in all colours of the rainbow, and the colour also has significance, the spiritual aspect of which we'll look at a little later. Physically, colours make a difference, too. Some birds have dark wing tips; this darker colour contains melanin, which gives the feathers additional strength – especially useful in long flights. And the iridescence of the feathers of the hummingbird, for example, is caused by a layer of bubble-like cells that reflect the light in much the same way as a soap bubble does.

Birds can see a greater range of the colour spectrum than can humans, including ultraviolet light, and whereas a crow may simply appear to be black to our eyes, to another bird it will be colourful and sparkly. Next time you see a crow, look at it with new eyes.

The Message of Feathers
A Tool of Communication

A very pragmatic way in which the feather is used as a tool of communication is seen with the quill pen. The quill has been the most important tool in writing in the Western world. Calligraphers still prefer the feather quill pen to almost any other writing tool. The wing feather of the swan or, more commonly, the goose was used, and the quill pen was popular because the hollow, strong channel holds ink very well and is firm enough, yet flexible enough, to make the desired marks on the paper. The nib can be shaped or sharpened very simply, and feathers were cheap and relatively abundant.

I love the continuation of the idea that Mercury invented the alphabet by watching the flight patterns of birds, and we draw that same alphabet using a part of a bird's wing …

The Prayer Stick

The Pueblo Indians make beautiful staffs or prayer sticks with bundles of feathers on top which blow about in the wind. These sticks are used in several ways; they might be set up in a field of maize or corn, or perhaps on top of a high place, as a way of thanking the Gods. The waving of the feathers, following though the logic, is believed to carry messages between the Gods and Mankind.

There's a description by a Pueblo Indian Chief, Don C. Talayesva, in *Pueblo Birds and Myths*, telling about the first time he saw the offerings of feathers at the Winter Solstice Festival:

> At Sunrise, my Mother took me to the eastern edge of the Mesa with everyone else in the village to place prayer feathers on the shrines. These sacrifices bore messages to the Gods in order to bring good luck. The people placed feathers in the ceilings of their houses and in all the kivas [temples]. They tied them to ladders to prevent accidents, to the tails of donkeys to give them strength, to goats, to sheep, dogs and cats to make them be fertile, and to the chicken houses to get more eggs.

The making of a prayer stick is an elaborate ritual, and the feathers of 72 species of birds are used. As well as the type of bird from whom the feather came, the type of feather used is also important – whether it be a wing or tail feather, for example, or a down feather or another type. The different kinds of feathers required are kept in boxes or wrapped up in cloth.

In addition, the wood from which the stick is made has significance and this, combined with the specific feather type, makes the prayer stick a powerful magical tool.

Feathers as Signs

> And the moment of greatest pleasure was when his wife, Cristina, picked up a white feather from underneath the table and handed it to her husband.
> 'Paulo, look what was down there.'
> And she put the feather on the table.

Coelho brightened, took his wife's hand and, deeply moved, said, 'Thank you, Cristina!'

For him, the fortuitous appearance of a white feather at his side is a sign of the impending birth of a new book. And, at that moment, we were just coming to the end of this book.

Juan Arias, *Paulo Coelho: Confessions of a Pilgrim*

This story of Paulo Coelho's feather omen is wonderful, and shows just what an important sign the feather can be. And because of the association that feathers have as messengers from another world, it is natural that we should regard them thus.

In *Sacred Feathers* by Maril Crabtree, Hazel Achor tells a story about the death of a close friend who was a member of her spiritualist circle. At the first meeting held after the death of her friend Claude, Hazel describes how she voices the feelings of everyone when she says out loud that she wishes that Claude was still with them. The group sits silently and they meditate about their lost friend for a while. After they finish,

> there in the centre of our circle was a large feather, similar in size and markings to an eagle feather or a large hawk feather.

Delores, Claude's wife, is delighted:

> 'That's the symbol we agreed on before he died – a feather! All through our lives, wherever we travelled, we collected feathers. He said that his spirit would send me a feather to let me know he was all right.'

Hazel's conclusion?

> Whether it was sent by Claude's spirit or whether we drew it to us from somewhere in the Universe, it remains a miracle of interconnectedness.

There are lots of other stories about feathers being regarded as carrying a sign or message that is very personal to the person receiving the feather.

SECRET SIGNS

Pueblo Indians use feathers in their dances, and the wearing of feathers signifies certain things. The different types of feathers used provide signals to observers of what is going on; for example, what kind of ceremony is taking place, or what society the wearer belongs to, or what authority they hold. Sometimes feathers are hidden about the person, for example in their moccasins, and form part of a secret known only to the carrier.

Feathers can carry messages from men to the Gods, as well as the other way round. Some Native Americans will tie feathers to trees whose bark has been stripped for use, or to the horns of slaughtered cattle. This is both as a sign of respect and in order to apologize to the Gods for the interruption in the natural process of things.

Bringing Feather Magic Into Your Life

In *Illusions*, Richard Bach describes a piece of creative visualization which involves a blue feather. Richard is told by his friend that whatever he wants to bring into his life, he has to start by imagining that it is already there. In order to demonstrate this, he is told to start with something small – he decides on a blue feather.

> 'Imagine the feather. Visualize it, every line and edge of it, the tip, the V-splits where it's torn, fluff around the quill. Just for a minute. Then let it go.'
>
> I closed my eyes for a minute and saw an image in my mind, five inches long, iridescing blue to silver at the edges. A bright clear feather floating there in the dark.

Richard waits all afternoon for his feather to appear, but there's no sign. Then, over dinner, he spots a carton of milk bearing the legend 'Packaged for Scott Dairies for Blue Feather Farms' … the blue feather might not have appeared in the precise way he had expected, but the blue feather came to him nevertheless.

I like the idea that the first thing Richard thinks of when deciding to try an experiment in creative visualization is a feather, since it's another reminder of the extraordinary power of these beautiful objects to carry messages.

However, there are other kinds of feather magic available to us.

DISCOVERING FEATHERS

The first thing to do is to become aware of feathers and to start to discover them around you. It's lovely if you have access to wide-open spaces but, if not, never mind, because birds are everywhere and, therefore, so are feathers!

You might want to start collecting feathers. They are beautiful objects in their own right, leaving aside any significance they may have for you. You'll soon start to recognize what birds the feathers come from – the soft grey of the pigeon, the iridescent black of the crow, the smart black and white of the magpie, and the dappled tawny and cream design of the buzzard. You might even be lucky enough to find the tiny blue wing-tip feather of the jay.

STORING YOUR FEATHERS

As I explained earlier, you should store your feathers with respect. Native Americans store their feathers in sacred places, wrapped in special cloth or bark with a sprinkle of tobacco. You might also choose to keep your feathers stored in glass jars – I am sure you'll find a way that suits your purposes.

USING YOUR FEATHERS

The colours of the feathers you are using have great significance. In general, wherever we are, whatever nationality we are, colours carry more or less the same meanings.

Here's a quick guide to colours; this is a very brief summary but it should give you the general idea.

- Red – vitality, strength, nobility
- Orange – divine love, fidelity, lust
- Yellow – renewal, the Sun, fertility
- Green – awakening, hope, tranquillity
- Blue – purity, imagination, unconscious thought
- Violet – temperance, spirituality, clarity
- Black – dark, night, the place of rebirth
- White – light, daytime, initiation
- Brown – earth, humility, camouflage
- Grey – mediation, orientation, neutrality

Remember that Native Americans hold the wing feathers of the juvenile eagle in great reverence because they are black and white, signifying night and day, male and female, and other polarities. You might apply the same significance to magpie feathers, for example, which are usually slightly easier to come by!

MEDITATION

Knowing what to do about different kinds of birds from the information contained within these pages means that you can use your feathers to connect with the qualities of the bird in question. I have a jar of swan's feathers which help connect me to the spirit of poetry; holding one of these feathers and knowing that this association with the swan has been there since well before pre-Christian times gives a sense of connection, of timelessness, and helps to orient the mind.

You may well find the feather or a crow or raven; knowing that this bird is famed in particular for its intelligence might help you to focus on intellectual pursuits. A small word of warning though: no amount of raven feathers as totem objects in an examination room will make up for a lack of revision, and the intelligence of the bird should tell you this!

There's also a section in this book relating different birds to their associated divinities (see page 496). Knowing that your feather is that of a dove, for example, will help you to connect with Aphrodite's energy. Among other things, Aphrodite is the Goddess of Love.

It is not essential to know the exact bird your feather came from. The feather itself carries enough information; simply hold it, examine it, and intuit its significance for you. You could also choose to meditate upon the qualities of the feather itself. As you know, the feather is an emblem of truth and justice, of lightness of body and spirit, and of mediation between the worlds.

FEATHERED OBJECTS

The Dreamcatcher

Originating from the Chippewa or Ojibway tribes, the original dreamcatcher was a round or oval frame containing woven strips of leather or cloth, decorated with feathers. These dreamcatchers were made to protect children from nightmares by trapping the 'bad' dreams in their web-like structures and only letting the 'good' dreams through. Dreamcatchers started to become more popular in the 1960s and 1970s as people became interested in American Indian culture and other tribes started to make them.

The Prayer Stick

The prayer stick is used to send messages or prayers up to the heavens. It can be as simple or as elaborate as you wish, but bear in mind that the making of such an object can be a meditative process in itself, and the energy that you put into its construction is as important as any other aspect of this object.

First you will need to find a stick; long or short is up to you. You could decorate it with painting or symbols, or you might choose to carve the stick. Once this is done, you should take your chosen feathers and tie them to the top of the stick with a suitable material – ribbon, or a strip of leather perhaps.

Finally, the stick should be pushed into the ground in such a place where the wind will lift the feathers and carry your messages to the Otherworld.

The Talking Stick

The talking stick is used to indicate that whoever is holding the stick has the right to talk – a useful thing to have in any household! The stick should be easy to handle and can be decorated however you wish. At either end of the stick feathers should be tied on. Keep the talking stick close to hand in case of family disputes, arguments, or noisy gatherings!

However you decide to use your feathers – for decoration, meditation or as means of communication – enjoy them!

Birds as international Symbols

Countries of the World

Anguilla – Mourning Dove
Argentina – Rufous Hornero
Australia – Kookaburra
Austria – Barn Swallow
Bahamas – Greater Flamingo
Bangladesh – Magpie Robin
Belgium – Kestrel
Belize – Keel-billed Toucan
Bermuda – White-tailed Tropic Bird
Bolivia – Andean Condor
British Virgin Islands – Mourning Dove
Burma (Myanmar) – Burmese Peacock
Canada – Common Loon
Cayman Islands – Cayman Parrot
Chile – Andean Condor
Colombia – Andean Condor
Costa Rica – Clay-coloured Robin
Cuba – Clay-coloured Robin
Denmark – Mute Swan or White Stork
Dominica – Sisserou
Dominican Republic – Palm-chat
Ecuador – Andean Condor
Estonia – Barn Swallow

Finland – Whooper Swan
France – Gallic Rooster
Germany – Eagle
Grenada – Grenada Dove
Guatemala – Resplendent Quetzal
Guyana – Hoatzin
Haiti – Hispaniolan Trogon
Honduras – Scarlet Macaw
Iceland – Gyrfalcon
India – Peacock
Indonesia – Javan Hawk-eagle
Israel – Dove
Jamaica – Red-billed Streamertail
Japan – Green Pheasant
Jordan – Sinai Rosefinch
Korea – Black Billed Magpie
Luxembourg – Goldcrest
Mexico – Golden Eagle
Namibia – Crimson-breasted Shrike
Nepal – Impeyan Pheasant
Netherlands – White Stork
New Zealand – Kiwi
Nicaragua – Turquoise-browed Motmot
Nigeria – Black-crowned Crane
Norway – Dipper

Panama – Harpy Eagle
Philippines – Monkey-eating Eagle
Poland – White Stork
Puerto Rico – Bananaquit
St Kitts and Nevis – Brown Pelican
Scotland – Golden Eagle
South Africa – Blue Crane
Sri Lanka – Ceylon Jungle Fowl
Sweden – Eurasian Blackbird
Thailand – Siamese Fireback Pheasant
Trinidad – Scarlet Ibis

Tobago – Cocrico
Turkey – Redwing
Uganda – Grey Crowned Crane
United Arab Emirates – Falcon
United Kingdom – European Robin
United States of America – Bald Eagle
Venezuela – Troupial
Western Australia – Black Swan
Zimbabwe – Fish Eagle

Bird Symbols of the American States

The National Bird of America is the Bald Eagle, which was chosen in 1782. However, each state has its own particular bird symbol:

Alabama – Yellowhammer
Alaska – Willow Ptarmigan
Arizona – Cactus Wren
Arkansas – Mocking Bird
California – California Valley Quail
Colorado – Prairie Lark Finch
Connecticut – Robin
Delaware – Blue Hen Chicken
Florida – Mockingbird
Georgia – Brown Thrasher
Hawaii – Ne Ne
Idaho – Mountain Bluebird
Illinois – Northern Cardinal
Indiana – Cardinal
Iowa – Eastern Goldfinch
Kansas – Western Meadowlark
Kentucky – Cardinal
Louisiana – Brown Pelican
Maine – Chickadee
Maryland – Baltimore Oriole

Massachusetts – Chickadee
Michigan – Robin
Minnesota – Common Loon
Mississippi – Mockingbird
Missouri – Bluebird
Montana – Western Meadowlark
Nebraska – Western Meadowlark
Nevada – Mountain Bluebird
New Hampshire – Purple Finch
New Jersey – Eastern Goldfinch
New Mexico – Roadrunner
New York – Bluebird
North Carolina – Cardinal
North Dakota – Western Meadowlark
Ohio – Cardinal
Oklahoma – Scissor-tailed Flycatcher
Oregon – Western Meadowlark
Pennsylvania – Ruffed Grouse

Rhode Island – Rhode Island Red

South Carolina – Great Carolina Wren

South Dakota – Ring Necked Pheasant

Tennessee – Mockingbird

Texas – Mockingbird

Utah – Seagull

Vermont – Hermit Thrush

Virginia – Cardinal

Washington – Willow Goldfinch

West Virginia – Cardinal

Wisconsin – Robin

Wyoming – Western Meadowlark

Bird Symbols of Canadian Territories and Provinces

The state bird symbol for Canada is the Common Loon.

Alberta – Great Horned Owl

British Columbia – Steller's Jay

Manitoba – Great Grey Owl

New Brunswick – Black-capped Chickadee

Newfoundland – Atlantic Puffin

Northwest Territories – Gyrfalcon

Nova Scotia – Osprey

Ontario – Common Loon

Prince Edward Island – Blue Jay

Quebec – Snowy Owl

Saskatchewan – Sharp-tailed Grouse

Yukon Territory – Raven

Early Birds:
A global alarm-clock

In Papua New Guinea, there used to be a system of telling the time based on which bird was singing at any point of the day. Inspired by this idea, and with the invaluable help of Dr Richard Thomas of Birdlife International in the United Kingdom (and bearing in mind there will be some latitude allowed for seasonal variations), we have compiled a 24-hour global alarm clock. Wherever you are in the world, here's a guide showing which bird will be the first to give you a wake-up call!

Starting in New Zealand, then, and tracking the rising sun around our planet, here are the early birds:

New Zealand – Great Spotted Kiwi
New Caledonia – Kagu
Australia – Laughing Kookaburra
Japan – Japanese Thrush
Indonesia – Blue and White Kingfisher
Siberia – White-billed Diver
India – Asian Koel
Kazakhstan – Black Lark
Arctic Russia – Great Grey Owl
Madagascar – Cuckoo Roller
Greece – Sardinian Warbler
South Africa – Cape Robin
United Kingdom – Nightingale

Senegal – Red Eyed Dove
Azores – Azores Bullfinch
Brazil – Alagoas Ant Wren
United States of America (Eastern Seaboard) – Northern Mockingbird
Ecuador – Screaming Piha
Guatemala – Ocellated Turkey
Mexico – Elf Owl
United States of America (West Coast) – Brown Thrasher
Canada – Canadian Warbler
Cook Islands – Rarotonga Monarch
Alaska – Mackay's Bunting

Bards and Blackbirds:
Birds in the Celtic tradition

"Three score birds and five and three hundred, bright like snow, golden-winged, sing many songs from the branches of the paradisal tree; it is a right language they sing together, but the ears of men do not recognise it."

Lady Gregory, *The Voyage of St Brendan the Navigator and Stories of the Saints of Ireland*

Relate now, O Bird of Achill
Tell us the substance of thy adventures;
I am able finely
To converse with thee in bird language.
The Hawk of Achill

As you might imagine, birds were very important in the Celtic world, and there are numerous fascinating traditions and stories attached to them or about them. In particular, birds were seen to be representatives of the Gods and Goddesses, and carried messages between the deities and mankind (however, these messages needed to be interpreted). It is also possible that birds may have been used as sacrificial animals to appease these aforementioned Gods, or to ask for some kind of benefit from them.

Birds could bring good omens or bad, of life or death. As with other cultures, it was largely believed that it was the bird's ability to move in another

dimension which gave it its magical powers, as well as the individual characteristics of different species. The flight of the bird was also symbolic of the human soul leaving its body after death.

Poets and musicians were accorded special status in Celtic times, and the Druid bards would wear cloaks made of bird skins and feathers, particularly the feathers of the swan, which had/has a particular connection with these skills. This affinity with the feathers of the bird, and the belief that the wearer would somehow take on the attributes of the creature, is identical to the motivation of the Native American shaman, and it is through customs like these that we can see just how closely the world is connected in terms of its instinctive spiritual beliefs and rituals, as opposed perhaps to those of organized religions.

The Otherworld

The concept of another world, literally, the 'Otherworld' or 'Sídhe', was an important part of the Celtic spiritual belief. The 'Sídhe' runs parallel to our everyday world, and if we are able to access it, then we will be able to understand what the birds have to say. In Celtic fables and legends, birds, with their ability to fly, are often regarded as being representatives of spirits from the Otherworld, too, while a recurrent theme of many stories is that of people changing into birds or vice versa. For example, Llew, or Lugh, was transformed into an eagle at the moment of his murder – an example of the liberation of the soul from the body.

The appearance of a seabird, such as a gull, would often be interpreted as providing a means to cross the invisible boundary into this parallel universe of the Otherworld – a logical interpretation, since these birds have the ability to exist in both the element of Air and of Water.

Divination

The Celts watched birds in order to divine information, in much the same way as the Etruscans, Romans, Greeks and others did. Combined with a close attention to other elements of the natural world, birds could guide and inform the seer, provided their behaviour was interpreted correctly. Both the flight pattern of birds and their calls and cries were considered relevant.

> If the Raven croaks over a closed bed within the house, this denotes that a distinguished guest, whether lay or clerical, is coming to you. If it be a layman who is to come, it is 'bacach! bacach!' the raven says. But if it is to be a man in holy orders, it is 'gradh! gradh!' it says; and it is far in the day that it croaks. If it be a soldier or satirist that is coming, it is 'grog! grog!' that it croaks; and if it is behind you that the Raven speaks, it is from the direction that the guests are to come.
> **Middle Irish Codex**

However, there was sometimes a conflict between these old practices and the relatively new Christian beliefs, which were beginning to gain a strong foothold. In a poem decrying the Old Ways, St Columba stated:

> It is not with the sneeze our destiny is,
> Nor with the bird on the top of the twig,
> Nor with the trunk of a knotty tree.
> Nor with an act of humming.
>
> I adore not the voice of birds
> Nor the sneeze, nor a destiny on the earthly world,
> Nor a son, nor chance, nor woman:
> My Druid is Christ the Son of God.
> **Peter Beresford Ellis,** *The Druids*

Birds that were particularly associated with prophecy and auguries included the raven and the owl. The Owl Goddess was Etach, whose cries could mean bad news or good, depending on their tone and the time of day that they were heard. The crow was the embodiment of the War Goddess, Erui, who was the Mother of All Ireland, and its appearance could be a harbinger of bloodshed.

The tiny wren, as the King of the Birds for Druids, was also one of the key birds in divination. There are medieval texts containing detailed descriptions of what each movement of a wren could foretell, so important was this bird.

Weatherlore

Of course, overriding all other subjects for divination would have been the essential desire to know what the weather was going to do – vital for any agricultural community. There were certain birds that were particularly associated with the changing weather patterns, and these included the curlew and the blackbird, whose calls could mean rain; the pigeon was said to bring better weather with it, and the lark promised sunny days and fine weather for anyone overhearing its song.

> A wish made on the first robin of Spring is bound to come true.

The Birds of Rhiannon

Like bird song, the power of music to transport us to 'another place' is profound. Poetry and music were and are fundamentally important to Druids, and Celtic folklore is full of stories about their power to break down the boundaries between the worlds.

In the *Mabinogion*, the Lady Rhiannon had birds that started to sing after a terrible battle, and caused the assembly to forget their woes and to lose all sense of time. This ability of bird song to make us forget where we are and to be transported into the Otherworld is also documented further:

> There were white birds with purple heads and golden beaks. They sang with sweet harmony while eating the berries and their music was melodious and magnificent. They would bring sleep to sick people or to those grievously wounded.

In addition, these mysterious birds could 'waken the dead and lull the living to sleep'.

Groups of three birds are a repeating theme in Celtic mythology, and could be said to be representative of the Three Fates. For example, Clíodna of the Fair Hair is one of the greatest Faerie Queens in Irish folklore. She is a supreme shape-shifter, and is said to be the most beautiful woman in the world. She is always accompanied by three birds, which have the power, from their gorgeous songs alone, to heal the sick.

Other Birds

THE COCKEREL

Although Julius Caesar noted that the Britons didn't eat chicken, nevertheless the cockerel was used as a bird of sacrifice and it was particularly associated with the festival of Imbolc in early February. The festival celebrates the coming of Spring and, of course, the cockerel is also associated with the start of a new day, telling everyone that the sun has arrived by its strident calls. This is a little grisly, but apparently the cockerel would be sacrificed at this time of year by being buried alive at the intersection of three streams. This may also have been to gain protection from evil spirits.

THE CRANE

Cranes often seem to have been associated with war, or the Gods and Goddesses of war. The emblem of the crane was frequently used on shields and helmets, and there's a legend that one of the Gods, Midhir, was accompanied by three cranes who could steal away courage from warriors and make them lose their will to fight.

> A Siberian Red Crane was the oldest bird on record, dying at a proven age of 82.

There's a particular belief, too, that cranes were women who had changed shape, and to eat crane-flesh was taboo. In Scotland, if you wanted to get rid of someone whom you felt had perhaps lived too long, then simply to feed them crane-flesh could do the trick!

Herons, cranes, storks and pelicans are related to the Gods and Goddesses that preside over the mysteries of reincarnation, acting as guides to the Underworld.

THE CROW

Crows were associated with war, most likely because of their appearance on battlefields where they would scavenge from the corpses. This also meant that the crow became associated with death and ill-omen for the Celts, and thus the bird became key in their auguries. The War Goddess, Badb Cath of the Irish tradition, actually means 'battle crow'. The Morrigan, or Morrigana, the Great Queen or the Phantom Queen, shape-shifted into a crow on occasion, although she more usually transformed into another closely related member of the Corvid family, the raven.

THE GOOSE

Again, we get a sense of the preoccupation of the Celts with battles and fighting when we realize that the goose was also a symbol of war. Geese have even been found in the graves of Iron Age Celtic warriors. Of course, geese are aggressive birds so it may be that this is why the association arose. Goose flesh was another taboo meat for the Celts, as geese were considered to be magical birds.

THE OWL

This bird has particularly unflattering names in Scottish Gaelic and Welsh; in the former it is known as the 'night hag' or 'cailleach oidche', and in Welsh the translation is the 'corpse bird', or 'aderyn y corff'. As with other cultures, there is a general belief that the owl is a bird of bad omen, probably because of the nocturnal nature of the creature and its association with darkness and hidden things.

THE RAVEN

A key figure in Celtic mythology, the Morrigan, the Great or Phantom Queen, was the Sea Goddess and also the Goddess of War, and could shape-shift into the form of a raven as and when the occasion demanded. If you see one of these birds close up you can understand why it has been ascribed this power; its eyes are particularly human-looking and seem to be all-seeing and shrewd.

The raven is particularly associated with darkness and death, and was said to dwell in the Underworld as well as on this earth. Ravens are birds of wisdom, too, and are able to warn of coming dangers.

THE ROBIN

Prior to the Christian belief system clouding some of the earlier Pagan ideas, the robin was the bird sacred to the oak king. It was regarded as a lucky bird, and its appearance meant the coming of Spring and better times. Later, the bird came to be associated with Christ and the nature of sacrifice.

THE SWAN

Another important bird for the Celts, the swan was believed to have the power to send people to sleep, and is depicted in many tales as being the spirit of a person, or vice versa. A popular symbol is two swans attached by a chain of precious metal, such as red gold; one of the birds is often seen attached to a Sun symbol, the Solar Wheel, as well.

There is a legend that the Sea God, Llyr, had four children, who were cruelly bewitched and turned into swans by their wicked stepmother, Aoife. The story goes that they had to spend 300 years in each of three places, which would mean that the children were exiled as swans for 900 years. Only when a Prince of the North married a Princess of the South would they be restored to human form, but at that point they would of course die immediately, because of their great age.

It is said that the swan children would meet on the north side of the Island of Rathlin, if they ever became separated, and indeed there's a bay on the north side of this island whose name, Attitudy Bay, translates as the Bay of Swans. These swans were reputed to sing so beautifully that it became a criminal act to kill a swan – a statute that remains in place today.

THE WREN

Although physically the smallest of the birds in the Celtic world, and indeed the smallest bird in the British Isles, the wren is one of the most important by far, being considered to be the King of the Birds. It is associated with prophecy and divination. In fact, its name in Welsh is Dryw, which is the same as the word for Druid.

There is, however, an unfortunate early history for the wren; it was sacrificed at the turn of the year, in a Wren Hunt, which is looked at more closely in the particular section about this bird (see page 278). This Wren Hunt tradition was prevalent throughout the Celtic world and took place generally round about the time of the Winter Solstice. One belief is that the wren was sacrificed at a time of winter, in order to make way for Spring, which was personified by the robin. There's another idea that, since the bird was so profoundly revered by the Druids, the incoming Christians tried to wipe out certain traces of this pagan belief system and the wren became a victim of this. However, even if this latter theory is correct, to kill a wren at any other time of the year was still regarded as having dire consequences for the community.

A Magical Gift

'On my 30th birthday, rather than having a party, I decided to take a few of my close friends to Waylands Smithy. This is an ancient pre-Christian structure, a longbarrow, with many ancient Celtic legends attached to it, and has always had a great resonance for me as being a very magical place. I was in a comtemplative frame of mind and it seemed greatly significant for me when I found a large black feather sticking up out of the ground on our walk to the longbarrow. Then inside, once our eyes got accustomed to the light, I found a small circle of pebbles and flowers on the ground as though someone had prepared a lovely surprise for my birthday. And in the center of this circle was another, identical black feather. It felt as though the Universe had given me a great gift that day.'

Phil, Torpantau

Birds of the New World: New Zealand

"Ka Tangi mai te riroriro
ko te tohu o te raunati,
ka tutu nga tane,
ki nga uwha, a wai na waka.

When riroriro calls, it is the sign of the summertime.
It is then that a man and a woman make love to
each other and the canoe slides easily through the water."

Maori bird song

Maori Bird Beliefs

The Maori, in common with other peoples throughout the world, believe that birds serve as messengers between man and his Gods.

There are many folktales and beliefs about the importance of birds in Maori culture. For example, when Maoui, a legendary superhero somewhere between a man and a god, seeks to slay the Goddess of Death, he takes with him the fantail, the robin and the whitehead as company.

The Tohunga – Maori Augurs

The Maori people also had their augurs, the specially appointed people who could interpret the signs given by birds. These people who read the signs in much the same way as did the augurs of Rome, Greece, etc., were called Tohunga, and they were expert at also catching birds to use for these auguries. As well as the flight of the birds, like their counterparts in other parts of the World the Tohunga thought that cloud formations and weather patterns (as well as other indications from the landscape) were to be considered in analysing the messages of the birds.

Kite Flying

The most divine of all the Gods, Rehua, was referred to as the Sacred Bird and was the ancestor of the kite.

As a form of sky-worship, and to further cement the connection between the material and spiritual worlds, the Maori practise kite flying, which forms part of a ritual of a cult of the sky. The kites are beautifully constructed from bark cloth, which covers a lightweight frame, and usually the kites are designed in the shape of birds with bird features painted on them.

Given that the bird-kite could carry messages between man and God, it is important that they fly as high as possible; some of the so-called 'cloud piercing' kind, or Manu Atua, have strings over half a mile (1 kilometre) long, and some of the kites are so big and strong that people can be picked up by them! The kites are constructed with singing and elaborate rituals, which are closely guarded secrets.

The Magical Bird – the Miromiro

The Miromiro, or Tom Tit, is a small black and white bird, and is a magical bird to the Maori, with many tales relating to its attributes. Despite its size, it had an important part to play in many rituals throughout a person's lifetime.

'Miro' means to twist or turn rapidly or to move quickly; the bird was given this name because it does indeed move fast, and can appear in the twinkling of an eye. To have 'he karu miromiro' – literally, a 'tom tit eye' – means that a person has sharp eyesight.

During the search for a bride, a young Maori man would inform his elders about his choice of a mate, and then the parents would organize the matter. However, if the young lady didn't find that the man was what she had in mind, there was an act of magic that a man was said to be able to perform which might persuade her otherwise, or else bewitch her. The bird usually entrusted with this magical role was the miromiro. The miromiro would be dispatched to the house of the girl, and settle on her head; the girl would then be compelled to get up and walk to the house of the sender.

The same charm could be used to bring back erring husbands or wives, and accordingly, the miromiro has the reputation of being a bird of love. Unfortunately, as yet I've been unable to find any documentary evidence to say that this ever happened!

THE SOUL BIRD

The Tarapunga is a seabird, a small gull, which settled around Mokoia Island and Rotorua. Sacred amongst the Maori, it was forbidden to shoot the Tarapunga or otherwise hurt it in any way, since it played host to human souls who would enter into the bird; the leaders of the flocks would have been tribal elders.

The Tarapunga was accorded its sacred status after a flock of them flew up early one morning, warning the Maori of the close proximity of an enemy who had come to attack their island. In the event, there was a terrible massacre, but the fact that the birds had tried to send the warning was never forgotten. The birds were declared 'tapu', or sacred, because they had acted as if they were human beings.

Land of the Flightless Bird

Because New Zealand is such a long way away from any other land mass, and because there are no major predators such as lions, tigers and the like, there is a very large proportion of flightless birds located on both the North and South Islands.

Before the advent of mankind and other, more predatory mammals such as cats and dogs, there were 18 different species of flightless birds in New Zealand; today, only seven species survive. The existence of all these birds hangs in the balance, but conservationists are working very hard to redress the balance.

Some of these extinct birds are worth looking at, since they have attained legendary status.

THE MOA

The moa is believed to have been the largest bird in the world. Fossil evidence shows that the moa had lost any vestige of wings entirely, and had grown to its colossal size probably thanks to its diet – entirely vegetarian, the bird liked to eat sticks and coarse fibrous leaves from the forests it chose to live in. This diet would have needed space in the bird's stomach to digest, so therefore its body needed to grow very large to support it. Weighing in at 500 pounds, the moa must have been a daunting sight.

Many flightless birds have been made extinct because of predators such as rats, but the New Zealand Wood Rail, or Weka, has actually added mice and rats to its diet.

There's controversy about just when the moa became extinct and how this happened; the debate centres around whether the bird was extinct before the arrival of the Europeans on the shores of the island. Because the flightless birds were easy to capture and made good meat, they were easy prey for the first settlers.

In 1866 the Governor of New Zealand paid a visit to the west coast and met Wormy Hukanui, a Maori chief. There he asked about the Moa and was told by one of the Maori natives, Keeo Papa, that when he was young he had joined in the hunting for the Moa. The following comes from a report published in the *Transactions of the New Zealand Institute*, Volume 21, from 1888.

The young men stationed themselves in various parts of the old plains, and when a moa was startled it was pursued with wild shouts, and sticks, and stones, until they were tired, when another detachment would take up the running … until the moa was exhausted, when a chief would administer the coup de grace.

Because the veracity of his story was questioned, Keeo Papa provided further evidence by telling the visitors exactly where the ovens were which had been used for cooking the giant bird. Accordingly, several men were sent out to dig in the specified place, and unearthed a huge stone, blackened with fire, which had obviously been used for cooking. Then a Maori oven was uncovered, which measured more than five feet (1.5 metres) in diameter and contained blackened stones and charred bones that were obviously from the moa.

Keeo Papa told the Governor's party about the bird's plumage, which he described as a brown colour with feathers similar to those of the emu. He also described how the bird was a fierce fighter, striking out with its huge feet.

THE LAUGHING OWL

This was a large owl; its call sounded like someone laughing, hence the name. The early Europeans saw the bird primarily on South Island but a few were still living on North Island.

Sadly, the very last laughing owl was reported dead in 1914. The reasons for its extinction? Well, evidence from archaeological surveys show that the owl was eaten; it could also be possible that introduced rodents and the like hastened its demise by eating the bird's chicks and eggs.

TE HOOKY – THE NEW ZEALAND EAGLE

This huge bird lived only in New Zealand. It must have been an incredible sight, with its three-and-a-half-foot (3-metre) wingspan and huge claws. It is possible that the eagle would have fed upon the moa. As to its extinction, again it is commonly believed that hunting by early settlers did the damage.

THE STEPHENS ISLAND WREN

A tiny, flightless bird, the Stephens Island Wren was only ever seen by one European, David Lyall, who was the lighthouse keeper on Stephens Island. Ironically, the last wren was killed by Lyall's cat; Lyall has described the bird as 'running about like a mouse' so it must have been an easy target for the puss!

The Huia

One of the better-known extinct birds, along with the moa, the huia was endemic to New Zealand. It was a crow-like bird with a marked difference between the bills of the male and female, and it's likely to have been in decline before the European settlers came to New Zealand.

However, the fact that the bird was hunted as a curiosity for private homes and museums did not help at all. In addition, the bird was very tame – unsurprising in many creatures that have no predators and do not know that they have anything to be afraid of.

In 1867, Sir Walter Biller gave this account of his encounter with the huia bird:

> We heard the soft flute-like note of the huia in the wooded gully far beneath us. One of our native companions at once imitated the call and in a few seconds a pair of beautiful huia, male and female, appeared in the branches near us. They remained gazing at us only for a few instants, then started off up the hill.

In the 1880 Maori chiefs realized that the huia was getting scarce, so made it illegal to kill the birds. However, in 1902 the Duke of York was given a huia feather to put on his hat; after this everyone wanted to follow suit and the feathers of the huia became extremely sought-after. The hunting began again, and by 1920 the bird was extinct.

New Zealand Today

It's sad that all these birds have become extinct; however, we seem to be better informed now, and more able to recognize the dangers faced by birds close to the edge of survival. The Royal Forest and Bird Protection Society plays a key role in ensuring that as much as possible is done to ensure that rare birds get a fighting chance of survival. It has 40,000 members in New Zealand and 54 branches.

THE KIWI

Of course, the kiwi is New Zealand's most famous bird. It is the national emblem of the country, with New Zealanders nicknamed Kiwis. A flightless bird, the kiwi is nocturnal and lives in burrows. Some say the kiwi more resembles a badger than a bird, what with its habits and its feathers, which seem to resemble fur. Kiwis have extremely acute hearing and are able to stalk in the opposite direction from any interlopers in its wooded habitat, so they are becoming more difficult to spot in the wild. However, according to the Royal Forest and Bird Protection Society, the bird will be extinct on both islands in just 15 years' time unless drastic action is taken.

HOW THE KIWI LOST ITS WINGS

This is an ancient Maori tale, which I apologize for abbreviating slightly!

Once upon a time, the God Tanemahuta was walking through the forest, worried that the trees, his children, were starting to get ill. He called all the birds together to see if they could find the cause of this illness.

'I need one of you to come down from the treetops to the forest floor so that we can see what is affecting the trees so badly, so that they, and subsequently your home, will be saved. Will anyone do this?'

All the birds shuddered to think of living on the cold, dark, dank forest floor instead of up in the air and in the treetops. One by one they refused the task; but the kiwi, seeing the bigger picture, said that he would come and live on the forest floor to see if he could help save the trees and his fellow birds' home.

Tanemahuta warned him, 'Do you realize that if you do this, you will change entirely; your legs will become thick and strong so that you can run on the ground; you will lose your beautiful colouring since you will need to blend in with the forest floor so you will be safe from predators; and most of all, you will never be able to fly or see the light of day ever again?'

The kiwi sighed to think of all this, but decided to go ahead with his promise.

The other birds were given various punishments for their laziness or cowardice; but the reward for the kiwi was to become New Zealand's best-known and most loved bird.

THE KAKAPO

Another endangered species which the Royal Forest and Bird Protection Society are doing their very best to preserve (at the time of writing there are believed to be only 86 left in existence), the kakapo is also flightless. It is the largest parrot on the planet, and again, it is believed to have attained its bulk by the need to accommodate enough volume in its stomach to break down a fibrous diet. The kakapo is nocturnal, a habit it evolved in order to protect itself from its predators, such as eagles.

The kakapo is a long-lived bird – some reports have it living for 60 years.

THE FANTAIL – PUKEKOHE

There are actually 16 different Maori names for the fantail, one of which, Tiwakawaka, is also one of the names of the demigod and folkloric superman already mentioned, Maoui. Maoui reputedly settled in New Zealand a thousand years ahead of the main migratory people.

There's a story about how Tiwakawaka challenged the explorer Nukatawhiti when he arrived at the islands by canoe. Tiwakawaka the demigod performed an angry dance to frighten the intruder away, and it is the dance of the fantail that inspired the Maori war dance most often seen performed before international rugby matches, the Haka.

At one point, Maoui got angry with the fantail for refusing to tell him where he could find fire, and shook the bird hard, squeezing him until he went pop-eyed – this accounts for the bird's appearance. But the fantail got its revenge.

Maoui decided to visit the Goddess of Death, Hinenuitepo, to see if he could arrange for man to live more than just one cycle of life before dying. Maoui thought that the best way to achieve this would be to simply kill Hinenuitepo. Maoui's father described the Goddess so that Maoui would recognize her. She seems to have been a giantess, with eyes of greenstone, teeth of flaked obsidian, and matted seaweed for hair.

Maoui chose several birds to accompany him on the mission, including the fantail. He himself travelled with them all to the Underworld disguised as a sparrowhawk. The general idea was that Maoui would enter the womb of the sleeping Goddess and kill her from within. Shape-shifting into a worm, he told the birds sternly that on no account must they laugh or the Goddess would awaken. Maoui entered the womb of Hinenuitepo; however, no sooner had he done so than the Tatahore bird burst out laughing and the fantail danced noisily up and down with delight. Hinenuitepo woke, closed her legs and strangled Maoui.

THE SADDLEBACK – A WEATHERBIRD

The saddleback has a band of reddish colouring running across the bird's back, which is said to have happened when Maoui, the man-god, managed to capture the Sun. Maoui beat the Sun mercilessly so that it could only move slowly across the sky, giving us longer daylight hours. All this effort made Maoui thirsty and he asked the saddleback to fetch him some water. The bird pretended not to have noticed, so Maoui seized the bird and as a result singed its feathers with his hand, which was still hot from the heat of the Sun. Maoui then threw the bird in the water.

The Maori believe that the saddleback is closely associated with water, and it is called upon when rain is needed.

Following this theme, the great ancestor and priest of the Terra tribe, Ngatoroirangi, had two saddlebacks as pets, and these birds, much like Odin's ravens, had magical powers. They were able to predict which way the wind was going to blow and any change in the weather. The birds were believed to have helped to steer the canoes out across the Pacific when the early settlers arrived on New Zealand. The bird's calls were also said to be reliable barometers; the note of one was said to be a sign of good weather, while the other's, shriller cry was said to be a warning of rain.

PIPIWHARAUROA – THE CUCKOO

Pipiwharauroa
Te manu i whiti mai
I tarawaahi
Me to o ano ki te wae mau ai
Nau mai
The shining cuckoo
The bird that has crossed hither
From beyond the sea
With the O carried in its foot
Welcome

The cuckoo to the Maori is the harbinger of Spring and good times ahead; it's also possible that the first settlers in New Zealand had followed the flight of the cuckoo to the islands. The migratory effort of the cuckoo to New Zealand is extraordinarily strenuous, and the bird is said to carry a small pebble in its claws, which it licks in order to combat thirst on its long journey.

THE BIRD WOMAN – KURANGAITUKU

The Kurangaituku recently featured on a stamp of New Zealand, and a very scary-looking creature she is indeed; a giantess, with green skin, the body of a woman, and the huge wings of an eagle.

It's likely that Kurungaituku started out life as a huntress, of Amazonian stature, who became mythologized as the bird woman and the personification of female power. In any case, Kurungaituku liked to keep birds and animals as pets at her home in a cave on Puhaturoa. One day she was out hunting and her lip was accidentally skewered by the spear of a young chief, Hatupatu. Angry, she took him prisoner and added him to her collection of pets.

> Cuckoos' eggs differ in colour from bird to bird, and the females will lay their eggs in the nests of birds whose eggs are the same colour as their own, even though the sizes may differ considerably.

Hatupatu was the only 'pet' that didn't enjoy his status, and he longed to escape. The big problem was that all the other birds and animals watched him as closely as did the bird-woman. One day Kurungaituku asked Hatupatu what he'd like as a special treat. Hatupatu, thinking fast, asked her to hunt for him some bird which lived a long way away, thinking that he might have time to escape. Accordingly, once she had gone, Hatupatu set about killing all the other pets so that they wouldn't give him away. However, he missed the tiny warbler, who hid in a chink in the wall; as soon as Hatupatu ran out of the cave the warbler immediately flew away to tell his mistress what had happened.

She was home in just three strides. Infuriated, she set off after Hatupatu who, using a magic spell, made a cave open up for him so that he could hide. Once he thought she had gone Hatupatu set off again for his home, but Kurungaituku caught sight of him and pursued him again. The only thing the young hunter could think to do was to lead the bird woman though the treacherous grounds past the boiling cauldrons of Whakarewara, and poor Kurungaituku fell into the cauldrons and the ground swallowed her up …

THE SECRET LANGUAGE OF BIRDS

Birds of the New World: Australia

Australia is home to some fascinating birds, and I've selected just a few to explore here: the Cassowary, the Lyrebird, the Megapode, the Bowerbird and, of course, the Kookaburra.

There are also the usual smattering of myths concerning birds which are able to either foretell rain, or which can bring it, as might be imagined in a country where rainfall is at a premium. The storm birds in question are the channel-billed cuckoo or the koel. If it is a detailed forecast you're after, it is believed that the number of Black Tailed Cockatoos which fly over at any one time will let you know precisely for how many days it's going to rain.

The Lyrebird

This bird is so called because the tail of the male lyrebird, when fanned out in courtship display, forms a beautifully perfect lyre shape, although this doesn't happen as often as the depiction of this display on stamps and the like would suggest! Lyrebirds like to dwell in scrubland and forests in Eastern Australia. They're quite territorial and not often seen since they're quite shy. They can fly, but don't do so very often, preferring to run with occasional leaps through the undergrowth. Lyrebirds are splendid mimics, and can copy the cries and calls of other birds and animals incredibly accurately. They can also emulate engine sounds, chain saws and the like!

In the Blue Mountains, there's a range called the Three Sisters, and there is an Aboriginal Dreamtime tale involving the lyrebird, which describes how the mountains were formed.

The sisters are named Gunedoo, Meenhi and Wimlah. The girls lived with their father, Tyawan, in the Blue Mountains, which are not far from Sydney. The father was pretty fearless on the whole, but did have a terror of the local monster, the Bunyip, who lived (very inconveniently) in a deep dark hole close to the family, but who fortunately seemed to spend a lot of his time sleeping.

One day Tyawan had to go on a journey, so he left the girls on a ledge where he assumed that they would be safe. However, a centipede happened along and, girls being girls, they were extremely nervous about the insect; they threw a rock at it. The rock missed the centipede but crashed down the mountain and awoke the Bunyip. The monster was very angry at having his slumbers disturbed, and started to lurch towards the sisters.

Tyawan hadn't got very far before he heard the commotion, and was able to cast a spell, turning the girls into stone to protect them. Thwarted in his hunt, the Bunyip turned his attentions to Tyawan, who transformed himself into a lyrebird. However, in doing so he lost the magic bone that he had used to cast the spell, and without it he was unable to transform either himself back into a man or the three huge stones back into his beloved daughters.

It is said that the cry of the lyrebird is Tyawan, still searching on the forest floor for the magic bone.

The Kookaburra

A member of the Kingfisher family, the Laughing Kookaburra – also known as the Laughing Jackass – is possibly Australia's most famous bird, immortalized in song and famous for its strident call, which sounds exactly like manic laughter. This 'laughter' has an incredibly human quality, and can sound alarming to someone who isn't expecting it and hasn't heard it before. The laughter of the Kookaburra punctuates both ends of the day, both at dawn and dusk, and the birds are so punctual that they are known as the 'Bushman's Clock'.

This bird is valued not only for its apparent good humour, but because of its habit of eating snakes. Australia has a fair number of poisonous snakes, so anyone willing to take care of a few of them is welcomed. The bird will either approach the snake from behind, seizing it by the head and then flying off and dropping the snake from a great height to kill it, or it might decide to batter the snake senseless on a nearby branch before consuming it. This habit of killing snakes has elevated the Kookaburra to the status of a deity.

Why the Kookaburra Laughs – a Dreamtime Tale

A long time ago, before the time when there was a sun, there were only the moon and stars in the sky, and there were no people on the earth, only animals and birds.

One day the Emu, Dinewan, and her friend, Brolga, started quarrelling; they had been sitting in a wide-open space, and their argument was so vociferous that everyone could hear it; it was causing quite some disturbance. Brolga got so angry that she rushed over to Dinewan's nest, grabbed one of the eggs, and threw it with all the force she could muster up into the sky, where it broke with a huge great cracking noise. Astonished, Dinewan and Brolga watched as the huge yolk spilled on to a massive pile of wood, which burst into flame, illuminating everything around it, and making what appeared to be a new world.

The Spirits decided to keep this fire going, building it up during the day and letting it die down at nightfall, and things have been different since that fire started. However, it wasn't always easy to choose the right time to stir up the fire again. The Spirits had the idea to appoint someone to wake them up when it was time to tend the fire at either time of day. But who to choose? They needed someone punctual, reliable and loud.

One day one of the Spirits was passing the forest and he heard the Kookaburra's laugh.

'That's the sound we need!' the Spirit decided.

Kookaburra was brought to meet the Spirits, and was told their requirements; that he should laugh his loudest every morning just before the last star faded, and at night he should do the same, just as the first star rose, so that the Spirits would know when to tend the fire. If the Kookaburra didn't agree, the Spirits said, there was no way they could continue unaided, and they would have to leave the fire to die out, and the World would be a dark place once again.

The Kookaburra thought it would be churlish to let everybody down and agreed to do the job. And so the fire of the Sun is tended every morning, building up to a frenzy by midday, and is allowed to die down every evening. However, children are not allowed to imitate the call of the bird, just in case he thinks there's someone there to relieve him of the job, and he goes away.

The Cassowary

One of Australia's large flightless birds, the Cassowary likes to live in forests and is for the most part hard to spot, being mainly nocturnal. It's a fierce fighter, though, and this, combined with its notorious bad temper, means that it's probably best to get out of the way if you disturb one. The Cassowary is also a native of New Guinea, where the native people believed it was worth inviting the wrath of this huge bird, since some of the Cassowary's feathers are used as the decoration for people's septa, the piece of skin between the divide of the upper lip and the nose. Cassowaries are formidable birds; they hiss and growl and thunder through the forests. One strike of their incredibly sharp claws is enough to rip open a man's stomach – indeed, the Cassowary is perhaps the only bird on the planet that is big enough and powerful enough to kill a man … watch out!

What Bird Would You Be?

'I'd be a Cassowary … It doesn't fly, which might make it an odd choice I guess, since the power of flight is so attractive to human beings. But they are magnificent birds with brightly coloured feathers. They're also very dangerous … I could have also chosen a peregrine falcon, but I wanted to choose something unlikely and unique.'

Andy, San Francisco

The Megapode

Native to Australia and also south-east Asia, the Megapode is a chicken-like bird whose name means Big Foot. They are unique in the bird kingdom in that they do not rely on their own body heat to hatch their eggs; instead, they scratch up a great deal of vegetation, making a huge mound about 6 feet (2 metres) high and 20 feet (6 metres) in diameter. This might use all the debris from the forest floor for quite a large area.

As the vegetation begins to rot, it generates heat. Once this heat is judged to be sufficient by the bird, the female climbs up to the top, scratches a deep hole in the top, and deposits her eggs. The eggs take up to nine weeks to hatch, whereupon the chicks scratch their way to the surface and emerge, fully feathered, to say hello to their parents!

The mounds can be used year after year.

The Bowerbird

From Northern Australia, the Bowerbird, part of the Bird of Paradise family, has incredible building skills; and as well as this, they seem to have an amazing aesthetic sense. The birds can be divided into four groups, depending on their specialist building skill: the avenue builders; the maypole builders; the stage builders; and the ones who don't build at all, called, appropriately enough, the no-builders.

The bowerbird builds the most elaborate structures in the bird world. When the bowerbirds' constructions were first found, people thought that they had been built by children rather than by a small bird. These structures are not for nesting in, but are to attract a female; once she's decided on her mate, the female bowerbird will construct a small, simple nest in which to lay her eggs.

The simplest constructions are built by the stage builder. The stage builder will clear an area about four feet in diameter, and will then cover the space with leaves, replacing the leaves as they wither.

The maypole builder places sticks and twigs around the base of a tree to a height of around 4 feet. After this, he'll build a smaller similar structure around the base of a neighbouring tree, and fill in the space between the two so that it looks like a thatched roof. The whole will then be decorated with flowers, shells or berries, and the faded flowers will again be replaced with fresh ones as required.

The avenue-making bowerbirds are considered to be the real experts, though. A space is cleared, around about 4 feet (1.2 metres) in diameter; then an avenue of sticks is planted to make an avenue about 3 feet (90 cm) long and 16 inches (40 cm) high in the case of the Spotted Bowerbird of Australia. Different species of birds may make their avenue smaller, but it will be the right size for the bird to walk through without brushing its wings.

The avenue will then be decked in flowers, leaves and shells; and the final touch sees the bowerbird take a fibrous piece of scrub and then use this as a paintbrush to apply a pigment made usually from charcoal, saliva and other substances. During the course of construction the bird will stand back to admire its handiwork, occasionally shifting some of the decorations around until the desired effect is achieved.

The bowerbird is deified. Djuwe was the Great Bowerbird, who is said to have taught men how to build the special shelters that are used for initiation ceremonies and dances. The spirit of this great God is believed to reside in the bird.

Peacocks and Palaces:

Birds in India

"Where I hover like a bird soaring
Through skies innumerable,
And vanish beyond the range of mortal vision,
Self-sustaining, not needing food or drink
Even so, my God, I could not know thy price
Nor say how great is Thy name."

Sri Rag

In India, both birds and animals are revered and are often represented as Gods and Goddesses, such as the National Bird of India – the Peacock – which carries the soul of Lord Karttikeya among others. Some of the early Vedic manuscripts describe birds as one of the symbols of the friendship of the Gods to human beings, and it was a bird that first brought food to mankind.

Birds are also a symbol of intelligence. The bird's nest, high in the top of a tree, is the representation of Heaven in Hindu belief; in order to get to the 'nest', the soul would need to shake off the material world and fly there. The Upanishads describe the soul as being a migratory bird, the Hamsa, which translates as the goose; since the belief in reincarnation has the soul migrating from body to body, this seems appropriate, but of course the ultimate aim is for the 'nest' to be reached where there will be no more need for transmigration.

Lessons from Birds

There's a legend about a young man, Jaimini, who is confused about some of the issues raised in the Indian epic, the Mahabharata. His teachers are unavailable, although his second teacher advises Jaimini to travel to the Vindhya Mountains, where he will find the information he seeks from four birds, called Pingaksha, Vivodha, Suputra and Sumukha. These magical birds were not only very well-versed in the scriptures, but could both understand and speak the language of human beings. The wisdom imparted by the birds to Jaimini can be found in a book called the *Markandeya Purana*.

The Language of the Birds

There are also instances in which ancient Indians had mastery over the language of the birds. King Kekaya was one of these people. He overheard the conversation of a pair of birds living in his courtyard, which made him laugh, and his wife, who wasn't privy to this magical language, was quite insistent that Kekaya should tell her what the birds had said. However, it was forbidden to repeat anything, and the king eventually divorced her since she refused to take 'no' for an answer …

Indian henna tattoos often feature bird symbols, which have specific meanings; for example, a dove is said to give a blessing for a journey.

The Rukh or Roc

This giant bird is first mentioned in a series of tales called the Jatakas, dating from around the fourth century BC (which actually formed the basis of many of Aesop's fables). It later appears in the tale of Sindbad the Sailor from *The Arabian Nights'* tales – see the section on mythical birds for more details (page 48).

The Peacock

The Peacock is the symbolic bird of India. Although its
numbers have been diminishing, there is a concerted effort
to help the bird survive, and it is now covered under
Schedule 1 of the Wildlife Protection Act of 1972. This
subject is covered in more detail in the section about
the Peacock (page 446). The Peacock is often domesticated in and around some of the villages.

As well as being associated with Karttikeya, the Peacock
is also the bird of Krishna, and Krishna is often depicted wearing
a peacock feather in his hair. Sarasvati, Goddess of knowledge, science
and art, is also depicted riding a peacock.

The peacock feather plays an important part in both decoration and ritual,
and the Bhil tribe would wear clothes constructed from peacock feathers.

The Pigeon

Unusually, in Hindu culture the pigeon is regarded as an ominous bird, and
there are even charms to ward off any ill effects the bird might bring about:

> Oh ye Gods, if the pigeon has been sent as the messenger of Nirriti [a
> destructive God] and has come to find us, we are prepared to sing his
> praises and we shall prepare a ransom.

The Owl

The God of Death, Yama, would sometimes send an owl as his messenger of
death, rather than his more usual two dogs.

The Raven and the Crow

There is a tribe, called the Maratha, who believe that the spirits of their ancestors reside in the bodies of crows. Therefore this bird is especially revered.

In the Mahabharata, the raven is a messenger of death, and the crow seems to be the bird that carries the most information about the goings-on in the Heavens. It is therefore an important bird in divination. People who are keen to attain a heavenly state are advised to be kind to the crow.

The crow is also an important bird at the time of year when departed ancestors are remembered, and by feeding the crow, people feel that they are also feeding their lost loved ones. Crows and ravens can be seen in the places where Hindus carry out the ritual burning of corpses, which could account for the association.

The Goose and the Swan

In the Mahabharata, the wild goose, because of its form and its whiteness, is the symbol of God, and of the pure soul. It is the supreme bird and is equivalent to the Sun. Varuna takes on the form of the Goose or the Swan, and the Lord Vishnu is pulled through the air in a chariot drawn by geese.

The Parrot

A symbol of love and of fertility, the image of the parrot often features at weddings. This is possibly because the parrot imitates things, as lovers imitate one another in the early days of infatuation. Parrots are also associated with heaven and the notion of infinity.

In an ancient series of stories called the Avadanas, the parrot is chosen as the King of the Birds over the owl because, argues the parrot, the owl might be a good nightwatchman but it is inclined to fall asleep during the day!

The Garuda

Another mythological half-bird half-man figure, and an important bird in the mythology of India, the Garuda is covered extensively in the 'One World, One Tribe, One Bird' chapter of this book. But I liked the following anecdote.

A woodcarver at Kanchipuram, who was a keen devotee of Vishnu (the Garuda is the bird associated with this God), carved a beautiful statue of Garuda. Because the woodworker carved the bird correctly, with due reverence for the wood and the image, when complete the bird came to life and flew away.

> Like birds of dusk settling on the trees
> To roost for the night
> Some joyous, some sorrowing; all lost in themselves.
> When dawns the day and gone is the night
> They look up at the sky and resume the flight.

This is a story from India about something that happened three years ago:

A dear friend of mine lost her father in a very dramatic way. A week after her father passed away she was so depressed she could not get up from bed. She stayed that way until she started hearing a strange sound in her flat; it came from the kitchen. She started to look for a logical answer to the sound, which sounded like a bird in distress. After a day she opened up an air-regulator in the kitchen and there was a bird, stuck. She released it and let it out of the window. The next morning the bird was back sitting at her window looking at her, and after a while it just flew away and she never saw it again.

She called me and told me of her experience, and also that she now believes in reincarnation (this was an atheist who never believed in any kind of spirituality or religion) and that she was sure the bird brought her a message from her father. The bird gave her a feeling of happiness and a lust for life.

That bird experience opened new doors in her soul and she left behind the bed and the sorrow. Everyday since then she is taking small steps towards spirituality and God. As her friend it is a great happiness to see her dealing with her loss in such a constructive way.

Sonja, India

Essential weatherbirds: Birds of Africa

"Some birds have stopped me dead in my tracks. In Tanzania in January I saw the Great Bustard in the Ngorongoro Crater. This magnificent [male] bird would stroll around the crater floor looking for a mate. The bird was one of the largest birds I've ever seen and was almost as high as a wildebeest with magnificent plumage."

Alan, UK

Because the state of the weather is, of course, a critical matter in many parts of Africa, there are lots of stories and lore concerning birds and the weather, so it's worth looking at some of these beliefs.

The Lightning Bird

As in other places around the world, the notion that birds bring thunder and lightning is prevalent in Africa, too. The Amandebele people give the name 'Inyoni Yezulu' to their white-necked fish-eagle; the name means 'Bird of Heaven' and indeed the bird flies at a great height and its droppings are said to possess magical qualities. The Hammerkop or Tufted Unmer also has an association with lightning, as does the peacock. To ward off the lightning bird, its image was carved into soapstone or wood and then placed on the roof or by the doorway of the dwelling place.

Another name given to the lightning bird is 'Impundulu' – this name is also given to electric trams, which tend to spark as they drive past. The bird is said to dart down to earth so quickly that all people ever see of it is the lightning flash as it streaks through the air. Where the bird strikes it lays a huge egg, which isn't a fortunate sign for anyone who might happen to be living close by. The egg should be dug up and destroyed.

There is an apocryphal tale about the finding of some of these 'lightning eggs' in Mashonaland. After a lightning strike, a witch-doctor was called in to try to spot the place where the eggs would have buried themselves. Eventually she stuck a horn into the place where she said the eggs were to be found. After some time digging, sure enough, inside a small hole were found two rather ordinary-looking eggs. By this time a large crowd had gathered and there was some suspicion cast at the woman, who was believed to have placed the eggs in the spot while no one was looking in order to corroborate her pronouncement. One of the eggs was inadvertently dropped, to the great consternation of the crowd, but it proved to be rotten; no untoward lightning strikes came about as a result of the egg's breaking, and all the pieces were duly thrown into a nearby river.

The Hornbills' Trick

Female hornbills are sealed into their nesting area, often a rock crevice. Both the male and female help to construct this 'wall', leaving just enough space for the female to get her beak through to receive food. This is so the chicks will be protected from tree snakes and monkeys.

The Chimungu

The Chimungu is the lightning bird of the Baronga people, and is a hawk that buries itself in the ground wherever its 'lightning' strikes. A potion made from the earth at the spot where the strike is made is said to have the effect of allowing thieves to be detected.

> The African Palm Swift will 'glue' a pad of feathers to a palm, and then fix her eggs, upright, on to this tiny platform using her saliva as a fixative.

The procedure for making this potion is, first, to identify the spot where the Chumungu has struck by finding scorched grass or earth. The village chief will then cast bones over the spot and then the local expert is sent for. The expert will proceed to dig at the designated spot with a long black stick, and will eventually find the bird, whether dead or alive. He will take the bird home, and grind it to a fine powder after first roasting it.

The lightning bird was once reported to have been seen by a young girl who had been hoeing a vegetable plot. She described it as being a large black bird, with the curling tail feathers of a rooster or cockerel. It had landed, apparently, in a pool of water near to where she was working, scratched her quite violently; then it flew away into the sky again. The claw marks were visible on the girl's body and it is possible that she had been struck by lightning, which she identified with the bird she saw.

Caruya, Lord of the Storm

The people of Buziba, which is on the shore of Lake Victoria, hold that lightning is caused by tiny, sparkling red birds which nest by the side of the lake in the rocky areas there. Caruya, the Lord of the Storm, sends these birds out when he feels the need; the flashing of their collective wings is said to be the lightning, with the thunder being the rushing sound made by their many wings all flapping together.

Rain Birds

Rain is vital to Africa, and as you might imagine there are many and varied methods of attracting water to an area. Although the professional rain-doctor is a very important person and plays a key role in summoning rain, there are rituals in which everyone can play a part.

There's a bird called the Insingi, or the Ground Hornbill, which is killed and thrown into a pool if there's been a period of drought for some time. When the rain does eventually come, it is believed that the sacrifice of the bird will have caused the precipitation, since the heavens are weeping for the loss of the bird. The Insingi is also believed to call for rain by its cries – as well it might!

The Ingungulu, or Bateleur Eagle, is another bird which is believed to be able to call for rain. Thankfully, however, this bird is not used as a sacrifice.

Birds As Messengers

The key messenger birds in Africa include doves and pigeons, the guinea-fowl, the fish-eagle, the raven and the rooster. The Mockingbird also has a place as a messenger, from a legend about him revealing the return of a great African leader from the Moon. And the croaking raven carries a message of death for people in many parts of Africa.

Pharaoh and phoenix:
Birds in ancient Egypt

Many of the birds of Ancient Egypt were given divine status, and were attached to the many Gods and Goddesses, with elaborate mythologies being built up around them. Ancient Egyptian art, hieroglyphics and the like show numerous divinities that share the attributes of birds and animals.

We've looked at the Benu, the Egyptian extrapolation of the Phoenix, in the chapter about mythological birds; here we'll have a look at some of the 'real' birds associated with Ancient Egypt. When I say real, I have to tell you I've included the Sphinx – impossible not to!

There are several birds used in the written language system of the Egyptians in addition to those detailed below, including the eagle, who represented the letter A and the sparrow, which represented the enemy and also stood for lustfulness and bad luck. The crow represented discord in the hieroglyphic system, while the swan meant music.

The Sacred Ibis

The ibis is an extremely ancient bird, and fossil records show that it has been around for at least 60 million years. The birds' involvement in the history of mankind, and particularly in Ancient Egypt, stretches back for just a small part of this time – approximately 5,000 years.

The Egyptians venerated the ibis and believed that it was the assumed shape of the God Thoth, who was the Scribe of the Gods and whose job it was to document the life story of every human being on the planet – the ibis represented knowledge. Thoth was known as 'Lord of the Holy Words' and the name means 'three times very, very great'.

Thoth was also the spokesman for the Gods and carried messages for them: 'Ra has spoken, Thoth has written.' It is interesting to realize that Thoth is identified with the Roman God Mercury, and his Greek counter-part, Hermes, the 'messenger of the Gods', who is believed to have created the secrets of the alphabet by observing the patterns made by the shapes of birds' wings. It is another example of the bird as a messenger. Thoth appears as having the head of an ibis, and as a lunar deity he also sometimes appears with a crescent moon over his head. Another belief was that the ibis-headed Thoth had actu-ally created the world, which hatched from the 'world egg'. Thoth accomplished this act by the sound of his voice alone.

The ibis image is an integral part of Egyptian hieroglyphics; its elegant form is easily recognizable in statues, carvings, friezes and the like, too. The Egyptians believed that there was a part of the soul, called the Akhu, and this was written as an ibis. The birds were even mummified with a great deal of ceremony and would be buried with the Pharaohs. Thousands of mummified ibises have been found, particularly at Sakkara, and in fact the birds were bred specially to be embalmed so that pilgrims could make offerings.

Up until relatively recently the ibis was believed to be extinct. However, it has recently been rediscovered near Palmyra – this discovery is described more fully in the chapter about bird conservation (see page 503).

The Falcon or Hawk

Because of its ability to soar high and fast, the falcon also formed a very important part of the bird 'power' of the Ancient Egyptians. From early on the image of the falcon served as a general term for a God, and the falcon itself was considered to be the 'king of the air'. As such, it became the symbol for the God Horus, in particular.

Horus had many aspects, one of them being that of the God of the Sky, who protected the Earth with his outstretched wings. His eyes were the Sun and the Moon. Often the symbol for Horus can be seen as a winged disc – a logical extension in symbolic form for all these concepts.

Another falcon-headed God was the God of War, who was associated with Apollo. He can be distinguished from Horus in that the solar symbol surmounting his hawk head is accompanied by two feathers, one either side of the disc. The Sun god Re is also depicted as having the head of a hawk, as is Sokar, the mortuary God, who often appears with a greenish tinge.

Maat and her Ostrich Feather

The Goddess Maat personified all the rules of existence, embodying truth, the law and the natural order of things. She is depicted wearing an ostrich feather, because, unlike many other feathers, which have one side longer and deeper than the other to aid in flight, the ostrich feather is perfectly symmetrical, since the bird is flightless. This symmetry came to represent balance, truth and the scales of justice.

The Vulture Goddess

The vulture, a sacred bird and symbol of the maternal principle, is the form taken by the Goddess Nekhbet, who was the representative of Upper Egypt. She was paired with the Snake Goddess, Wadjet, who had dominion over Lower Egypt. Nekhbet can often be seen suckling the royal children, and even the Pharaoh himself.

The Sphinx

It would be impossible to ignore the sphinx when looking into the birds of Egypt! Personified in the huge stone statues with which everyone is familiar, the sphinx was half-woman, half-bird, with the body of a lion, who, despite her current appearance in Egypt, actually guarded the road to Thebes in Greece, and would ask travellers a riddle before they were allowed to go any further. If the riddle wasn't answered to the satisfaction of this fearsome creature, she would eat the unfortunate passers-by.

Just in case you ever find yourself confronted with the Sphinx at any time in the future, I can reveal here both the riddle that was asked of Oedipus and his answer; you never know when this information might come in handy. Determined to remove the Sphinx, the courageous Oedipus approached her, and was asked:

> Which is the animal that has four feet in the morning, two at midday, and three in the evening?

Oedipus replied, correctly:

> Man; as a child, he crawls on all fours. As an adult, he walks upright on his two feet; and as an old man he needs to support himself with a stick.

The Egyptian Vulture cracks open ostrich eggs by using a stone held in its beak.

The Sphinx was so annoyed that her question was answered correctly that she threw herself into the sea.

The Winged Gods:

Birds in ancient Greece

"Then, turning with the word, Athena flies
And soars, an eagle, through the liquid skies.

Vision divine! The throng'd spectators gaze
In holy wonder fixed, and still amaze ..."

Homer, *The Odyssey*

Did you know that Greek Goddesses were meant to be able to take wings and fly? The poem above refers to Athena transfiguring herself into an eagle ... easy when you know how (if you're a Goddess) but a tricky one to master, I should think.

Jason's ship, the Argo, with which he searched for the Golden Fleece, was built from the sacred oak found at Dodona, and the Argo itself could speak and translate the Language of the Birds. Again, a useful navigation tool if you could decipher what it was saying ...

The Mystery of Migration

The migration of birds must have been a very intriguing thing for ancient people all over the world; how could the birds simply disappear? The Greek writer and philosopher Aristotle was one of the first on record (around 300 BC) to make observations about the migratory habits of certain birds, noticing that doves, pelicans, geese and swans seemed to disappear at the start of the Greek Winter.

One of Aristotle's theories was that these birds travelled to warmer climes at the onset of cold weather. However, other conjectures made by Aristotle and other naturalists at the time were not quite so accurate, but gave rise to certain beliefs, which persisted until relatively recently, about the apparent disappearance of birds in the winter. One of these theories was hibernation, and another of Aristotle's theories – that swallows, storks, kites and doves would simply sleep the cold season away in burrows and hollows – lingered for a very long time. In fact, an American ornithologist, Dr Elliott Coues, counted 182 papers dealing with the hibernation of swallows alone.

It is a salutary lesson about our ability to make faulty observations fit our theories. There was another belief that swallows would gather to hibernate in reedy marshes, their combined weights sometimes bending the reeds to the point of collapse until the birds drowned; somehow or other, seemingly corroborating this, there are reports of fishermen catching not only fish, but swallows, in their nets in these areas.

An even more bizarre theory about the whereabouts of birds in the winter was posited by Aristotle. This was the theory of transmutation. It seemed logical that, as one bird often arrived just as another left, that these were one and the same bird, but wearing different plumage so as to be able to cope with the colder weather!

The Harpies

There are some interesting bird/human hybrids in Greek mythology. The Harpies were said to be extraordinarily beautiful winged girls in early stories. Later on, they became more monstrous creatures, bearing the faces of ugly old

Green sandpipers
sometimes use
abandoned nest of
squirrels as their
homes.

women and possessing gnarled talons. The names of the Harpies are Aello ('Stormswift'), Celaeno ('Dark') and Ocypete ('The Swiftling') and it is likely that they were representations of different types of storm winds.

Among other things, the Harpies were employed by the Gods to punish people for various crimes. One of these unfortunate beings was Phineas, who had his sight taken away by Jupiter as a punishment for his cruelty. The punishment was compounded, because whenever Phineas was given food, the Harpies would swoop down and take it away from him as he stumbled around blindly.

The Sirens

Other bird/female hybrids were the Sirens. Having the head of a beautiful woman and the body and wings of a bird, in early Greek mythology the Sirens acted as prophets, but they are most famously known for their mesmerizing, beautiful voices, which they would use to lure unwitting sailors on to the rocks surrounding the islands on which they lived. The reason for the hybrid appearance of the Sirens was because they didn't intervene when their friend Persephone was abducted by Hades, the God of the Underworld; as punishment they were given the bodies of birds by Demeter.

There were probably three sirens – Thelxiepeia ('Enchantress'), Aglaope ('Glorious Face') and Peisinoe ('Seductress'); one was said to play the lyre, another the lute and the third would sing the fatal, sailor-luring songs. In the *Odyssey*, Odysseus had been warned about the danger of the Sirens' songs, and he and his crew stuff their ears with wax so that they simply couldn't hear anything. When they passed the same way again, however, Odysseus decided he'd like to hear the songs, so he ordered his men to lash him to the mast tightly so that he'd be able to hear the songs and yet not succumb. It must have been torture – apparently the melodies were amazing but the lyrics even more enticing, promising knowledge, wisdom and a quickening of the spirit. Odysseus begged to be untied but his crew just tied him tighter to the mast.

Another man who escaped the lure of the Sirens was Orpheus. His method was to take out his lyre and simply drown out their songs with his playing. If anyone resisted their singing, the Sirens were meant to drown themselves in the sea.

Pandora's Box

The story of Pandora's box is pretty well known. However, what is not quite such common knowledge is that the one remaining thing in the box, Hope, took the form of a small bird. When Pandora's curiosity resulted in her unfastening the cords which bound the box and opening it, all the pestilential things which we have on this planet today are said to have flown out in the form of moths, stinging and biting everyone in the way, and then disappearing out of the door. Hope, the bird, was left in the box, but upon her release she quickly set about healing the scars and wounds left by the evil moths.

The Hoopoe, the Swallow and the Nightingale

Tereus, the son of Ares the God of War, had assisted the king of Athens, Pandion, in his fight against Thebes. As a reward, the king's daughter, Procne, was given to Tereus in marriage. Some little while later, Tereus and Procne returned to visit her father, and a banquet was thrown in their honour. Procne's younger sister, Philomela, danced before the company. Such was Philomela's beauty that Tereus was instantly smitten, and he devised a plan to abduct this lovely young girl. He told the king that Procne was ill and would need the care of her sister, so accordingly all three returned to Thrace.

Philomela of course rejected Tereus' advances, but he was so enamoured that he attacked her on the long journey, and so that she couldn't tell her sister what had happened he ripped out her tongue. To make matters worse, he then imprisoned the unfortunate girl in a cold dank dungeon. However, embroidery was a skill possessed of many of the upper classes in Greece, and during her time in captivity Philomela embroidered a cloth, depicting what had happened to her, and convinced one of the jailers to take it to Procne.

Procne was furious, and set out to rescue her imprisoned sister. Once free, the sisters devised a plan that would punish Tereus for the terrible things he'd done to Philomela. The Ancient Greeks were a bloodthirsty lot – Procne's revenge was to murder her own son by Tereus, Itys. She then concocted a recipe, and served up Itys's body to his father. As Tereus ate the last morsel, Procne took the boy's head from a leather bag and flung it on the table. Not surprisingly, Tereus fainted, and Procne and Philomela set out in some haste for Athens.

When he had recovered, Tereus took his sword and set out in pursuit of the murderesses. He soon caught up with them, and was about to kill them when Procne begged the Gods for mercy. The Gods intervened, and transformed Procne into a nightingale, Philomela into a swallow, and Tereus into a hoopoe. Legend has it that the nightingale calls out the name of her murdered son, 'Ity, Ity, Ity', both day and night; the swallow, having no voice, mutters the name of her attacker; and Tereus, the hoopoe, calls out 'pou-pou-pou', 'pou' meaning 'where?' in Greek.

Incidentally, before people start writing in to correct me, I've related the original Greek version of events, which has Philomela as the swallow and Procne as the nightingale. In their later reinterpretations, the Roman poets swapped the swallow and the nightingale around.

The Halcyon Birds

Perhaps the most famous bird-related Greek legend of them all is that of the Halcyon Birds ...

Ceyx was the king of Trachis. He was a good and popular king, and the country was happy and peaceful. He was an extraordinarily handsome man, not surprising in view of the fact that his father was Hesperus, the Day Star, and his wife, Halcyone, was incredibly fond of her husband.

However, Ceyx's brother died, and following his death all sorts of unfortunate-sounding prophecies had been made. Not unnaturally, Ceyx was worried by this, and decided that he would make a journey over the sea to visit the Temple of Apollo at Delphi, to get a second opinion from the Oracle there.

Halcyone had a premonition that the journey wasn't a good idea. She tried to persuade Ceyx that he should maybe postpone the trip because of the renowned savagery of the winds at that time of year. He refused to give up the idea, so Halcyone then said she'd rather go with him and face the dangers together than be left at home wondering what was happening.

Obviously, Ceyx was worried about his wife's fears, but all the same he was determined to go. He didn't want Halcyone to take the same risks, and so he insisted that she stay at home.

I promise, by the rays of my father the day star, that if fate permits I shall return before the moon will have twice rounded her orb.

And with that he set off, leaving Halcyone, with a sudden presentiment, to fall to the ground in a faint. As she came to, blinded by tears, the last she saw of her husband was him standing on the prow of his ship, waving back at her. She waved back until the ship was no longer visible, then went home and tried to allay her anxiety.

Meanwhile, at sea, Ceyx was less than halfway on his journey to visit the Oracle at Delphi when the winds started to pick up, a little at first, but soon reaching the full crescendo of gale-force. The little ship was soon in trouble. The storm raged, with thunder and lightning and lashing rain. Worst of all were the winds. They were terrible, changing direction on a sixpence and whipping the ship around in all directions, the sails useless against the onslaught. The sailors were petrified; although they were all experienced seamen, they'd never come through anything like this before. Ceyx was afraid, too, but he was glad that his beloved wife Halcyone was safe at home. Then the final blow; the mast of the ship was struck with lightning and the vessel went down. Clinging to a spar, Ceyx's last wish was that his body would be brought to shore so that Halcyone would know what had happened.

Back home, Halcyone was counting the days until the return of her husband. Every day she prayed for his safe return and that he should be faithful to her while he was away, and not fall in love with anyone else. Every day, she laid out a new set of clothes for him, as a sort of charm that would ensure his safe return. Her prayers were directed mainly to Juno, who eventually took pity on Halcyone. Juno sent Iris, Goddess of the Rainbow, to fetch Somnus, the God of Sleep, to give Halcyone a vision, a dream, so that she would know what had happened.

Somnus woke one of his sons, Morpheus, who was able to take on the shape or form of any human being. Morpheus accordingly went to the bedside of Halcyone, and took on the form of Ceyx, except that he looked as he would as if drowned – his skin pale, his eyes sunken, his hair and beard soaked with water. Then Morpheus spoke to Halcyone:

Do you recognize me, my beautiful wife? Or is my appearance too strange and terrible for you to know your husband? Your prayers and thoughts have been in vain; the storms which you warned me about swept away my ship and everyone on board has drowned. I come in person to tell you this so that you'll know it is the truth.

Reaching out in her sleep for her husband, Halcyone woke up, realized what had happened, and in the nature of all good tragedies, started to wail and gnash and tear out her hair.

She ran down to the sea, remembering the last few moments she spent with Ceyx, when she spotted a distant object on the horizon. Trying to see what the floating object might be, she climbed up on to a barrier, part of the coastal defences, and waited for the tide to bring the thing nearer.

It is the body of Ceyx.

In her grief, Halcyone jumped from the barrier, and as she did so, a miraculous thing happened – she started to fly like a bird, suddenly she had wings. She called, lamenting, and the sounds which issued from her sounded like the keening cries of a seabird. Halcyone flew out to the body of Ceyx and wrapped her wings around his limbs. As she did so, Ceyx came back to life, and turned into a bird, too; the agent of the transformation was Halcyone's father, Aeolus, Lord of the Winds, and there they both are, still.

The Halcyon Bird is of course the Kingfisher. As a gift, Aeolus granted the kingfishers Ceyx and Halcyone a period of seven days, twice, every Winter, when the winds were kept imprisoned so that the birds could nest on the water. In Greece today, there is often a period of calm in the middle of Winter, when the seas are still and the weather becomes quite balmy with a promise of Spring. This time is called the Halcyon Days, which refers in general to any period of calm delight, either at sea or otherwise.

The Wryneck

An unassuming bird of the woodpecker family, the wryneck had great importance as a magical bird in Ancient Greece. The wryneck has an unusual capacity to be able to twist its head around without moving its body at all, and it is this characteristic which could be a contributory factor in the bird's importance, although no favours at all were done for the poor bird.

As a solar symbol, there was a ritual whereby the bird would be spread eagled on a wheel and spun around, clockwise and then anti-clockwise. A writer at the time described the ritual:

> Witches regard this bird as suitable for employment as a love charm.
> For they take it, bind it to a wheel and whirl it round while uttering incantations.

In time, the wheel, as part of a spell to charm a potential lover, was employed without the use of the bird, although the connections between the bird, the sun, the wheel symbol and love charms is still steeped in mystery.

Messengers
from the fourth dimension:
Birds in ancient Latin America

The ancient civilizations of Latin America – the Aztecs, the Peruvian Incas, the Mayans and the rest of the Latin American world – are extremely rich in bird imagery and bird lore. Birds feature heavily in the ancient books, the codices; indeed, in the Nahua Borbon Codex, 13 birds were used to depict time itself – an early indicator of how time flies, perhaps?

This is just a small glimpse into some of their customs and beliefs.

The Dimension of Fire

The Ancient Mexicans believed that the universe was composed of between 9 and 13 different 'heavens', and that the birds belonged in the fourth and fifth heavens, which were also the domain of fire. Birds travelled to Earth from this higher dimension, and if man could become sufficiently enlightened, then he should be able to understand the language of the birds.

The Mexicans love their birds; they had a profound knowledge of their behavioural patterns, their flight patterns and their 'song' or language. Because of Mexico's fantastic biodiversity, there are many different varieties of birds, more than in either Canada or the United States. Many towns and villages still have place-names which have associations with birds. Aztlan or Aztatlan,

for example, means 'Place of the White Herons' and was the place of origin for the Aztecs; there's also Cuautla – 'Where the Eagles Abound'.

The Aztecs and the Gift of Language

As with most cultures, the Aztecs have a story about a great deluge. Their story goes that most of mankind was wiped out by a terrible flood; there were just two people who were fortunate enough to have escaped, a man called Coxcoxtli and a woman called Xochiquetzal, who managed to escape in a boat. They were lucky enough to find some dry land on top of a mountain, and had many children. The gift of languages was given to the family by a dove; unfortunately there were so many different languages that the children couldn't understand one another.

Quetzalcoatl

Although not strictly a bird, the God Quetzalcoatl plays such a major part in the mythology of the Aztecs that it would be impossible not to mention him. The name comes from Quetzal, a bird also called the Trogon. The Trogon is a beautiful bird, a little larger than a sparrow with iridescent green feathers and a crimson underbody; its tail is long, eight to ten inches (20–25 cm), and curved.

The Quetzal, which is the National Bird of Guatemala, is believed to die of a broken heart if kept in captivity.

Quetzalcoatl translates as 'the Quetzal Feathered Serpent' and the motif of the feathered serpent is really a symbol of evolution, because of course feathers actually started out as scales. The imagery of the serpent and the feathers also combines the ideas of Heaven and Earth. The Feathered Serpent became the deity associated with the priesthood of the Aztecs. The precursor to Quetzalcoatl was a Yukatan God, Cukulcan, whose name also means 'bird snake'.

Quetzalcoatl was the God of Wind and the great Creator. He was also one of the Four Lords of Creation whose domain was in the West.

Huitzilpochtli and the Hummingbird

Huitzilpochtli is another of the Aztec bird-gods. He was said to have been born after a crown of feathers fell from the sky onto the lap of his mother.

Another of the four Lords of Creation, with his domain in the South, Huitzilpochtli was a God of War, and indeed the attributes of the hummingbird were believed to have been war-like, too, hence the association. Despite their size, or perhaps because of it, hummingbirds are territorial and aggressive and will not hesitate to attack not only each other, but also much larger birds, should necessity demand it, sometimes even coming to blows with hawks or owls. Their long beaks have a weapon-like appearance. In terms of manoeuvrability, the hummingbird is supreme; it can move backwards and forwards and also upside down, and its flight pattern is decisive and swift.

The hummingbird was thought of as one of the Spirits of the Ancestors, and parts of the hummingbird have a totemic use, either to enhance strength or to bring love, because as well as being the bird of war, oddly enough the hummingbird was believed to be a love-token too. This belief has carried through to the modern day, and parts of hummingbirds are eaten or carried about in the hopes that the magical powers of the bird will be imbued to those who possess certain parts of it.

It was Huitzilpochtli who told the Mexicans the sign they should look for so that they would know where to build their great city …

Mexico City, the Eagle and the Cactus

Mexico City was founded where the long-awaited sign from the Gods was spotted – an eagle perched on a cactus on an area of marshy water. The eagle was engaged in the act of strangling a serpent. This image was engraved on to the Great Seal of Cortez and remains the emblem of Mexico to this day.

The eagle, unsurprisingly, was as important a bird to the ancient Mexicans as it was in the rest of the world. A manifestation of the Sun, the Golden Eagle is to be seen on the flag of Mexico and is the country's national emblem. The eagle represented military strength, and often featured on shields and the like; the best Aztec warriors were known as Eagle Warriors. The eagle that inspired this imagery would have been the Harpy Eagle. A massive bird, the Harpy has a seven-foot wingspan (just over two metres) and is a heavy bird, living high in the forest canopies.

The Vulture

The vulture also held an important place in the bird world of the ancient Latin Americans. These birds are superb flyers, and are able to soar at great heights, like the eagle, with relatively little visible effort. Their habit of eating rotting flesh and the like provided an invaluable service where there was no sanitation or plumbing, and the birds were seen as transformers of waste and decay, rendering everything clean and wholesome again. In addition, vultures only take what they are given; they do not kill in order to eat. The Turkey Vulture's name in Latin, *Cathartes aura*, has the same root as the word 'cathartic'.

The image of the vulture was used on Peruvian knives used for human sacrifice; and in many stories across Latin America the vulture is associated with fire, and said to be its keeper. The vulture is also associated with agriculture, probably because of its habit of circling the fields (which are burned down on an annual basis) looking for groggy animals. The main God of the ancient Costa Ricans, Sibu, took the form of a vulture and gave the people the information they needed to become a civilized agrarian people, showing them which seeds to plant.

The Condor

Another important bird, the condor is a manifestation of the Sun. It's worth bearing in mind that the condor is the world's largest flying bird and with a wingspan of 12 feet (3.5 metres) the Andean Condor is an incredible sight. The condor can glide for ten miles without flapping its wings; no wonder it held such an important place in the mythology and symbolism of the Latin American peoples. Preferring high places, the condor will breed and roost at heights of 10,000 feet and upwards. The bird features heavily in art, including on textiles and pottery.

The Bororo

The Bororo people of Brazil essentially believe themselves to be people of the macaw; the story goes that their God turned them into birds, before turning himself into the Sun. Most Bororo keep birds, and when a bird dies it is accorded due ceremony, and wrapped in a mat and buried behind the house. Macaws are held in great reverence and never killed, since the birds are believed to hold the spirits of their ancestors.

In Argentina, the Grey-breasted Parakeet dwells in colonies; these are high structures constructed from twigs, with each pair of birds occupying its own private 'apartment'.

Peruvian Feather Work

Feather work was a very important craft for the pre-Columbians; not much of it exists today, but what is left is extremely valuable. The working of the multi-coloured feathers was a painstaking art, requiring patience and dexterity. Birds were kept specifically for their feathers and were plucked at the appropriate time of year to provide material for these works of art, and dealers in feathers established themselves in close proximity to the craftsmen.

Feathers were also used extensively in clothing, such as cloaks and head-dresses, and to decorate certain ritual items. The colour of the feathers was an important factor; for example, yellow feathers were representative of the sun; red stood for fertility and power, but also for blood; and blue was for the sky, communication and water. The colours of the feathers were also used to denote the rank or status of the wearer.

A Mayan Myth – How the Birds Chose their King

A long time ago, but not so very long ago in the great scheme of things, Halach-Uinic, the Great Spirit who presided over everything, was growing rather tired of the constant bickering and arguments between the birds, so he told them that they must decide among themselves who was going to be their king.

All the birds quite naturally thought that they each held the attributes suitable for such an important job. The Cardinal, with its red feathers, was sure that its beauty would be enough to get him the vote. The Mockingbird, however, was convinced that its beautiful voice would convince all the other birds that he was best for the job, and accordingly he set about impressing everyone with a spectacular series of trills and elaborate melodies. The Turkey, however, stepped into the fray and told all and sundry that *he* was the best bird to be king because of his incredible strength.

And so it continued all day long; all the birds showing off one after the other, and for Halach-Uinic the noise was worse than ever. Only one bird kept quiet, and that bird was the Quetzal, whose name was Kukul. Kukul was quite a shabby-looking bird so he believed that his appearance wouldn't be the sort of thing that the other birds would expect in a king.

However, Kukul was also an ambitious and clever bird, and went to see his friend the Roadrunner.

'My friend, I wonder if we might come to some arrangement. You're too busy to take on the role of King; but if you could loan me your beautiful feathers for a while, I think I might find a way to become the ruler, and if this happens then I'll share all my riches with you.'

Although he wasn't too keen at first, the Roadrunner finally agreed, and waited patiently while the Quetzal plucked his feathers and adorned his own shabby body with them.

Soon the Quetzal was transformed; his feathers were iridescently green and sparkling in the sunshine, and his tail swooped elegantly around in a huge glittering arc. He preened himself a little, caught sight of his reflection in a lake, and then made a grand entrance into the circle of still-squabbling birds. They were all hushed at the sight, and then a slow chorus of 'oohs' and 'aahs' started to swell.

Halach-Uinic was delighted with the transformation and decided to put an end to the arguments once and for all:

'I have decided that the Quetzal, Kukul, should be King of the Birds.'

All was well, but in the business of his important new job, Kukul completely forgot about his promise to the Roadrunner.

After a few days the other birds realized that the Roadrunner was missing, and started to put two and two together; they went off to find him, and discovered him almost dead from cold and starvation, shivering in the forest. They quickly fed him, and he revived, and they heard the story of what had happened.

So all the birds donated a few feathers each to the Roadrunner, and that's why today the Roadrunner has such an oddly coloured coat. But his friendship with the Quetzal certainly isn't what it once was.

THE SECRET LANGUAGE OF BIRDS

Thunderbirds and rain dances:

Birds of the Native American peoples

"We have learned to be patient observers like the owl. We learned cleverness from the crow, and courage from the jay, who will attack an owl ten times its size to drive it off its territory. But above all of them ranks the chickadee because of its indomitable energy for life."

Tom Brown Jr, tracker

There are so many different tribes of Native American peoples, and so many myths and stories concerning the important birds that you will have to forgive some generalizations. Huge tomes have been written on the subject of the Native American peoples and the significance of their birds and animals that all I can do here is offer a brief insight into the subject.

The Totem

The root of all Native American belief systems is that of totemism. A totem, according to the *Larousse Encyclopaedia of Mythology*, is

> an object, a being, a force of nature, which is generally looked on as the ancestor of a group or clan or individual, who takes its name and identify themselves with it.

Possibly the best-known extrapolation of the idea of the totem is found in the totem pole, a large piece of wooden sculpture featuring various animals and birds. The pole itself carries the same symbolism as the tree, that is, of transcendence and of reaching new heights and a new understanding of the world.

The totem animal or bird would be given or revealed to the Native American at puberty. For boys, this assumption of an animal spirit guide would often coincide with circumcision – a process of saying goodbye to the ignorance of the child, and embracing the spirituality and knowledge of the adult.

Many of the Indian tribes and clans bear the names of animals or birds; indeed, there is an actual Bird Clan among the Cherokee, consisting of the Thunderbird, the Eagle, the Pigeon and the Hawk or Warrior. The Bird Clan has special names that it gives to its members, such as Ahuperewiga ('Transparently Clear Wings'), Hegheniga ('Young Swan') or Keredjusepga ('Black Hawk').

The Native Americans believe that everything in nature – birds, rocks, trees, plants, everything – has a power, a spirit, which can reach out and influence others and which we, in turn, can influence. There are many names for this spirit, this numen; we'll call it the manitou.

In order to get in better touch with their totem birds and animals, Indian peoples would use feathers and sometimes other parts of the creature, such as skins or furs, in their rituals in order to take on the spirit, or manitou, of the totem. This inevitably meant that some birds would need to be hunted and then either killed or kept in captivity. Today, some of us might find this repugnant, but bear in mind the following statistics, taken from the book *Pueblo Birds and Myths* by Hamilton A. Tyler; by the way, a 'mesa' is a plain.

In 1893 there were two captive eagles on the First Mesa ... Against this we may set the numbers killed by the Anglos ... The Big Bend Eagle Club alone made the following number of kills of eagles from aeroplanes: 1941, 657; 1942, 667; 1943, 1,008; 1944, 800; 1945, 867; 1946, 819.

Thankfully, we are now far more aware of the damaging effect mankind can have upon the animal and bird kingdom, and eagles are a protected species.

The Eagle

The importance of the eagle in Native American legends and rituals cannot be overstated. Their feathers were used on the war flags of Creek Indians; for the Cherokee, the feathers were sacred items and could only be worn by their elite warriors. The Iroquois had the eagle as their King of the Birds, who never actually visited the Earth himself, but would send delegates to carry out various tasks. Similarly, the Pawnee believe that the eagle is the King of the Sky, and the Natchez equate the bird with a great God.

The Pueblo valued especially the feathers of young adult Bald Eagles, since they have a black tip to their tail feathers which disappears as the birds grow older. An eagle would be kept tethered and its tail feathers plucked as appropriate. In fact, this particular tail feather was considered to be as valuable as a horse.

CATCHING THE EAGLE

The catching of the eagle for such a purpose was, as you might imagine, a highly risky and dangerous endeavour, especially as among the Plains Indians it was taboo to actually kill the eagle. One of the methods used by the Pueblo Indians to capture the eagle was to dig a pit; at the bottom of the pit would be a bowl of water, which would act as a mirror. The outside of the pit would be disguised with foliage, and fastened in among the greenery would be a rabbit as a lure for the bird. Once the bird had alighted upon the rabbit, then it was apparently a relatively straightforward matter for the C'haiani, or eagle catcher, to trap his prey.

The Eagle Killer

For some tribes such as the Cherokee, although it was not taboo to kill the eagle, the task was placed in the hands of a specialist professional killer. The event was something that involved the whole community and certainly was not to be taken lightly. The eagle killer would be conversant with the special prayers to be offered after the event to apologize for the sacrilege.

If the eagle were killed at the wrong time of year or in the wrong way, then all kinds of calamities could befall the tribe, so the job of eagle killer was a very important one. The killer would usually be called in from some way away so that a discrete distance was kept between the tribe and the killer.

The eagle killer would set out alone for the mountains, and would then start a process of fasting and meditation or prayer; this would take about four days. After this the hunter would kill a deer to leave as bait for the eagle. The eagle killer would then sing songs to call the eagle down from the sky, and once the eagle had alighted on the bait the bird would be shot. The killer would then ask the eagle for forgiveness and tell the bird not to blame the tribe. Once back at the tribal domain, the announcement would be made that 'a snowbird has passed'; this was so that the eagles, if they happened to over-hear the conversation, would not realize that it was one of their own kind that had been killed.

After the eagle had been left for four days, to allow parasites and vermin to leave the body, then the feathers – magical, sacred items – would be stripped, again by specialists who knew precisely what they were doing. The feathers would then be wrapped in a fresh deerskin and taken to be stored in a round hut built specially for the purpose.

Then the eagle dance would begin, after the feathers had been offered food and drink. Only the best warriors and most holy Spiritual Elders would be permitted to wear the feathers or carry them in the dance.

Tradition vs Modernity

Whereas for the Native American Indian the respect for the body and the spirit of the bird was paramount, how many of us today eat birds or use their feathers (for mattresses or pillows, for example) without any thought or consideration of the sacredness of that being? It is one thing to hunt a bird or animal as a means of survival or spiritual welfare, because in the chase and subsequent capture a relationship is built between the hunter and the hunted which implies a mutual respect. It is something completely different to eat a bird or animal as part of a prepackaged ready meal, where perhaps both the life and the welfare of the animal have been given scant, minimal attention, and where our involvement with a living being is even more removed from the reality.

However, in recent years there has been a conflict between the rights of Native American peoples to be able to carry on with their traditions, and the bureaucracy of a 'foreign' government who is trying to uphold laws pertaining to the protection of certain rare or endangered creatures. Fortunately, the way in which these issues are being tackled should serve as an inspiration. Native Americans and the US government are working alongside one another to ensure that the birds remain protected whilst the rights of the tribes remain intact.

The US Fish and Wildlife Service

A unique organization, the United States Fish and Wildlife Service is located in Oregon. Part of its role is to ensure that Native American people retain the right to own parts of certain sacred birds, while ensuring that the birds themselves remain protected. If you are a bona fide tribal member, then an approach to the Fish and Wildlife Service will provide you with, for example, the eagle feather you might have the right to own as part of a long-standing tribal tradition. As Pat Durham from the Service says:

> In a nutshell, the Federal Government will allow for possession, transfer and gifting of regulated parts and feathers but prohibits unauthorized takes (killing, harming, harassing) and any commerce of those items.

Pat goes on to explain that a particular tribe in New Mexico have established an aviary for eagles in order to address their own cultural and spiritual needs regarding this particular bird. This is a fantastic innovation, which is beginning to be emulated by other tribes.

The Owl

As in many other cultures, the owl is regarded with some ambivalence, due to the sounds it makes and its nocturnal nature. The Cherokee name for the dusky horned owl is Tskili, which is the same word for witch (reflecting the 'strix' or 'strega' of European culture), and indeed owls were generally believed to carry the spirits of dead people or witches. If an owl feather were to be soaked in water and the eyes of a child bathed in this water, then the child would be able to remain awake all night.

In Hamilton Tyler's *Pueblo Birds and Myths*, he describes the bird thus:

> Owl, like some kind of awkward, winged Satan, is exiled from the Sun's world to become a creature and symbol of the dark.

However, this nocturnal knowledge can also be put to good use, and this information gives the owl a great deal of wisdom.

There's a Cochti story further drawing the parallel between owls and witches. A hunter, out late and finding that the night was drawing in, decided to go no further but to wait till dawn, taking shelter in a chink in the rocks.

As he waited, crows and owls started gathering from all directions, perching on the branches of the trees. The birds changed themselves into men and women, and then one of them opened a fissure in the rock revealing to the hunter a huge cave, which proceeded to fill up with witches and wizards who continued to arrive in the shape of owls and crows – even the hunter's own wife was there.

> Owls are among the few birds who can see the colour blue.

The hunter quickly went home and discovered his wife's eyes, which she had removed from their sockets; these he rendered unusable and then went away again. The next day he returned home to find his wife with a veil over her eyes. He took away the covering and discovered that his wife had the eyes of an owl.

Another sign of witchcraft would be the wearing of owl feathers and crow feathers, either openly or surreptitiously. There's an anecdote about a Zuni war chief who was a prosecutor of witches and a well-known character. He was accused in the middle of a trial of keeping owl feathers in his moccasins and was forced to remove his footwear; the accusation proved to be true.

The Thunderbird

The Thunderbird, or Wakinyan to some of the Plains tribes, forms an important part in the bird mythology of the Native Americans. It is worth bearing in mind that this giant bird is an extrapolation of the energies of nature, and that the stories which surround it are a way of explaining some of those energies and their duality, for example, how the thunderstorm can be an alarming thing but also brings with it great benefits.

The Plains Indians held that there were four differently coloured thunderbirds representing the four cardinal directions, the Western Thunderbird being the most powerful and holding precedence over the other three. It was considered extremely rash to approach the nest of a thunderbird, with the ill-advised intruder often being swept away by violent storms and the like. The symbol of the thunderbird is a jagged red lightning strike, often seen in textile art or paintings.

The Indians of British Columbia had a notion that the thunderbird was not a giant bird at all, but was in fact the ruby-throated hummingbird. This little bird actually makes quite a thunderous sound with its wings.

We've already had a close look at the thunderbird in 'One World, One Tribe, One Bird' so I won't repeat myself here; however, because the thunderbird forms such an important part of bird lore for all Native American peoples it might be interesting to have a look at one of the birds which inspired the legend – the condor.

The Condor

The condor is the world's largest flying bird, having a wingspan of up to 12 feet (3.5 metres), and one of its ancestors, *Teratornis Incredibilis*, was the largest flying bird ever to have lived on the planet, with a wingspan of 17 feet (5 metres). It is the Californian Condor that is most likely to have given rise to thunderbird legends, although the bird is in danger of extinction right now. The condor is featured in designs and legends in many different tribes, and in legends is usually depicted as a benevolent friend of mankind, providing education, knowledge and food in times of need.

A Song from the Ghost Dance - Arapaho

My father
My dead father
took me to visit with the spirits
and he turned into a moose
he turned into a moose

I fly the circle
I fly the circle
all around the edges of the earth
and wear the two wing feathers
the two wing feathers as I fly

My father
my father
As I look at him
look at him
he begins to turn into a bird
to turn into a bird

Adapted by David Ossman, from James Mooney

The Raven and the Crow

The raven and the crow are, of course, closely related. The raven plays a major part in many creation myths for Native Americans and, indeed, the Tlingit peoples hold that Man was created out of leaves by a raven, who also gave all the other birds their feathers and various attributes. There are also many stories, including from the Haida people, about how the raven opened a huge box and freed the sun, the moon and the stars.

To the Cherokee, the raven is a great hero because he was responsible for bringing fire to the world of men. The fire had been caused by the Thunder God and was residing in the hollow of a tree, but its retrieval meant that the raven became scorched and blackened, which accounts for the bird's appearance today. To the Iroquois, both the raven and crow were favoured since they were reputed to have brought seeds and grain to mankind from the place where the Sun came from.

The Apache Indians felt that the birds would signal the approach of an enemy, and some Plains Indians have a 'Ghost Dance', calling upon a Messiah who would restore the world to the safe place it was before the arrival of the White Man, in which the raven and crow play a prominent part. Although there are many benevolent aspects to the crow in American Indian society, there was still a slight fear of the bird; the Pueblo would not use the feathers on prayer sticks because of the birds' habit of eating carrion, but it was permissible to use them on masks and the like.

The Magpie

Part of the Corvid family to which ravens and crows belong, the Sioux believed the magpie to be an omniscient being. The Pueblo associated the bird with the East and the coming of dawn, probably because of its black and white feathers showing both the darkness of night and the light of day.

The Buzzard

In a similar vein to the stories of the raven, the buzzard – used as a folk-name in the USA for Turkey Vulture – also plays a part in the creation of the universe for some Native Americans. It is considered to have healing abilities, possibly since it feeds on carrion yet never becomes ill itself. In fact, to eat a little of the flesh of the buzzard, or to use buzzard 'stew' as a wash, was believed to prevent smallpox, and was used in a major smallpox epidemic among the Cherokee in 1866.

> The Honey Buzzard is aptly named; it eats wild bees and their honey, along with other insects and grubs.

A buzzard feather placed over the door of a cabin was believed to keep away witches. This association may possibly be due to the fact that the buzzard is a bird of the day – as opposed to the owl, which, as we have seen, is closely associated with witchcraft, being a nocturnal bird and therefore associated with darkness.

The Goose

The White-fronted Goose was said to have brought tobacco to mankind. Tobacco is particularly important as a magical herb, since the smoke carries messages to and from the Otherworld in much the same way as feathers.

The Turkey – The Earth Eagle

For the Pueblo, since the Mountain Turkey lives close to the ground, it was considered to be the earthly equivalent of the eagle. The beautiful feathers of this bird form an important part of magical rituals and since the birds are easily domesticated the feathers are abundant on masks, prayer sticks and the like. It is also likely that the turkey was not eaten but was kept purely for its feathers alone, these being more valuable than the meat of the bird.

It was believed that turkey feathers would help the dead to return to earth before they rose again as clouds, so the feathers were an important part of funerary rites. Pueblo bodies were wrapped in blankets, and these blankets were often made of turkey feathers, to speed the spirit to the next world. Also, prayer sticks with turkey feathers would be given to the relatives of the deceased.

The Chickadee and the Titmouse

To the Cherokee, the chickadee is regarded as a messenger, or the bearer of news. So is the titmouse, but the titmouse is said to be a little sparing with the truth!

Rain Birds

Naturally, the need for rain would be of paramount importance at certain times of the year in order to ensure good crops and to maintain healthy animals. There's a firm belief that certain birds are associated with wet weather, so feathers and other totems would be used accordingly to bring about the desired rainfall.

The swallow and the swift are included in this group of birds. Zuni priests believed that they have the ability to call or sing for rain. Feathers from the birds would be offered and the offering would be made at night. The priests would use Jimson weed in minute quantities to help them see the birds in the dark and also to be able to understand their language.

The feathers of the swallow were used particularly in this ritual because, as a Zuni Indian says, 'These birds fly around before rain and after. The rain priests use their feathers. They are hard to get.' The difficulty in obtaining the feathers of swifts or swallows would make them even more effective as a charm.

The hummingbird is similarly associated with rain for the Pueblo; this is perhaps because the bird is a nectar-eater, and nectar, like water, is moist. Since the bird was also a tobacco-bringer, smoke was used by the rain priests, who blew it in all directions to encourage the rain.

The use of hummingbird feathers, as especially sacred items, is restricted to the rain priests. Obtaining the feathers is pretty tricky and involves a delicate sort of lariat, which doesn't harm the bird. There's a lovely story about how the hummingbird gained its rainbow colours, which also explains more about the little bird's relationship to water.

How The Hummingbird Got Its Colours

The Zuni mountains have lava deposits all the way down the Eastern side; these were caused by Kaupat'a, the Volcano Demon. The volcano was the result of a gambling match between the demon and the son of the Sun; the demon lost, and in his anger caused the volcano to boil up, setting fire to the trees and bushes and causing a huge conflagration in the landscape.

Several birds were burned or killed during the volcano, but the brave little hummingbird flew to all directions of the compass to speak to the rain clouds to convince them to come and put out the fire. As he flew on this desperate mission he flew through a rainbow and absorbed its colours. The clouds obeyed the call of the hummingbird and came to help, eventually stopping the flow of molten lava and therefore saving the remaining birds and people.

The Dove

The dove always returns to water at night to drink, which it has to do given that its diet consists mainly of dry seeds and husks. Therefore the dove has become associated with water, too; the bird also has the ability to search out springs, which is, of course, an especially useful attribute.

The cries and calls of doves are said to be a call for rain, and some of the Pueblo rain songs imitate the calls of doves. The call of the Mourning Dove in Santa Ana, 'ho-'o G'Owai, G'Owai!' is translated as 'Water, pool of water!' and there's a traditional song, sung as corn is being ground, a verse of which goes:

> Dove, you liar,
> You are always telling the corn maidens
> That there is water over here and over there.

A Parallel universe of Magic:

Birds and shamanism

"Birds of Heaven, five Markut*
Ye with the mighty copper talons,
Copper is the moon's talon
And of ice the moon's beak;
Broad thy wings, of mighty sweep,
Like a fan thy long tail,
Hides the moon thy left wing,
And the Sun thy right wing,
Thou, the mother of nine eagles,
Who strayest not, flying through the Yaik,
Who weariest not about Edil,
Come to me, singing!
Come, playing, to my right eye,
Perch on my right shoulder!"

* Bird of Heaven

From *The Song of an Altaic Shaman*

Although we now tend to associate shamanism almost exclusively with Native American cultures, almost all societies, all around the world, have their shaman traditions. These may vary in some ways, but at their heart they are very similar, and all involve the imagery of birds as a key component. The names and connotations may differ, however; exchange the word 'shaman' for 'dervish' or 'witch' or 'witchdoctor', and you'll see how our perceptions can alter.

What is Shamanism?

In looking into the association of birds with shamanism, it is as well to define precisely what shamanism means, or, at the very least, what is meant by it for the purposes of this book. It is a term that has become quite fashionable and which is bandied about somewhat these days, perhaps without people fully understanding precisely what it stands for, and though the explanation is simple, the consequences of shamanism are profound and far-reaching.

The *Students English Dictionary*, published by Ogilvie and Annandale in 1913, defines shamanism as:

> An idolatrous religion of Northern Asia and elsewhere, characterised by a belief in sorcery, and in demons who require to be propitiated by sacrifices and rites.

Whereas the *Concise Oxford Dictionary*, published in 1978 by the Oxford University Press, has the following listing for shaman:

> Priest or witch-doctor of class claiming to have sole contact with gods etc.

And in the 1995 edition of the *Concise Oxford Dictionary*, we have the following definition:

> A person regarded as having access to the world of good and evil spirits. esp. amongst some peoples of Northern Asia and North America.

Amazing how things can change with the passage of time, and how subtle shifts in understanding can make a huge difference to our perceptions!

The description I prefer, however, and the one which appears to be the most apposite with regard to this book, is from Joseph L. Henderson, who gives the following explanation in *Man and his Symbols*, which was edited by Carl Jung:

> the shaman ... whose magical practices and flights of intuition stamp him as a primitive master of initiation. His power resides in his supposed ability to leave his body and fly about the universe as a bird.

Though our basic needs are exactly the same as those of 'primitive' man, for most of us, our lives now are very different from theirs. To adopt many of their methods of tuning into the forces of nature, such as the ritual sacrifice of various animals and birds, or ingesting psychotropic substances, no longer makes any sense for most of us.

Ted Andrews says in his *Animal Speak* that we need to 'honour and attune to the natural world and the animals within it'. And for me, shamanistic abilities include the power to be able to 'tune in' to both the seen and unseen worlds around us, to realize that animals, birds and all things natural are equally as important as mankind, and that everything is connected. Ultimately, it means being aware that the nature of linear time is something which we as human beings have invented as a convenient and necessary guide, but which need not control us, and finding a place within us which enables us to climb out of the constraints of both time and matter, to embrace the physical and the spiritual and the intellectual, but to be able to free ourselves of their restrictions when necessary.

There's a further qualification in Mercia Eliade's book, *Shamanism; Archaic Techniques of Ecstasy*:

> Though the shaman is, among other things, a magician, not every magician can be properly termed a shaman. The same distinction must be applied in regard to shamanic healing; every medicine man is a healer, but the shaman employs a method that is his and his alone ... The shaman specialises in a trance during which his soul is believed to leave his body and ascend to the sky or descend to the underworld.

The Bird – The Mother and Father of the Shaman

The Eagle

There is nothing coincidental about the roots of language; there are clues everywhere if we have the linguistic skills to be able to understand enough to make the connections.

The Yaku world for Eagle, 'Ai', is also the name of the Supreme Being, God, the Creator, the Great Spirit, whatever we choose to call it. Ai Toyon is 'the creator of light', and the Lord of all the birds is the two-headed eagle, Toyon Kotor, which sits at the top of the Tree of Life. The tree is full of the nests of the children belonging to the Creator. Sometimes, the branches of this World Tree – which we look at more closely later in this section – contain the souls of future shamans.

In the section about the Eagle (page 409), we discover how Siberian shamans believed that the very first shaman had an eagle for a father and a human being for a mother. This myth is found elsewhere in the world – the idea of a supernatural being impregnating a human to produce a hybrid child of exceptional talents.

The Vulture

In Anatolia, in Turkey, there are excavations in the Neolithic settlement of Çatal Hüyük of a room that has been called the 'Vulture Shrine'. The Çatal Hüyük culture dates back to 6500 BC, and the vulture is painted several times around the room in various guises, but often it hovers close to a human body which is missing its head. That the vulture must have been important to these people is seen in the fact that the bird appears in a God-like form. It seems to be biting the heads off the bodies. This could be an analogy for the removal of the soul, perhaps. Another of the pictures shows a human being dressed in a vulture skin, and again, we can understand the importance of this if we remember that the vulture was held to be a sacred bird because of its habit of 'recycling' souls. In addition, the vulture was a 'psychopomp', which is a shaman, animal or bird, which is believed to conduct souls from this world to the next.

OTHER BIRDS

The Yakut shamans hold that each shaman has for a mother a Bird of Prey, which sounds rather terrifying; this huge bird is supposed to have the head of an eagle, with an iron beak, hooked talons and a very long tail. The bird will only ever be witnessed by the shaman twice in his or her lifetime: first, at the shaman's spiritual birth (this is not the same as the physical birth), and then at his or her physical death.

At this second appearance, the bird carries away the soul of the shaman to the Underworld, and leaves it to ripen on the branch of a pitch pine tree. Once the soul is ready, the bird carries it back to Earth, and the body is cut into pieces and distributed among the spirits that bring death and disease to mankind. Because each part of the body is assigned to a particular malady, the shaman will in the future be able to conquer these diseases. (This is reminiscent of the way homeopathy works, namely, to take a little of a poisonous substance in order to know it and therefore to conquer it.) Once the disease spirits have eaten the body, the evil entities depart, and the bones are reconstructed by the bird-mother; then the shaman awakes as though he's just been sleeping … and is therefore reincarnated.

In another legend of the Great Bird Mother, the bird lays eggs in the branches of a tree, in the North; some eggs will hatch in one year, some in two years, while the most powerful shaman of all will take three years to hatch. Once the shamans have hatched out of the eggs, they are given by the Bird Mother to a sort of demon-shaman, who allows devils to come and dismember the bodies. Again, as in the tale above, the parts are fed to demons in order that the shamans will be able to conquer them.

In further additions to this theme, some stories relate that the body of the shaman lies unconscious and ill while his soul is transformed into a bird or animal, or in some cases even a human. His power or strength is kept hidden in the leaves of a tree until such a time as it is returned to him.

This, for me, is a reminder that some of the 'demons' that torment us, though they can seemingly tear us apart, are never so terrible once they are faced. Symbolically, this could be one of the meanings of these tales.

The Magic of Flight

It is the idea in the last paragraph that starts to hint at the vital importance of birds to the shaman. The notion of flight, or ascendance, is key. It equates to the idea of somehow being able to 'climb out of' time or to transcend the barriers that we humans have constructed around ourselves as a convenient way to operate in the everyday world we usually experience.

The sight of a bird ascending into the sky is a simple image. It is something most of us see every day of our lives on this planet, and since birds have been here so much longer than human kind it's no surprise that the symbol is so powerful. If we then take the premise that the 'Gods' are above us, in the Heavens, then the idea starts to come together nicely that birds bring messages.

> The penguin is the only bird which can swim but which cannot fly. However, it can jump six feet into the air!

However, there is an alternative way of looking at this; that is, that all planes of existence are to be found within our own consciousness. To go 'above' need not be a physical act for us, because, of course, we don't have the privilege of real wings; our wings are metaphorical.

Another attribute of the bird is its ability to see things from a height, to see the world in a different way from a mere ground-restricted view. If we step outside of ourselves and persuade ourselves to see things from above, then we add a whole new dimension to our thinking. Whatever our problems are, whatever issues or needs, if we can 'fly above' them, then we literally expand our minds.

It's this expansion that lies at the heart of all shamanistic practice.

NOT JUST FOR THE SHAMAN ...

The ability to fly is a power that is accorded to all people with magical abilities, whether or not they are called shamans. Yogis, for example, have a long tradition of being able to levitate. In India, an ancient text, the Pancavimsa Brahmana, tells us, 'The sacrificer, having become a bird, soars to the world of heaven.' And in Buddhist writings, the ability to fly is accorded importance, too, and the ability to fly as a bird is listed as one of the four magical powers. However, the Mahabharata makes the following distinction between bird flight and magical flight:

We too can fly to the heavens and manifest ourselves under various forms, but through illusion.

It is worth assuming that witches and wizards are shamans, too; they hold similar powers of healing and foreseeing the future, and being able to direct or control 'natural' phenomena in some way, and of course they are all supposed to be able to fly. We also know that the witch or wizard was believed to be able to assume the shape of a bird, particularly a raven or crow, and this is identical to the ability of the shaman to take on the form of a bird to cross over into the 'Otherworld'.

Although we tend to imagine the traditional witch on a broomstick, the witch trials of England in the seventeenth century only mention a broomstick once. In a witch trial in 1712, a Jane Wenham was accused of flying; however the judge, a Sir John Holt, remarked that there was no law against flying, and reduced the charges against her!

Witches' powers of magical flight were, in fact, said to have been gained by applying magical ointments or unguents, although some of the ingredients would appear to be rather unsavoury and certainly not to be tried at home. The 'fat of young children' seems to form a constituent part in many recipes, for example!

Among the Turks of Central Asia the power of flight is also attested to: 'Ahmed Yesevi and some of his dervishes could change into birds and so have the power to fly.'

As human beings, flight is a gift which we have chased for centuries; think of the early attempts at flight for example – men strapped into clumsy wooden contraptions which would more likely than not disintegrate into pieces upon the first take-off. Physical flight, without mechanical help, will remain the last bastion of the unknown. But the idea of being able to fly is not so very different in essence to that of the shaman. Although the shaman's 'flight' is symbolic of transcendence rather than a physical attempt, the fascination is the same. And just because we may not have witnessed something with our own eyes, and though logic would dictate otherwise, who's to say that flight is not possible for us human beings? We need to keep an open mind.

> In Medieval Europe, witches were said to ride on the backs of geese.

Familiars

Readers who enjoy the Western tradition of fairy tales will be familiar with the concept of an animal or bird with whom a human enjoys a particularly close relationship – the witch and her black cat, for example. But these creatures – who can act as guides – are not restricted to fairy stories.

Shamans are shown certain things, and given access to hidden knowledge, by familiars, and these often as not take the form of birds, with the eagle, crow, goose and owl being among the most common. The creature could appear to the shaman in a dream, or a trance, or a vision, and reveal, wordlessly, what the shaman needs to know. In particular, bird familiars carry the most important messages from the Gods. Sometimes the shaman will summon these 'spirits' and will then allow them to speak through himself as his own consciousness is suspended in a trance-like state. Among the Yakut, the most powerful shaman will have an eagle as his guide, or familiar spirit.

The talent of shape-shifting is also accorded to all magicians, sorcerers and shamans. For me, if given the choice between a 'ground' animal or a bird, I'd choose the latter every time.

The Secret Language of the Birds

It is essential for the shaman, once he or she is in contact with the birds as messengers from the Gods, to be able to understand what they are saying – to be able to understand the language of the birds. This can happen at a theoretical level, or the shaman might be powerful enough to truly understand this secret language.

As part of their initiation, many shamans have to learn to imitate bird sounds and calls. When in trance, the shaman may speak in tongues that appear to be like no other language on earth, or otherwise, bird sounds will be heard that are rich in meaning. These are all mystical, magical matters. Sound itself is a powerful thing, and when rendered into song it is a transportive element too. There is an old German word, 'galdr', meaning 'magic formula', which comes from the verb 'to sing', which applies specially to the songs and calls of birds.

For the shaman, the ability to master the language of the birds at one time might have involved ingesting the flesh of the snake, or perhaps some other magical animal. Its value lies in the belief that knowledge of the language of birds will provide the translator with the key to prophecy and future knowledge; and to become a bird will bestow the ability to travel beyond this world, and this time.

It's to be remembered that in most Creation myths, there was only one language between all creatures. This 'paradisal' state is what is being sought.

BIRDS AS SHAMANIC MESSENGERS

There are many different ways of understanding what a bird is trying to tell us; it's not down to a literal understanding of their language alone. There are stories of shamans regarding the actions of certain birds as indicators from the Gods, too. For example, to the Magyar shamans of Hungary, the death of a shaman means that a new leader has to be chosen, and this person will often be indicated by omens. The sign could be that a bird such as a goose alights on the roof of a house in which a child lives, or where a baby is about to be born; the child or baby would then be accepted as the new shaman.

Reaching the Heavens

In order to ascend to the heavens, the shaman needs to associate with the creatures who can facilitate this flight – primarily, of course, birds. Joseph L. Henderson, in *Man and his Symbols*, reminds us that,

> The bird is the most fitting symbol of transcendence. It represents the peculiar nature of intuition working through a 'medium', that is, an individual who is capable of obtaining knowledge of distant events – or facts of which he consciously knows nothing – by going into a trance-like state.

Shamans are often chosen by birds, or by the spirits of ancestors appearing in their form. Mircea Eliade relates a story from the Bororo Shaman tradition:

> The Bororo shamans … are chosen by the soul of a dead person or by a spirit … The future Shaman walks in the forest and suddenly sees a bird perch within reach of his hand, then vanish. Flocks of parrots fly down towards him and then disappear as if by magic.

Smoke is another 'connector', and to further cement the connection with birds, the smoking pipes of Latin American shamans were often carved in the form of a bird; the substances used in the pipe would have been conducive to his journey into the Otherworld. Tobacco, a sacred herb, produces the smoke that also acts as a transmitter/receiver between the worlds.

The shamans of the Koryak hold that they need to find their own totem animal which will protect them while they are engaged in shamanistic practices, which involves the setting aside of 'normal' consciousness in favour of being able to communicate with the Otherworld, or the world of spirits. The raven is one of the common guardian spirits, along with the dear, the wolf, the eagle and the seagull.

Water Birds

Water birds are representative, in the beliefs of the far north of Siberia, of the shaman's ability to descend into an Underworld, especially a submarine one.

Making the Connection

One of the most important aspects of making this connection, the connection with the higher parts of the spirit, and with the birds, lies for the shaman in costume. Feathers form a major part of the costume of the shaman, no matter what part of the world he or she originates from. They are mentioned virtually everywhere, and the reason for this is obvious!

As far as possible for some traditions, the shaman's costume not only carries the feathers of birds, but will seek to resemble the shape of the bird, too. The Altaic shamans favour the owl; the boot of the Tungus shaman's costume actually is shaped like a bird's foot. The most extreme form of these bird costumes goes to the Yakut shamans, since the foundation for their costume is a large iron bird skeleton. Drums, which form a large and important part in many rituals, are also decorated with feathers.

Headgear, too, will feature feathers, and often has the appearance of a bird's head. In *Shamanism; Archaic Techniques of Ecstasy*, Mircea Eliade tells us that 'the bird costume is indispensable to flight to the other world; "they say that it is easier to go, when the costume is light"', and, further, 'a Shamaness flies into the air as soon as she acquires her magical plumage'.

In the world of the Ancient Celts, the use of a feathered cloak was said to help the wearer connect with the spirits. The feathers of the swan were particularly suitable for bards, since the swan was the bird most associated with the art of poetry.

The Catalyst

In many of the shamanic processes, we see a grave illness or near-death experience providing a catalyst for the life-shift to come. This is not uncommon or restricted to what we may think of as the conventional shaman. William Fiennes, for example, in his book *The Snow Geese*, undergoes a life-threatening illness prior to the awakening of his interest in birds that speeds his recovery and inspires his journey to follow the migratory path of the geese; this changes his life.

In some of the shamanistic traditions, the death experience is emulated if not actually experienced. Fasting, hallucinogens and arduous experiences can all bring about the desired effect, which will divide the old life from the new: a 'rebirth'. Amongst the Araucanians in Chile, for example, a young woman will collapse and appear to be dead; upon awakening she will declare that she is now a Shamaness. The taking of hallucinogenic herbs, often a part of the process, can also cause the purging of both the body and the mind; again, this can be as apprehended as similar to the near-death experience, an experience which provides a watershed in the life of the 'candidate'.

A similar ritual, which was part of the initiation ceremonies in Ancient Greece, India, Tibet and elsewhere, involved the candidate being locked away in darkness for some time, before being let out into the world. After such an experience, the world would be revealed in all its full beauty, and the notion of flight or transcendence would be easier to assimilate.

Dreams

As well as the 'trigger' state of illness, either 'natural' or self-imposed, the budding shaman can also be shown important facets of his or her new nature via dreams. There is an account of a shamanistic dream, triggered by a serious bout of smallpox, which took place during the initiation of a shaman. Part of this dream concerns birds:

He was carried to the shores of the Nine Seas. In the middle of one of them was an island … a young birch tree rose to the sky. It was the Tree of the Lord of the Earth … The tree was surrounded by seas, and in each of these swam a species of birds with its young. There were several kinds of ducks, a swan, and a sparrow-hawk.

Mircea Eliade, *Shamanism*

Eventually, the dreamer is shown in his dream how to drum, and then he finds that he is flying with the birds.

The World Tree

Celtic myth, the Kabbalah, myths from Asia, India, the Americas, Siberia, Persia, Turkey, Scandinavia – all feature the parable of the World Tree, whose branches signify the steps of the Soul to Heaven. In the tree are birds; these birds represent the souls of men. The tree is part of the symbolism related to ascendance, and it is no accident that the Celtic word for 'oak', 'Dair' or the Welsh 'Drws', has the same origin as the word for 'Druid' or 'Door'. The tree, with the bird-souls in its branches, signifies a way into another world, and to climb a tree enables us to see the world from another angle – literally, from a higher place or plane.

Max Ernst – A Latter-day Shaman?

Max Ernst, who was born in 1891 and was a key figure in the Surrealist art movement, had a very unusual muse – his pink cockatoo, Loplop.

Loplop died on the night of January 5th, 1906, which coincidentally was the same day that Max's sister was born. Although he was aged 15 at the time, the collision between the death of the bird and the birth of his sister was to have a profound effect upon the artist's life and work.

Max called Loplop 'The Superior of the Birds', and ascribed his own life to that of a bird; writing about himself in the third person, he describes the detail of his 'birth':

Max Ernst had his first contact with the sensible world, when he came out of the egg which his mother had laid in an eagle's nest and which the bird had brooded for seven years … Max Ernst died the 1st August

1914. He resuscitated the 11th of November 1918 as a young man aspiring to become a magician and to find the myth of his time. Now and then he consulted the eagle who had hatched the egg of his pre-natal life. You may find the bird's advices in his work.

Beyond Painting and Other Writings by the Artist and His Friends, *translated by Dorothea Tanning*

Most of Ernst's experimental artistic techniques, such as collage, frottage (the art of making rubbings) and his ability to go into a trance-like state to give his 'hypnogogic visions' full rein, he ascribed to the influence of Loplop, and this practice is very akin to the techniques used by shaman.

He describes the visits of the supernatural bird:

I was visited nearly every day by the Superior of the Birds named Loplop, my private phantom, attached to my person.

Ernst would also assume the guise of Loplop from time to time, wearing a strange bird costume and headdress. A latter-day shaman if there ever was one …

Shamanism in Our Lives

The shamans who have been discussed here belong to a time before our 'modern' world and all the things we find we have to concern ourselves with. Yet a return to their notion of making direct contact with the essence of the natural world is just as valid and vital now as it was then, especially if we are to retain our sanity and remember what truly is important.

Each individual's journey is unique; the catalyst for change can never be predicted. The most important thing to remember is that you are on this journey already, and that to be aware, and self-aware, is the most important aspect of the quest. The magic is always there, although some times we are more receptive than at other times, and it's worth keeping in mind that the 'dark' times are all part of the journey, too.

We are all shamans. We all have access to every possibility, every skill, talent or power, in the universe. Once we truly understand this, then anything is possible.

Then we can truly fly like the birds.

The Wings of Desire:
The alchemical nature of birds

" **A** lchemy … We know, on the other hand, that the name and the thing are based on the permutation of form by light, fire or spirit; such is in any case the true meaning indicated by the Language of the Birds."

Jean-Julien Fulcanelli, *The Dwellings of the Philosophers*

Alchemy is a massive subject, and I don't want to pretend to you that this section will give you anything approaching its depths of detail. If the idea of alchemy holds any kind of fascination for you, then there are tomes on the subject, some of which are mentioned in the bibliography at the back of this book.

Excitingly, though, in looking into alchemy we meet our old friend Thoth, or Mercury, or Hermes again; remember how the alphabet was said to have been invented by Mercury as he watched the flight patterns of cranes? In his aspect as Thoth, he preserved arcane knowledge prior to the Great Deluge; much of this information includes the roots of alchemical practice.

The Language of the Birds

Alchemists use the symbols of birds and animals to describe various procedures and transformations that take place in their laboratories, often with the aim of hiding certain processes in order to keep them wrapped in a cloak of mystery and, in former times, away from the interference of the authorities. Alchemists often work with volatile substances; the word 'volatile' comes from the Latin, 'volatilis', which means flying, so using birds as a method of describing these mysterious transformations is entirely appropriate. Indeed, the depiction of wings indicates the volatility of a chemical. Just as the shamans use the imagery of birds, flight and wings to signify ascension so do the alchemists.

What is Alchemy?

The truth is hid in plain sight …

The general definition of alchemy, and the most common answer to this question, is that alchemy is the transmutation of base metals into precious metals – lead into gold, most commonly – by means of a mystical and obscure ingredient often known as the Philosopher's Stone. However, there's much more to alchemy than will probably ever meet the eye.

The very word 'alchemy' has become the stuff of fantasy, conjuring up images of cobweb-ridden subterranean laboratories, with the alchemist in a cloak embossed with symbols, stooping in the half-light over a glass vial full of a chameleon liquid which bubbles and smokes dangerously. However, as we shall see, this definition is simplistic in the extreme; there's far more to alchemy than a supposed material gain.

What is Gold?

He who knows gold, obtains gold. Tone is verily its gold. He who thus knows what is gold, obtains the gold.
Brihadaranyaka Upanishad

In China, gold was drunk because it was believed to confer immortality, and the Vedic writers of India declared that gold was immortality, and that immortality was gold. This helps us get to the heart of what alchemy is really about, and what we are looking at via the symbols of the birds. The real transmutation that takes place is that of the human soul.

What we are aiming for is to be conscious of the gradual evolution of a person. The material world gradually fades in importance as the spiritual nature of the person develops, and the 'base metal' of materialism turns into the 'gold' of spirituality.

Fulcanelli, a mysterious alchemist who was/is at great pains to conceal his true identity, reminds us that, in order to possess the gold, man must 'be the gold'. We therefore start to understand that the search for the Philosopher's Stone is not a simple matter of material gain.

The Hidden Ingredient

Hic lapis est subtus te, supra te, erga te et circa te.
This stone is beneath you, above you, in you, all around you.
Jean-Julien Fulcanelli, *The Dwellings of the Philosophers*

The Philosopher's Stone, when eventually discovered, meant that the alchemist enjoyed perfect knowledge. Physically, there were many recipes for the Stone concocted over the years. The search for this grail-like substance was a metaphysical task, too; another term for the Philosopher's Stone was the 'Spirit of Truth', and alchemists would undertake a spiritual programme of purification and ritual in order to attain this elusive element. The Philosopher's Stone was also an elixir of life, reputed to give immortality to the possessor.

To possess the Philosopher's Stone meant that the alchemist would have true understanding and experience of the unity of all things.

Our Perceptions

Although we tend to think that the aim of the alchemist was to take base metal and turn it into gold, or to find the mystical, magical elixir that would give us the secret of immortality, this very literal interpretation can also be used metaphorically. At the heart of alchemy lies the notion of transformation; most importantly for our purposes here, this applies to the spiritual nature of mankind.

For latter-day alchemists, this transformation of the soul, which involves its blossoming and 'awakening', is a crucial part of the process.

The Secret Language of the Alchemists

Alchemists used a secret language based on birds and animals to describe the processes of (al)chemical change, and I have taken this very profound imagery, which, as Jung realized, is archetypical, to enable us, via a meditative process, to discover our 'totem' or 'spirit' bird. In doing so, we may understand more about ourselves.

This may seem to be an unusual melding of shamanistic processes with alchemy, but in many ways the strands they follow are similar – the ascent or flight of the soul after various tests and rituals, part of which can involve the removal of everything which went before and a conscious rebirth of the individual.

Bird Symbolism in Alchemy

Given what we know about the symbols of various birds, and the general meaning that all birds carry for transcendence, multidimensional existence and the ability to access the Otherworld, it is no surprise that the alchemists use birds in their secret language. Alchemists use allegory and mystical language to describe many of the processes, both physical and metaphysical, which they undertake as part of their work.

Here, then, is a very simplistic guide to the meanings of bird symbols in alchemy.

Two contending birds are symbolic of the male/female nature of Mercury; this aspect is sometimes also shown as one bird ascending and the other descending.

The Crow

Because the bird is black, it represents a stage known as 'nigredo', which is the first stage in the alchemical process. It represents blackening, mortification and a symbolic dying to the world.

The Eagle

Flying high in the clouds, the eagle represents the free, spiritual aspect of the Prima Materia, that is, nature in her raw state. The double eagle stood for the male/female element of Mercury. Often the eagle and the lion were seen together, and they symbolize wind and earth – wind the volatile principle; earth the fixed principle.

The Peacock

The astral world is represented by the shifting iridescence of the peacock's tail. This stage is representative of the sudden realization of the spiritual plane as a real entity rather than as an imaginary realm.

The Pelican

The destruction of the old in order to make way for the new. The legend of the pelican piercing its breast with its own beak to nurture its young gives some indication of the notion of the sacrifice of the self that is involved.

The Phoenix

As the phoenix needs to be immolated in order to be born again, the symbol of this bird in alchemy means the sublimation of the physical in favour of the spiritual.

The White Swan

The white swan represents the interface between the earth and the heavens, this world and the next, the seen and unseen worlds, and the material and physical.

Finding the Gold Inside – Your Spirit Bird

Know Thyself
Written above the entrance at the Oracle at Delphi

In order to claim the Philosopher's Stone – in order to glimpse the 'oneness' of everything and the interconnectedness of every single piece of the universe in which we live – first of all we must know ourselves. Sometimes we can get a tantalizing glimpse of self-knowledge, which seems as though a curtain has lifted somewhere in the psyche.

The search for Knowledge is a life-long challenge, and there are many ways to find the Truth. Some will find glimpses of it in music, or art; a study of yoga, tai chi or something similar can be beneficial, since theses practices seek to unify mind, body and spirit. Some find the connection via meditative practices and chanting.

The following section of this book leads the reader through a process of creative visualization based on the symbolic birds used in the alchemical process. The ultimate goal is to find the bird that the reader most associates with in his or her innermost heart. In discovering our inner 'bird', we may take a little step further in discovering our own nature, and will be a little further on in our pursuit of our personal Philosopher's Stone.

Perhaps the best way to approach this exercise is to read it through a few times, then carry out the visualization once you are familiar with the order of the birds in question.

Preparing Yourself and Your Surroundings

Before undertaking the visualization, make sure that you will not be interrupted. Find a quiet space, outdoors or indoors; if indoors you might want to light some candles, burn incense or play some soft background music. If outdoors, make sure that you are wearing warm clothing and that you will be undisturbed.

If you have the feathers available of the birds mentioned, this will definitely help you to make the connection; you will need the feathers of a crow, a swan, a peacock, a pelican and a phoenix. This latter is a little difficult to come by; however, nothing is entirely impossible, so be prepared to unexpect the expected.

If you are comfortable sitting in one of the seated positions in yoga, then do so. Or you may prefer to stretch out on your back, head to the north, following the natural polarity of the Earth. Make sure that you will be warm enough; bear in mind that you will be motionless for as long as the exercise takes, and that our bodies can get a little chilly if they are still for a period of time.

Have a pen and notebook to hand to write down your experiences for later analysis.

Whatever your chosen position, become aware of your breathing. Start to count your breaths in, and out; and in, and out. Work up to a slow count of six while inhaling; pause; then a s-l-o-w count of six as you exhale. Follow this count for several minutes.

Concentrate solely on your breath, the cool inhalation and the warm exhalation, and the slow counting, as your body starts to relax and your mind stills itself from the 'radio interference' and chatter. Allow your mind to become empty, ready to receive.

When you feel ready, begin the process.

1. The Crow: The Blackening

The Crow represents the Blackening; it is the beginning of the process in understanding who and what we are. It encourages us to examine the space inside us, to face the void; to understand that the nature of death is not simply an end, but a state of change in a timeless process. We need not fear death, but embrace it as a great adventure.

Imagine the encroaching gloom of a darkening sky. From a distance, a crow comes flying slowly towards you. Visualize this beautiful black bird as it flies slowly but determinedly into your field of vision.

What exactly does the crow look like? Which direction did it fly from? Is the bird looking at you, or away from you?

See the glimpses of light lustring the bird's feathers. Some say that the crow is black, but if you look again you will see that its feathers are in fact all the colours of the rainbow. Like birds, whose ability to perceive colours is far superior to that of humans, we need to see things as they really are; not simply as we are told to see them.

You already know that the coming of the crow represents the knowledge that we must die to be reborn. The appearance of this bird means that you are ready to let go of the past and embrace the Now that is you.

As you examine this beautiful bird, you will find that you start to associate with it more and more. It may be that you become one with your crow and start to see the world from a different place. Go with this; there's no need to describe what you might encounter, but make a close mental note of what you see and experience. Go where the crow takes you, and enjoy your journey. Do not be afraid of the darkness that the crow brings; remember, the world was created from a place of blackness – embrace it.

Eventually the crow will fade away. You can finish your visualization now, if you choose, by gradually realigning with the world; as soon as you are ready, relax into awareness, and write down the journey of the crow.

If you wish, you can carry on to the next stage. Let the crow fade away; then make inner space for the White Swan.

2. The White Swan: The Whitening

The White Swan represents the brightening of the Inner World. In contrast to the blackness of the Crow, the whiteness of the Swan may dazzle you as your mind awakens into the second part of its illumination, as the spirit world and all your potential and capabilities are glimpsed.

If you are entering the second stage anew, repeat the relaxation and deep breathing exercises. If you are continuing straight away after your encounter with the crow, become aware of your breathing again, and take a few moments to clear your mind.

Let your mind be still. In the darkness, a light appears on the horizon – the Sun, gradually brightening into the day through the many hues of the sunrise. When it's light enough, you see a swan, beautiful, graceful and majestic.

You already know that the swan represents the union of the physical world with the spiritual world. You know that the coming of this bird shows that you are ready to acknowledge the connection between your body and your soul.

Observe the swan. Which direction is it coming from? Is it flying? If so, what does the sky look like? Is it swimming? What kind of water is it swimming on? What are its surroundings?

Get closer and closer to the brightness of the bird's snowy white feathers until your whole field of vision is filled with their soft whiteness. As you look at the swan, you are filled with wonder at its brightness; you start to become that brightness, and as you do so, you become as one with the swan. Let the bird take you wherever it will. Concentrate on seeing what the swan is seeing. Are you floating? Are you flying? What can you see? Are you on the water or in the air?

Relax on your journey with the swan. Let the bird take you and show you things you've never seen before. Let your spirit interact with the material world and be aware of the unity of everything.

As the brightness of the swan fades away, become aware of where you are. You may choose to wake to the outside world slowly and gradually and write down your experiences, or you may decide to carry on to the next stage in this alchemical visualization.

3. THE PEACOCK: THE AWAKENING TO THE INNER WORLD

You are aware that the peacock represents the inner awakening to the astral world, the sídhe of the Celts. You are about the experience the world without the limits of time or the impositions of any kinds of restrictions at all. This is a rare opportunity and should be relished.

As the brightness of the White Swan gradually fades away, you become aware once more of your breathing, before you delve again into the inner world.

The first thing to notice is where you are. What are your surroundings? Are you alone or are there people? Are you indoors or outdoors? Is it day or night? Perhaps you're in a foreign city, or you could find yourself in familiar countryside. Take time to observe your surroundings closely and commit them to memory.

Soon, you will notice your peacock. Watch the bird closely.

Which direction is it coming from? Is it flying, or walking? Is it perhaps roosting in a tree? Is its fantastic tail furled or unfurled? It doesn't matter either way. Let your peacock come towards you and, as it approaches, realize the full iridescence of its astonishingly gorgeous feathers – all the colours of the rainbow packed into the tiniest of filaments; the whole, as you are aware, symbolizing the astral world as you become acquainted with this magical domain for the first time. You are bewildered by the vast potential stored in such a minute part of the cosmos as the feather of a peacock.

Gradually, the dazzling array of colours, which twinkle and shine in a confusion of hues, starts to separate into their individual components. You realize that whoever said there were seven colours in a rainbow was severely mistaken, as you start to get a glimpse of what's really there. There are no words yet invented to describe what you are seeing, so just watch. Relax, and unexpect the expected, as the peacock takes you on a journey into uncharted territory.

Allow yourself to fall into an even deeper state of relaxation as you become one with this beautiful bird. Remember that it is the steed of Gods and Goddesses from all over the world. Go with the peacock wherever it takes you, committing to memory the places you see and the experiences this bird gives as a gift to you as you awaken to the possibilities of the astral planes.

Gradually, your journey with the peacock comes to an end. Knowing you can access this new world again at any time, you start to become aware of your surroundings in our lovely material world, and realize what a gift you've been given – the ability to see things as they really are, a glimpse of the oneness of everything.

At this point it would be advisable to suspend your journey into the alchemical realms of the soul, and write down your experiences so far. We are more than halfway through the journey, and these birds have taught us many things, but the next stage is difficult and will require further efforts of concentration.

4. The Pelican: Sacrifice of the Self

This next stage is pivotal. It involves a 'letting go' of the ego, which can for many seem like dangerous territory, and sometimes our feet will be stepping on to the shifting sands of the unknown for the first time. You are aware of the imagery of the pelican, which was supposed to pierce her own breast to nourish her babies. The pelican stage of our awakening effectively turns us back into children, so bear in mind that children know no fear because they have no experience. The pelican stage in your personal alchemical process makes it possible to experience a profound awakening to who and what you really are, and marks the penultimate stage in your personal transformation.

Begin again with the relaxation and deep breathing exercises described previously.

This time, it may not be necessary to visualize the pelican. Look carefully at your surroundings and commit to memory what you are seeing. Is it night or day? Where are you? Are you in a familiar place, or a strange one?

You see something approaching in the distance. Look closely to see what it is.

It might be the pelican; or it might be yourself.

Be careful to take a good hard look and tell the truth about what you see, because the bird and you are the same being.

The pelican sacrifices itself by piercing its own breast to feed its young. In the same way, we need to cast aside with love our old, material selves to nourish the spiritual aspect of our nature.

If a pelican approaches you, be absorbed into its warm kindness, realizing the nature of love and compassion. Through the eyes of the bird, see yourself for what you really are; analyse yourself as kindly as you would examine your closest and most beloved friend. Very often we are far nicer to other people than we are to ourselves, and we can be cruel to ourselves while comforting our friends. Stand outside yourself for a moment, and realize that you are your own best friend. Give this friend some advice. What are this person's best points? What could be improved upon?

What are the good qualities of this friend? What are their failings?

As you search inside, remember that you are outside, looking in; be rigorous, but kind, and above all, know the truth. The pelican gives you a wonderful opportunity to come to terms with your true nature, and helps you to appreciate that you are divine.

At this point you may either choose to become aware of your surroundings, surrender to the world we inhabit and write down your experiences, or you may choose to continue your journey.

5. THE PHOENIX

The final stage in our alchemical exploration sees our meeting with the Phoenix, a supposedly mythological bird which renewed itself by setting itself on fire in order to give birth to itself once more – the ultimate experience of being born again, with all the self-awareness and realization of the truth that this entails.

As we begin our journey again, you should remember that the exercises in deep breathing and the relaxation techniques are essential to the process of unifying the mind, body and spirit. Breathe even more slowly and deeply, counting all the time but delaying the pause between the inhalation at the top of its scale and the exhalation. Become aware of your body a little at a time, and allow yourself to relax even more deeply than ever before.

You enter a new world.

Although it may have familiar elements, there are things you've never noticed before. The colours may be different; the sounds and smells may be distinctive yet foreign.

Describe this environment to yourself, and commit it to memory.

From out of nowhere comes a fabulous bird; it is the phoenix.

Although the phoenix is believed to be a mythological bird, because there was only ever one at a time and because they created the means of their own rebirth, the phoenix you see is as real as any other bird you've ever seen. Describe this creature, taking note of every tiny detail. Which direction did it come from? Did it fly directly or on a skewed path? Did it fly through the air, or skim through the water, or through a wall of fire?

The experience of the phoenix is very personal for everyone; forget about what you've ever known, and see what's really there – take your time.

Suddenly, the phoenix perches on a nest of some kind – you decide what. Then it raises its head to the sky, gives a long, deep, musical sigh, and flames start to play around its body. As you watch the flames, imagine what they feel like, and be aware of the chemical changes that would take place in your own body. What would this feel like, knowing that this is an essential part of the process of change in order to be reborn?

As you become subsumed by the cold heat of the fire, you feel yourself begin the change; and it is here that the real alchemical process begins.

Your Bird – Your Gold

The final part of this guided meditation needs to follow straight on from the Phoenix. As the bird is subsumed by the flames, become aware of your breathing. Slow it down even further.

As the fire dies down, you notice a large, golden egg in the centre of the dwindling flames, red patterns dancing on the lustrous surface.

Concentrate on the egg.

You may find that you are inside the egg, or you may be an observer. There's no need to hurry. The egg will hatch of its own accord, and revealed inside will be your bird.

Watch and wait … breathe slowly and deeply and be carried by the realms of your imagination.

Soon, the first fissure appears in the egg, and part of it falls away as the bird inside is born.

This is your bird, part of your own inner gold, part of the Philosopher's Stone, part of knowing yourself.

The bird hatches fully grown into the world.

There's no need at first to give the bird a name. Observe it; what are its feathers like? What colour is the bird? See the shape of its wings as it stretches and shakes for the first time. Notice all aspects of your bird. It could be that this is a bird you have never seen before, or it could be a bird you see nearly everyday.

Communicate with your bird. Let it carry you away if you like.

When you are ready, become aware of the world around you, and realize where you are. You will gradually adapt to the everyday world, and ease yourself back into consciousness.

You may wish to describe the bird inside, either by writing or drawing, or discussing it with friends. You might find that it equates to one of the mythical birds described elsewhere in this book.

I hope you enjoyed this journey to find your Totem Bird, and that you continue to explore your inner self in order to discover the gold within.

Accounts of the Guided Meditation

When I was writing the guided meditation above, I asked several friends if they would try the process to ensure that the instructions were easy to follow. Natalia, who lives in Italy, and Theo, from the UK, very kindly agreed that I could use their notes in this book. Your experience will be very different but the following accounts might give an idea of what is possible.

NATALIA'S TOTEM BIRD

1. The Black Crow

I'm used to doing yoga, so I'm familiar with the slow breathing involved, but what I wasn't prepared for was just how quickly the crow appeared; one minute I was relaxing into the darkened place in my mind, the next I was looking into the eye of the crow, very close up; the bird just stared at me; the whole thing was very realistic – the crow was so close I couldn't seem to pull back to observe anything else about it apart from it's eye. Then I found myself sort of being absorbed into the eye of the crow – this was all very fast – then I was rushing above the sea, a real sense of purpose, either inside the crow or being the crow; the sky was dark and the sea was dark and it was quite comforting, in fact, a sort of warm velvety blackness. Then I started to see a light on the horizon and realized that I was approaching the rising sun and that the next part of the process had started without me even trying.

2. The White Swan

As the sun got brighter, lightening the sea, the rushing slowed down and I realized that the crow had simply disappeared. The swan came floating towards me, sort of swimming through the air, definitely floating, not flying; it was as though it was suspended between the sky and the water, extremely beautiful and glowing with whiteness.

A feeling of incredible stillness came over me, a real contrast to the rushing of the crow. It was as though the wind could blow straight through me, and the closer the swan got, the deeper this feeling of tranquillity. It's funny; I've experienced this feeling sometimes after deep meditation. There was a sort of wordless communication between the swan and me, and I realized that I could carry this feeling of tranquillity with me all the time if I chose; this feeling of emptiness inside, the feeling that I was the centre of the universe, a sort of hub around which everything else revolved.

I had intended to carry on with the meditation, but found that I was becoming aware of my surroundings and that perhaps it was time to leave the swan behind, although part of me was regretting not climbing on to its back and taking a ride!

But I realized that the swan had already taken me somewhere – to the still place inside myself – and I find now that I can get there whenever I choose. I've been given a kind of short-cut, if you like, because of what the swan showed me.

3. The Peacock

It was about a week before I found time to explore further, and after the deep breathing exercises I'm afraid to say I fell asleep, but then I had a dream that was oddly vivid and relevant and also a part of the process.

I found myself in India. I was close to the ground scratching among small stones and I realized I was a bird with clawed feet. There was chaos all around; noise, confusion, sounds, it seemed to be some sort of market place; millions of colours everywhere too and it felt frightening and confusing.

Then there was an old man who beckoned to me, and the next moment I was in a sort of marble verandah, open on three sides with some sort of building it was attached to. The old man had an old-fashioned paint colour chart and he was patiently showing me the colours … I know that this dream was in colour because everything was so incredibly vivid. As the old man showed me, I started to feel calmer, then other irrelevant things happened and I woke up.

I realized that I'd had a glimpse into the shifting colours and seeming chaos of the astral world, but in a very interesting and lateral way; from the chaos in the streets to the order of the old man and his colour chart. I'm still contemplating the meaning of it.

4. The Pelican

This one is brief. I started the meditation and was plunged into exactly the same feeling I'd had when the call came through to tell me that my mother was very ill with a rare disease; that feeling of the rug being pulled from under your feet. This call triggered months of panic and was one of the most awful days of my life, perhaps even more awful than the day she died, because we had been prepared for that, but not for this call.

I hadn't realized just how I'd carried this feeling around with me. By confronting it again, it feels as though I have been able to come closer to some personal healing around the whole awful episode. But it wasn't what I had expected.

5. The Phoenix

I was keen to resume the meditation so continued a couple of hours after the Pelican stage.

It seemed to take ages for the phoenix to appear, then I realized I was probably just trying too hard, so I relaxed and after a short while I saw what appeared to be a mechanical bird. Then I realized that this was my phoenix, except it was covered in jewelled, jointed armour, very colourful and shiny, like a very expensive clockwork model.

More than anything I wanted the phoenix to take off the armour so that I could see what it looked like, but the bird wouldn't do this for me; the phrase 'More than my life's worth' kept echoing through my head.

I understood implicitly that the phoenix wasn't ready today; the armour of the bird and the phrase told me this. I decided that, symbolically, I was not ready to let go of everything yet, and that to progress further through the phoenix stage and on to finding my own bird, was something that I had to wait a little longer for.

I liked Natalia's account of her guided meditation because she made a profound realization during the phoenix stage in particular – she realized that she wasn't yet ready to go further.

Here is Theo's account. His experience is very different from Natalia's.

THEO'S TOTEM BIRD

I did this meditation all at once one Saturday afternoon, not feeling great to be honest since I'd been suffering from flu. Because I was feeling drowsy it seemed to be easy to get straight into my first bird.

1. The Black Crow

It's a blustery day with the kind of light you get in the Winter; steely and hard. A crow flies in from the North, feathering its wings to stay on course, which make the wings appear to rise and fall, first left, then right. It's looking right at me, its strong, deltoid beak slightly open. Somehow I travel on with it to a noisy rookery where it alights on a nest and regurgitates some food – red, raw meat – for its two young. The noise of cawing in the canopy is intense, yet strangely comforting.

2. The White Swan

I feel the cool wind again and then I'm standing by a lake. A swan is coming towards me out of a low, setting sun. The sun makes it hard to look at. It's so bright. The swan stops and preens its feathers with its long beak. It looks at me from time to time to make sure I'm paying attention. I lose myself in its soft down.

3. The Peacock

Then I'm standing by a house with low gables. On the roof is a peacock, its sharp claws scrabbling noisily on the tiles. It lets out a fierce scream, jumps down and then puts its tail up. By moving its neck to one side it invites me to dive into its tail, which I do. I discover it is like water with petrol on it. I swim in a trillion colours. Totally lost.

4. The Pelican

Now I'm standing on a sandy shore. A pelican flies from the East, along the shore and offers me a fish from its pouch. I accept and swallow it whole, gulp by gulp, like a bird. Then I am a pelican too. We fly together westwards across the sea, which glimmers below. I dive down and catch a fish and offer it to the other pelican. She accepts it. We fly on towards the sun; our lazy wings beat together.

5. The Phoenix

The sun is on fire. Then I realize that the sun has been hiding a volcano. Streams of super-heated red magma rush from openings on its slopes. Playing in these streams is a phoenix, a nondescript bird much like a parrot but with no colouring. Not grey, not pale, just no colour at all. The phoenix is almost lost in the incredible brightness.

Bubbles rush up and slowly burst through the magma, releasing little clouds of acrid chemical gas. One especially large bubble bursts and in it is an egg, white and large. The egg breaks open to reveal a raven, which blinks, stretches its so-black wings and flies towards me. It is my bird.

The striking thing about Theo's account, for me, is his vision of the phoenix, which appears with no colour, and is possibly the last thing we'd expect of this bird.

Do persevere with your own alchemical transformation. Have no preconceptions about what might happen, and eventually you will discover your own inner bird … in good time.

Elemental Birds:

Earthbirds, waterbirds, airbirds, firebirds

"This magical power of understanding bird-talk is regularly the way in which the seers of myths obtain their information."

Halliday, *Greek Divination*

For this next section, I thought it would be useful to have a look at some individual birds in more detail, examining their physical characteristics and idiosyncrasies, as well as some of the mythology, legends and folklore associated with them. After all, if we are trying to understand the Secret Language of Birds, it is as well to realize that communication is never via the spoken word alone; the traits attributed to the birds by ancient cultures are a valid part of understanding what we're dealing with. Comprehension happens on many levels, and in understanding a little more about certain birds we should be able to make a deeper connection to them.

Birds do not use the notion of 'time' in the same way that we do. They do not have clocks or watches, or alarm bells, or blackout curtains. They have carried their stories with them for generations, for thousands if not millions of years, and what 'ancient' man saw in these creatures has exactly the same relevance today. Some of the sections will deal with 'ancient' civilizations, which immediately plunges us into the realms of 'past' and 'present'; however, for birds, there is only the 'now'.

For the sake of simplicity, I have divided up the birds into the elements that seem most to represent them – earth, air, fire and water. Some of the

birds could fly into more than one category, of course – this is not yet an exact science! You may wonder about some of the associations; why, for example, does the owl belong to the Water Element? It is because the Owl is often connected with hidden knowledge and with the moon, and the moon is associated with water. Other clues about the Elements of the Birds are contained in each of the descriptions.

This is by no means a comprehensive list of all the birds in the world. That would be impossible in a book such as this. I have concentrated on the ones that seem to be best-known and therefore most likely to form a part of our everyday lives and of our collective consciousness.

Chickadee

Earth

> Melodious silence greets my morn
> As icy prisms suspended at my pane
> Refract the advent of a fresh-fallen fantasy
> Mottled only by the whimsical fluttering of
> A chickadee on undaunted wing.
> My reverie envelops me
> In a vast blanket of glistening unsullied snow,
> An illusory mask for winter's sallow earth beneath.
> Still waters stand in frigorific splendour as
> Evergreens bough their ice-laden limbs in reverence
> To the glacial touch of the vernal crocus,
> The chickadee and I
> Shall appertain this pristine dream as one.
> **Nancy Ness,** *The Day of the Chickadee*

CHARACTERISTICS

The chickadee is a small bird, part of the titmouse family, just five inches long. It is found in all parts of the USA and Canada although is not resident in the UK. They like to nest in woodland areas, in hollowed-out stumps and the like, although they will also congregate in a more urban environment, where food is more plentiful – especially in the colder months, since the bird is not migratory. The chickadee will keep warm by puffing out its feathers, but if the temperature drops below 10 degrees, then bird feeders form a vital part of the equation in keeping it alive.

The chickadee is so called because this is what the bird seems to sing; it also seems to be saying 'Spring Soon' or 'Sweet Weather', so no wonder the bird is popular! As well as sounding happy, it's a cheerful sight, too, having a black cap and chest and white cheeks. The birds are gregarious, easy to train, and happy to feed from bird feeders close to human habitation, although if the chickadee considers itself to be in danger this little bird will actually spit, making an explosive sound at the same time.

NATIVE AMERICA MYTHS

Unsurprisingly given the chickadee's distribution, many of the stories about it come from America. The Indians of Labrador believed that the chickadee was the keeper of the time, and recorded the moons and the seasons. The bird kept these records by cutting small notches in its beak. Although man emulated this by keeping similar marks in a stick, in case of any confusion the chickadee had the last word.

The Cherokee call the bird 'tsikilili' and believed that it was the bearer of news and messages, which it would convey by various means. For example, perched by the house could mean one of two things: either that an enemy was after you, or that a long-lost friend would soon be in contact.

There's a story about a witch, called Spearfinger, who terrorized an entire tribe, waiting for vulnerable travellers who she would then kill and, stabbing into the bodies with her finger, extract the liver, which she then ate. No one could catch Spearfinger since she kept her identity a secret, but the chickadee courageously landed on her head and so she was discovered.

What Bird Would You Be?

'An Andean Condor – it might not be the prettiest of birds to look at, but once in flight is a breathtaking sight and simply commands respect.'
Rachel, UK

The Dove and the Pigeon

Earth

> The dove alone expresses
> Her fervency in kisses
> Of all most loving;
> A creature most offenceless
> As those things that are senseless
> And void of moving.
> Let us so love and kiss
> Though all envy us:
> That which kind and harmless is,
> None can deny us.
> **Thomas Campion,** *What Harvest Half So Sweet Is*

CHARACTERISTICS

Although pigeons and doves are from the same family and the name given is pretty much dependent on where you are in the world, there are some distinct differences in the birds. These birds, in one form or another, are found all over the world. Their song for the most part is quite repetitive and easily identifiable, being perhaps a little monotonous, if soothing.

Both doves and pigeons are able to suck up water, a talent unique to the species. Both pigeon parents also produce a curd-like substance called, appropriately enough, 'pigeon's milk', which the chicks take directly from their parents' mouths.

The nests of both the dove and pigeon tend towards the flimsy, wherever the bird has chosen to build it, whether in a tree, in a building, on a cliff ledge – in fact, the nest is so notoriously badly made that there's a legend about it. The magpie, who builds quite a thorough nest that even has a roof, decided she ought to teach the dove how it should be done. But the dove got bored very quickly, and just kept saying 'That'll doo-oo! That'll doo-oo!' until eventually the magpie got very irritated and left the dove to its own devices.

The best-known dove in America is the Mourning Dove, which can be found in every single state except for Hawaii.

THE DOVE – THE BIRD OF MESSAGES

The fact that there are so many stories associated with pigeons and doves would indicate that these birds were domesticated for man's use very early on. One of the prominent roles of both birds is concerned with the carrying of messages, both of a practical and spiritual nature.

We've already looked at the role of the carrier pigeon; this bird has been used for thousands of years as a go-between, and man has known for generations of the bird's long-distance flying ability, its ability to orientate itself, and its endurance over foreign terrain. In the Bible, it was the dove who returned to Noah, after all, with news of dry land, carrying a sprig of green olive leaves in its beak.

This ability to navigate has been the subject of several experiments, and the conclusion so far is that the birds seem to do some calculations by the sun, and they also have a built-in mechanism that allows them to determine the whereabouts of heavenly bodies. Beyond that there's still a lot to learn about just how these birds manage to find their way, although recent research is pointing towards the bird's ability to orientate itself via the Earth's magnetic fields.

The Feminine Aspect and Love

Dove associations are uncannily similar the world over. From American Indian beliefs through to Ancient Egypt, the bird is associated with the feminine, the mother, the moon, and all aspects thereof. That the dove is sometimes associated with sorrow and mourning is probably more to do with its melancholy voice, and perhaps its sober colouring, than anything else.

There are several constellations featuring birds; for example, there is Columba the Dove, who is depicted holding an olive branch.

The bird is also associated with love. This could be to do with the fact that doves are notoriously fertile, since the birds will leave the nest just two to three weeks after hatching and will begin to breed soon after; they also have two clutches of eggs in a season. In addition, the birds are very affectionate with one another, and the image of two turtle doves caressing one another is known the world over.

Egypt

We know that doves were kept, and domesticated, in Egypt at least as far back as 3000 BC. In addition to being a symbol of love, the dove was also a symbol of innocence.

Greece

The dove is the bird of Aphrodite, Goddess of Love, who was said to have been born from an egg that had been brooded by a dove. Athena, the Goddess of Wisdom, also shares some of the dove's attributes, as does Zeus; the birds are said to have fed him when he was a baby in a cave in Crete. Once again in Ancient Greece we find the symbol of the dove with the olive branch, as depicting the renewal of life and of hope.

At Dodona, there was a sacred oak tree, and in the branches was perched a dove which was said to have oracular powers. The three priestesses at the shrine were also known as 'doves', and they would announce the oracles while hidden in the foliage of the surrounding trees, as though the doves were speaking.

ANCIENT ROME

The dove is the symbol of Venus, who is, of course, the Roman Goddess of Love, and a counterpart to Aphrodite.

One of the Sirens is said to have followed the message from a dove to find a place to found a city. This was the city that became Naples.

Today, the many pigeons in St Mark's Square in Venice are fed by visitors and apparently fly around the area three times daily, it's said, in honour of the Trinity. There's a belief that as long as the pigeons are present in the dome of St Mark's, then the sea will never fully encroach upon the city.

AMERICAN INDIAN LEGENDS

Among Native Americans, the dove is representative of death and rebirth, the cycle of reincarnation, and is often depicted with a sprig of leaves in its beak, just like the one from Noah's Ark.

The Pueblo Indians associate the dove with water (the feminine element again, and possibly because of the ability the bird has to suck up water), and believe that the calling of the dove will show them where to find springs. There's a logic there, since the dove returns to watering places at night: because it eats dry seeds and grains it is essential for the bird to find water, so its calling would be a good indicator of the location of these essential watering-holes. Because of this association with water, the feathers of the dove were worn in masks during rituals that were performed to bring much-needed rain for crops, although the use of the feathers on prayer sticks was taboo.

> Dread the anger of the dove.
> *Proverb*

In a story which has a great deal of similarity with the dove being sent out from the Ark to find dry land, there's a Cherokee legend about a time when there was a great famine, and the pigeon was dispatched to see if she could find anything to eat. She returned with news of a country that was rich in 'mast', which is a nutritious combination of chestnuts, acorns and beech-nuts. Again we see the bird as a messenger of hope, as the animals promptly moved to this fertile country.

Celtic Lore

Running contrary to what's generally believed of the dove — as symbolic of peace and hope — are some stories from Wales.

Here the dove is seen as a bringer of disaster to coal miners. The appearance of a dove hovering near the mouth of a coal pit in 1902 was enough to cause 300 men to refuse to go to work. The incident is described in the *South Wales Echo* of July 15th:

> The men have been whispering their fears to each other for some time past, but the drastic action of Monday was probably the outcome of so-called evil omens which are said to have been heard in the mine … there is of course the usual tale of the dove hovering over the mouth of the level …

Reputedly, the bird had been spotted in the vicinity prior to the Senghenydd, Llanbradach and Morfa Colliery explosions.

There's also a tale in Wales of a dove that would appear near a lake that had formed in the crater of an extinct volcano, known as Llyn Dulyn, or Black Lake. The dove is said to represent the descent of the soul of a beautiful but wicked woman into the Underworld.

Mecca

Doves are protected in Mecca as a sacred bird. Indeed, doves tend to flock in large numbers around the mosques, and it is considered to be bad form to disturb these birds. Special niches are left in the walls so that the birds have somewhere to roost.

There is a story that Muhammad trained doves to take seeds from his ears; the faithful, seeing this, assumed that the Holy Ghost had assumed the shape of the dove and was speaking directly to the Prophet. In fact, Shakespeare makes reference to this in *Henry VI*:

> Was Mahomet inspired with a dove?

Judo-Christian Beliefs

The symbol of Israel is the dove, and it is seen as the spirit of God.

The dove and the turtle dove were the only birds that were allowed to be sacrificed; in Jewish belief, a white dove was regarded as an acceptable substitute for a lamb. The doves were domesticated, as elsewhere in the world, since time immemorial, and were kept in dovecotes. There also used to be a system of betting on racing doves, in the same way that some countries have this tradition even today, although the practice, as gambling, was frowned upon.

In the New Testament, there are numerous references to the dove as a symbol of the Holy Spirit, and as such the dove often depicted in art hovering over the head of the Virgin Mary. The following is from the account of the baptism of Christ found in Matthew's Gospel:

> The heavens opened, and He saw the Spirit of God descending like a
> dove, and lighting upon Him.

References are made to the dove being an emblem of love, devotion, gentleness and peace. Additionally, it may be a relief to some that, although the Devil can assume many forms, the dove, as a symbol of the Holy Spirit, is denied to him as a shape-shifting tool.

India

In Gujarat, it's a tradition to build very beautiful and ornate dovecotes, known as Chabutras. These take the form of a platform, raised about five or six feet off the ground and covered with a roof or dome, the whole often having climbing plants or flowers growing up and around it. Although these elaborate bird houses can be a home to other birds, such as peacocks, sparrows and mynah birds, their main use is as a dwelling for doves or pigeons; indeed the name 'Chabutra' comes from the Gujarati for pigeon, which is 'Kabutari'. The Gujaratis believe that the souls of people assume the form of birds and animals, so in taking care of the birds in this way they are showing their affection for departed human spirits.

The reverence in which the bird is held is shown by an incident that took place in Mumbai in 1921. Two European boys killed a couple of doves in the street, and the horror which ensued was enough to close down the stock exchange and cause the threat of a widespread strike of Indian workers.

Paradoxically perhaps, to Western minds at least, the Hindu God of death and destruction, Yama, has a pigeon as a messenger ...

JAPAN

In Japan, the dove got itself a reputation as a messenger of war. This harks back to a tale about a mythical hero called Yorimoto, who, being chased by enemies, took refuge in the hollow of a tree. Because a pair of doves flew out of the hollow as the enemies passed by, they assumed that no one was there, and Yorimoto survived to become Shogun. He declared that the birds had brought him luck.

> I had a very vivid dream, of mountains somewhere ... Then there were many planes, they looked like World War Two planes, and they were dropping white paper doves which were fluttering through the air onto the valleys below. A few weeks later my dream came true – white paper doves had been dropped on to Nepal from planes.
>
> *David Antony, Wales*

What Bird Would You Be?

'Well it wouldn't be a bird of prey that's for sure, don't fancy being a bird living in a huge mass, not keen on crowds, I'd probably starve, I'm not competitive enough ... Seashore birds have a wonderful landscape, so that's possible. Then again, doves have a special place to be and are a wonderful symbol of peace, dovecotes are usually situated in calm and lovely surroundings ... that's it; I'd be a dove!'

Gill, Wales

The Magpie

One for sorrow
Two for mirth
Three for a wedding
Four for a birth;
Five for silver
Six for gold
Seven for a secret
Never to be told;
Eight for Heaven
Nine for Hell
And ten for the devil's ain sel.
Anonymous

CHARACTERISTICS

The magpie is a member of the incredibly intelligent Corvid family, to which ravens, crows, rooks and jays also belong. They are easily recognizable birds, and are to be found in both the Southern and Northern hemispheres. They have beautiful black and white markings, which look a little to me like a very smart uniform, and they're noisy and boisterous, usually appearing in groups of three or four. It is the black and white markings that give the bird part of its name – 'pie', meaning 'pied'. 'Mag' was added, and means 'chatterer'.

Blue jays are believed to forget where they store their winter food supplies.

The magpie is of course famous for being attracted to bright and shiny objects, which it will take away if at all possible and stow in its nest, which is usually pretty huge – between one and three feet (30–90 cm) in diameter – and very bulky. The nest will be used year after year and gets scruffier as time goes on and it is added to! Unusually, a magpie's nest usually has a roof and is entered through the sides.

We use the term 'magpie' to apply to anyone who collects too many possessions, or who hoards things away.

Weatherlore

Like many other birds, the magpie has its place as a weather forecaster. In France, if the birds build their nests low down in the trees, then a season of storms and gales can be expected. Conversely, if the nests are high up then it is expected that good weather will follow. In fact, if the weather is stormy, one magpie will leave the nest in search of food and will feed both birds, but if the weather is fine then they'll both go out. This gives rise to the belief that a lone magpie is a bad sign for fishermen.

In Mongolia, it was generally supposed that magpies were actually in charge of the weather and could control it. Therefore it was as well to stay on the good side of the bird!

Britain

The beliefs about the magpie in Britain are pretty ambivalent, but it is generally held to be a bird of ill-omen, unfortunately, and is sometimes viewed as an extrapolation of the Devil, which may be due to the influence of the early Christian Church where the poor magpie used to be seen as representing dissipation, vanity and evil. In Scotland, the bird is even called 'the devil' and is believed to have a drop of the devil's blood in its tongue.

There's a popular counting rhyme about magpies, which has subtle differences depending where in Britain you are. The most popular version I could find is at the beginning of this section. It is possible that the 'opposites' in the rhyme, and the general ambivalence about the magpie, is because of its black/white, night/day colouring.

The magpie rhyme is another representation of signs from the birds; this time, counting the birds will give us the information we're seeking.

> The day I went to have my scan at the hospital with Tymen, my second child, my mother saw 4 magpies in her garden and rang me to say that it would be a boy. (She didn't know that I was 10 minutes away from having the scan which told me exactly that.)
> *Lyndall, UK*

If you see an unacceptable number of magpies, there is a way to counter the bad effects, which is to take off your hat and bow three times to the magpie. In Yorkshire there's a slightly different twist: if the magpie has a 'bad' message, the person will cross their thumbs and say

> I cross the magpie
> The magpie crossed me
> Bad luck to the magpie
> And good luck to me.

One of the reasons for the magpie's reputation as a bird of ill omen could be that it was written that the magpie refused to get into the Ark but instead perched on the roof, where it chattered all day long. There's also a legend that the magpie failed to wear full mourning to the crucifixion, which would also account for the bird's bad publicity in some quarters.

EUROPE

In Sweden, sorcerers take the form of magpies on Walpurgis Night, and in the rest of Scandinavia, it's popularly supposed that witches take the form of magpies, or used them as transport. Even its name, 'Scadi', denotes a sense of loss, or evil. This belief holds in Germany too.

The word 'gazette', used to apply to a journal or newspaper full of interesting titbits of information, is derived from the Italian word for magpie, 'gazza'. In Rome, barbers used to keep magpies as pets in their shops.

The bird has its best reputation in Norway, however, where its confident, gregarious and fearless qualities are looked upon favourably. Because the birds like to live close to people, the Norwegians even tie a sheaf of corn to the top of the house at Christmas so that the birds can also take part in the celebrations.

CHINA

Contrary to the lore associated with magpies in Europe and the UK, in China the birds are seen as emblems of good luck and happiness. They even call the bird the 'Happy Magpie'.

However, there's also a story that the husband of an unfaithful wife learns about her deception from the magpie, since the man gives his wife a mirror, which turns into a magpie and tells the husband what the wife has been up to in his absence. The association with the mirror could be because of the attraction shiny objects have for these birds. Another version has the couple breaking a mirror in half; the superstition being that if one partner was unfaithful to the other, the half mirror would turn into a magpie and fly to join its other half. This is why mirror backs in China are even now often decorated with images of the bird.

The Manchu and the Magpie

The Mongolian Manchu dynasty believed that the magpie was a sacred bird, and it was a symbol of the imperial rulers. This is because of a legend about the founding of the dynasty.

A Goddess, Fokulon, was out by a lake when a magpie flying overhead dropped a red fruit. Fokulon picked it up and ate it, and nine months later she gave birth to a baby boy, Bukulirongshun. This boy became the founder of the Manchu dynasty.

Bukulirongshun and his descendants were skilled and heroic fighters, and were seen as a threat by neighbouring provinces. These formed an alliance with the idea of destroying the new tribe. A young boy, Fancha, was the only one to escape the massacre that ensued, and he did this by running as hard and as fast as he could until he could run no longer. His enemies were after him and had nearly reached him when a magpie suddenly alighted on his head. Fancha used his wits and stayed as still as possible, so that, in the gloaming, he looked like a tree; his potential murderers went on their way. So the Manchu dynasty was saved, by a very thin thread, and the magpie has been considered sacred to them ever since.

Ancient Greece and Rome

The magpie used to be sacred to Bacchus (in Rome) and to Dionysus (in Greece), Gods much associated with wine drinking and revelry. This is because the bird loosened tongues under the influence of alcohol, and caused secrets to be revealed.

The Pierides were the nine daughters of King Pierus, who had the audacity to challenge the Muses in a singing contest. The Pierides lost, and were transformed into magpies, and the Muses retained their status as the Goddesses of the Arts.

NATIVE AMERICAN LORE

In general the magpie is seen as a friend and helper to man. Indeed, the Sioux see the magpie as having God-like powers and status, of being omniscient. While for the Pueblo, the black and white colouring of the bird held special significance, since it was emblematic of East and West.

There's a nice tale about a Shasta Indian boy who fell in love with a girl, and asked her to marry him. The girl was so excited that she told everyone; when there was no human being left to share the happy news, she ran into the forest to tell all the animals and birds, too. As a result, everywhere the boy went he was congratulated. Tired after days of the constant chatter, he thought to escape to the forest, but of course it was even worse here; the magpie, voluble at the best of times, was the loudest with her teasing, and eventually the boy shouted out, 'Women and magpies, a curse on you all! Just like the magpie, women can't keep quiet!'

> To a woman and a magpie tell your secrets in the marketplace.
> *Proverb*

And that's why, apparently, women and magpies like nothing better than to chatter away all day long.

What Bird Would You Be?

'I'd have to be a magpie – I love the uniform, and I'd love to have a nest lined with precious jewels and sparkly things.'
Lee, France

The Nightjar or Whipoorwhil

Earth

> The buzzing dor hawk round and round is wheeling
> That solitary bird
> Is all that can be heard
> In silence deeper far than deepest noon.
> **William Wordsworth,** *Canto First*

CHARACTERISTICS

The Latin name for the nightjar/whipoorwil is 'Caprimulgus', from 'capra', meaning nanny goat, and 'mulgus', to milk, but which is commonly translated as the sinister 'goatsucker'. This eerie name was first ascribed to the nightjar by Aristotle, apparently. It got the name because of its reputation for stealing milk directly from the udders of goats, thereby causing the animal to go blind. This is patently untrue, but it gave the nightjar a semi-vampire status, which has stuck for some reason.

Since the nightjar and the whipoorwhil are essentially the same bird, for the purpose of avoiding confusion I'm going to refer to the bird as the 'caprimulgus' except where there are marked traits in either bird.

A nocturnal bird, the caprimulgus is not often seen. It has plain, tawny brown feathers which blend in very well with the landscape, and if you were to spot the bird during daylight hours you might well find that what you're looking at resembles a pile of dead leaves, since the bird sleeps lying motionless on the ground or resting along a bare branch. It lays its eggs very simply on the bare ground too. The caprimulgus is so well camouflaged that often it will almost be trodden on before flying away suddenly into the undergrowth. If the bird does feel threatened, it will move its eggs or even its chicks to another location.

With its small legs and feet, the bird only shuffles a few paces if it needs to, which isn't very often. Feeding primarily on insects, which it catches at night, the caprimulgus needs to live in places where insects are plentiful. It has a wide gaping mouth, which is useful for capturing insects during flight. Cleverly, most baby caprimulgi hatch when the moon is full; this makes it easier for their parents to go hunting for food for the chick.

The whipoorwhil has a particularly unusual characteristic; it's the only bird that has been proven to hibernate during winter months. Previously, modern ornithologists had scorned the idea that birds could hibernate, and had ascribed the stories of the Arizona Indians, about the bird who slept its winters away hiding in crevices in cliffs, as mere folklore. However, in 1946 it was discovered that this 'legend' was fact.

THE STRANGE SOUND OF THE NIGHTJAR

Perhaps the most unusual feature of the nightjar is its very peculiar call. Since it comes out at dusk to feed on flying insects, this is the best time to hear the strange sound the bird makes. It has been described as a 'churring' sound, or like an engine revving up for a few moments at a time. The first time I heard it, I had no idea that the sound was being made by a bird. It's a strange, alien sound, especially if you're not expecting it; it sounds like the old-fashioned children's toy, a piece of card with two holes in with elastic threaded through – the card is twirled around then the elastic pulled taut so that as the card spins fast it emits a sort of whirring sound.

Only nocturnal birds have an external ear. Despite this, all birds have a keen sense of hearing.

Because the nightjar will make this sound as it flies, it can be even stranger. You are in the twilight, the bird is invisible, yet these sounds move in the air all around you; it is quite startling and spooky.

I have also discovered that if you wave something light-coloured – just a piece of cloth for example – the nightjars seem to be attracted to it and will follow you, making their ghostly sound as they go. (In case you're wondering what on earth I'm doing wandering the hills at night in the pitch black waving bits of cloth about, I'll explain that I have two black dogs with white-tipped plume tails – the discovery was purely accidental!)

THE BIRD OF FAERIE REALMS

Because of its twilight habits and its strange, otherworldly calling, the caprimulgus is associated with the world of fairies, elves and the like, and with Puck in particular, a mischievous spirit who would make trouble for people walking home late at night. Because lots of inexplicable things were ascribed to the faerie realms, and the nightjar seemed to be present at the same time, the two have become interlinked.

The USA

In America, the whipoorwhil is associated with death, probably because of its nocturnal nature and eerie, ghost-like calling. This is reflected in some of the bird's colloquial names: 'corpse bird' or 'corpse fowl', for example.

There's a variety of the bird called Heinrich's Nightjar, which is also known as the Satanic Nightjar. The cry of this species is reputed to be the sound it makes as it tears out people's eyes …

> He seemed in ultimate peace
> Except he had no eyes. Rigid and bright
> Upon the forehead, furred
> With a light frost, crouched an outrageous bird.
> Anthony Hecht

Native America Lore

The supposed origins of the nightjar are quite alarming. The Arawak say that it constructed itself from the brains scattered from a cracked human skull …

The Omaha Indians have a legend about the repetitive call of the bird. Because the cry sounds a little like a question, it was believed that if they replied 'No' and the bird then stopped calling, it would signify a death. Conversely, if the bird kept up its questioning, the person would live for a long time.

The Bible

Adam and his first wife, Lilith, were said to have been created back-to-back from the same dust. But Lilith found many things unacceptable, since she thought herself, quite rightly, to be the equal of her husband. She left Adam, and was punished by God for failing to do as she was told. Since then, if she is spoken of at all, it is with hushed tones.

THE SECRET LANGUAGE OF BIRDS

She is associated with the nightjar, which is one of her nicknames; the New English Bible carries the phrase

Marmots shall consort with jackals, and he-goat shall encounter he-goat. There too the night-jar shall rest, and find herself a place for repose.
Isaiah 34:14

VIETNAM

We end on a positive note concerning the much-maligned caprimulgus. The Montagnard peoples of Southern Vietnam refer to the nightjar as the 'black-smith bird'. They believe that to dream of the bird will enable you to master the craft of iron working!

What Bird Would You Be?

'A whipoorwil ... a large American bird which sleeps horizontally, its nest is a mere pile of leaves on the ground, and wakes everyone up at night with its loud "whippa will whippa will".

'At such times the delightful mellowness which one hears, with the birds in the distance, gives rise to an almost painful, penetrating shrillness. The more deliberately uttered song is invariably preceded by a strong gutteral sound not unlike that produced by striking an inflated rubber bag.'
Janette, New York

The Ostrich

Earth

> The ostrich roams the great Sahara
> Its mouth is wide, its neck is narra
> It has such long and lofty legs
> I'm glad it sits to lay its eggs.
> **Ogden Nash**

CHARACTERISTICS

The largest of all the birds on the planet, the adult male ostrich can stand up to eight feet (2.5 metres) tall, and can weigh 300 pounds (135 kg); a daunting sight close up. The ostriches of 50 million years ago used to live in Southern Europe, but now their main territory is in central Africa, although they are pretty adaptable – as recent trends in ostrich farming in Finland have shown.

Of course, the ostrich is flightless. If there is a threat the bird would prefer to run away, but if necessary it will fight furiously, using its muscular legs and feet and its sharp claws, which are strong enough to tear open a man.

Ostriches seem to thrive well in captivity, although they don't domesticate too well. They have been encouraged to pull carts, but when the bird gets bored or tired it will simply sit down and refuse to go any further.

A MYTH DEMYSTIFIED

If we say about someone that they are likely to 'bury their head in the sand', we're alluding to the alleged habit of the ostrich, and we mean that the person is likely to ignore problems or pretend that they don't exist.

However, the ostrich doesn't bury its head in sand at all! Ostrich eggs are laid in a large hole in the sand; this 'nest' is often shared by two or three mother birds and can contain as many as 30 eggs. The eggs are huge – six inches (15 cm) in diameter and weighing up to three pounds (1.5 kg). If the ostrich feels threatened, however, it will lay its head down flat against the ground to try to disguise itself and the place where the eggs are hidden; this habit could have given rise to this particular myth.

> Now when the time comes for it to lay some eggs, the ostrich raises its eyes to heaven and looks to see whether the Pleiades are visible. Nor will it lay until the Pleiades appear. When, however, it perceives that constellation, round about the month of June, it digs a hole in the Earth, and there it deposits the eggs and covers them with sand.
> *The Book of Beasts,* **twelfth-century Latin bestiary**

Another myth is that the ostrich is stupid because it has a habit of eating stones. In fact the small stones and pieces of grit help the bird's digestion – especially useful since the ostrich has no teeth. However, like the magpie, the ostrich is inordinately fond of shiny objects and will consume jewellery, broken watches, bits of glass, bottle tops and the like, all of which usually don't do any harm. In fact the stones that may also have been swallowed by the ostrich will help to grind these objects down.

This habit of eating metal objects is reflected in depictions of the bird, which is often shown with a piece of iron such as a key in its beak. Indeed, Shakespeare knew about this habit too:

> I'll make thee eat iron like the ostrich, and swallow my sword.
> **Henry VI**

THE OSTRICH FEATHER

Ostrich feathers are extremely beautiful, and since they belong to a flightless bird, they can afford to be fluffy and decorative. Their usage has included adorning the helmets of knights during the crusades for identification purposes to being employed in ladies fashions, particularly in the nineteenth century, when ostriches began to be bred purely for their plumes.

The Ostrich Egg

Ostrich eggshells have been recovered from Etruscan tombs, and also from burial places in Egypt and Africa. The shells were often decorated, and could be used as water-carrying vessels, as the eggs are large and the shells are strong.

The Islamic World

The ostrich egg is an important symbol in Islam, and is used as a decoration in mosques to indicate the qualities of faith and patience.

There is a legend about Barak Baba, a twelfth-century Dervish leader, who rode an ostrich, which actually flew a little way because of Barak's incredible powers.

Egypt

The Goddess Maat is depicted wearing an ostrich feather. She is the Goddess of Law and Justice, and the feather is a fitting emblem since, unlike other birds' feathers, which are often longer and slightly heavier on one side than the other for ease of flight, the ostrich plume is perfectly balanced on both sides.

When the dead were brought before Osiris to be judged, the person's heart was weighed against the ostrich feather on the scales of Maat; it was believed that the heart could be weighed down by sins. In Ancient Egypt, therefore, the ostrich feather epitomized truth and justice. The God Shu, the God of Air and Space, also used the ostrich feather as his symbol. The feathers were also used in the fans of the Pharaohs.

Ancient Rome

Ostrich meat was a prized delicacy and would be eaten at the feasts of Emperors.

The Dogon

The ostrich, to the Dogon tribes of Mali, is a sacred bird, and ostrich eggs are placed on the tops of the roof spires of their sacred buildings; the egg symbolizes creation. The ostrich itself is representative of water and light, and the bird is shown in Dogon art as a series of undulating lines, zigzags and concentric circles. The ostrich is also believed to hold supernatural powers.

How Man Found Fire – An African Story

In African folklore, Mantis is a sort of superhuman being, a God, who has a benevolent attitude towards the bushmen …

A long time ago, the bushmen didn't have fire; they didn't have anything to keep them warm at night, and nor had any of them ever tasted just how delicious cooked food could be. But Mantis had noticed that the ostrich always seemed to have food that smelled different, and amazing, and very unlike anything that was the regular diet of the other creatures. So Mantis watched the ostrich and saw that he took something bright, and red, and flickering from underneath his wing, and dipped his food into it. After this happened, the tantalizing smells arose again, and Mantis decided he must take this magical substance back to his people.

However, he also knew that the stubborn ostrich would never share the magical thing; he would have to trick the bird. Accordingly, a few days later he went to visit the ostrich.

'Hello, Ostrich; I've got a treat for you. There's a tree nearby with incredibly delicious-looking plums on it, which you, with your great height, should be able to reach easily.'

The ostrich was very pleased at being taken notice of by Mantis, let alone the prospect of a treat, so off he went to find the tree. Mantis made him stretch higher and higher to reach the juiciest plums on the top of the tree. As the ostrich reached further and further upwards, standing on tip toe, the fire underneath his wing was revealed. Mantis grabbed it quickly, and ran off with it.

The ostrich was terribly upset about the theft of the fire, and although it was really too late, ever since then he has kept his wings close to his sides and to keep safe the tiny bit of fire that wasn't stolen.

What Bird Would You Be?

'It would have to be an ostrich ... I have no head for heights so its ground-based existence would suit me. Also, I'd never have to worry about what to wear to parties again.'
Alexandra, Greece

The Partridge

Earth

On the twelfth day of Christmas my true love gave to me
Twelve drummers drumming
Eleven pipers piping
Ten lords a-leaping
Nine ladies dancing
Eight maids a-milking
Seven swans a-swimming
Six geese a-laying
Five gold rings
Four calling birds
Three French hens
Two turtle doves –
And a partridge in a pear tree.
Anonymous

CHARACTERISTICS

The partridge is a prolific breeder, laying between 10 and 20 eggs at a time; sometimes the nest is shared by other birds so will often contain up to 40 eggs. Partridges are extremely well camouflaged when nesting; their colours blend in perfectly with the brown of the leaves and bracken it lives among.

The courtship ritual of the partridge is unusual in that the male and female will take it in turns to chase each other. The partridge does tend to run rather than fly. When they do fly there's a lot of effort from the wings, which appear to whirr around; the distances flown are not very far, though.

Unfortunately for the partridge, it's one of the most popular game birds for hunters. It nests on the ground and can fly almost vertically upright when disturbed, a characteristic which makes it a favourite amongst marksmen, and which is similar to the pheasant and the quail.

THE NAME

The name of the partridge originates from the Greek 'Perdesthai', which means to make an explosive noise. This could refer either to the bird's rasping call, or to the sudden flurry of noise when the bird is disturbed and, almost literally, 'explodes' from its nesting place.

In *The Book of Beasts*, a twelfth-century Latin bestiary, we are told 'Perdix the partridge gets its name because it makes that sort of noise'.

A SECRET MESSAGE

The familiar Christmas song, quoted in part above, is not the simple piece of doggerel which it appears to be. During the period 1558 to 1829, Catholics in England were persecuted to the point that it was actually illegal to belong to this faith. Punishments for anyone caught practising the Catholic faith were severe, including torture. So the song was written as a code to help young Catholic children remember the tenets of their beliefs, with the various peculiar items of the twelve days representing various aspects of Catholicism. The 'partridge in a pear tree' was representative of Jesus Christ, and the 'true love' is God.

CHINA

In China the partridge's cry is interpreted as a love call, despite its discordant sound. This is probably because of the fecundity of the bird. The partridge also used to be regarded as an antidote to poisons.

In Greek Myth

Daedalus was from Athens, a master craftsman and inventor. His skills were reputed to have been taught to him by the Goddess Athena herself. However, Daedalus had a nephew, Talos, whose skills looked set to outshine those of Daedalus. When Talos invented the saw, apparently from the jaw of a snake, Daedalus descended into a fit of jealousy so great that he tried to murder Talos by pushing him from the top of the Acropolis. Athena intervened, and turned the boy into a partridge; hence the Greek name for partridge is Perdix, which was the name of Talos's mother.

Birds often emulate each other's behaviour, for example, buzzards can sometimes be seen hovering like kestrels.

Thereafter, the partridge was afraid of heights, as well might be expected, and this is why the bird stays close to the ground.

In Christian Myth

Perhaps because of the enthusiastic mating habits of the bird, in Christian allegory, the partridge is regarded as being symbolic of temptation and damnation. In *The Book of Beasts*, the fertility of the partridge is described thus:

> Desire torments the females so much that even if a wind blows towards them from the males, they become pregnant by the smell.

As such, the poor partridge is seen as an incarnation of Satan, and stands for theft, deceitfulness and slyness. However, conversely, the bird also represents the truth of Christ.

The Pheasant

Earth

> See! from the brake the whirring pheasant springs,
> And mounts exulting on triumphant wings:
> Short is his joy; he feels the fiery wound,
> Flutters in blood, and panting beats the ground.
> Ah! What avail his glossy, varying dyes,
> His purple crest, and scarlet-circled eyes,
> The vivid green his scarlet plumes unfold,
> His painted wings and breast that flames with gold?
> **Alexander Pope,** *Windsor Forest*

CHARACTERISTICS

Pheasants are perhaps among some of the most beautiful and exotic-looking birds in the bird world, with their long tails, occasional crests and jewel-coloured feathers. The pheasant nests in scrubby ground, and although the bird is incapable of very long flights, it can rise from the ground almost vertically and very swiftly – characteristics that have, unfortunately, made it a favourite among game bird enthusiasts, alongside the partridge.

Originally from central and southern Asia, the bird was introduced to America by the British in the late eighteenth century, while its presence in Britain in the first place is attributable to the Romans. The name of the pheasant originates in a Greek word, which translates as 'bird from the River Phaesis'.

CATCHING YOUR PHEASANT

In Europe, peasants were not permitted to go out hunting, and so had to devise more ingenious ways of attracting useful birds and animals. The pheasant could be lured by mirrors; attracted to its own beautiful reflection, the bird was then easy to snare.

CHINA

Unsurprisingly given its origins, most of the lore about pheasants comes from China, where, symbolically, the pheasant represents male energy, light, beauty and luck. The bird was the emblem of the Emperor Yu, who in turn was seen as 'the Regulator of the World'. As a reminder of the bird's special status, a golden-coloured pheasant with long tail feathers was the symbol of an official working for the Civil Service.

> Pheasants are fools,
> if they invite the
> hawk to dinner.
> *Proverb*

The pheasant is also associated with the Goddess Li, who was, perhaps unusually, the personification of the female energy of fire and the Sun, both usually male attributes in themselves.

There are also tales associating the pheasant with the weather; when the hen bird calls out to the cock, it's seen as a sign of thunder. The belief that the pheasant could bring about thunder meant that in Spring people would dance about in imitation of the bird in the hope of enticing the rain to fall.

JAPAN

The pheasant represents maternal love, protection and duty. It is believed to be able to predict earthquakes – a useful attribute in a country where these calamities occur relatively frequently – and so the pheasant is Japan's national bird symbol.

In Shinto myth, the pheasant was the messenger for the divinity who regulated the world, Ame-wakahiko.

MALAYA

The Argus Pheasant, who does not have the brilliant colours of some of the rest of his species but instead is a drabber brown colour, decided that he wanted to change his appearance, and so asked the crow to help him out by painting him in more exciting colours. The crow obliged, painting the Argus in the colours he preferred, and was so pleased with his handiwork that he asked the pheasant to return the favour. However, the pheasant didn't endear himself to the crow; he simply tipped a bottle of ink over his friend, giving the crow the black feathers that we know him by.

When we lived in the country the Guinea Fowl used to roost on the flat roof of the next door holiday cottage and visitors used to complain. I told the story to our local vicar who said he had never eaten Guinea Fowl. He was a very 'hunting, shooting, fishing' bloke so, being less enlightened than I am now, I said he could have them if he could catch them. Eventually I caught them myself and put them into a chicken shed and told him to take them away as they were such a nuisance. He decided to give them a 'sporting chance' – this meant letting them out of the pen and shooting them, not very sporting if you ask me. In any case, they delicately walked down the ramp and then took off. The vicar took a shot at them, missed completely and utterly, and hit the tin shed of the workmen who were having tea! They all came out screaming and yelling at the vicar – it was very funny – and all the birds escaped!
Liz, UK

What Bird Would You Be?

'**I**'d choose the pheasant ... for the feathers alone; as long as I had a mirror to admire myself, I'd be perfectly happy.'
Giovanna, Rome

The Quail

Earth

When the hawk's eye darkens
The little quail
Begin to chirp.
Basho

Characteristics

The quail looks like a miniature version of a partridge, and likes to live in among tall grasses and undergrowth at the sides of fields or meadows. They nest on the ground, and are monogamous but prolific breeders, some laying up to three clutches of eggs in one year. Like their larger cousin, they have unfortunately been a regular favourite with hunters.

Because for the most part quails don't migrate and tend to stay within just a few miles of where they are born, certain distinctive features peculiar to the birds' geographical location usually remain intact within the gene pool. The exception to this rule is the Quail of Eurasia, which will migrate from Europe and Western Asia into Northern Africa. It is the migratory species of the bird which is the one with the most stories and the source of much of the bird's symbolic meaning.

The Witches' Bird

When quail do fly or migrate, they do so by night. It is perhaps because of its associations with the nocturnal hours (also the time for lust, of course) and also possibly because of its fertility, the quail is said to be one of the birds of witches, and as such represents devilish powers and black magic for some people.

China

The quail is an important bird in Chinese symbolism. It is a bird of fire, and of the colour red; as such it represents Summer. Because of its high fertility, it is associated with love, or, more exactly, with the heat of desire. Additionally, there's an association between the quail and the phoenix in Chinese myth.

Greek Myth

The daughter of Coeus and Phoebe, Asteria, was incredibly beautiful, and the God Zeus, who always seems to have had an eye for the ladies, was very keen to make her acquaintance … However, Asteria was vehemently insistent that she wasn't interested in Zeus. The only way she could escape his attentions was to transform herself into a quail and throw herself into the sea, at which point she transformed again into an island, Ortygia, which means Quail Island.

According to early Greek writers, the quail wasn't eaten as much as some other birds, since the bird would eat plants poisonous to human beings, such as the hellebore. To eat the bird, apparently, could result in the eater being poisoned and he or she could also suffer from epilepsy.

Rome

Quail were domesticated and kept as pets, and for the Romans, as well the bird symbolizing sexual prowess and lust, the quail also signified victory in battle and courage.

Phoenicia

There was a Phoenician extrapolation of Hercules who was called Melkarth, meaning 'King of the City'. Melkarth apparently died on an annual basis, and was revived by the quail when the bird was held to his nose by the Phoenician equivalent of the healer Ascelpius, who was named Esmun. Therefore the quail became a symbol of renewal and resurrection.

Robert Graves, who relates this story in *The White Goddess*, tell us that 'The quail is notorious for its pugnacity and lechery.'

The Bible

When the Children of Israel were in the wilderness and hungry, as well as the manna bread which appeared, quails also appeared to allay their pangs of hunger. A huge flock arrived one evening and were promptly eaten!

Hindu Myth

In Vedic stories there appear twins, the Ashvins, who represent day and night, light and darkness. They are responsible for bringing back to life the quail, which was swallowed by a wolf.

What Bird Would You Be?

'A quail ... I don't know why in particular, but I think they are meant to belong to witches and I quite like the idea of being a witch.'
Selena, Rio

The Sparrow

Earth

> I have two sparrows white as snow
> Whose pretty eyes like sparks do show;
> In her bosom Venus hatcht them
> Where her little Cupid watcht them.
> **Michael Drayton,** *The Muses' Elysium*

The sparrow used to be so common in the UK as to be virtually unnotice-able. Books about birds written just 20 years ago had not noticed that these small, pretty, supposedly commonplace birds were at the beginning of a dramatic decline. I find the rate at which the sparrow has declined very alarming. It seems to be a herald of something far, far worse, and I hope that the more we realize what a precious asset we have in all our birds, the more inclined we will be to do something about this catastrophe.

CHARACTERISTICS

The House Sparrow has been around almost as long as man has been a land settler, and the bird used to like to live in close proximity to man, feeding on grain and small insects, and often nesting in buildings. It is a small, brown bird, fairly nondescript, with an attractive cheeping call. Their nests tend to be rather scruffy in appearance – a bundle of sticks which appear to have been shoved together. Indeed, sometimes they will be happy to 'squat' the aban-doned nests of other birds.

The age of the sparrow can be derived from its name, which has Anglo-Saxon origins.

GREECE AND ROME

Because the birds proliferated, they were sacred to the Love Goddesses, Venus and Aphrodite, and were also said to be Cupid's bird. This profligacy was not approved of at all by Aristotle, who referred to the birds as 'wanton'. Perhaps because of their success in breeding, sparrow's eggs were considered to be an aphrodisiac.

IN AUGURY

The sparrow, humble though it is, has its place in world history, and its signif-icance was not unnoticed by the augurs who were employed to predict what might befall when the combined fleets of the Greek states were lined up to attack Troy. The augur Calshas noticed a serpent seize nine sparrows who had been perched in a nearby tree, and he interpreted this sign as meaning that Troy would not fall for another nine years; this prediction proved to be true.

In Christianity

Perhaps because it was so common and plain-looking, the sparrow is associated with meekness and lowliness. The sparrow is described in the New Testament as being sold 'two for a farthing'.

There's also a story that does the sparrow no credit at all. While Christ was on the cross, the sparrows are said to have proclaimed to all and sundry,

He is living! He is living!

while the swallow was doing its best to persuade the tormentors that it was time to cut Him down. This placed a curse on the head of the sparrow.

Bohemia

In Bohemia, farmers employ several charms and tricks to try to keep sparrows off their grain crops, since they are considered to be very destructive. One of these arcane practices was to take a splinter from a coffin, or even a bone from a corpse, and place it upright in the field. I have been unable to find any documentary evidence supporting the efficaciousness of this practice.

The Tongue-Cut Sparrow – A Classic Japanese Folktale

Once upon a time, but not so very long ago, in a remote part of Japan, lived an old man and his wife.

One morning the wife opened the screens and stepped outside to find a tiny sparrow, all alone, on the doorstep. Very carefully, the old lady brought the sparrow into the house and fed him. After he was fed and had warmed up, she tried to make him fly away, but he didn't want to leave her. The sparrow seemed to have decided to stay, because every morning at sunrise he was to be found on their rooftop, singing beautifully, and this made the old couple very happy, that a wild animal would choose to befriend them in such a way.

However, there was an evil old woman who lived close by who hated to be woken up so early. She caught the sparrow and slit his tongue, so that the little bird would never sing again.

Because the sparrow could not sing, he was very ashamed, and flew away. The old lady and her husband were very sad, and decided to go and look for him. They went everywhere, asking,

'Have you seen a little sparrow, who can't sing? His tongue has been cut, you see.'

As you might imagine, many people thought the old couple were quite, quite mad. They were sent on a wild goose chase by people until they thought to ask the animals the whereabouts of their little sparrow friend.

The bat sent them across a bridge and over a mountain. Then they came to a crossroads but had no idea whether to go left or right. So they asked a field mouse.

'Take the road which goes down the mountain and through the woods,' he replied, so the old couple followed his advice.

At last, they found where the little shame-faced sparrow was hiding, and despite his embarrassment he came flying out to meet them. He introduced them to his wife and children, who all came and bowed down, and after a rare feast they danced a very special 'sparrow dance' in honour of the kind humans.

At last it was time to go, and as a gift the sparrows offered the couple one of two baskets. One was very light and appeared to have nothing in it; the other was very heavy, and stuffed with mysterious things. The elderly couple decided to take the lighter load; they didn't want to take too much from the birds, but made the excuse of the length of their journey home and the fact that they were tired.

Once back at home, they opened the basket and found that, contrary to their expectations, it contained priceless silks and lots of gold. Now they would be rich enough for several lifetimes.

The wicked woman who had slit the throat of the sparrow had been spying through her screen, and saw the riches coming out of the basket. She was horrified that this old couple should now have so much wealth, so went the next day to apologize and make amends, and no doubt to see what she could gain from the situation.

'How may I find the sparrow, so that I might apologize in person?' she asked.

The old lady thought the very best of everyone and so sent her to the forest where the sparrows lived.

The sparrow did everything to make the wicked old woman very welcome. She was fed, and they danced the dance, and at last she was offered the choice of two baskets.

I suppose we can all guess which one she took? That's right – of course she chose the heavier of the two.

She virtually ran all the way back home and pulled the screens tight to ensure that no one would be able to see the riches she was expecting to pull out of the basket.

But … once opened, the basket let out a stream of poisonous creatures, who bit and scratched and stung. The wicked old woman screamed in horror and crawled to the door to get away from them, but once she was outside the creatures picked her up and flew away with her – and that was the last anyone ever saw of her.

What Bird Would You Be?

'A sparrow … When I was little my mother raised one from its birth. We called it Scooter. It would follow me around the house all the time. I thought I was teaching it to fly by holding it and spinning round in big circles. Then one day it packed its bags and flew the coop. Till this day, when I see sparrows, I think of Scooter.'

Marc, Detroit

The Turkey

Earth

> We have given our plume wands human form
> With the massed cloud wing
> Of the one who is our grandfather,
> The male turkey,
> With the eagle's thin cloud wings
> And the massed cloud tails.
> **From a Zuni Indian prayer for rain**

CHARACTERISTICS

Turkeys were introduced to the rest of the world from the sixteenth century onwards, from Mexico, where the Indians had domesticated them. Fossil evidence in the Americas of the birds dates back 40 million years, so their origins are quite plainly in this region. The birds spread through the rest of the world because, in 1511, the king of Spain made an order that every Spanish ship returning from the New World should bring back five male and five female turkeys, and soon the bird was a common sight throughout Europe.

Turkeys are brilliantly coloured birds, with various feather patterns and markings, and they also possess a distinctive red wattle under their bills. They prefer to live in open woodland or mixed forests, and although they are strong fliers, reaching up to 50 miles per hour on short flights, they don't tend to fly very far and do not migrate. They also nest on the ground, although they will roost in treetops in quite large numbers.

When the Pilgrim Fathers landed in America, turkeys were so common that they could be bought for a couple of cents a pound, although the cutting back of the woods and the vast culling of the birds means that they no longer run wild in New England.

Although the Bald Eagle was chosen as the National Bird of the USA, Benjamin Franklin for one was far more enthusiastic about the turkey. He suggested that the eagle was a bird of 'bad moral character' and that the turkey was a courageous bird, who would have no compunction in attacking any redcoat which entered the bird's barnyard!

A Weather Bird

The turkey become restless before storms, and as such is a good indicator of harsh weather to come.

Because the turkey in America comes from the mountains, which are also home to the rain clouds, in Native American belief the bird was closely associated with rain. Hence, the feathers were often used to carry messages between man and the Gods; turkey feathers are left along certain trails in order to indicate where the rain was desired to fall.

The Jewelled Fowl of the Native Americans

To the Toltecs, the turkey was the 'jewelled fowl', because of its sparkling colours, and was the ultimate food for festivals and ritual occasions. This is still the custom today in the USA and the UK, where it usually takes pride of place at Thanksgiving and Christmas meals. Among the Native Americans, however, nothing of the turkey would be wasted; after it had been eaten, the feathers would be used as ornamentation, and the bones used to make musical instruments or whistles.

Turkeys can have heart attacks.

Not surprisingly given its origins, the turkey is an important bird to Native Americans. One particular tribe, the Creek, have a special dance in honour of the turkey at the Fire Festival that marks their New Year.

The turkey symbolizes the fertility of both the male and the female, possibly because of the bird's polygamous habits, but it may also be because the male's wattles swell during courtship or when in an argument with another male. The hen is also one of the most fertile of birds. The hen birds have a habit of choosing their male and then attracting his attention by lying down in front of him. Turkeys also tend to have collective nests for their eggs.

Because it is an important bird to Native Americans, and also because it lives close to the ground, thereby being the polar opposite of the high-flying eagle, the turkey is sometimes called the Earth Eagle and is representative of the Earth Mother.

A Sacred Bird

Most Pueblo Indians would never eat turkeys, but kept flocks of the birds for their feathers alone, so it is highly likely that the turkey was considered to be sacred. However, there is some dispute about this! When Coronado, a Spaniard, sent soldiers to the Pueblo people in Acoma, he wrote:

> Wee found heere Guinea Cockes but few. The Indians tell me in all these seven cities they eate them not, but that they keep them only for their feathers; I believe them not, for they are excellent good, and greater than those of Mexico.

It seems that the birds would have had far more value as providers of feathers for prayer sticks and the like than they would have had as mere meat, because of course the feathers would always grow back again.

In Pueblo funeral rites, whole turkeys would sometimes be buried along with the corpse, and occasionally the bones are still found. Prayer sticks decorated in a specific way with turkey feathers would be given to the families of the deceased.

The Wagtail

Earth

> A baby watched a ford, whereto
> A wagtail came for drinking;
> A blaring bull went wading through;
> The wagtail showed no shrinking.
> **Thomas Hardy,** *Wagtail And Baby*

CHARACTERISTICS

Wagtails are small, slim, elegant little birds, who tend to feed close to the ground, and are immediately identifiable because, as their name suggests, their tales wag up and down continually when they're on the ground. They have an undulating flight pattern, and call while on the wing.

There are many species, including: the yellow wagtail, the pied wagtail and the grey wagtail. Wagtails like to live by water, along streams amid mountains or by marshy inland lakes. They nest in trees and shrubs, and are sometimes happy to occupy the abandoned nests of other birds.

JAPAN

The wagtail has an important part to play in Japanese tales of the beginning of the world. Apparently the first man and woman, Izanagi and Izanami, learned about how to procreate from the little bird. As the serpent revealed 'hidden knowledge' to Adam and Eve, the wagtail played a similar part in Japanese myth. Accordingly, the bird holds sacred status there.

The Ainu people worship the wagtail as being responsible for the Earth's creation. They have a story that relates how the wagtail trampled down the swampy, slushy earth into mud which would be habitable by mankind. Sent down by Kamui, who had invented the world, the little wagtail was aghast at first when he realized what a muddy mess everything was. However, undaunted, he set to work to trample the swampy mud and dry the earth by stamping on it with his feet and fluttering it with his wings.

FRANCE

There's a French legend that relates how the wagtail initially had no tail at all. When he was asked to go to the wedding of the lark, in desperation he asked to borrow the tail of the wren. He was so pleased with the way the tail looked that he conveniently forgot to return it, and is said to keep on wagging it to reassure himself that it's still actually there. The wren, of course, seems to have very little tail to speak of!

Greece

The Greeks held the wagtail to by a symbol of love, and they also linked it to magical potions, primarily love potions.

Celtic Lore

Merlin, the seer and magician and sometime educator of the young King Arthur, asked all the birds to help him build a new water course. The wagtail was reluctant to get his feet wet, and so refused to help in the task. Merlin's punishment was to change the colour of the wagtail's feet, previously white, to black.

In Ireland, the pied wagtail is said to have a drop of the devil's blood mixed in with its own. This could simply be because of its colour, since pied plumage often seems to carry diabolical connotations – the magpie and the stone chat share this dubious privilege!

What Bird Would You Be?

'It might seem a strange choice but I'd probably go for a wagtail ... they're cute and comical but there's something of a hidden mystery about them, something indefinable.'
Michael, Germany

The Wren

Earth

> He who hurts the little wren
> Shall never be belov'd by men.
> **William Blake,** *Auguries of Innocence*

> a single wren
> Which one day sang so sweetly in the nave
> Of the old Church that, though from recent showers
> The earth was comfortless …
> … yet still
> So sweetly mid the gloom the invisible bird
> Sang to itself that there I could have made
> My dwelling place, and I lived forever there,
> To hear such music.
> **William Wordsworth,** *The Prelude,* book 2

Characteristics

In the USA the bird is known as the Winter Wren; in Europe simply as the Wren. Wrens have a wide range across North America, Europe and Asia.

The wren is tiny; it is usually less than four inches (10 cm) long. The bird is one of the smallest in the UK and used to feature on what was also the country's smallest coin, the farthing. When seen from behind and relatively close up, the wren has a reddish appearance and it is this which has given it a reputation of being one of the birds responsible for bringing fire to Mankind.

Wrens tend to nest fairly close to the ground in dense, shrubby undergrowth; this can make them easy prey for cats. They're quite well camouflaged, with their rather plain brown markings, but they are voluble and often their nesting places are revealed either by their harsh chatterings and scoldings or by their fluent, melodic singing – in fact their singing is so loud you wonder how such a small bird can make such a big noise!

The tiny wren sings all year long; their song is not simply part of their mating ritual, since the birds also use sound to alert one another to each other's presence. Between pairs, wrens sing duets; if you have wrens around and you listen, you'll start to notice the 'question and answer' responses from pairs of birds chattering or singing to one another.

The nest of the wren is large and bulky, with a domed roof and a side entrance. The nest is constructed entirely by the male, who seems to be terribly keen on home improvements; he'll often build up to half a dozen nests within his territory, and once a likely-looking female wren has been attracted, she'll choose her favourite spot for the pair to settle in and raise their young. The female will also add 'the woman's touch' by lining the nest and generally making it fit for occupancy – raising it from bachelor pad status to a family home.

The King of the Birds

The belief that the wren is the king of all the birds, despite its diminutive size and modest demeanour, is accepted in ancient traditions in the UK, France (where it's called Le Roitelet, and 'Poulet de Dieu' in Normandy), Spain, Germany, Italy and Scandinavia, where the name for the bird actually means 'king' – as does the name in both Greek and Latin. This belief is shared by some Native American tribes too, including the Ojibwas.

There's a popular legend as to how the wren got this status. The eagle challenged all the birds to a race, to determine who should be the king. But the wren was so small that the eagle didn't even bother asking him to participate. The wren, far from being insulted, thought that this was quite funny, and accordingly had a think about what to do …

The eagle, of course, flew faster and higher than all the other birds, and as he reached the summit of his performance he shouted out, 'I'm the King! I'm the King of all the Birds!'

However, just as he was about to begin the descent, the wren popped out from underneath the magnificent ruff of feathers around the eagle's neck, and flew just that little bit higher, thus using intellect and lateral thinking over physical strength and size. As a consequence of the wren's victory, the angry eagle flew up into the air with the wren and dropped him from some great height; the wren was fine, but ever since then he has gone about with only half a tail, which was said to have been damaged in the fall.

This explains why the wren is not able to fly terribly high. Another version of the story has a similar contest to see who should be king, except

> The fox is the most cunning beast in the world, barring the wren.
> *Proverb*

this time the bird who flies lowest will be the winner. Once again the wren is triumphant, since it is small enough to be able to fly down a mouse hole!

The real 'king' of the birds is said to be the gold-crested wren, barely an ounce in weight, who is reputed to travel about tucked into the fluffy feathers between the back wings of an owl.

The Sacred Bird of the Druids

As well as its royal status, the wren is also held to be sacred in many belief systems, and, in particular, it is one of the birds revered by the Druids. Indeed, the Irish word for wren is 'drui', which is interpreted as 'the druid among birds'. Similarly, 'drwy' has the same meaning in Welsh.

The wren plays a large role in stories of mystery and magic from ancient pre-Christian times, and was said in Irish tradition to be a 'Magus Avium', which is to say a sorcerer amongst birds. In Celtic auguries, the wren has great significance.

The wren and the robin have always been closely associated in the British Isles, with the pair either being supposed to be married or related in some way. It is true that they occupy similar habitats.

The Bird of Witches

Following in the theme of the magical powers that are ascribed to the wren, it is also considered to be a bird of witches. The feather of a wren can protect against magical spells and sorcery so is a useful item to have around the house.

In Christianity

Possibly as a way of adopting some of the existing belief systems, in Europe, the incoming Christians took the wren to be the bird of the Virgin Mary; in Scotland it was called 'the Lady of Heaven's Hen':

Then said the wren
I am called the hen
Of Our Lady most cumly;
Then of her Sun
My notes shall run
For the Love of that Lady.
From *The Armonye of Birds, 1555*

THE HUNTING OF THE WREN

Now, we come to a very great paradox. Everywhere, it was considered that one of the most unlucky things to do was to kill a wren. In England, to do so would make the killer break his own bones; in Scotland, such an act would cause the cows to give bloody milk.

However, this taboo on the killing of the wren was lifted just once a year. Then, all the rules concerning the protection of this tiny bird were overthrown, and it was customary to hunt it down, a practice that was accompanied by a great deal of ritual.

The reason for this has been obscured in the mists of time, but since the wren had been one of the sacred birds of the Druids, and the ritual slaughter would take place on one of the new Christian saint's days – St Stephen's Day on December 26th, it could be supposed that the killing of the wren was symbolic of the ousting of the old pagan beliefs. In her intriguing and comprehensive book, *Hunting the Wren*, Elizabeth Atwood explains the allegation that the wren had 'a drop of the devil's blood in it' in order for its executioners to justify such an inhumane act.

There's another legend that supposedly justifies the wren hunt, too. Apparently, the first Christian martyr, St Stephen, was about to make good his escape from prison when a wren alerted the guard by flying in his face. This resulted in Stephen's death. And in Ireland, it was supposed that the bird was killed because it was a witch.

Whatever the reasons, the ritual took place all over the UK, the Isle of Man, and in some parts of France.

Once the bird was killed, it would be placed either in a beautifully decorated circular bower, or, in Wales, in a little 'wren house', which was a beautifully made wooden box, just like a small house, with doors and windows, decorated with ribbons and streamers. The dead bird in its elaborate coffin would be carried from place to place, often by four men who would make a pretence of struggling under the weight of their burden.

It could also be that the killing of the wren was symbolic of the ending of Winter and the making way for the coming of the Spring, although on the Isle of Man the wren was hunted for its feathers, which were regarded as charms against shipwrecks. Legend has it that the bird could turn itself into a Siren-like creature, who would lure sailors to watery graves, so the feather would act as a talisman against such a happening.

EGYPT

There's a very odd little story concerning the wren in Ancient Egypt. Pliny, the Roman naturalist, reported that the wren acted as a toothpick for crocodiles in this country. The story had first been related by Herodotus in the fifth century BC, and it's likely that the bird who carried out this task would not have been the wren at all. However, due to a copying error the wren has been given the credit for this unusual occupation!

GREECE

The Greeks thought it was unlucky to see a wren at a wedding because the bird makes several nests. As usual, Aristotle has a remark to make about it:

> The wren inhabits shrubberies and holes and cannot easily be caught. Now it is shy and of feeble habit, but endowed with great ability of getting food and knowledge of its craft.

It's also worth bearing in mind that the wren gets its genus name from the Greek word 'Troglodytes', meaning 'cave dweller'.

NATIVE AMERICAN LORE

To the Pawnee Indians the wren is 'the laughing bird' or 'the happy bird'. (It may be purely coincidental that the Breton word for the wren also translates as 'happy'.) The bird is loved because it greets the sun with the loudest song despite the fact that it is such a small bird.

The Cherokee thought that the wren got up early in the morning to report the latest news to the Council of the Birds, including telling them about the sex of any new babies which had been born.

HOW THE WREN GOT ITS FEATHERS

Once upon a time, the wren, seeing that mankind didn't know about the gift of fire, decided that she would find some in Heaven, and bring it back to Earth.

When she was struggling through the little hole between the two worlds, carrying the precious burden of a few flames, the little wren scorched herself and lost quite a few of her feathers. All the other birds decided to give a feather each to help compensate for the loss, which had also left the wren with a tiny flash of red. However, the owl refused to help out; this is why the owl only appears at night, being too ashamed to face the other birds during the day.

What Bird Would You Be?

Caroline and Alan are married to one another; it must be a good match, because each chose the wren without the other knowing!

'I can't decide between two extremes ... a Buzzard and a Wren. I'll go for a Wren, just looking at one now out of the window, amazing little things.'
Caroline, UK

'That's pretty tricky ... There are so many different birds, some of which have been rightly or wrongly endowed with human characters making some birds that I like tricky to choose. I think I would actually like to be a bird that hasn't been discovered yet ... But if I have to pick one then I think the Wren, because if I am a Wren then there are a lot of us, but we are good at going unnoticed.'
Alan, UK

The Blackbird

Water

> O blackbird! Sing me something well;
> While all the neighbours shoot thee round,
> I keep smooth plats of fruitful ground
> Where thou mayst warble, eat and dwell.
>
> The espaliers and standards all
> Are thine; the range of lawn and park;
> The unnetted black-hearts ripen dark
> All thine, against the garden wall.
> **Alfred, Lord Tennyson,** *The Blackbird*

Characteristics

Possibly the first thing you'll notice about the blackbird is its lovely song; in the eighteenth century, Joseph Addison wrote in the *Spectator*

> I value my garden more for being full of blackbirds than of cherries, and very frankly give them fruit for their songs.

The blackbird tends to perch on a high vantage point and will sing really sweetly and often quite loudly; if there's a sudden threat or the blackbird feels there's danger around, however, he will change his tune to a one-note call, repeated over and over. The blackbird's song is especially prevalent at twilight. Blackbirds are also great mimics and can imitate car alarms and the like quite effectively!

> Cherries are bitter to the glutted blackbird.
> *Proverb*

As Joseph Addison observed in the quote above, blackbirds do like to eat fruit and berries and are one of the more friendly garden birds. They're quite territorial, too, and part of their song is used to stake a claim on their 'patch'.

Blackbirds in the USA were named because they look like their European counterpart. However, the American birds are a different species altogether.

Sing A Song of Sixpence ...

The old nursery rhyme refers to a custom at royal banquets in Europe of placing blackbirds under a baked pie crust; when the pie was cut into, the birds would fly away, creating a memorable spectacle for the guests. China pie funnels are still made in the shape of blackbirds today in memory of this tradition.

Celtic Lore

In *The Druid Animal Oracle*, Philip and Stephanie Carr-Gomm tell us that the blackbird is one of the five sacred animal totems and that the bird holds as much meaning for latter-day Druids as it did for their more ancient counterparts. The blackbird's very name in Gaelic, Druid Dubh, translates as 'Black

Druid'. In the tradition of birds as messengers, the bird is seen as a caller to the gateway between the two worlds, and invites us into the Otherworld, or the parallel reality.

ITALY

There are many stories describing how black-coloured birds got their colour, since it used to be believed that most of them started out being white and received their black colouring as some sort of punishment. This isn't just an Italian anomaly, but there's a lovely story from that country about how the blackbird got its colour. Apparently, the blackbird climbed up the chimney in order to try to keep warm in the middle of winter. Of course, when the weather got warmer and the blackbird emerged, he was as black as soot. The cold spell at the end of January/beginning of February in some parts of Italy is still called the 'Blackbird Days'.

THE PATIENCE OF A SAINT

There's a fable about an Irish saint, St Kevin, who was apparently praying in a temple, with one hand outstretched to the sky. Suddenly, a blackbird egg fell into his hand, and so Kevin simply stayed in what must have been a pretty uncomfortable position until the bird hatched out!

This story equates with a tale about Buddha. A blackbird laid an egg on his head, and Buddha simply went into a deep meditation until the chick had hatched.

THE WHITE BLACKBIRD

The following is a tale from the Basque region of Spain.

Once, there was a king, who had three sons. Unfortunately for the King, he was blind, but one day he was excited to hear about a white blackbird, which was said to have the power of restoring sight.

The eldest son offered to go and find the bird, and although the King was worried about the potentially dangerous journey and tried to persuade his son (whom we'll call Jack) that he'd rather be blind than put his boy in any danger, Jack decided he'd go off on the quest in any case. So he saddled up a horse, took a large amount of money, and went on his way.

One night Jack stopped at an inn, where three incredibly beautiful girls asked him if he'd like to join them for a game of cards. At first our hero declined the offer, but eventually the lure of the gorgeous girls was too much to resist. Unfortunately, he's not a great card player, and within a short space of time he has lost all his money, and his horse, and has also run up other debts which he can't honour; as a result, Jack ends up in prison.

Meanwhile, back at the castle, the family is wondering what could have happened to their eldest son. The second son – Tom – decides that he'd better go and see, and perhaps he'll find white blackbird at the same time. So, with a saddled horse and a bag full of money, off he goes. In the great tradition of fairy tales, the fate of Jack befalls Tom, too, and now they're both in prison together.

Meanwhile, back at the castle, you can imagine there's some cause for consternation about the non-return of either of the sons. There's one boy left, remember, and Joe (that's his name) decides that it really is up to him to try to find out what might have happened to his two brothers and, of course, search for the white blackbird. The King is by now very frightened and loath to see the boy go, but Joe is insistent. So his father gives him the very best horse, a huge sack of gold, even a loan of his crown, and off Joe goes.

Predictably enough, eventually Joe stumbles into the inn, where the three young ladies again ask the third brother to join them for a game of cards. Joe, however, has his eye on the end game – the discovery of the whereabouts of his brothers and the white blackbird that could restore the sight of his much-loved father; he refuses all the entreaties of the young ladies and goes on his way early the next morning.

As chance would have it, the next morning is the day his brothers are to be executed, although all Joe sees is two men being led to their deaths. Enquiring why the executions must take place and discovering that it's because of gambling debts, Joe pays off the money, although as far as he's concerned the two men are total strangers. Joe also pays off the debts of another man who has been recently executed in order that his family will not have to live in shame.

Soon Joe is at what he believes to be the end of the journey – the palace of the King who has the white blackbird.

Although he asks very nicely if he might have a loan of the bird, in the true tradition of fairy tales, things aren't that easy. The King asks Joe to fetch him the daughter of a lord, who lives quite a long way away. With a sigh, off goes Joe, and at the door of the palace where the lovely girl lives, he is met by a fox. The fox offers to look after his horse while Joe fetches the girl, and also advises that the girl should put on one of the beautiful dresses she owns, since usually she wears old clothes and doesn't always look her best.

Accordingly, Joe does as he's told. With one of her beautiful but neglected gowns on, the girl looks amazing, and starts to sing, bringing all the courtiers and attendants running to see what's the matter. Her father, is infuriated that someone has 'woken up' his daughter in this way, and poor Joe has to explain hastily that he has the very sincerest of intentions, and only desires to find the white blackbird and thus restore the sight of his father. As chance would have it, the girl's father asks Joe to carry out a task for him, too. He is to go to yet another fine house again miles and miles away, and fetch a horse; once the horse is the property of the lord, then Joe can take the girl in exchange for the white blackbird.

Joe sets out once more and eventually finds the house of the man with the incredible horse. And lo and behold, as he's on the doorstep the fox appears again and advises that the boy should saddle up the horse with an incredibly ornate saddle, which he'll find hanging in the stable; this will enhance the appearance of the steed. The fox also warns that there will be trouble when this happens, because the horse will be so pleased with himself that he'll start to make a terrible racket and everyone will come running to see what the matter is.

Sure enough, this happens, and Joe feels that he's in dire danger, but the appearance of his crown saves the day. The owner is impressed by the thought of royalty in his house, and Joe is given possession of the magnificent horse, and gallops as fast as he can back to the lord with the lovely daughter. When the girl sees the horse, however, she can't resist jumping on to its back, and she and Joe escape together to the abode of the king with the white blackbird.

When they get there, they don't have to say or do anything. The blackbird flies out of a window and settles on the hand of the girl, so our couple are once again on their journey.

Back home, however, the two eldest sons, freed from a certain death by the intervention of the youngest son, obviously have not learned any lessons. They have told their father all sorts of untruths and slanderous tales about how Joe simply ran away with the best horse, the money and the crown.

So when Joe arrives back, crown intact, cash intact, with an additional incredible horse and the most beautiful and magnificently dressed girl any of them have ever seen, and not forgetting the white blackbird, of course, the brothers decide that the only thing they can do is to throw poor Joe down the well, and take the riches, the horse, the girl and the magical blackbird for themselves.

THE SECRET LANGUAGE OF BIRDS

However, the horse runs away with the girl on his back, and the blackbird, not wanting any part of this, flies away with them. Luckily, once again our friend the fox comes to the rescue. He lowers his tail into the well, enabling Joe to climb out and run to his father's house to explain what has happened.

The ending, of course, is that Joe gets the girl and the horse, and no doubt eventually the kingdom. The magical white blackbird restores the sight of the King, who is able now to see for himself what has happened, and the two elder sons are exiled into the desert, where, as the legend has it, 'if they had lived well, they would have died well'.

What Bird Would You Be?

'A blackbird ... When I was a teenager I had a Welsh/Arab mare called Solitaire. I loved her dearly and spent all my free time exploring the countryside with her. One of our favourite rides involved crossing the River Tees and having a good gallop along a forest trail on the other side. I have strong memories of summer evenings; Solly and I ambling through the country lanes on the way home from that ride listening to blackbirds singing. Every time I hear a blackbird now it takes me back to those summer evenings.'

Penny, UK

The Crow

Water

> My roost is the creaking gibbet's beam,
> Where the murderers bones swing bleaching;
> Where the chattering chain rings back again
> To the night-wind's desolate screeching.

To and fro, as the fierce gusts blow,
Merrily rocked am I;
And I note with delight the traveller's fright
As he cowers and hastens by.
Eliza Cook, *The Song of the Carrion Crow*

Although the crow and the raven, of the Corvid family, have a particularly close connection, and in some instances can be treated as the same bird, nevertheless I feel there are enough marked differences to give them both separate attention, which is what they deserve.

CHARACTERISTICS

Crows are present throughout almost the entire world. They are absent from very few places, although New Zealand is one of the few countries where there are no crows to be found.

Crows have a very varied appetite and will eat almost anything they can find. It's this adaptability that is one of the contributory factors to the survival of the bird. In addition, the crow can co-exist quite happily in places where mankind is prevalent. Crows can in fact get to be very fond of individual human beings, and can make good if unlikely pets.

The Corvids are believed to be the most intelligent of birds. They have their own language and the meaning of their calls and cries are apparent to anyone who has the opportunity to listen to them; there are warning cries, calls of alarm, and murmurs of endearment. Crows can also be taught to speak human words, although there are other birds, such as the parrot, which have more aptitude for this.

As we've mentioned, the crow and the raven are often confused with one another. The crow is the smaller bird, however, by several inches. In France, it's said that bad ravens make priests, whereas bad crows make nuns – so differentiation is simple!

Bird of Language

Because of the crow's skill with vocalizations, it's considered to be a songbird, although it's rarely if at all heard actually singing. In his book *The Human Nature of Birds*, Theodore Xenophon Barber tells us that researchers have managed to distinguish 300 different kinds of crow calls, and that crows seem to have their own form of regional dialects:

> Many 'linguistic' complexities have already been found in these crow calls: There are local dialects among crows in the United States; isolated groups of crows do not understand the calls of 'mainstream' crows, and crows on both sides of the Atlantic understand some but not all of each other's calls.

For this skill, perhaps, the crow has proved a popular bird in augury; indeed, there was a Tibetan method of divining messages from the Gods that relied exclusively on the calls of the crow.

Myth, Folklore and Magic

The poem at the beginning of this section is about the Carrion Crow; its funereal appearance, and the fact that, according to Dr Samuel Johnson, it 'feeds on the carcasses of beasts', have given it a spooky reputation. As if this wasn't bad enough, Malphas, who is effectively considered to be the Grand President of Hell, takes on the form of a crow, and will deceive most people who make sacrifices to him. The crow is seen as a symbol of death, darkness and cold; contrary to its habits the bird is also perceived to be unsociable.

Despite its association with matters dark, the crow has always been perceived as a magical bird, with certain arcane powers. Crows can tell us what's happening just by the way they fly. And fairies are apparently able to take on the shape of the crow, which they will do if they want to get up to no good.

However, there's an instance of the crow trying to do someone a favour and being repaid very poorly. The Argus Pheasant had asked the crow to paint its plumage, which the crow did, and a very good job he did too. He then asked the pheasant to return the favour. However, the careless pheasant simply spilled a bottle of ink over the crow, and didn't even stay around to say sorry.

A Weather Bird

Weather prediction is just one of the magical skills associated with the crow. Its croaking portends rain, as this old English rhyme shows:

Crow on the fence
Rain will go hence
Crow on the ground
Rain will come down.

Another sign of rain being on the way is if crows are seen walking into water in the evening!

Europe

Starting with the positive, in Czech lands the crow is said to bring babies, in the same way as the stork. And in France, the city of Lyons, named after the Celtic God Lugh, carries a crow on its coat of arms.

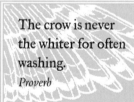

The crow is never the whiter for often washing.
Proverb

However, it was common knowledge that during the Summer months, when the crow was moulting, it was visiting the Devil in Hell, because the bird seems to disappear at that time. In fact, the moulting tends to make the bird a little depressed and subdued, so it's less voluble and therefore less noticeable at this time. But we can never know for sure ...

Rome

In ancient Rome, one of the key jobs of a bridesmaid was to scare the crows away from the scene of the wedding. It was believed that two crows would be a lucky sign, but that one on its own could spell disaster for the marriage, so best to be safe, just in case. Crows were believed to live to be a very great age, and 'to live the life of two crows' meant just this.

GREECE

There's a deal of ambivalence with the crow in Ancient Greece, although there's no change in the imagery of the crow as a bird of ill omen. To 'go to the crows' meant to the average Greek the equivalent of 'go to the Devil'. It was believed that, once upon a time, crows were white; there are several tales of the bird being turned black as part of a punishment.

For a crow to land on a roof was a sure sign that one of the inhabitants would die; Athena apparently ensured that crows never landed on the roof of the Acropolis.

However, as a bird of augury, it was the crow who announced to Apollo the birth of Hermes as the twelfth Olympian, i.e. the twelfth God. Alexander the Great seems to have crows on his side, too; they led him across the desert to a temple, where the oracle told Alexander that he had achieved God-like status. And let's not forget that the crow was one of the birds of Apollo!

CELTIC LORE

Similar to the Roman belief, in Celtic lands one crow was held to be an unlucky sight, whereas two meant the opposite. The crow is closely associated with Celtic creation myths, and Bran, whose name was synonymous with that of the Crow God, and whose legend you can read about in the section on the Raven (page 60), had a close association with the crow too, which, according to Robert Graves in *The White Goddess*, was 'his oracular bird'.

The crow was also seen as a healing bird, a bird of medicine, as well as being associated with war and battle; again, the latter could be because the carrion crow would be seen at the aftermath of battle scenes. The Morrigan, who in Celtic legend was the 'phantom queen' or 'the great mother', has a Gaelic name, 'An Badb Cath', which means 'The Battle Crow'.

NATIVE AMERICAN LORE

In many tales from the Indian tribes, both the crow and the raven take on roles as creators of the world. The crow is a skilled shape-shifter, like his larger cousin the raven, and he holds the key to several of the sacred tribal laws. Additionally, the crow is held in reverence as having brought the first grains and seeds to mankind from the Gods:

> … carrying a grain of corn in one ear and a bean in the other from the field of the great God, Cautantouwit in Sowwaniu, the Southwest, the happy Spirit-World where dwelt the Gods and souls of the great and good …

thereby enabling agricultural skills. This means that the Indians don't seem to mind so much if the crows help themselves to a little bit of young corn or other crops.

However, the attachment of the crow to death and doom has its place in Native American belief, too; the Navajo believed that wicked members of their tribe would become crows after they died. And the early Christian missionaries were nicknamed 'crows' because of their black garments.

> Scottish herdsmen used to make offerings to the eagle and to the hooded crow, asking them to spare their flocks.

THE GHOST DANCE

For the Plains Indians, the Ghost Dance was a preparation for the arrival of a supernatural being, a saviour who would change things back to how they were before the Europeans came. The central bird in the dance and the ceremony was the crow, as being a direct messenger from the Spirit World.

THE FAR EAST

Again, the crow is seen as a bird of ill-omen, but in Shinto, the crow is a holy bird, and is one of the messengers of the Gods. They are often kept at temples.

Yata-Garasu is the three-legged crow that was sent by the Goddess Ameratsu to help Emperor Jimmu in battle. Yata-Garasu was the bird belonging to this Goddess. This three-legged symbol associates the crow with the Sun, in this instance, and the three powers of heaven, earth and man. The number 3 is also the number of light and goodness, with the most extreme example of this being the Sun: the Emperor of Japan was sent a crow by the emissary of the Sun-Goddess to help his armies.

THE SECRET LANGUAGE OF BIRDS

Similarly, in China, Confucius said in his Chinese history, entitled 'Ch'un Ch'iu', that 'the spirit of the Sun is a crow with three legs'. This association with the Sun would seem to indicate that the crow brought good fortune.

INDIA

In Hindu myth, the crow is the bird which the God Varuna rides upon. In Northern India, it was popularly supposed that the crow had one eye, which it would switch between sockets! There are also tales of crows being carried on board ships and then being sent out to find land; the sailors would follow the birds, a ruse which usually worked.

PITY THE POOR CROW!

It seems that the dark suspicions attached to the crow in many cultures are not easily thrown off; even a vet, who you might think would be more pragmatic, seems to have an aversion to this bird, as the following anecdote relates.

> I found an injured crow in a field close to my home recently. At first I couldn't see it, all I could hear were some rasping birdcalls, which sounded quite distressed for some reason. I tracked where the calls were coming from and suddenly saw the bird. It was quite ragged-looking and seemed unable to fly; at my approach it rose about a metre or so into the air before falling back. I went home and found a cat box, not quite sure what I was going to do but thinking I'd like to help in some way.
>
> The bird was quite easy to catch. I simply walked up to it and picked it up gently and put it in the box, no problem. Back home, my husband took the crow out of the box and handled the bird, spreading its wings, first the left one and then the right one. He said there didn't seem to be any sign of damage, but there were lots of feathers missing. It seemed like a nice enough bird.
>
> It was typically, a Sunday, so eventually I found an emergency vet.
>
> The vet's reaction was extraordinary. She put on thick rubber gloves before handling it, and then kept going on and on saying what

repulsive birds crows were; that I was wasting my time and hers; she pointed out that it had fleas; and I think she used the word 'disgusting' five times in all. I was quite pleased when the crow, either annoyed at being handled so roughly or cross about the insults being hurled around, suddenly gave a loud screech and twisted round and bit the vet good and hard on her wrist just where the gloves ended.

Clever bird. But what I couldn't understand was why the vet would assume any injured animal to be unworthy of any attention; surely it's the job of a vet to look after any injured creature which comes into her care?

The second thing I wondered was why she had had such a strong reaction against the bird; it was almost superstitious; what had the crow done to deserve all this? It might have had a few fleas, but it had not been responsible for, say, land mines or nuclear weapons; why did the vet give this bird such a hard time?

I must add that I brought the crow home and treated it kindly; within three days it had recovered from whatever was bothering it, and flew away, although I see her most days – her feathers are still raggedy so she's easy to spot.

Sarah, UK

The Duck

Water

> Four ducks on a pond,
> A grass bank beyond,
> A blue sky of spring,
> White clouds on the wing;
> What a little thing
> To remember for years –
> To remember with tears!
> **William Allingham,** *A Memory*

CHARACTERISTICS

There are some 200 different species of duck, spread right around the planet. Some ducks are freshwater birds; others belong in the sea. Although the different kinds of ducks have differing habits, most tend to be ground nesters; if possible the duck will choose an island surrounded by water as being the safest bet against predators.

All breeds of duck can swim and many of them can also dive; they'll dive for fish, sometimes to depths of up to 100 feet (30 metres). The duck has been successfully domesticated by man for thousands of years, used for its eggs, its meat and for its feathers.

One of the most abundant ducks is the eider duck. A large sea bird, its feathers are in incredible demand and are used as stuffing for the most luxurious quilts and pillows. Indeed, the word 'eiderdown' is pretty much interchangeable with 'quilt'. There are farmers who farm these ducks specifically for their lovely feathers, and there are strict rules pertaining to the birds' welfare.

DUCKS AND DRAKES

Although the title of this section is Ducks, it is worth remembering that the male of the species is the drake!

Surprisingly, for such a universally popular and well-loved bird, a favourite with small children and their parents who enjoy feeding these lovely birds with their somewhat comical aspect, the duck is associated with some very peculiar beliefs. One of the most mystifying is the superstition that to see a duck hanging upside down is symbolic of negative or evil influences, or bad spirits, which fall away from the bird as it dangles.

THE DUCK AND THE DEVIL

For such a pretty and innocuous bird to be associated with the Devil would seem to be a curious thing. However, a thirteenth-century pope, Gregory IX, preached a vehement denunciation of the practice of the worship of a particular demon, Asmodi, who appeared to his followers as a duck. After various shenanigans, such as dancing around Asmodi and kissing him, the revellers would throw themselves into an orgy and while away a few hours in satanic ecstasies, which I doubt would have involved much bread-throwing.

Not a Daffy Duck

The citizens of Freiburg in Germany raised a monument to a duck, which is said to have saved thousands of lives during the Second World War. Although there had been no official warning of an impending air raid, the bird had disturbed everyone enough for them to run for cover, as it took to the streets with frantic flapping and quacking.

WEATHER LORE

If migrating ducks arrived anywhere earlier than usual, this was said to presage harsh weather ahead. In addition, the breastbone of the duck used to be used in the same way as that of the goose or turkey, as a means of prognosticating the weather. Although the close examination of the breastbone at one time probably had other meanings, we are left with the belief that if the bone was a dark colour, then the winter would be severe, and mild if the bone was of a lighter colour the weather would be kinder.

There's another belief that if ducks seem to be quacking louder than usual, then they're telling us it's going to rain.

GREECE AND ROME

Following the theme of the duck as a reliable predictor of the weather, Athaneus described the skill thus:

Divers and ducks, both wild and tame, are a sign of rain when they dive, of wind when they flap their wings.

Unsurprisingly, given its diving abilities and proximity to water, the duck was the bird of Poseidon.

Similarly, in Rome, because of the duck's association with water and its ability to forecast bad winds, the duck was Neptune's favoured bird.

THE EGYPTIANS

The Egyptians kept domesticated ducks as far back as 5,000 years ago, and the bird was associated with Isis. The duck, skimming along the surface of the water prior to take-off, also symbolized the soul taking off and leaving the material world behind.

The pintail duck in particular was sacrificed to the Sun God, Ra, and the bird was used as a hieroglyphic.

> If ducks quack after 10 p.m. in Essex Falls in New Jersey, they are breaking the law.

THE FAR EAST

In China and Japan, a pair of Mandarin ducks represents a happy marriage, faithfulness and loyalty. As such, the image of the duck is used frequently in art, both in 'high' art and in more populist forms such as greeting cards, etc.

INDIA

The Brahminy Duck, as you might imagine from its name, was especially favoured by the priests, and abbots of the monasteries wear robes in the colour of the duck's feathers.

Celtic Lore

The duck was a symbol of the Sun. There are some archaeological finds, knows as the Urnfield Deposits, dating back to 1300 BC; these show the duck with the solar wheel symbol, and they also show the bird flanking a boat which carries this same sign.

The Goddess Sequana, of the River Seine in France, is depicted as a duck.

Latin America

The duck was seen as the alter ego of the human soul, and therefore the Olmec shaman, present in Ancient Mexican times, would wear a mask depicting the bird.

The Aztecs held that the ruddy duck was able to predict coming storms from the beating of their wings in the water.

Native American Lore

The duck is a rather special bird, since it seems to be as much at home on the water as it is in the air, and because of this Native Americans regard it as a sort of mediator between the sky and the water.

For the Pueblo, although all water birds are significant, the duck is the most important, ranking just below the eagle and the turkey. Duck feathers were valuable totem objects, particularly the beautiful iridescent blue-green wing feathers of the mallard – the colours indicate both the sky and the water.

The Zuni believe that the duck is the preferred form taken by a soul when it is returning home.

A Creation Myth

There's a Yokut story about the creation of the new world after the great flood, and the important part the duck had to play in it.

After the flood, the water had covered all the Earth, and there was no land at all. However, one day, out of the sky, came a huge eagle, with a crow taking a ride on its back. The eagle was tired of flying and they were looking for a place to land, when luckily they spotted a tree stump rising up above the surface of the endless water.

After a few days of eating fish that they were lucky enough to catch as they leaped out of the water, and feeling fortunate to at least have a perch, the birds started to wonder how they might possibly be able to improve upon their situation. A little bit of land would be a lovely thing, but there seemed to be no sign of the waters receding.

One day, however, the crow and the eagle were surprised to see a duck swimming around their perch. They noticed that every time the duck dived for a fish, it would come up with a little bit of mud in its beak.

This excited the crow. Being an intelligent bird, he realized the possibility that if the duck could bring up enough mud from the bottom of the sea, then perhaps they'd be able to form a small island at the very least. How to make the duck understand what they wanted was another matter, but the birds stumbled on the method of leaving fish by the stump for the duck, who was grateful for this. When the duck took the fish, the crow would carefully scrape the soil from his beak and add it to the small mound, which had started to build up.

The duck worked hard, bringing up mud from the bottom of the ocean, and before long the pile was starting to resemble land. Although the crow and the eagle had said they'd split the pile equally, and share everything, the acquisition of land turned the heads of both birds and the gathering of mud started to become a race. Eventually, as you might imagine, the waters started to subside and the piles of earth provided by the duck proved incredibly substantial; in fact, the mud belonging to the crow became the Coastal Mountain Range in California, and the eagle's portion became the Sierra Nevada Mountains. The duck, however, was quite happy to remain in the water …

What Bird Would You Be?

'Any bird, really, which is at home both in the water and in the air ... Probably a duck, because they are incredibly beautiful but understated, and also they get fed with more interesting things than many other birds!'
Vivien, New York

The Heron

Water

I have to tell you that today I woke up with the intention of telling you about the eagle, since the day's dawning was bright and I thought we'd be in the midst of sunny weather, entirely befitting this magnificent solar bird. But then there was a thunderstorm – pretty dramatic, and worrying since this house has twice been struck by lightning – and after the storm the skies clouded over. I went for a walk and found three heron feathers, almost exactly the same grey colour as the sky, so changed my plans.

The apparent luxury of going where you're led to or drawn to isn't such a difficult thing. Watch out for the signs, have the courage to follow them, and you'll find all will be well ...

The heron shares many traits with the crane and the stork; all three are similar wading birds.

CHARACTERISTICS

Birds from the heron family are among the oldest avian creatures on the planet, dating back some 100 million years. The family is widespread around the world.

The heron is a distinctive bird to spot in flight, having a kink in its neck (the heron has neck vertebrae of differing lengths). They're also a beautiful sight by a stream or river, standing stock-still on one leg as they watch for fish in the water. Herons rank high in the bird intelligence stakes too, and often use bait when fishing.

Herons have a particular kind of feather, unique to the species, which are called powder-down feathers. Unlike other feathers, the powder-down feathers are never shed; the feather continues to grow, but the edges start to fray. As the name might suggest, the fraying is the start of the breakdown of the feather which provides the fine powder used by the bird when it preens the other feathers. The powder is useful for removing dirt, such as oil. The heron lacks the oil glands present in other wading birds, but these specialized feathers do the job just as well.

Herons' nests are shallow and saucer-shaped, and are added to every year. Therefore they can get quite large.

> The Osprey is said to be able to lure fish to the surface by means of an oily substance contained in its body.

A STRANGE HABIT

Herons and cranes are both said to arrange the small fish they catch into the shape of a wheel, which is also a symbol of the sun. Robert Graves, in *The White Goddess*, reports having seen this for himself on the banks of a river in North Wales; it must have seemed a magical thing.

CELTIC LORE

The heron used to have an association with the moon, and on the Isle of Angus in the Hebrides the bird is said to grow either fatter or thinner following the waxing and waning of the moon, to such a dramatic extent that it was believed that the bird could not stand at the time of the new moon, since it was so weak. Conversely, it couldn't stand during the time of the full moon because it was so very chubby!

The Cailleach, the hag-like woman of Celtic myth, sometimes appeared as a heron.

Ancient Egypt

The heron – or at least the Purple Heron – could have been one of the birds that influenced the fable of the Benu, which seems to have transformed into the phoenix. The heron was a bird of the Sun, renewal and resurrection, and was associated with the Nile, since it was often seen by the river.

Cambodia

The heron is a popular bird in Cambodian myths and legends, and one of the superstitions concerned with it is that it presages fire if it lands on a house.

Hebrew Lore

The heron is one of the 'unclean' birds, as listed in Leviticus chapter 11. This means that the bird would have been held as sacred. The Hebrew name for the heron is 'Anaphah', which implies that the bird has a bad temper.

What Bird Would You Be?

'I used to get up 5.30 a.m. and practise my kung fu over looking the river. I loved the view, the peacefulness of the river and the energy it gave me. There was this one heron I named Mr Stalky, who I imagined to be an old kung fu master, he would be there almost every time I practised, watching me, as if saying, "Very wise student, you must spread your wings like me, be light as me but strong ... most of all be happy!"'
Linda, UK

What Bird Would You Be?

'Heron: Vigilance, quiet, patience, divine and occult wisdom, life, transformation – what you'd expect pretty much, but the stuff that really got me is that the heron is sacred to Poseidon, and was employed by Athena as a messenger. I can't say more here than that both these Gods played a *large* part in my upbringing, and that being back in Orkney late last year, was more than a little significant.'

Luke, Barcelona

The Lapwing

Water

> O lapwing, thou fliest around the heath,
> Nor seest the net that is spread beneath.
> Why dost thou not fly among the cornfields?
> They cannot spread nets where a harvest yields.
> **William Blake,** *The Blossom*

CHARACTERISTICS

There are 38 species of plover, of which family the lapwing is a member. Plovers are to be found in any part of the world that is free of ice. The name comes from the Latin 'pluvia', meaning 'rain'.

Members of the plover family like to live in mud close to rivers, or on marshy moorlands, and their eggs are laid in shallow saucers scooped out from the earth, lined with shells or pebbles. The nests are very well camouflaged.

The lapwing itself is a pretty bird, with green wing feathers and an attractive black plume on its head. It was once prevalent in farmer's fields, but the use of chemicals has forced this bird to the safer dwelling places mentioned previously. The lapwing was a favourite of King Solomon – as related in the Qur'an, as part of his army of birds, the lapwing brought Solomon news of the Queen of Sheba and was the trusted confidante of the king; there are further details about this in the first chapter.

The name of the lapwing has a lovely origin, coming from the Old English 'Hleapwince', which means 'leap with a waver in it' or, alternatively, 'run and wink', which quite accurately describes the seemingly erratic flight of this bird.

Lapwing chicks are able to be up and about very soon after they have hatched, being able to run immediately if there's danger. This precociousness gave rise to the phrase 'running about like a lapwing with a shell upon their heads', coined by Ben Jonson, and which is taken to mean someone who behaves rashly.

The lapwing plays a prominent part in bird lore, and has magical and mysterious qualities, as we shall see.

THE LAPWING'S CRY

The lapwing has a peculiarly haunting, ethereal cry; this call has resulted in a number of alternative names for the bird, such as the Peewit, the Weep and the Teewheep. The call has an eerie sobbing quality, and this has meant that the bird has become associated with sorrow for some. Combine this with the fact that this calling is likely to be heard in the lonely places inhabited by the bird and we can start to understand why some of these associations have been made.

GREECE

This very peculiar piece of information comes from Aristotle. I have tried to verify it but, unfortunately, no further evidence seems to be available; make of it what you will:

> When the crocodile yawns the plover flies in and cleans its teeth, and so obtains its food. The crocodile appreciates the service and does not harm it, and when it wants to come out it shakes its neck so that it doesn't get bitten.

If anyone has any evidence of this I'd be pleased to hear about it! It's very similar to the story about the wren acting as a toothpick for crocodiles, first posited by Pliny, which is related in that section …

The Greeks called the lapwing 'Polyplagktos', which translates as 'luring on deceitfully'; this refers to the bird's habit of calling potential predators away from the hidden nest.

THE BIBLE

In Leviticus, the lapwing is mentioned as an unclean bird, a bird of taboo, which was counted as sacred and therefore which should not be eaten. Other 'unclean' birds include the swan, the eagle, the ibis, the raven and the owl, so the lapwing is in distinguished company. Again, it is probably the bird's known ability to keep a secret that made it so special.

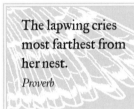

The lapwing cries most farthest from her nest.
Proverb

There's another legend, too, which says that plovers were the transmuted souls of Jews who had assisted at the Crucifixion. This gave rise to another folk name for the plover, which is sometimes called the Wandering Jew.

SWEDEN

There's a Swedish folk tale about the lapwing's cry. Apparently, the bird used to be one of the servants of the Virgin Mary, but stole a pair of her scissors one day. Caught out, the punishment for the unfortunate girl was to be turned into a bird with a forked wing, and to be made to fly around the fields confessing 'Tyvit! Tyvit!' meaning 'I stole them! I stole them!'

THE SEVEN WHISTLERS

Part of a folk tale that is so ancient that its origins are shrouded in mystery, the Seven Whistlers were an ominous phenomenon, who gave warnings to mankind from the Otherworld. The lapwing or plover is associated with the Seven Whistlers, and indeed there's an old Gaelic name for the bird, the

'Guilchaismeachd' or 'Wail of Warning'. The myth of the Seven Whistlers is not restricted to the Celtic tradition, but also appears in Portugal and other places. There are rumours of mining disasters that took place after the Whistlers had been heard, and in some parts of Britain legend has is that the phenomenon is caused by six whistlers in search of the seventh; once the seventh whistler is found, then the world will end.

KRISHNA AND THE LAPWING

The generosity of Lord Krishna is indicated in the following Indian folk tale.

The battle of Kurukshetra was just about to take place; the elephants were ready to march forward at the first blast from the conch shell, and the archers were poised ready to attack. The tension was almost unbearable; the banners were fluttering, and the army was ready and poised to fight to the death.

In the long silence before the battle commenced, suddenly the plaintive cry of a lapwing was heard. She had built her nest in a grassy hillock very close to where the battle was due to take place, and was terribly anxious about her eggs. Her plaintive 'Wheep! Wheep!' attracted the attention of Lord Krishna, who took pity on the little bird, and called a halt to the battle preparations.

He gently placed a huge elephant bell over the nest and the lapwing so that she would be protected from the din of the battle. She was safe for the 18 days that the fighting raged all around her, protected by the mercy of Krishna.

What Bird Would You Be?

'I'd be a flamingo ... they eat bacteria which turns them from a dull grey to a vivid pink, and a lot of them apparently spend much of their time in quite acidic water that could burn a human's skin ... quite strange but this appeals to my sense of adventure.'
Rhodri, UK

The Loon

Water

> If the rain goose flies to the hill
> Ye can gang to da heof when ye will;
> But when sho gangs to the sea,
> Ye maun draw yir boats an flie.
> **Rhyme from the Shetland Islands**

CHARACTERISTICS

Another name for the diver, particularly the Red-throated Diver, the name 'loon' comes from the Icelandic 'Lomr', meaning 'awkward person'. It's possible the bird was given this name because, although it is graceful in the water, once on land the bird is barely able to stand; they can shuffle a few paces at a time, but not with any ease. Also, the loon has particularly dense bones, another factor to take into consideration when explaining why the bird is better suited to water than land.

The call of the diver is particularly distinctive. It can be either an unearthly, human-sounding wail, or a cacophonous, spooky laugh. This vocalization has given rise to many of the myths associated with the bird.

As you might expect from its name, this bird can spend long periods underwater; because of this there was a suspicion that the divers were in contact with entities from the 'lower regions', i.e. Hades. Again, it is the bone density of the bird that helps it to stay under the water for long periods. Whereas most birds have hollow bones, the loon has solid ones. They can dive deeply, too; one was caught in a fisherman's net 240 feet (73 metres) below the surface of the water, and dives of up to five minutes have been observed, although this is unusual.

Although clumsy on land, once in the air the loon is an efficient flyer and can reach speeds of up to 60 miles per hour.

Sadly, the loon population isn't what it once was. Coastal oil spillages and acid rain have affected its numbers in recent years.

THE BIRD OF VISION

There's a story about the loon restoring sight, which crops up from Greenland through to Alaska and beyond. The story goes that the bird approached a blind boy, suggesting that the boy might be cured if he did as the bird told him. The bird told the boy to dive three times into a nearby lake; this the boy did, and indeed his sight was miraculously recovered.

This story is especially interesting since graves in Alaska have been discovered that contain early Eskimo skeletons, which have had artificial eyes inserted in the sockets; the skulls of divers accompany the skeletons, and the divers have also been given artificial eyes. Perhaps the eyes are to equip both bird and man with what they'll need to see their way through to the Otherworld.

THE WEATHER BIRD

As befits a bird that spends so much of its time in the water, another name for the loon is the 'Rain Goose', and it's supposed that if they were particularly noisy, then the weather would be likely to change.

In Norway, the cries are also meant to predict rain, or that someone is going to be drowned; and in the Faroe Islands the bird was meant to miaow like a cat before rain. If the weather was going to be fine, however, the bird would have a different call entirely – a sort of 'gaa gaa gaa' sound, apparently. If the bird is heard calling directly overhead, then it is believed to be escorting a spirit to the 'other side'.

NATIVE AMERICAN MYTHS

The Thomson Indians similarly believe that the call of the loon heralds rain, and will imitate the voice of the bird – which does indeed have a rather human quality – if rain is desired.

There's an Indian belief that both the loon and the crow were once men. Two men were out fishing, so the story goes, and the unsuccessful fisherman attacked the more successful one, whose nets were full, by hitting him on the head and cutting out his tongue before stealing the fish. The poor fisherman who'd been rendered dumb got to the shore but the only sound he could make was like that of the loon; so the Great Spirit transformed him into the bird, and his attacker was transformed into a crow.

There's also an Algonquin legend about a loon that chose to become a man. The tribe who were believed once to have been loons is called the Kwimiuk.

The Algonquin hero, Kuloskap, was chasing his enemy, a giant wizard called Winpe. A flock of loons appeared, and Kuloskap asked their leader, Kwimu, what they wanted. Kwimu answered that he would like to be Kuloskap's friend and servant. Therefore Kuloskap taught them their cry, which they were told to use whenever they needed help. Shortly thereafter, the birds were transformed into men.

SHAMANISM

Because loons were seen as messengers of men to the world of spirits, shaman in America and Siberia use rattles shaped like the bird.

What Bird Would You Be?

'I'd be a loon – I enjoy its song and the way they can stay underwater ... wonder if they sing underwater too?'
Dave, USA

The Nightingale

Water

Adieu! adieu! thy plaintive anthem fades
Past the near meadows, over the still stream,
Up the hill-side; and now 'tis buried deep
In the next valley glades:
Was it a vision, or a waking dream?
Fled is that music: Do I wake or sleep?
John Keats, *Ode to a Nightingale*

CHARACTERISTICS

The nightingale is a nondescript-looking bird – small and brown – and it is usually hidden in the shrubs or thickets it prefers for nesting. Despite its name it often sings during the daytime, but anyone who has ever heard this bird's song at night will never forget it. Its song is even more delicious in the dead of night than it is during the day, when it can be appreciated properly since it's likely to be the only bird song audible at that time. In the United Kingdom, its song can generally be heard between the months of April and June.

WHY THE LOVELY VOICE?

Apart from the fact that the nightingale sings alone and at night, and is therefore more audible than many of the lovely bird songs that you can hear during the day, there's an Italian story explaining how she got such a beautiful voice. When God was painting the birds, the shy nightingale, who had been hesitant to come forward, was overlooked and there was no paint left to colour her. So God gave her the most perfect voice as some comfort for her plain appearance.

The Latin name of the nightingale, 'Lucerna', comes from the word meaning 'light', and it takes that name because the bird signals the dawn of a new day with her song.

The Greeks and the Nightingale

The night-time song of the nightingale wasn't welcomed by everyone. A Greek poet commented,

> Leaf-loving nightingale, loquacious sex,
> Sleep quietly, I beg, and cease your din.

In the section about birds of Ancient Greece (page 180), you can read about the legend of Procne, who was transformed into a nightingale, so there's no need to repeat it here. The act of transformation came about because of a tragic series of events, and it's this ancient myth that seems to have given the nightingale the reputation of singing a lament. The actual song of the nightingale does not sound sad at all, however, it can seem a little plaintive – the bird does not sing in company, like other birds, but it always sings alone.

There's another Greek legend, which connects Zeus with the nightingale.

The Queen of Thebes had only one son, and she was insanely jealous of her sister-in-law, Niobe, who had several children. The Queen decided to redress the balance and murder some of Niobe's children, but unfortunately she killed her own child, Itylus, by mistake. Zeus decided to do the only possible thing in the circumstances and turned the murderous Queen into a nightingale, so that she could sing of her sorrow for ever more.

Something slightly more grisly, now: in a typical case of sympathetic magic, the Greeks believed that to eat the flesh of the nocturnal nightingale would ensure that a person would stay awake and watchful.

> According to the great violinist Paganini, Stradivarius made his celebrated violins from 'the wood of trees on which the nightingales sang'.

Arabian Lore

> The nightingale with drops of his heart's blood
> Had nourished the red rose, then came a wind,
> And catching at the boughs in envious mood,
> A hundred thorns about his heart entwined.
> **Hafiz**

The poem by Sufi poet Hafiz shows how the Arabs linked the nightingale, or rather the Persian equivalent, the bulbul, with the rose, and believed that the singing of the bird would cause the rose to flower. The bird would sing on until it simply died of joy.

Oscar Wilde used this legend as the basis of his story, 'The Nightingale and the Rose', here reinterpreted and abbreviated.

A young student, talking about the girl he loves, exclaims that she would love him if he could bring her one red rose. The romantic nightingale, overhearing the conversation, is convinced that the student understands the meaning of true love, and sets off to find him the red rose he needs. But all the rose bushes in the garden are the wrong colour, and the red rose tree has been blighted by frost. There's only one way that the nightingale will be able to obtain a red rose for the young student:

> 'If you want a red rose,' said the tree, 'you must build it out of music by moonlight, and stain it with your own heart's blood. You must sing to me with your breast against a thorn. All night long you must sing to me, and the thorn must pierce your heart, and your life-blood must flow into my veins, and become mine.'

The nightingale decides to make this sacrifice, in the name of what she supposes is true love:

> 'Love is better than life, and what is the heart of a bird compared to the heart of a man?'

But the student, lying near the tree where the nightingale is singing one last song for the tree, is ignorant.

> The student looked up from the grass, and listened, but he could not understand what the nightingale was saying to him, for he only knew the things that are written down in books.

In the morning, the nightingale is dead, but she has created the most perfect red rose, which the student finds and takes to the girl. In a very sad twist, which echoes the idea that the nightingale sings a tragic song, the petulant girl discards the rose, since

A nightingale cannot sing in a cage.
Proverb

'I am afraid it will not go with my dress ... and besides, everyone knows that jewels cost far more than flowers.'

The student, with the implication that he is as ignorant as he ever was, declares:

'What a silly thing love is! It is not half as useful as logic, and it is always telling one of things that are not going to happen, and making one believe things that are not true ... I shall go back to Philosophy and study Metaphysics.'

What Bird Would You Be?

'**I**'d be a nightingale, they seem to be such optimistic birds, heralding each new dawn with the most beautiful song.'
Landsley, UK

The Owl

Water

Under black yews that protect them
the owls perch in a row
like alien gods whose red eyes
glitter. They meditate.

Petrified, they will perch there till
the melancholy hour
when the slanting sun is ousted, and darkness settles down.

From their posture, the wise
learn to shun, in this world at least,
motion and commotion;

impassioned by passing shadows,
man will always be scourged
for trying to change his place.
Charles Baudelaire, *Owls*

Characteristics

There are some 137 species of owls around the world. Before we start looking
at some of the many and varied spooky superstitions that are attributable to
the owl, let's have a look at some of its general characteristics. Physically, owls
are incredible birds. Their huge eyes are one of their most noticeable features,
large and staring, which can account for between 1 and 5 per cent of the
creatures' total body weight. Its extraordinary vision is enhanced by the fact
that its neck will swivel an astonishing 270 degrees. Literally, the owl can see
behind itself!

What many people don't realize is that, as well as its incredibly keen
eyesight the owl has extremely acute hearing too. The ears are also not
arranged completely symmetrically on the owl's head; this improves the bird's
directional hearing even more.

Owls are notorious for their calls, which often pierce the stillness of the
night as a ghostly reminder that the darker hours are not the time of slum-
ber for everyone. They are also extremely efficient killers. Apparently, a Barn
Owl will kill ten times the amount of small rodents in one night than
would a cat, although in the past owls had been killed by farmers and the
like in the mistaken belief that the cat is the more effective hunter. Because
small rodents tend to congregate where humans live, since there tends to be
more scope for foraging, this means that the owl is usually not far from
human habitation either.

Owls prefer to live alone and usually only come together when they need
to breed; except for Barn Owls, owls will often separate once the baby owls,
the owlets, have learned to fly the nest. Most owls will not even bother to
build a nest, preferring instead to lay their eggs in the disused nest of another
bird, or perhaps in the secure hollow of a tree. This does mean, unfortunately,
that some eggs get broken, and some owlets will fall from the perch, but

generally if they are left on the ground the parent will be able to find it and will continue to feed the baby bird.

Most famously, perhaps, the owl is a nocturnal bird, preferring to do its hunting by night. There's always an exception to the rule, of course, and in this case it's the Short-eared Owl. This owl builds a proper nest, rather than laying its eggs in the crook of a tree, it is happy to hunt during the day as well as at night. The Snowy Owl has a unique ability to adjust its iris to take into account the prevalent light conditions, and will also hunt during daylight hours. They're clever birds, Snowy Owls; the babies learn to 'play dead' at an early age, and can both swim and run, both little-known facts about this particular owl!

Owls are of course known for their silent flight. Despite the large wingspan of the Barn Owl, it is able to fly without announcing its presence to its prey. This is because there is an adaptation along the front edge of the wings of the owl — a sort of fringe — which facilitates this noiseless flight.

Of the 137 species of owls on this planet, the tiniest is the Elf Owl, which is just five and a half inches (14 cm) long, and lives in Mexico and the American Southwest. This little owl lives mainly in forests and woods, and has an astonishingly loud voice for such a small creature — its call sounds a lot like the barks and yappings of puppies, apart from during the breeding season, when the birds can be heard singing beautiful duets together in the moonlight.

The word 'owl' comes from the Anglo-Saxon 'ule' and means 'to howl', although the Italian name for the owl comes from the Latin 'strix', which means 'witch', and the modern Italian version of this word is 'strega'. Pliny wrote about 'striges' being women who could transform themselves into birds of prey by using their magical powers. These women would allegedly fly around at night looking for infants to slaughter.

Just for the record, the traditional sound of the owl, the 'tu-whit, tu-whoo', is made by the Tawny Owl!

Symbols and Superstitions

Possibly more than any other bird, the owl is dogged by ominous beliefs and superstitions; as I was researching this chapter I started to feel rather sorry for the owl. Pliny called this creature the 'funeral owl and monster of the night'. But if we take into account the habits of the bird we can start to see where these old beliefs have come from.

Because it's a nocturnal bird, there has always been a sense of mystery surrounding the owl. Anything that happens in the dark speaks to us of the mysterious, the secretive, the occult or the hidden. The face of the owl, particularly the Barn Owl, with its dominant, staring, forward-facing eyes, also looks unusually human and full of intrigue.

Eagles, owls and hawks have a 'third eyelid', called a nictitating membrane, which enables them to look directly at the Sun.

The owl is, unsurprisingly, a symbol of the moon, the feminine principle, darkness, mystery, prophecy and wisdom. This latter characteristic is attributed to the bird because, of course, she sees the things that sleeping creatures do not. The owl is said to be unable to bear sunlight, being related instead to the light of the moon. Moonlight, of course, is light reflected from the sun, and acts as a mirror of the sun; hence we can understand why the owl has come to be associated with clairvoyant power, the power of 'second sight'. Also because of its association with the moon, the owl is said to be gifted with powers of fertility and seduction, because night-time is the time for such matters, of course.

The imagery of the owl as bringer of all things dark and ominous is found time and time again throughout literature. In *Macbeth*, the three witches include an 'owlet's wing' in their satanic concoction, their 'charm of powerful trouble'.

If you've ever seen a Barn Owl gliding past you at night, you can begin to understand the fears and superstitions surrounding this bird. They're like huge white ghosts, much bigger than you would imagine; they fly without a sound, and their otherworldly, spectral appearance is enough to cause goosebumps in the most stoic of observers!

You can easily imagine why the bird came to be associated with witchcraft, simply because of its appearance alone. Indeed, in the USA, the Barn Owl is often known as the 'ghost owl'. As well as their appearance, the calls of owls have an eery, haunting quality, especially since you're more likely to hear them at night than during the day, and the stillness and dark all adds to the shiver factor.

Because they often inhabit empty buildings, the owl became associated with actually causing the ruin and dereliction, which is of course both nonsensical and unfortunate for the owl, further promulgating the legend. However, it is easy to see how superstitions arise.

The Greeks

For the Ancient Greeks, the owl was, above all else, a symbol of wisdom. It was also believed that it was the bird of prophecy, and could bear tidings of either triumph or evil, according to the circumstances of its appearance.

The owl was the guardian of the Athenian Acropolis, and was sacred to Athena, the Goddess of Wisdom. The owl that is often seen with this Goddess is the Little Owl. The reason for Athena's wisdom was attributed in part to the owl, her constant companion, who was said to whisper the secrets of what had happened during the night to her, thus giving the Goddess access to hidden information and knowledge, and the ability to see all sides of a situation. The bird was held in such reverence in Athens that its image was stamped on the back of the coinage of the day, and this coinage came to be known as the 'Owls of Laurium'. Indeed, there was a popular phrase at the time, to 'bring owls to Athens', which meant the same as our latter-day equivalent of 'taking coals to Newcastle' or 'selling refrigerators to the Eskimos'.

However, the Short-eared Owl, far from being a symbol of wisdom to the ancient Greeks, was considered to be incredibly stupid; there was a belief that if someone walked round and round the owl it would eventually wring its own neck as it tried to watch the person! Some Native Americans also shared this belief.

The Romans

The owl is a fatal bird, of evil omen beyond all sorts, especially at public auguries; it lies in desert places, and not merely those that are unpeopled, but those of hard access; monster of the night, it never utters a song but only a groan. It never flies where it intends, but is borne off at a slant.

Pliny the Elder

The Romans were not quite so keen on the owl as the Greeks; Nycteme was a Roman girl who, after lying to her father, was turned into an owl as a punishment. The owl was sacred to Minerva, who shares the same attributes as Athena, and was said to be able to make predictions and prophecies, since this Goddess had the power of 'second sight'.

In Ancient Rome, to place an owl feather near a sleeping person meant that you would be able to discover their secrets. This is indicative of the idea of the owl having access to hidden knowledge, having been abroad during the nocturnal hours when everyone is usually asleep.

Hecate, the Goddess of the Underworld, also had the owl as her ally – a suitable partnership, it would seem, since Hecate was also Goddess of magic, charms and enchantments, all talents attributable to the owl, too. It seems appropriate that Julius Caesar, Marcus Aurelius and Augustus all had their deaths foretold by the hooting of an owl.

NATIVE AMERICAN LORE

In Native American tradition, the owl is said to bear dreams to sleeping people: another belief related to its nocturnal nature. However, like every-where else, it seems, it is also a symbol of death, black magic and sorcery. For the Plains Indians, the owl was the ruler of the dark time, night, and the underworld, and owl feathers carried a great deal of ritual significance. Among the Algonquin, the owl would be personified in a statue and perched in the medicine lodge – this was 'the owl being, that guides into the Land of the Setting Sun, the land of the dead'.

In general, the owl is held to be the 'Night Eagle' because, like the eagle, it is both silent in flight and swift to kill. The owl and the eagle are considered to be opposites.

The Pawnee saw the owl as a symbol of protection, whereas for the Ojibwa, its meanings are evil and death. The Pueblo Indians saw the owl as the 'skeleton man' who was not only the God of Death but also the symbol of fertility.

To an Apache Indian, to dream of an owl meant that the dreamer would die soon. In a similar vein, to the Navajo tribe in particular, the owl is said to be the 'death bringer'. The Mojave Indians believed that you would become an owl after you die; the next stage in evolution would be to become a water beetle and, after that, pure air.

The Cherokee shamans believed that the owls could be asked questions, but also that if you needed to be punished then the owls would make you ill. They also hold the bird sacred because of its ability to see in the dark. The Cree peoples regarded the whistles of the owl to be a call from the spirit world, and the call would need to be answered using the same intonation. If there wasn't another return call, then the hearer would soon die. The Hopi

Indians believed that the Burrowing Owl was the God of the Dead and looked after all underground things, such as seed germination.

The Kwagulth people believed that owls could be both a deceased person and their newly released soul. Similarly, the Kwaikiutl Indians believed that owls were souls of people, and that if an owl was harmed then the person to whom the owl 'soul' belonged would also suffer a similar fate. The Lenape peoples thought that to dream of an owl meant that it would become their spirit guardian, or totem, and the Zunis would place an owl feather next to a baby to help it sleep.

The Navajo have a belief that the Great Creator told the owl, after creating it, that 'in days to come, men will listen to your voice to know what will be their future'. They saw the bird as the messenger from the supernatural, 'unseen' world, and also associated it with earthbound spirits or ghosts.

The Newuks of California thought that brave warriors would become Great Horned Owls after they died. This is similar to the belief in the Sierras that the same owl would rescue the souls of the dead and carry them into the Underworld. Tlingit warriors would rush into battle hooting like owls, to give themselves confidence and to strike fear into their enemies.

AFRICA

In Africa the story isn't any different. The owl is associated with witchcraft and sorcery, and to the Bantu the owl is the 'familiar of wizards'. The Swahili people believe that the owl brings illness, especially to children.

Zulus believe that owls are sorcerers, and the owl is considered to be a messenger of wizards and witches. It has a powerful role to play in the casting of spells because of its magical abilities. In Cameroon and certain parts of Nigeria, the owl is thought to be so incredibly evil that it is never mentioned by name, but instead is referred to as 'the bird who makes you afraid'. Because owls shared space with other creatures of the night, such as demons, ghouls and witches, there was a belief that they had a special relationship with these creatures and, if you asked them nicely, they could help to avert other bad spirits.

THE CELTS

In Ancient Britain, the owl represents the crone figure; in *The Druid Animal Oracle*, by Philip and Stephanie Carr-Gomm, we're told:

> Because the owl is sacred to the Goddess in her crone-aspect, one of its many Gaelic names is 'Cailleach-oidhche' (Crone of the Night), and the barn owl is 'Cailleach-oidhche gheal' (white old woman of the night).

This aspect of the owl as crone and as being a creature of the underworld, reoccurs throughout Europe. In the Celtic world, the owl was sacred to the Goddess Arianrhod, who was said to be able to see into the darkest corners of people's souls. She moves through the night spreading comfort and solace all around. She was a Goddess of fate and reincarnation – at last, a positive aspect of owl symbolism!

CHINA

Children born during the Day of the Owl (the summer solstice) were unfortunately believed to inherit violent tendencies. Owl stew would be served up to the servants of noblemen on this particular day, although whether this was some kind of ordeal of torture or purification is unclear! The owl was regarded as a horrendous creature who was said to have eaten its own mother, and is an extrapolation of huge amounts of yang (male) energy. Being associated with smelting, the bird was the symbol of Emperor Huang Ti, who was also the first blacksmith.

INDIA

The Hindu God of Death, Yama, generally had two dogs as messengers, but sometimes he would also have an owl. Lakshmi, the Hindu Goddess who is said to bring abundance and wealth, has the owl as her sacred bird. Since the owl is associated with fertility, the flesh of the bird is considered to be an aphrodisiac; conversely, the eating of this flesh could also turn a man into a fool!

In Southern India, there were meanings attached to the calls and cries of the owl. One cry meant that there would soon be a death; two calls indicated that success would soon follow for the listener. Three, and a woman would be married into the family, and four meant that there would be a disturbance of some kind. Five owl calls meant that the hearer would soon be making a journey, and six meant that there would be guests arriving soon. Seven calls were a sign of mental disturbance, with eight foretelling a sudden death. Nine was the ultimate number of calls for good fortune.

JAPAN

There's an island north of Japan that is home to an indigenous Japanese race of bird and animal worshippers called the Ainu. They hold the Eagle Owl sacred as a God of hunting, a divine ancestor and their 'Servant of the World', which is not surprising since the owl is indeed a magnificent hunter. They would raise a toast to the owl before going off to see what they could catch. For the Ainu, the Screech Owl warned against danger. However, they're not so keen on the Tawny Owl, because it was once believed to have failed to deliver a message to man that had come directly from the Gods. In addition, the Barn Owl and the Horned Owl were considered to be demonic. The Ainu believe that the owl, rather than being evil itself, warns of evil approaching, and they revere the bird in general as a messenger from the Gods.

AROUND THE WORLD

In Arabia, the owl is bad news; it is said to be a powerful spirit that carries away the bodies of children at night. Ancient Arabian lore says that the female owl had two eggs; one would make hair fall out, and the other would make it grow back again.

In Egypt, if you were given the gift of an owl, it would be best not to be too hasty in thanking the donor, since it should be taken as a hint that the recipient should take his own life. This is similar to the Ethiopian ritual whereby a man condemned to death would be taken to a table which had an owl painted on it; the man would then be expected to commit suicide. However, the talisman of the heart of an owl, if carried into battle, would give the bearer courage and would avert danger.

Australian Aborigines believe that the owl personified the soul of woman. This meant that both women and owls had sacred qualities. The bird is also a messenger of the God Muurup, who apparently had the antisocial habits of eating children and killing people. In general for Aboriginal people, the owl was considered to be bad news.

In Hebrew belief, the owl represents desolation and is considered to be 'unclean': not fit to be eaten. This belief follows through to Islamic law too.

In Sicily, the Short-eared Owl is probably the most feared of all the owl family, and if its call is heard, people will throw a pinch of salt into the fire to avert the omen. In Indonesia, in contrast, owls are associated with wisdom. Whenever someone wants to go travelling he will consult with the owls, who will either make sounds saying that it is safe to go, or that it might be better to simply stay at home. These warnings are always taken seriously.

> Baby owls decide among themselves who is hungriest, so when the parents arrive at the nest with the food, the most desperate babies are fed first.

The Maya-Quiche have a saying, 'When the owl hoots, the Indian dies.' Certain sorcerers were said to be able to transmute into owls. Aztec belief about the seemingly maligned owl isn't really any different from anywhere else. It was the embodiment of darkness, wet weather and storms. One of the evil Gods of the Aztecs wore a screech owl on top of his head. The Peruvian Incas' grave furniture often included a sacrificial knife whose blade would have the effigy of a god, half human and half owl. The owl often is depicted holding a sacrificial knife too, and a bowl to catch the blood of the victim.

To redress the balance somewhat, the Samoans believe that they were actually descended from owls. And in Yorkshire, in the UK, the owl is considered to be lucky!

WEATHER LORE

In England, the Barn Owl is said to be the best weatherman of all the different owl types, and it seems that whatever the weather is doing, if you hear the owl screech, then you should soon expect the opposite. So if the weather is absolutely appalling and you hear the owl, don't worry – it'll change soon!

For some reason, owls were also believed to be able to protect against lightning and because of this the Chinese placed figures of owls on their chimneys. In China, the owl is an ancient symbol, the emblem of the thunderbolt or lightning strike among other things, and apparently this is because, like the lightning, the owl brightens up the sky. This ties in with Europeans belief that owls could avert lightning strikes. In fact, in both Germany and England real owls were killed and nailed to doors in the hopes that this gruesome piece of voodoo would avert lightning strikes.

There's more weather lore associated with the owl. In Sussex in the UK there's an old saying, 'When owls whoop much at night, expect a fair morrow.' And finally we have the belief, from Newfoundland, that the hooting of the owl presages bad weather.

Owl Medicine

There are similarities around the world as to the supposed medicinal value of owls' eggs and the like. Many of these are cases of sympathetic magic, whereby there is a correlation between the qualities of the bird and the symptoms of the illness

In Belgium, an omelette made from the eggs of the Short-eared Owl is regarded as a cure for drunkenness. Similarly, owls in classical literature were meant to be able to cure alcoholism, and in the UK, alcoholism was also treated with the egg of an owl, which must have been a pretty difficult cure to administer since owl eggs are not that easy to come by. If you were wise you'd feed your children owls' eggs, too, since this would protect them from drunkenness for the rest of their lives.

Another strange custom in Britain was to serve up owl stew to children suffering from a formerly virulent disease, whooping cough. This is evidence of sympathetic magic, because the owl makes a sound similar to the cough.

There are some potions for eyesight, too. In Britain powdered owls' eggs were said to improve the eyesight, and similarly, in Northern India, to eat the eyes of an owl would ensure good eyesight. In Peru, boiled owl is said to be incredibly powerful medicine for just about any ailment.

In India, rheumatic pain would be treated with a paste concocted from the flesh of the owl.

What Bird Would You Be?

'I would be an owl. Nocturnal, bookish, knowing. '

Louise, London

'I wouldn't have expected to have said the owl a couple of years back, but I had a really gruelling shift for a while as a night nurse in a strange town where I knew no one. Sometimes the work was very sad and traumatic; more people pass away at night than during the day, and although sometimes there was a lot of activity there were some nights which seemed to stretch on forever. There was an owl which I'd see close to the hospital from time to time, though, and it was very reassuring; it was telling me that I wasn't alone, and that the work I was doing was valuable and appreciated.'

Clara, Ireland

The Pelican

Water

> A wonderful bird is the pelican:
> His bill will hold more than his belican
> He can take in his beak
> Food enough for a week
> But I'm darned to see how the helican.
> **Dixon Lanier Merritt**

CHARACTERISTICS

One of the very ancient birds, remains of pelicans dating back to 40 million years ago show very little change between the fossils and the bird we have today. It's so old that we can't even say for sure where the name came from. The large bill (it can hold up to 3 gallons, or 12 litres) isn't actually used for storing food, but for scooping up fish.

The pelican is a large bird; some of the white pelican species have a wingspan of over nine feet (3 metres) and, as you can imagine, to get airborne can be tricky if the wind isn't in the right direction. The bird will have to run awkwardly, pattering along, for some distance before he attains lift-off.

Pelicans have a great sense of unity and 'oneness' with their flock. They fly in a precision-built form, and tend to do everything together, even to the point of all facing in the same direction when resting or feeding. Another wonderful thing to see is pelicans fishing together. They will make an arc on the water, then all swim together, splashing the water with their feet and wings to drive the fish together into a school, where the birds can then take their pick.

There's a fantastic description of this by Pamela Conley, in *The Gift of Birds*. Pamela is out swimming and suddenly finds herself in an unexpected situation:

> My foot hit a fish and then the ocean began to explode around us. I froze with fear. I looked up and saw a hundred pelicans swarming down … Some were landing as close as two feet away, and in the centre of this hysteria I realised that they were swooping in on a school of fish and we were in the middle of a feeding frenzy … Then understanding replaced panic and I watched in awe as pelican scooped up fish with what appeared to be gallons of water.

AN INEXPLICABLE MYTH

> To his good friends thus wide I'll ope my arms;
> And like the kind life-rendering pelican,
> Repast them with my blood.
> **Shakespeare,** *Hamlet*

There is an ancient legend that the pelican would feed its young from the flesh of its own breast, which it obtained by puncturing its chest with its own bill. This resulted in the bird becoming a symbol of parental love, and also led to an association with the Christ figure because of the nature of the bird's supposed self-sacrifice. So the pelican became a popular ecclesiastical emblem.

In *The Book of Beasts*, which is a translation of a Latin bestiary of the twelfth century, is the following bizarre description:

> When these [children] … begin to grow up, they flap their parents in the face with their wings, and the parents, striking back, kill them. Three days afterwards the mother pierces her breast, opens her side, and lays herself across her young, pouring out her blood over the dead bodies. This brings them to life again.

NORTH AMERICA

The great age of the bird is indicated in the belief of the Seri people, a tribe who used to inhabit the island of Tiburon, in the Gulf of California. The Seri believed that the world was created by the 'Ancient of Pelican', a supernatural being possessing infinite wisdom as well as a beautiful song, who was responsible for raising land above the waters that had previously flooded everything in sight.

The island of Alcatraz, in San Francisco Bay, which used to be the site of the infamous prison of the same name, was so-called after the Spanish word for the pelican, since the birds used to nest there.

GREECE

Aristotle gives a very strange (and inaccurate) account of the feeding habits of the pelican, which is worth mentioning simply because it's so odd:

> Pelicans living by rivers swallow big, smooth shells. After cooking them in the pouch in front of the stomach they vomit them up, so that when they are open they may pick out the flesh and eat it.

THE SECRET LANGUAGE OF BIRDS

Hebrew Lore

In the Old Testament, the pelican is mentioned as being an 'unclean' bird, i.e. not to be eaten, and therefore considered sacred.

A Dreamtime Story – How The Opal Was Discovered

There's an Australian Aboriginal story, from the Wangkamura people, about how the opal was discovered …

Many years ago, the Wangkamura people decided to explore the Northern Territory. Logic decreed that the best explorer would be a bird, so accordingly they sent Muda, a powerful being who could transform from a man into a pelican.

Unfortunately, Muda fell ill, and had to rest on top of a hill. After a short while he started to feel better, and noticed that the ground beneath him seemed to be painted with the most incredible colours. He flew down from the hill and started to peck at the colours with his bill. Suddenly a spark flew out of one of the colours, and since the terrain was hot and dry, soon the flames spread for long distances.

But this meant that the Wangkamura people had the pelican to thank for two important discoveries; not only for fire, but also for the opal, which of course had been the source of the gorgeous colours that the pelican had been so curious about.

What Bird Would You Be?

'I'd be a sulphur-crested cockatoo … They are a beautiful bird, white with a golden crest. They have a strong beak but are in fact quite timid. They squawk dreadfully loud but can be taught to speak and will; if domesticated, become very faithful, and will fall in love with their owner. They make extraordinary companions too.'
Colin, Australia

The Raven

Water

> Then this ebony bird beguiling my sad fancy into smiling
> By the grave and stern decorum of the countenance it wore
> 'Though thy crest be shorn and shaven, thou' I said 'art sure no craven
> Ghastly grim and ancient raven wandering from nightly shore –
> Tell me what thy lordly name is on the night's plutonian shore!'
> Quoth the raven;
> 'Nevermore!'
>
> **Edgar Allan Poe**, *The Raven*

As I'm writing this, there's an almighty summer storm outside; the sky has gone from that dark, ominous slatey blue to an almost black colour; there have been thunderclaps and lightning flashes, and there's a scent of charged electricity in the air. All in all it seems like an apt day, mood-wise, to tell you about the raven.

Why this atmosphere should be reminiscent of the raven is perhaps a little unfair, but it is a mark of the anomaly that surrounds the bird. However, as the bird known to Native Americans as the Trickster, this paradox is perhaps only to be expected.

A couple of years ago I found an injured baby raven, and so had the privilege of seeing such an amazing bird close-up. The most arresting thing about these birds are their eyes, which are a piercing blue, with a very intelligent, beyond-human expression. I was lucky enough to be able to speak to Derrick Coyle, who is Ravenmaster at the Tower of London, and he told me some fascinating stories about the communicative powers of these birds. They have 30 or so different calls, as well as a system of body language, which is easy to read.

There are probably more legends attached to the raven – as a bird of mystery, sometimes of doom, of prophecy and omen, of language, and of its close relationship to humankind – than perhaps to any other bird. It's a prominent bird in folklore, and in some places holds even more importance than the eagle.

CHARACTERISTICS

The raven is prevalent pretty much everywhere, except for New Zealand, Antarctica and the southernmost part of South America. The Corvid family includes crows, jays, choughs, magpies and rooks as well as ravens, but here we're going to look exclusively at the raven, the undisputed 'king' of this group. The raven used to be the most widespread of the group, but nowadays seems to like to keep itself to itself after it was cruelly hunted quite extensively, and tends towards the wilder parts of the environment, such as mountains and other untamed parts of the landscape.

Although widely known as carrion birds, i.e. birds that prefer to eat dead animals rather than killing anything for themselves, the diet of the raven is incredibly adaptable – one factor which has ensured its success as a species. If it needs to, the raven will kill to eat.

The raven is surprisingly large, measuring up to 28 inches (70 cm), with a four-foot (120 cm) wingspan. They like to build their bulky nests on cliff faces. The birds are relatively long-lived, with some reaching an age of 30 or so years. The raven is monogamous, but if one of the pair should die it is replaced pretty swiftly with a young bird.

As befits an animal of extreme intelligence, the raven is a very playful bird, japing around simply for the fun of it. It will swoop and dive in the air simply for joy, and has been spotted sliding down snowy slopes. Derrick Coyle told me that there's a raven at the Tower called Rhys who likes to lie on his back and juggle with small plastic flowerpots!

Unsurprisingly for such a large bird, the raven has virtually no predators except for the Red-tailed Hawk and the Great Horned Owl, although it has been persecuted by man, who mistakenly believed it to steal large quantities of seeds and grain. It has been proven, however, that the raven kills plenty of pests so should really be regarded as the friend of the farmer rather than as a foe.

THE MOST INTELLIGENT BIRD?

It is with good reason that the raven is known as the Bird of Cunning; it has been found to be extremely intelligent, indeed, it is perhaps the most intelligent bird on the planet.

Ravens have an incredible ability to learn, and in addition they are one of the 'language' birds. In a recent experiment the raven was proven to be not only a tool user but also a toolmaker, putting a supposed 'bird brain' on a level with primates. The raven was put into a cage that contained a plastic tube with a small bucket of meat at the bottom. Various bits of wire were lying around, and the raven at first used one of these to try to get the bucket out of the tube. When after a few seconds this method clearly wasn't working, the raven fashioned a hook from the wire and succeeded at retrieving the food very swiftly. This experiment was carried out at the University of Oxford in 2002.

> The raven always thinks that her young ones are the whitest.
> *Proverb*

There's also a tale, related in Berndt Heinrich's book *Ravens in Winter*, about how ravens worked as a team to steal a husky's food. One bird led the chained dog away from his food, the bird hopping infuriatingly just out of reach; meanwhile the other raven ate his fill of the food from the dog's bowl.

Pliny, the Roman naturalist, relates a story about how raven, faced with needing to obtain water which was at the bottom of vessel with a narrow neck, dropped stones and pebbles into the container in order to raise the level of the water. This story also appears in Aesop's Fables.

WEATHERLORE

Many years ago, North American Indians, the Greeks, Chinese, Scandinavians and Siberians all believed that the raven could actually affect the weather. The Alaskan Eskimo believes that if there is an unprecedented period of rain then this is because someone has killed a raven. Berndt Heinrich relates how he was told about this myth during an unseasonably long period of rain; sure enough, he found a dead raven the next day, although whether it had been killed or not was impossible to tell.

In the USA, there's an old belief that to see a raven facing a sun which has clouded over will portend hot weather to come.

TERRIBLE PARENTS?

One of the more peculiar stories attached to the raven is that it refuses to feed its young until it can see what colour its feathers are going to be. This legend has imbued its way into Danish mythology to the extent that there's even a phrase 'Ravn-mudder', or 'raven mother', which is a euphemism for a bad mother. It could be that, because the baby ravens are red in colour when they first hatch, the mothers fly away in alarm. There's also a belief that God feeds the baby birds on insects for four days until they start to grow feathers and the mother returns to the nest.

LANGUAGE

Several raven myths involve them having a language, which is understandable by humans only if we have the key to it. Ravens can also be taught to speak human languages.

Derrick Coyle at the Tower of London told me that ravens not only have 30 to 40 calls, which are discernible as language, but that they also have a body language which is easy to analyse. If a raven is approached by a member of the public but is not in the mood to 'chat', the bird will puff up its head feathers. They will also spread their wings to designate territory. Further, Derrick has a raven that talks, and which talks intelligently: Derrick will feed the raven and perhaps say 'This is for you', and the bird will reply 'That's for me'.

It's believed that the bird sees everything and knows everything; obviously, it may not be appropriate for the raven to reveal its secrets to just anyone. The raven is one of the 'mimicking' birds, and can copy the sounds of other birds. It may be that the idea of the raven's language has proliferated because the raven's calls and cries possibly sound more 'human' than those of many other birds (the Greek word for crow, 'Coax', actually means 'croaker'). I was standing on a mountain recently and saw two ravens enjoying their mating ritual of tumbling and swooping from the sky; one was making comical 'pop pop pop' sounds whilst the other was croaking delightedly – it really was – that's the only way to describe it!

That the bird has established its own language is indisputable. The young have a particular cry to ask for food; the female has a call summoning her mate. Emotionally, some sounds are obviously angry; others, such as between mating birds, sound affectionate and intimate. The raven uses its body as well as its voice to communicate. An Alaskan hunter describes how the body language of the bird gave him a very specific message: the raven had been dipping and diving over a specific point in the woods, fanning its tail, and generally behaving in a noticeably peculiar manner. The hunter recalls, 'I had the distinct impression the raven was trying to show me something.'

Accordingly the hunter trusted this instinct and was rewarded with finding a moose.

The belief in this ability of the raven to converse with humans is widespread, and extends to Germany, Siberia, India, and pretty much everywhere where the bird exists. In Hans Christian Andersen's *The Snow Queen*, a raven is there when Gerda is looking for her little friend Kay, who has been abducted by the evil queen of the icy wastes; the bird says,

'Listen to me ... but it is so difficult to speak your language! Do you understand Ravenish? If so, I could tell you much better!'

Leaving aside the world of fiction for a moment, there's an account in an article in *International Wildlife* magazine, dated 1984, of a description of two ravens flying across an icy wasteland in Alaska. The birds are making a lot of noise as they go. The reporter turned to his companion, an Inuk, asking 'What did they say?' The Inuk replied immediately, with a smile:

'Tulugak (the wise raven) say, "Tuktu tavani! Tuktu tavani!" ("The caribou are there! The caribou are there!")'

BIRD OF DEATH AND ILL OMEN?

It's interesting to observe that associations with the raven as a harbinger of death, or indeed any supposedly negative symbols associated with it, are restricted to more recent times and seem to be confined in particular to Europe. It could well be that the association has come about because the bird was often seen in battle fields where it would feed upon slain corpses, although the spooky black appearance of the bird might also have something to do with it, as this Old English verse indicates:

They left behind the butchered bodies,
Flesh for the raven, the black-coated bird
With the horny beak ...
From *The Battle of Brunanburgh*

Any bird that is coloured black seems to be automatically regarded as a bad omen. Again, this is probably because of the association with the night and concealed, occult things.

In India, the Mahabharata uses the raven as a messenger of death. However, in order to interpret this we have to understand how different cultures view death, and we have to accept that this does not necessarily mean that in this case the raven is a bird of ill-omen. There is a biblical story associated with the raven which gives the bird a bad press. According to the eighth-century Old English version of Genesis below, it was the first bird to be sent out from the Ark, but never returned, possibly because the land was too far away to fly back to the ship:

> The son of Lamech let a black raven
> Fly out of the Ark on an empty flood.
> Noah believed that if in his flight
> He did not find land, the bird would be forced
> To search the wide expanse of the sea
> For the ship. But his hopes were all deceived:
> The fiend soon fell on rotting corpses;
> The dark feathered bird did not come back.

To cap it all, there's a European belief that the raven was the preferred 'shape-shifting' appearance of witches and devils. In Germany, on Walpurgis Night (April 30th) witches are said to fly to their diabolical Sabbats in the shape of ravens.

Norse Mythology

In Norse mythology, the God Odin was known as 'Hrafnagud', the word 'Hrafn' being the Norse for raven. In accord with the intuition we have that ravens see everything and know everything, Odin possessed two ravens, one black and one white, who were named Hugin and Munin – 'Thought' and 'Memory' – who would go flying out to gather information which they would give to Odin, thus keeping him several steps ahead of anyone else.

Odin's daughters, the Valkyries, would often take the shape of ravens. Danes and Vikings would bear the emblem of the raven on their sails as homage to Odin, and the symbol was regarded as a token of good luck. The weaving of the emblem was a ritual in itself. If the wings of the symbolic bird spread wide on the sail then the journey would be thought to be a profitable one, whereas if the wings drooped then difficulties could be expected.

In contrast to the biblical story, which besmirched the raven for its failure to return to the ark, when Vikings were navigating by sea for new territory, they would let loose a raven from the deck of the ship and the direction the bird flew in was noted. If the bird failed to return then the sailors would set their course to follow the bird in the sure belief that it had found land. It is said that Greenland, Nova Scotia and Iceland were found in this way, the explorers following the path set by the raven.

BIRD OF PROPHECY AND PREDICTION

> Of inspired birds the ravens are the most prophetical. Accordingly, in the language of that district, 'to have the foresight of a raven' is to this day a proverbial expression.
>
> **Thomas Babington Macaulay,** *The History of St Kilda*

In Ireland, the raven's calls were interpreted in the arts of prediction. 'To have a raven's knowledge' meant, in Ireland, that the person in question had the gift of prophecy or second sight.

ANCIENT ROME

The ancient Romans, renowned for their ability to discern messages from the Gods via their auguries, or interpretation of messages from the birds, had the raven as one of the most important of all their birds of omen. While it was believed that other birds could signal a meaning or an event, the raven was the only bird with the power to understand for itself what the omen signified. In addition, both the Greeks and Romans interpreted signs from the number and nature of squawks and croaks given by the bird, the direction they came from, and the time of day in which they were heard.

THE CELTS

Ravens were a sacred bird to the Druids, and the Irish hero Cúchulain possessed two of these birds, much like the Norse God Odin. The birds would warn of the approach of an enemy.

A key figure in Celtic mythology, the Morrigan, took the shape of the raven, and the bird was also closely associated with Morgan le Fay, the Queen of the Fairies. These fairies were not of the Tinkerbell variety but were far more interesting beings – the Dark Fairies or Dubh Sídhe – who often appeared as ravens, too. It's believed that when King Arthur eventually returns, he will come back in the form of a raven.

In Wales it is said that a raven has the power to restore the sight. And in Ireland, the Goddess of War, Badb, took the form of a carrion crow, which is an aspect of the raven.

THE DREAM OF RHONABWY

From a tale in the Welsh *Mabinogion* comes the story of Rhonabwy. The troops of King Arthur slaughter the ravens of Owen in a huge battle; the surviving ravens react in a manner more violent than anyone could have expected and turn on the army and hack them to pieces:

> They heard almighty tumult, and a wailing of men, and a croaking of ravens, as they carried the men into the air, and, tearing betwixt them, let them fall piecemeal to the earth.

THE RAVENS OF THE TOWER OF LONDON

The Tower of London has had ravens living within it since 1078, but not many people are aware of the reason why. The custom's origins are firmly entrenched in Celtic folklore.

Bran the Blessed was the Welsh King, and his sacred bird was the raven – indeed, 'Bran' actually means 'raven'. Bran was the protector of the whole of Britain. His sister, Branwen, was married to an Irish King who didn't treat her very well. Branwen was able to speak to a starling, and convey her plight to the bird. The starling flew to Bran to tell him about his beloved sister's problems. Accordingly, Bran went to fight his Irish brother-in-law.

Bran was decapitated after an almighty battle with the Irish, but luckily his head was still able to speak and could utter prophecies. The head requested to be buried in a part of London then called White Mount, so that Bran could continue to protect the Islands. White Mount later became known as

Tower Hill because the Tower of London was built upon it. The ravens are there as a homage to Bran, and to ensure that as long as ravens are there, Britain will be safe from any enemy or invader.

During the Second World War the Tower was bombed and the ravens went missing. In a hush-hush operation under the orders of the Prime Minister, Winston Churchill, young ravens were hastily brought from the Welsh hills to replace the lost birds in order that all would be well – as indeed it was, eventually.

Today, there are seven ravens continually in residence at the Tower. The flock has the sinister collective noun of an Unkindness.

GREEK MYTHOLOGY

The raven was sacred to Apollo, who was also the patron of augurs. As with many black birds, there are tales that the creature had once been white and the blackness had been sent as a form of punishment. The raven informed Apollo that his lover, Coronis, had been unfaithful to him. Apollo accordingly killed Coronis who was pregnant at the time, and after this act, in a fit of remorse, turned the raven black. When Coronis's body was on the funeral pyre, at the last moment, Apollo relented and took from the flames Coronis's child, who was just about to be born. The child became Ascelpius, the God of Medicine.

In Greek lore, the raven is a symbol of the Sun, from whose God it is said to bring messages. It is also sacred to Athena and Ascelpius. The raven is reputed to have given the information as to where to place the Omphalos, or central stone, at Apollo's oracle at Delphi.

CHINA AND JAPAN

In Japan, the raven is seen as a messenger of the Gods, and in both countries it is seen as a lucky bird and a symbol of devotion within the family. There's a Shinto legend about ten ravens that flew from the mulberry tree to bring light to the world. Had Yi the Archer not been able to shoot nine of the birds, the light they bore would have been so bright that the world would have caught fire! The red raven in particular was a symbol of the generosity of the Sun.

Hebrew Mythology

We have already seen how the raven was the first bird to be sent from the Ark to look for land. In Hebrew belief, the raven was considered to be 'unclean', i.e. not to be eaten, and therefore carrying sacred properties. But the raven is not all bad in stories from the Old Testament. Elijah was shown where to find food by the ravens when he was being hunted by Ahab:

> 'I have commanded the ravens to feed thee there' … And the ravens brought him bread and flesh in the morning, and bread and flesh in the evening; and he drank of the brook.'
> **I Kings 17: 4-6**

A lovely instance of the raven being a very practical kind of messenger from God.

St Antony was fed by ravens during his quest to find Paul the Hermit, who had been brought a half loaf of bread by the birds every day for 60 years. Once Antony arrived, however, the clever birds are said to have brought a whole loaf!

Egypt

The raven was a symbol of malevolence and destruction among the Egyptians.

Africa

The raven is a benevolent character in Africa, assuming the role of guardian spirit and guide. It is also seen as a bird that will bring a warning of impending danger.

Native American Lore

As elsewhere in the world, the raven carries its dichotomy into the American Indian world, too, and appears as both hero and villain, God-like figure and trickster. The raven's most important role, however, is as creator of the world, or at least as having a large part to play in that creation. The Tlingit peoples of the North West Pacific have the Raven as creator of the World; the bird also created the Sun and made it available to mankind.

The raven, while never as evil as it sometimes appears in recent European stories, is nevertheless often portrayed as a bit of a rascal, a quality which is in keeping with the playful nature of the bird. One belief is that the raven invented mosquitoes purely to annoy people! Indeed, it's believed that everything the raven created, in his God mode, was made purely for his own amusement. Man was initially hewn out of rock, but flesh made us mortal and therefore far more fun … The raven invented many things to make things difficult for mankind and therefore more amusing to himself, but never with any malicious intent. The raven is the best shape-shifter of all the animal kingdom and can change into anything or anyone in order to obtain what he desires.

To many tribes, the keen sight of the raven means that the bird is able to help them in the dark; the raven can guide the soul on its last journey. Rather than being seen as a creature of darkness, the bird is seen as having the ability to see through the darkness and this positive aspect runs counter to the many European stories as the raven as a harbinger of doom.

The Bird of Shamans

The raven is fundamentally important in all areas of the Pacific Rim, and in particular amongst the Koryak peoples. The Koryak believe that the universe was created by a raven, namely Big Raven, also known as Quikil. Quikil was the first man; he is the father and the protector of the Koryak as well as the most powerful shaman and a supernatural entity. Big Raven could be called upon to help in times of distress. Many Indian peoples will talk to the raven as to a God.

The shamans of the Koryak hold that they need to find their own totem animals which will protect them while they are engaged in shamanic practices, which involve the setting aside of 'normal' consciousness in favour of being able to communicate with the 'otherworld', or the world of spirits. The raven is one of the more common guardian spirits, along with the dear, wolf, eagle and seagull.

C.W. Nicol, a documentary filmmaker, has filmed in North Eastern Siberia, Alaska and Japan in a quest to discover more about raven mythology, and while in Kamchatka was introduced to a Koryak shaman, an old lady by the name of Maria. She told Nicol lots of raven stories, including how the raven brought up land from the bottom of the sea, and formed mountains by skiing on the land. A steaming volcano was a sign that the raven and his compatriots were cooking meat.

A Haida Myth – How the Raven Discovered the First Men

The Haida people of the Pacific North West have a legend that tells how the raven discovered the first men. The raven was seemingly alone on a beach after the subsidence of the Great Flood. He had had enough to eat for once, and was keen to find something to interest his febrile imagination since, being alone, he was quite bored and needed something with which to entertain himself.

The raven came upon a giant clamshell half-buried in the sand and prised it open, only to find small creatures with two legs inside. These were of course the first men. Although they were frightened of the raven at first, they soon overcame their shyness and came out of their shell. Soon the raven realized that the creatures were all male; there were no females, and he got tired of their ceaseless activity since they seemed to need so much looking after. The raven was about to put them back into the shell, but decided instead to see if he could find any girls.

He didn't have to look very far. The girls were hiding inside other seashells, clinging to the rocks at the edge of the sea. The raven gathered together as many as he could without hurting them, and brought them to the boys.

At first both parties were shy, and tried to cover their nakedness with strips of bark and cloth, but soon they began to relax and to enjoy each other's company. The entertainment factor these creatures provided together ensured that the raven was never bored again. In addition, he felt an obligation to protect them, since he had discovered them in the first place.

And the Raven, never flitting, still is sitting, still is sitting
On the pallid bust of Pallas just above my chamber door;
And his eyes have all the seeming of a demon's that is dreaming
And the lamplight o'er him streaming throws his shadow on the floor;
And my soul from out that shadow that lies floating on the floor
Shall be lifted – evermore!

Edgar Allan Poe, *The Raven*

I remember the ravens wheeling over dead plough land in winter, they had made a home in a clump of scotch pines, twisted by the channel winds. It was our island in the middle of the plough. My sister and I stood and watched them, shrieking over our heads, muffled against the January weather and we felt something stranger and more sad than we could ever express.

Martin, New York

What Bird Would You Be?

'A raven, definitely ... No other bird I can think of is as gloriously dark as the raven. From the almost liquid, jet blackness of their feathers, to their associations with death, the raven is truly the rock and roll star of the bird world ... Ravens are opportunistic to a fault, a quality I have always admired and aspired to.'

Ash, New York

The Stork

Water

at dusk
a stork speckled sky

storks are flying
to the northlands
as their generations
taught them

light fades
to evening

smooth sleek gliders
homing to the darkling woods
where secrets sleep
with the storks.
Tom Berman, *Storks*

CHARACTERISTICS

The stork appears in many countries in the world. There is fossil evidence that storks have been around, in exactly the same form as we see them today, for 50 million years. There are images of storks in the caves of Lascaux in France dating back to the Stone Age. They can still be seen nesting on tops of houses in parts of Germany and Poland, where householders are happy to have the birds in close proximity and, indeed, encourage them on to their roofs by putting baskets and platforms there – in previous times cartwheels were popular for this purpose – to provide the birds with bases for their nests. These nests can become very large, often six to eight feet (up to one and a half metres) in diameter. The storks will return to their nesting sites year after year, after their migrations. If the birds don't return to these sites it is considered a very bad omen indeed.

Although storks are often believed to be monogamous, this is not always the case. They may change partners after migrating, and seem to be more attached to the nest to which they are returning than to their former partners.

I love the following description from a Latin bestiary of the twelfth century, especially the image of the crows as sort of outriders!

> These messengers of the Spring, these brotherly comrades, these enemies of serpents, can migrate across the oceans and, having collected themselves into a column on route, can go straight through to Asia. Crows fly in front of them as pathfinders, and the storks follow like a squadron.

The largest of all the storks is the Jabiru (this is the bird's Amazonian Indian name), which can be discovered living anywhere from Argentina to Mexico. But perhaps the most popular American stork is the Wood Stork, protected for many years by the Audubon Society, and which lives in huge colonies of anything up to 5,000 birds in cypress swamps and the Everglades. These birds feed by stirring the mud with their foot, then grabbing at whatever animal or fish it might have disturbed!

The stork doesn't have a singing voice, but it can rattle its bill, and the bird communicates a lot by gestures such as flapping and strutting.

How the Stork got its Name

In Sweden, the story goes that when Christ was on the cross, the bird flew around him, calling, 'Starke! Starke!' which means 'Strengthen! Strengthen!'

Caring for their Parents

One popular story about storks is that they look after their parents in old age. Indeed, in Rome there was even a 'stork law' (Lex Ciconia) passed which ensured that the good citizens would emulate the stork and ensure that their own parents were well taken care of in their dotage.

The stork's an emblem of true piety:
Because, when age had seized and made his dam
Unfit for flight, the grateful young one takes
His mother on his back, provides her food,
Repaying thus her tender care for him,
Ere he was fit to fly.

Beaumont

THE BRINGER OF BABIES

Perhaps the most popular myth about the stork is that it brings babies. It is still a popular explanation for small children, when they ask where they came from, to be told that 'the stork brought you', and indeed the image of a stork carrying the precious bundle of a baby is a very popular emblem on christening cards, cakes and the like. Indeed, the reddish pink marks on the eyelids of a newborn child are often called 'stork bites'.

It's a myth which seems to be prevalent the world over; there's even a Sioux legend which describes how 'One day, a stork paid this happy couple a visit and left for them a fine big boy.' It could be that this legend started because, as a water bird, the stork is associated with the 'waters of creation', but in reality this explanation is pretty tenuous; why hasn't the crane, for example, or other similar wading birds been credited with carrying babies?

Another link could be the regular return of the stork to its nesting place at the start of every new season. In addition, storks are very good mothers, even being known to pull out their own feathers in order to keep their babies warm. Another extrapolation of the myth is that the stork is meant to be able to make any woman pregnant simply by a glance …

THE ENEMY OF SNAKES

Throughout the world the stork is held to be the enemy of, and slayer of, snakes and serpents. Reputedly, Poseidon sent the stork to remove all the snakes on the island of Tenos, which is in the Aegean Sea.

ANCIENT GREECE AND ROME

Aristotle advised against killing or harming this bird in any way, since it was supposed to protect the home from lightning. The stork was sacred to Juno, who was the Roman Goddess of the home, children and the family. In Greece the stork represented the essence of woman as the mother, the nurturer, and as such was dedicated to Hera.

There's a Greek myth that may well explain in part the role of the stork in bringing babies. Gerana was reputedly an Ethiopian woman, extraordinarily beautiful, who lived in Egypt. She had no respect for the Gods or Goddesses, and particularly hated Hera and Artemis.

When Gerana had a son by her husband, Nicodemus, Hera turned Gerana into a stork as punishment for her disrespect. After that, all Gerana cared about was how to get her son, Mopsos, back. She tried to abduct him but the other members of her tribe saw her and, not realizing she was his mother, drove her away.

ANCIENT EGYPT

The stork came to be associated with the Ba, or soul of a person, and the Ba was shown with the body of stork and the head of a human. It was believed that the soul could leave the body by night but would return at the right time every morning – again, a reference to the punctual nesting and migratory habits of the bird. It was for the same reasons that the stork also came to be associated with reincarnation and the transmigration of souls.

CHINA

In China the stork shares some symbolism with the crane and the heron, unsurprisingly, since the birds have a similar appearance. It is believed to live to a very old age, and indeed, up-to-date research and the ringing of storks shows that the Chinese are right – storks can live for up to 70 years.

The Chinese believed also that the stork had the ability to carry people up to Heaven, particularly the souls of soldiers who had died valiantly. They regarded the stork as a messenger sent directly from the Gods.

CHRISTIAN MYTH

The stork represents piety, a virgin wedding, and chastity. It is referred to as 'vestal', meaning that the bird is innocent, like the vestal virgins. It also indicates peace and a happy and blessed marriage.

HEBREW LORE

Continuing on the maternal theme, the Hebrew word for stork is the same as 'kind mother'.

In the Old Testament, the stork is said to be one of the 'unclean' birds, i.e. that it should not be eaten. This would mean that it was considered to be sacred. There is a verse in Jeremiah that says:

> Yea, the stork in the heaven knows her appointed seasons, and the turtle dove and the swift and the swallow observe the time of coming, but my people know not the law of the Lord.

Meaning, of course, that the stork and the other creatures mentioned had listened to God, but that the people hadn't.

NATIVE AMERICAN MYTHS

The Arawak hold the stork in great esteem; like the hummingbird, the stork is credited with bringing tobacco to mankind.

THE FARMER AND THE STORK – AESOP'S FABLE

One day, a farmer found a large flock of cranes eating corn that he'd just planted. Justifiably infuriated, the farmer threw a large net over the birds with the intention of killing them all.

However, one of the birds was a stork.

'Please don't kill me – I'm not a crane, you see, I'm not like these other birds. I'm a fantastic mother, and I take good care of my ageing parents … so please spare me.'

However, the farmer would have none of it.

'Whatever you say, you were with the birds who keep stealing my corn, and I don't like it. I'm afraid you'll have to suffer the same fate.'

The moral of the story? You are judged by the company you keep; or, birds of a feather flock together.

What Bird Would You Be?

'I'd be a stork … storks get to see interesting places, their flight patterns are energetically immensely efficient (and beautiful to watch), they don't have very many natural enemies (except for humans, alas) … to me they seem like natural aristocrats. So, put me down for storkdom.'
Tom, Israel

'It would have to be a bird of paradise … their long tail feathers and dramatic colours make them very beautiful. The males also have to perform an extravagant dance to attract the females, which I quite like the sound of!'
Debbie, UK

The Swan

Water

My clothes are silent when I walk on the earth
Or rest at home, or ride the waters.
Sometimes my wings and this lofty air
Lift me high above the houses of men,
And the heavens carry me far and wide
Over the world. My feathered wings
Whistle loudly, singing a shrill
And melodious song when, moving high,
I pass like a soul over land and sea.
Anonymous, eighth-century riddle

The swan is one of the more important birds in terms of its meaning, its use in art and literature and as an archetype. The swan itself actually appears 'otherworldly' – the bright white feathers making the bird the very personification of light itself, so its appearance alone is really enough to justify its importance, but there are other aspects of the swan which make it crucial in the world of birds.

CHARACTERISTICS

There are several different kinds of swan, but the one we usually think of – the beautiful, graceful white bird – is the Mute Swan. The Mute Swan was domesticated early and used for its meat, being raised in captivity. Later it became to be prized more for its beauty, and is still used as an ornamental creature to this day.

The swan is one of the heaviest birds and needs a good take-off area, a smooth lake, in order to be able to get airborne. If you've ever seen a swan on the 'runway' you'll know just what a huge amount of noise and flurry the bird has to make to take to the skies. Conversely, the landing can appear to be a little undignified and the bird can be lost in crashing waves of water as its feet hit the surface first, but its proper dignity is soon restored.

Swans mate for life. They are extremely devoted to one another, and stay together for the whole year. They can be very territorial; for example, the Tundra Swan will have a territory of a square mile, which they will actively defend from 'invasion' by other swans! Swans are long-lived and it's believed that they can survive for up to 80 years.

Swans are large enough and strong enough to break a man's arm if they choose to; close up their faces can seem to be remarkably bad-tempered. They prefer colder weather and are not suited to hot climates.

THE BIRD OF ROYALTY

In the UK, this swan is still under the protection of the Crown, and a licence is needed to breed them or deal with them in any way, a piece of officialdom which is believed to date back to before the twelfth century. Swan's meat is a delicacy restricted to the household of the reigning monarch. In fact, if you stole a swan's egg during the time of Henry VII, you'd be imprisoned for a year and a day! There was even a Swan Master attached to the court.

It wasn't just in England that swans were the birds of nobles or royalty. In Germany, it was customary to take an oath upon a swan in the same way that religious texts are used in courts these days. Swans were so well-protected that there's even a report of a man who was imprisoned for six months simply for walking too close to the edge of a lake that had swans upon it, with a hooked stick over his shoulder!

THE SPIRITUAL ESSENCE OF THE SWAN

Because the swan is distinctively a bird that belongs both to the air and the water, it's seen to be a 'bird of life'; it's also the 'bird of the poet' because of an ancient belief, again prevalent throughout the entire world, that the swan contained the soul of a poet. Indeed, Shakespeare was called the 'sweet swan of Avon' by Ben Jonson. It's worth bearing in mind too that the swan is a supernatural bird, and has magical powers.

The swan is the bird who looks after the souls of dead children and guides them to the Otherworld.

THE SWAN SONG

The silver swan, who, living had no note,
When death approached, unlocked her silent throat.
Leaning her breast against the reedy shore
Thus sung her first and last, and sang no more:
Farewell, all joys; O death, come close mine eyes;
More geese than swans now live, more fools than wise.
Orlando Gibbons, *The Silver Swan*

It's a commonly known fact that the swan is meant not to sing. It is a lesser-known fact that, curiously, the very name 'swan' comes either from an Anglo-Saxon root – 'sounder', meaning 'sonnet' and 'sound', or from a Sanskrit root which bears the same meaning.

Indeed, the swan doesn't really sing, but when annoyed it will make a honking or trumpeting sound. When they are in their migratory flight swans do keep up a constant calling to one another, the noise of which used to be believed to belong to a pack of 'demon dogs' called 'Gabriel's Hounds' or 'The Devil's Dandy Dogs'. The sound of the large wings soughing through the air is a different matter, though …

As for the actual so-called 'swan song', it's first mentioned by the Roman writer Pliny, but strangely there's no evidence that the swan sings its only song before it dies, although the expression is immediately understood and has become a part of our common belief about the bird – we understand the analogy immediately even though there seems to be no evidence whatsoever to support this notion. Socrates said that the birds did not sing because of grief but from joy that they were going to meet their God.

SHAPE-SHIFTING BIRD

There's a recurrent theme in myth, legend and literature all over the world, from Ireland to India and everywhere else in between, of swans turning into people and vice versa. Particularly we find tales of the swan turning into a beautiful girl who comes to live with a human man for a period of time before something happens to make her return to her own world once more.

This version of the story, from *The Arabian Nights*, is typical. Hassan of Bassorah visits a place inhabited by bird-maidens. When they take off their feather garments, the bird-maidens are transformed into beautiful women. Hassan captures the clothes of one of the maidens in order to keep her in human form as his wife. She is able to regain her feathers and flies away from him. Hassan sets out on a quest to regain his wife and after many adventures succeeds in finding her.

There's another version of the story from Russia. 'Sweet Mikhail Ivanovich the Rover' is a Slav tale that begins with Mikhail the Rover about to shoot a swan, which warns him, 'Shoot not, else ill-fortune will doom thee for evermore!'

On landing the swan turns into a beautiful maiden. When Mikhail tries to kiss her she warns that she is an infidel. However, if he takes her to the holy city of Kiev, then she might be received by the church and thus be free to marry him. So off they go.

In a similar South German legend a swan speaks to a forester who is about to kill her. The beautiful maiden in this case says that she would be his if he could keep her existence a secret for one year. He fails and thus loses her.

Celtic folklore brings us the legend of the Children of Llyr, which is explained more fully in the section about the Celts (page 143). When King Llyr's first wife dies, he marries a wicked woman called Aoife. Jealous of Llyr's children by his first wife, Aoife turns them all into swans.

And we mustn't forget Tchaikovsky's ballet 'Swan Lake', which is another version of the swan maiden story!

A Mysterious Find

Recently in England there was the discovery of mysterious pits, in Cornwall, which contained a lining of swan's feathers and swanskin. In the centre of the pits were small pebbles and quartz stones, and in other pits were discovered eggs containing unhatched chicks. Whether or not the pits were part of some swan cult has yet to be established.

The Chained Birds

Another universally used image is that of two or more swans joined together with a silver chain. This image occurs in Greece, Persia, Europe, India and elsewhere, although precisely what the significance of this chain is, is now lost to us.

GREECE

Appropriately enough, given that the swan is the bird of poets, in Ancient Greece it was dedicated to the Muses.

Perhaps the most famous story in Greek mythology is the story of Leda and the Swan. Leda was the wife of Tyndareus, and Zeus fell in love with her appearance. He determined that he'd make love to her, and so, while Leda was bathing in a pool one evening, Zeus transformed himself into a swan and came to her. Leda later bore two sets of twins, Pollux and Helen (who became known as Helen of Troy, the infamous beauty whose face 'launched a thousand ships'), who were the children of Zeus as the swan, and Castor and Clytemnestra, the children of her husband.

There's another version of this story, though, which has Nemesis, who was Goddess of the Peloponnesian Swan Cult, being seduced by the Swan/Zeus, something she's not at all happy about. So she leaves the egg, which is found and cared for by Leda.

The swan is also sacred to Apollo, the God of poetry and prophecy. There's a story that he was born 'on the seventh day', and on the day he was born, seven swans flew around his birth-island, Delos, seven times. Apollo has the ability to change into a swan.

In addition, Aphrodite, the Goddess of love, was drawn in a chariot pulled by swans, as was Eros/Cupid, her son.

> Cormorants were kept by James I on the Thames at Westminster; they were semi-domesticated and used to fish for their master.

INDIA

The swan is a key bird in Hindu mythology. For Hindus the swan operates in both the physical and spiritual planes and represents the material world and the spirit world.

It's believed that the swan, rather than the goose, laid the egg from which the universe hatched. The mythical bird, the Hamsa, takes the form of two swans. The Hamsa is a symbolic representation of the spirit of ultimate union, and the mating habits of the birds themselves would corroborate this. The Parama Hamsa, or Supreme Swan, is representative of the Universal Self.

Brahma is seen riding on a swan, which is also credited with the ability to distinguish good from bad. Sarasvati, the wife of Brahma, also rides a swan. She is the embodiment of education, music and wisdom.

CELTIC MYTHOLOGY

Ireland was referred to as the 'swan abounding land' by a poet in the seventeenth century, and indeed there's a wealth of mythology about the bird here. One of the beliefs was that the souls of people would take on the form of swans, so consequently it was considered appallingly bad luck to kill or injure the bird.

The swan is a central figure in much of the Celtic mythology that is associated with birds.

As in the Greek myth of Leda and the Swan, the shape of a swan is often assumed by 'Otherworld' people, spirits, faeries and the like, who wish to come to the earthly realms for some reason.

The Goddess Brighit's symbol is the White Swan, and therefore it is no surprise to find that among other attributes, Brighit was the Goddess of poetry. She also has healing powers attributed to her, and these powers are drawn upon by reciting poetry at magical wells dedicated to her.

In the Druid world, the swan represents the bard, muse or poet. Swan feathers were used to make the bardic cloak, with the feathers ascribing shamanistic qualities to the wearer.

NATIVE AMERICAN LORE

The swan is able to call up the four winds, according to the Navajo tradition, and the Great Spirit employs swans to carry out its wishes. The bird is symbolic of grace for many of the tribes, including in the Seneca, Aztec, Yaqui, Cherokee, Cheyenne and Mayan belief systems.

Swan feathers were used as part of the ornamentation of headdresses for several tribes.

SERBIA

In Serbia, the Vila, who are blonde, wraith-like nymphs, could assume the forms of swans, and Serbian women have a custom that they curtsy and say a prayer to the first swan they see at springtime.

NORSE MYTHOLOGY

In Norse mythology, the swan was the embodiment of the Valkyrie.

JAPAN

The Ainu live in the north of Japan, and hold a particular reverence for birds and animals. For them, the swan was the equivalent of an angelic being that lived in heaven. When the equivalent of a civil war all but wiped out the race, so the story goes, the swan descended to the last remaining Ainu child, reared him, then, when he was old enough, married him to ensure the survival of the race.

THE UGLY DUCKLING

One of the most famous stories about the swan is about the ugly duckling who is taunted by the other birds because of its appearance. Eventually the poor 'duckling' grows into a swan, one of the most beautiful birds, and so has the last laugh.

This is a story beloved of children, since it reflects insecurities and is ultimately reassuring; all will be well in the end.

What Bird Would You Be?

'I'd be a swan, because they're ugly when babies, beautiful when grown, couple up for life, are gnarly when angry, and serene when all's good. And they don't do much flying, instead effortlessly gliding on still waters that run deep.'
Ysanne, Los Angeles

The Albatross

Air

Often, to pass the time on board, the crew
will catch an albatross, one of those big birds
which nonchalantly chaperone a ship
across the bitter fathoms of the sea.

Tied to the deck, this sovereign of space,
as if embarrassed by its clumsiness,
pitiably lets its great white wings
drag at its sides like a pair of unshipped oars.

How weak and awkward, even comical
this traveller but lately so adroit –
one deckhand sticks a pipe stem in its beak,
another mocks the cripple that once flew!

The Poet is like this monarch of the clouds
riding the storm above the marksman's range;
exiled on the ground, hooted and jeered,
he cannot walk because of his great wings.
Charles Baudelaire, *The Albatross*

CHARACTERISTICS

There are at least 13 species of albatross, and the bird is well known to deep-sea fishermen and sailors all over the world. The albatross is a master of flight; they are so aerodynamically perfect that they can glide effortlessly, switching direction with minimal effort. Possibly the best-known of the species is the Wandering Albatross, which has a wingspan of 12 feet (3.5 metres); this makes it the largest of all living, flying birds.

Nests are usually found on small islands, and albatrosses breed in colonies. The nest is simple, often just a scrape in the ground lined with leaves or feathers. Both parents share in the incubating of the egg, which is just as well, since it takes between 65 and 81 days to hatch, according to the species. The courtship rituals of the albatross are famous; they perform peculiar-looking dances, bowing to one another, click their bills together, and emit strange-sounding nasal groans.

Albatrosses like to follow ships, and fishermen used to catch them to eat. Now, however, the bird is seriously endangered and is under protection. Because of their habit of following ships, the albatross sometimes lands on board deck. The bird then has great difficulty in taking off again, since it can't get high enough to make it over the rails. This causes such annoyance that the poor albatross will often vomit up their stomach oil in frustration. Once on land, the albatross is ungainly and ungraceful, the exact opposite of how it appears in its natural element, the air.

The name 'albatross' comes from the Portuguese, 'Alcatraz', meaning 'large sea bird'. Confusingly, the Island of Alcatraz, off San Francisco, which used to house the infamous prison, was named because pelicans are also called 'Alcatraz', but with a different meaning. In this case the name comes from the Arabic for 'bucket', a reference to the large sack under the pelican's bill; pelicans used to nest on the island.

There's a commonly held but erroneous belief that the bird is stupid; this is also reflected in a couple of folk names for the bird – the 'Mollymawk', from the Dutch 'Mallemok' meaning 'stupid gull', while in Japan the bird is called the 'Kakadori', which translates as 'fool bird'. Even the word 'goon', meaning a bit of a fool, comes from a slang name for the albatross, 'goon' or 'gooney'. One of the reasons the bird is supposed to be stupid is because it seemingly has no fear of man and is very trusting.

SOULS OF DEAD SAILORS

One of the prevailing legends about the albatross is that it holds the soul of a dead sailor; this gave rise to the belief that it was extremely unlucky to kill them. Everyone is familiar with the Coleridge poem, 'The Rime of the Ancient Mariner', which describes this; it would be impossible to write about the albatross without mentioning it so here's a brief excerpt:

At length did cross an Albatross
Through the fog it came;
As it had been a Christian soul
We hail'd it in God's name.

'God save thee, ancient Mariner!
From the fiends that plague thee thus! –
Why look'st thou so?' – With my cross-bow
I shot the albatross.
And I had done a hellish thing,
And it would work 'em woe:
For all averred, I had killed the bird
Which made the breeze to blow.

The killing of the albatross signifies disaster; even now, when we speak of 'having an albatross around our neck' we refer to a seemingly insurmountable problem.

Weather Bird

When you're at sea, the weather is of paramount importance, so it's no surprise that the albatross has an association with the weather. The presence of the albatross circling a ship was believed to herald storms, high winds and bad weather in general.

Greece

The species name for the albatross, Diomedeidea, is after a Greek hero, Diomedas, a hero of the Trojan Wars.

Easter Island

In the Pacific islands, the albatross was believed to be a messenger from the Gods, and was meant to be able to sleep on the wing. The bird is revered as a deity, and indeed, on Easter Island, one of the famous Easter Island statues has the beak of an albatross.

They were also believed to build a nest that floated like a raft.

The Bluebird

Air

When ice is thawed and snow is gone,
And racy sweetness floods the trees;
When snowbirds from the hedge have flown
And on the hive-porch swarm the bees –
Drifting down the first warm wind
That thrills the earliest days of spring,
The bluebird seeks our maple groves
And charms them into tasselling.
Maurice Thompson, *The Bluebird*

CHARACTERISTICS

A member of the thrush family, the bluebird is native to America. The Pilgrim Fathers called the bird the Blue Robin after the Robin Redbreast they'd left at home. The bluebird has a soft warbling song, somewhat quieter and gentler than that of other species of the thrush family. They like to live in open woodlands, and nest in holes in tree trunks and the like, although they will happily occupy bird boxes if placed in the right position. In the wild, bluebirds prefer a home with a south-facing entrance, so bear this in mind if you're inspired to put up a nesting box!

There are three types of bluebird: the Mountain Bluebird, the Western Bluebird and the Eastern Bluebird. Bluebirds used to be relatively common, but are rarer now, and the population is down by 90 per cent of what it reputedly used to be, because of a lack of breeding places caused by land development. Bluebirds are fertile, sometimes having two or three broods in one season, and are not monogamous birds; they'll often change partner after broods.

The symbolic association with the colour of this bird has played a key part in some of the beliefs that have sprung up around it. These are generally all from the Native American quarter, which is not surprising given the bird's origins.

The Blue Factor

In any bird that displays so prominent a colour as to have it as part of its name, the colour will provide an important clue as to the symbolism of the bird. Blue is the colour of spirituality, of transition, of a change about to come. It is also a colour closely related to creative expression. For some tribes, blue was associated with the South, and therefore the place of the Sun, an auspicious direction. Conversely, for other tribes blue was associated with the North and the blue of ice or coldness.

The Bluebird of Happiness

As a harbinger of Spring the bluebird brings joy. However, its reputation as the Bird of Happiness is a relatively recent development and is due to the Maeterlinck play *The Blue Bird*, which is about a little boy and girl who go in search of this elusive creature.

Native American Lore

As befits such an important bird, the bluebird features in several Native American myths, and has a position as King of the Birds for some, since the God Tirawa sent the bird to see what was happening after the Great Flood. The bluebird returned with news, whereupon Tirawa promised that the little bird would become Chief once mankind returned to Earth once again. That's why the image of the bluebird is often displayed on ceremonial pipes.

Because the bluebird is a harbinger of Spring, it is a bird of hope, and of better times to come. The Pueblo Indians use bluebird feathers on the prayer sticks that are used specifically at their solstice gatherings, to send a message to the Gods to send the bluebird soon, and Spring with it.

The suggestion of the colour blue as indicative of rites of passage is associated with the time when a young girl becomes a woman; and so the bluebird, for Hopi Indians, is representative of change and fertility. Another Hopi myth is of a place called Sichmo, or the Flower Mound. In the Otherworld, all the flowers of Summer bloom in Winter, and when the world is turned topsyturvy, the bluebird is there to help with the turning – again, a reminder of this bird's role at important times of transition.

The Western Bluebird heralds the rain for some tribes, and its feathers are used on prayer sticks to bring about the desired precipitation. The Navajo have a belief that two bluebirds stand at the doorway of the House of God.

The Crane

Air

> At dawn you shall appear
> A gaunt, red-wattled crane
> She whom they know too well to fear,
> Lunging your beak down like a spear
> To fetch them home again.
> **Robert Graves, from** *The White Goddess*

CHARACTERISTICS

When we look at the time that birds have been on the planet, it is an incredible thought that the Sandhill Crane has been on earth for 10 million years; it is one of the oldest species on the planet.

A migratory bird, the Sandhill Crane, which breeds in warmer climates, doesn't need to escape the cold in winter, so will stay put. When cranes do migrate, however, they fly in a distinctive 'V' formation so as to collectively optimize their aerodynamics and speed. They can cruise for long distances at speeds of around 45 miles per hour. In flight they look different from herons, with whom they are often confused; the crane extends its neck fully whereas the heron has a distinctive kink in its neck.

Cranes will fly at high altitudes, sometimes cruising a couple of miles above the earth's surface. Aesop characterizes the crane's ability to fly so high thus:

> to rise above the clouds into endless space, and survey the wonders of
> the heavens, as well as the earth beneath, with its seas, lakes and rivers,
> as far as the eye can reach.

Many species of cranes are threatened; their numbers have depleted in recent years. Cranes live for a long time – more than 50 years has been recorded – and they prefer to mate for life.

THE DANCE OF THE CRANE

One of the most unusual habits of the crane is its dance; although it can be a courtship ritual, this isn't always the case since often the birds will dance for the sheer joy of it. The dance involves the birds walking around each other with little steps with their wings half unfurled. They will also leap into the air – often as high as 15 or 20 feet (5 or 6 metres) – and then they bow to one another, and stretch; sometimes the bird will pick up pieces of stick or twigs and throw them into the air as part of the dance. The dance of the crane has, as you might imagine, given rise to many legends.

THE MYSTICAL BIRD OF MAGICAL SIGNS

The crane has a lot of mystery and magic attached to it, and one of the more fascinating legends, for me, is the story that the Roman God Mercury (or Hermes, his Greek equivalent) invented the alphabet by observing the wings of cranes during their flight. And these secret signs and symbols – the alphabet – were kept in a bag made of crane skin.

Indeed, we see these references to the crane being the bearer of language throughout lots of different cultures and societies. In Egypt, Mercury is represented as Thoth, who is said to have invented hieroglyphs; Thoth is symbolized by the ibis, which shares similar traits to the crane. In Africa, the Bambara believe that the crane was present at the birth of speech; in their secret initiation ceremonies it is declared, 'The beginning of all beginnings of the word was the crested crane. The bird said: "I Speak."'

THE VIGILANCE OF THE CRANE

Cranes often sleep with one foot bent upwards, and there was a belief that a stone would be held in the claws. The stone would be dropped to waken the other birds if there was any sign of danger, or if the crane fell asleep; therefore the bird became symbolic of vigilance.

THE CRANE'S STONE

During the long migratory flights of the crane, it was popularly supposed that the bird swallowed a stone, which would act as ballast during the long journey. Once the destination was reached, the stone would be regurgitated, and at this point became very valuable – it had the power to turn anything it touched into gold.

ANCIENT GREECE

The migrations of cranes are so regular that the ancient Greeks used the appearance and disappearance of the birds as a way of checking their calendar. As soon as the cranes departed, sailors would bring their ships up on to the beach for the winter months.

The crane was a solar symbol for the ancient Greeks and as such was dedicated to the Sun god, Apollo, who was believed to disguise himself as the bird when he visited Earth. Not surprisingly, the exuberant dance of the crane was seen as a celebration of life itself and prophesied the coming of Spring and the sunshine.

In *The White Goddess*, Robert Graves relays the legend of Ibycus, which tells us a little bit about the association of the crane with poets and poetry. Ibycus was a sixth-century poet, who lived most of his life on the island of Samos. He was attacked by robbers and left for dead. Although the wound proved fatal in the end, Ibycus managed to call on a flock of passing cranes to help him find his murderer. The cranes hovered over the heads of the bandits while they were at an open-air theatre, and one of the party, frightened by the birds' presence, confessed to the murder.

> When the crane attempts to dance with the horse, she gets broken bones.
> *Proverb*

In another myth, Gerana was an extraordinarily lovely woman; unfortunately she was also extraordinarily vain. Apparently Hera and Artemis were so annoyed by this vanity that they transformed the woman into a crane, which explains the Greek name for the bird, which is 'geranion'.

EGYPT

A two-headed crane was apparently spotted flying over the Nile, and this presaged a period of unrivalled wealth.

CHINA

In China the crane represents longevity and faithfulness; both traits which are, of course, true to the bird. It is also seen as a messenger between the Gods and humans, and is regarded as carrying the souls of deceased people to paradise. The dance of the crane represented the power of flight and, ultimately, the arrival in the Land of the Immortals, and the dance was copied by humans using stilts. In Taoism, the crane is the symbol of immortality. Further, the Chinese believed that 'heavenly cranes' or 'blessed cranes' represented wisdom, and carried on their backs wise men, legendary sages, on their flights between the worlds.

Just as Greek fishermen used the birds as a form of calendar, in China the punctual migratory habits of the crane indicated the time to sow crops or when to harvest them.

JAPAN

In Japan the crane is called the 'bird of happiness' and 'Honourable Lord Crane'. Pictures of cranes, symbolizing longevity, are given to old people and are a reminder of their great age.

It was believed that cranes could live to be a thousand years old, and that they accomplished this by practising a particular kind of breathing technique, which humans should try to emulate. In addition, the Immortals were carried about by cranes, and crane eggs were an ingredient in a magical potion that was said to give immortality to the imbiber. There's a legend about a mighty warrior who managed to increase Japan's territory; on his death his soul assumed the form of a crane.

During an eleventh-century Buddhist ceremony, hundreds of cranes were set free as a thanksgiving for a successful battle. Each of the birds had a prayer attached to its leg carrying the name of a soldier who had been slain in the battle. This again was symbolic of the belief that the bird would carry the spirits of the departed to Heaven.

There's another story about cranes being labelled; Emperor Yorimoto attached tags to the legs of cranes in an early attempt to track both the movements of the birds and their age. It was rumoured that some of the birds labelled in this way were still around, several centuries after the death of the Emperor.

Interestingly, the red and white colours of the crane have become an important part of Japan's national identity. The Japanese flag carries these colours, and they are also used in bridal dresses, denoting fidelity.

INDIA

For some reason, in India cranes were seen as harbingers of treachery, and there's a crane-headed Goddess, Balgala-Mukhi, who is the embodiment of all mankind's destructive instincts. The crane is also the symbol of Kali. However, Ramakrishna, who was believed to have been the reincarnation of Buddha and Krishna, is said to have fallen into a faint as a child in 1842, when he was astounded by the beauty of a flock of cranes flying against a stormy clouded sky.

CELTIC LORE

In Celtic mythology the crane was often contrasted unfavourably with the swan; sometimes the crane was seen as a bird to be wary of. Despite this, the crane is one of the four sacred birds in the ancient British and Irish belief systems, along with the raven, the swan and the eagle. It was taboo at the time to eat the flesh of the crane.

Again, there are links between the crane and the alphabet, and Philip and Stephanie Carr-Gomm, in their *Druid Animal Oracle*, tell us that

> Since it was known only to the Druids, the term 'Crane Knowledge' came to be used to denote knowledge of the Ogham [an ancient alphabet, the tree alphabet] in particular, and of arcane science in general.

The book goes on to relate how, once Christianity started to supersede Druidry and the Old Ways, the wiser priests were referred to as 'Crane Clerics'.

There is a darker side to the crane in Celtic lore, since it is associated with the 'hag', Cailleach, who is the dark side of the Goddess figure, and presaged death and bad luck for some. However, the Grandmother of Fion managed to save her grandson from falling over a cliff by assuming the shape of a crane and flying down to rescue him, so it's not all bad!

The crane was also associated with Pwll, who was the King of the Underworld. Three cranes are said to guard the entrance to his domain.

EUROPE

In Germany, the crane was sacred to a God with similar traits to those of Mercury or Hermes. In Europe in general the bird represented loyalty and vigilance, and this latter trait is illustrated by the story related under 'The Vigilance of the Crane', on page 362.

Interestingly, the word 'pedigree' comes from the Norman French 'pied de grue', which means 'crane's foot', the shape of which is said to show a similarity with the arrow-shaped diagram used on family trees.

What Bird Would You Be?

'My bird? That's easy. It's the North American Thunderbird. Why? My people believe that this elusive giant causes thunder by flapping its wings and lightning by flashing its eyes ... Free electricity indeed!'
Dion, USA

The Goose

Air

If we took all of our goose mothers
And sat them in a row
Would they but once perform a V
Or tell us when to sow?

The blue-green earth we cherish not
Came from their golden egg
And yet we leave the common lot
In autumn fields to beg

But what of fine democracy
Of taking turns in flight?
One cuts the wind and points the V
And portions out the night

When the cornfields turns to ice
She flies her secrets south
And whispers coyly 'silly goose'
Spread wide across my mouth
Sarah Coursey, *Goose 234*

CHARACTERISTICS

There are at least 20 different types of geese; all are possibly amongst the oldest of the bird species (there's evidence of this since goose images are carved into prehistoric sites around the world), and all are migratory. They're territorial birds, and over the years have been used as 'guard dogs' by many. Geese mate for life, and both parents play an equal part in the raising of the goslings. Because the goose and the swan are so similar, belonging to the same family of birds, it's understandable that they are often mixed up in mythology and folklore; however, there are some distinct differences.

Inky Feathers

Of course, in talking about birds as messengers, it's important to remember that one of the best feathers for using as a quill is the goose feather – I have one here. It's about 14 inches (35 cm) long, creamy white, and the end has been bevelled and then cut to a blunt square point. There's a vertical nick dividing the point. The hollow stem of the feather provides a perfect reservoir for holding the ink, and the feathers of the goose or swan were the favoured feathers for quill pens from the Middle Ages until the nineteenth century.

It seems appropriate, then, that the goose was universally acknowledged to be a mediator between Heaven and Earth.

Talking about the feathers of the goose, it's worth mentioning also that goose down is notoriously soft, fluffy and durable, and its use in mattresses and quilts probably gave rise to the idea that the goose was a symbol of marital fidelity, fertility and happiness.

Geese Growing On Trees?

Possibly one of the oddest ideas about any bird I've come across is the notion that geese used to grow on trees. This was first mentioned in the eleventh century, and then again in the twelfth, on a Genoese map which has the following annotation for Ireland:

> Certain of their trees bear fruit which, decaying within, produces a worm which, as it subsequently develops, becomes hairy and feathered, and, provided wings, it flies like a bird.

There's another old piece of British folklore which supports this bizarre theory, with a twist: goose eggs were said to grow in trees. They would hatch, out would pop the bird and, being unable to fly, they would fall into the water below. This is why the goose was ranked with fish in the Middle Ages and was therefore permitted to be eaten on Fridays by Pope Innocent III!

It is likely that this piece of misinformation related to the Barnacle Goose; here's a quote from John Gerard, from 1597:

They are found in the North parts of Scotland and the Islands adjacent, called Orchades, certain trees whereon do grow certaine shells of a white colour tending to russet, wherein are contained little living creatures; which shells in time of maturity doe open, and out of them grow those little living things, which falling into the water do become fowles, which we call Barnacles; in the North of England, brant Geese; and in Lancashire, tree Geese.

If anyone does manage to spot any egg-bearing trees, please do contact me in person. After all, we should keep an open mind about these matters.

Mother Goose

The Mother Goose legend, about a fairy bird mother who delights children with nursery rhymes and stories, actually has its origins with a real person – an early Queen of France, Bertrada, whose son Charlemagne went on to become the founder of the Holy Roman Empire. Bertrada was a patroness of children, but unfortunately she had such large and inelegant feet that she received the nickname 'Berte aux Grand Pied', or Bertha Goosefoot. After she died a mythology grew up around her, and the Mother Goose stories began.

Weather Bird

The bird was the bird of the Norse God Wotan, who was the God of Storms, and indeed the goóse can be associated with wild weather. There's an old Scottish rhyme:

Wild geese, wild geese, ganging to the sea
Good weather it will be;
Wild geese, wild geese, ganging to the hill
The weather it will spill.

The breastbone of the goose, in common with other birds, was used to predict the weather and what the seasons held in store:

If the November goose-bone be thick,
So will the winter weather be;
If the November goose-bone be thin,
So will the winter weather be.

The goose was also meant to be able to predict the weather in other ways; for example, the bird's body language could indicate whether or not rain was coming. There's a sixteenth-century English poem about this:

When the rain raineth and the goose winketh
Little wots [knows] the gosling what the goose thinketh.

As well as being able to predict whether or not it would rain, the goose was also able to tell whether or not it was going to be frosty – an important skill when valuable crops could be ruined by an unanticipated freeze. This useful piece of information would be deduced by the flight formations of the birds.

Nowadays, the breastbone of the goose isn't really needed as a weather forecasting tool, but is instead snapped to give the winner of the larger part the power to make a wish.

Egypt

The goose image is found in Egyptian tombs dating back to at least 3000 BC, since the souls of the pharaohs were depicted as geese. When a new Pharaoh succeeded to the throne, four wild geese were released at the cardinal points, into the four corners of the Earth, symbolizing the power held by the Pharaoh over all corners of his kingdom.

The bird was revered as a Sun symbol, and there's a reason for this. The goose is known today in children's stories as having laid the golden egg, and this simple tale originates in Egyptian mythology, since the golden egg referred to was the Sun, which was 'laid' by the Nile Goose and from which Re, the Sun God, was hatched. The goose is also a close companion of Isis, the Goddess of Love. Huge numbers of geese were offered in sacrifice, particularly by Ramses I, who killed 360,000 birds over a 31-year period.

Completely at odds with the reverence attached to the goose was the use of the bird as the emblem of a stupid person; the origin of our saying, 'Silly goose', perhaps? Despite this, the goose had the freedom of the Egyptian's house and garden, in spite of its occasional bad temper.

GREECE AND ROME

In Greek mythology, the goose is associated with Boreas, the North Wind. Before Cupid grew his own wings, he's seen riding a goose, both in Roman interpretations and in Asia Minor. Aphrodite, the Greek Goddess of love, is often portrayed as riding on a goose, too.

The Greeks used the birds to guard houses and, a little like dogs in some countries, they were companions for children.

THE CAPITOLINE GEESE

Geese saved the day for Rome in 388 BC. Gaulish armies had successfully invaded central Italy, and the only place not under their control was the Temple of Juno in Rome, high up on the Capitoline Hill; although the small army there was holding out bravely, the soldiers were under siege and weakening. The geese living in the temple, birds sacred to Juno, were also hungry. One night, the Roman guards were asleep when the Gauls decided to attack. The noise and flurry created by the angry birds awoke the Roman soldiers and the invaders were repelled, and this marked a turn in fortune for the Roman forces. Thereafter the geese were honoured annually in a procession, which carried a golden goose to the Capitoline Hill.

INDIA

The wild goose was sacred to Brahma, who is often shown riding one of these birds. A white goose in particular equates to the Sun symbol in India.

There's an old legend about the Buddha, too, who, when born as a Brahman, had three daughters. When he died he was reborn as a goose with golden feathers, which the daughters sold one by one in order to look after the family. When his wife decided (despite the protests of the daughters) to pluck all the feathers at once, however, they became the usual white feathers, and as such were worthless; a case of bad financial management, perhaps, which has similarities to the tale of the Goose with the Golden Egg that you can read about shortly.

CHINA AND JAPAN

Geese were regarded as envoys between Heaven and Earth. The white goose represented masculinity and light, and as a symbol of fertility and faithfulness, the goose had an important part to play in wedding ceremonies. The bird is still often given as a gift to the groom by the family of the bride, as a dowry.

In both China and Japan, the goose is inextricably linked with the moon.

NATIVE AMERICAN LORE

The Snow Goose is the symbol for Winter in the Native American medicine wheel.

The migration of Canada Geese, for Native American Indians, marks the passage of the Great Cycle of the Year, and serves as a reminder of changes and transitions in all our lives.

SHAMANIC BELIEFS

The shaman of the Altai Mountains, after the ritual sacrifice of a horse, would ride on the back of a goose to pursue the animal's soul. And after a visit to the King of the Dead in the Underworld, the shaman would return on the back of a goose.

CELTIC LORE

The mix up between the goose and the swan is probably more prevalent in Celtic folklore than anywhere else, and both birds were considered sacred. Caesar was the first to note to the sacred status of the goose and the swan in the Celtic British Isles, since he observed that the birds were not eaten, which is always a clue as to the esteem in which a bird or animal was held. This was possibly because of the goose's connection with the sun-egg. Indeed, although we now slaughter geese as a delicacy for midwinter feasts, it was originally considered very bad form to do so, because in killing off the goose we kill off hopes for the Sun's return.

In Wales, to see geese at night on a lake was considered to be very unlucky, since the birds could be witches. In fact this belief, that shamans, wizards and witches could shape-shift into geese, is prevalent throughout the world.

NORSE MYTHOLOGY

The goose was used as a grave offering in Scandinavian countries, probably because of the belief that the bird was able to migrate from this world to the next and could assist the spirit of the departed person on the journey.

The Goddess Freyja was said to possess the feet of geese or a swan.

THE WILD GOOSE

The Wild Goose, otherwise known as the Greylag Goose, is the precursor to all the other species of geese we know today.

There are not so many Wild Geese left now in the British Isles, and what there are tend to be restricted to the north of Scotland, but there are large flocks in the USA and William Fiennes, in his book *The Snow Geese*, tracked their journey along their migratory route. William was ill for a long time, and felt trapped during his period of recuperation. A new-found interest in birds, and in the snow goose in particular, inspired him to make this epic journey, and I'd recommend anyone to read the book.

Geese sometimes pine to death at the loss of a mate.

There's a gorgeous description of the birds as a huge congregation of 200,000 geese come to land on the ice at Sand Lake:

> Scarves of glitter furled through the flock when drifts of birds turned
> their backs and white wings to the sun, and sometimes the entire sky
> was lit with shimmer, as if a silver, sequined dress were rippling beneath
> a mirror ball, the sounds of goose calls and beating wings pounding the
> ice below.

The 'V' formation of groups of geese in flight is a beautiful thing to see. It looks like an arrowhead, full of intent and faith in the journey being made, all the birds spaced equally in a rhythmic and harmonic pattern.

Finally, here's the story of the goose that laid the golden egg, from Aesop's Fables – an interesting allegorical tale which I guess is telling us to be patient and to let the natural course of events unfold …

The Goose That Laid The Golden Egg

Once upon a time, a farmer went to check on his geese, and found to his utter surprise and delight that his goose had laid a golden egg! The egg was very heavy, being made of solid gold, and as you can imagine the farmer and his wife were more than delighted with this astonishing event.

Even more was to come. Every day after that, when the farmer went to check on his birds, the goose had laid another golden egg.

Of course, the farmer and his wife became very rich, and no doubt had a new-found popularity amongst the farming community. However, a strange thing happened. The richer the farmer got, the more greedy he became; he wanted more and more, until one day he had the bright idea that if he cut open the magical goose he could have all the golden eggs at once.

Of course, once the farmer had cut open the goose, he found that inside there was nothing at all – and, moreover, the goose was dead.

> Three grey geese in a green field grazing,
> Grey were the geese and green was the grazing.
> **Anonymous**

What Bird Would You Be?

'A Canadian Goose. Beautiful, majestic, a natural wonder of flight and survival. No predators and a command of the world's great wildernesses. Sailors believed them the angels of the seasons themselves as they signified the very soul of Mother Nature and her Green Man's regeneration of the world. Punctuating her births and moons with a journey so complex it was not for a mere mortal to understand, but for God himself to command. But have you seen them try to land? Hilarious!'
Bob, USA

'My choice of bird would be the wild goose, because of a song I remember ... The goose also expresses for me my own ambivalence between staying with what is safe and familiar, and the longing for the strange and adventurous, which has marked my life.'
Eleanor, UK

The Jay

Air

I am a wonder. I vary my voice,
Sometimes bark like a dog, sometimes bleat like a goat,
Sometimes honk like a goose, sometimes shriek like a hawk.
Sometimes I mimic the dusky eagle,
That war-bird's cry, sometimes I mock
The kite's voice, sometimes the gull singing
Where I sit glad. G suggests me,
Also A and R, with O,
H and I. Now I am named,
As these six letters clearly say.
Eighth-century riddle, *the Higora*

'Higora' was the Anglo-Saxon word for either the jay or the woodpecker, in case you were wondering!

Characteristics

As I'm writing this, there's a flock of jays over in the woods about 170 feet (50 metres) away. Although some people think that their harsh cries are annoying, for me they sound like they're having a nice time. They are sociable birds, and I think they're funny …

There are two types of jay we'll be looking at here: the Common Jay (*Garrulus glandarius*) and the American Blue Jay (*Cyanocitta cristata*). The Common Jay is found in temperate woodlands all the way from Britain to Japan, and tends to be more often heard than seen, although in cities it's happy to live in parks and tends to be less shy than it would be in its country habitat. As the poem above explains, the jay has a wide range of vocal abilities, as you might expect from a member of the Corvid family, but its warning chatter is very distinctive. Because jays tend to congregate in groups, several birds can give out the same warnings and it can become a bit of a cacophony! In Scots Gaelic, the name for the jay is Schreachag Choille, which aptly translates as 'Screamer in the Woods'.

Jays are lovely-looking birds, with a cheeky aspect; they have exquisite blue flashes on their wings. They prefer to stay near the cover of trees, especially among oak trees, since the jay is particularly fond of acorns, and the jay is believed to have been instrumental in the spread of oak forests because of its habit of burying acorns.

Ancient Greece and Rome

The musical and imitative ability of the jay is very high, and Cicero relates a tale about a Roman barber who had a pet jay in his shop. The jay was well-known for being able to imitate musical instruments, but one day the funeral procession of a wealthy man passed the bird, and after this the poor jay seemed to be struck dumb – either that or the bird had been deafened. However, it seems that the jay was merely absorbing what he'd heard, and few days later he created a perfect rendition of the trumpet parts he had memorized, although the bird had heard them only once!

Jays were also kept in Ancient Greece as pets, prized for their imitative ability. Aelian said of the bird, 'The jay is an excellent mimic of all other sounds, and best of all the human voice.'

The jay was sacred to Dionysus.

AMERICA

The Blue Jay is the American counterpart of the Common Jay, and lives for the most part in North America. The blue jay also likes woodlands but has adapted well to life in cities. The bird is boisterous, and unfortunately has a bit of a reputation as a bully! In addition, for some reason the jay never seemed to be seen on Fridays, therefore it gained the reputation of being the bird of Satan. The story goes that Fridays were the day that the bird carried sticks down to Hell for its master, presumably to keep those bonfires burning.

However, it's not all bad for this beautiful bird. The Blue Jay is one of the birds first credited with the discovery of the Earth.

NATIVE AMERICAN LORE

In Pueblo areas, the Jay is associated with war – its cries alone would be enough to give the bird this reputation. However, the 'bully' aspect has also been a factor. Jays like to 'mob' other birds in order to drive them away from the jay's territory. Jays don't restrict their mobbing activities to other birds such as hawks or owls, but will also attack men if necessary. The birds are particularly fearless.

Pueblo warriors or War priests will therefore carry the feathers of this bird, or use the feathers on the top of prayer sticks which would then be put in close proximity to the enemy so that they would be 'robbed of their wits'.

Jays are also believed to be able to kill ghosts – an extremely useful bird to have on your side, therefore. Here's a segment from a Zuni story relating to this sinister ability of the jay:

The people stared and chattered in greater fright than ever before at seeing the dead seemingly come to life!

'Akaa! Akaa!' cried a flock of jays.

'Hear that!' said the villagers. 'Hear that, and ask what's the matter!

The jays are coming; whoever they light on dies! Run!'

And they left off their standing as though chased by demons. On one or two of the hindmost some jays alighted. They fell dead as though struck by lightning.

Therefore the jays rescued the villagers from the ghosts, while also inadvertently killing some of the living too.

In Canada, the jay is said to warn the Eskimos if Indians from the Hudson Bay area approached their camp; so the jay wasn't regarded with much favour by the Indians in this area. However, for the Chinook people, the jay was a deity; he was a clown, a mischief maker, boastful and a trouble-maker, happy when making mischief either for himself or for other birds, or indeed for humans! The Winnebago people called him the 'jester'.

I tried your suggestion of associating a bird with a person. I decided that the jay was very like my friend Bobby – they're both highly intelligent, colourful, chatty, slightly mad-looking characters. I don't speak to Bob that much because he's halfway across the world. So, every time I saw the jay, he'd spring to mind. One day I saw two jays together, so I made an expensive phone call to see if anything special was happening … he told me he'd just met the girl he was going to marry. That was just six months ago. Sure enough, they married last week.
Wendy, USA

What Bird Would You Be?

'I think I would have to choose a jackdaw, as I tend to live with them all year round now in one of my chimneys ... they are determined, intelligent, resourceful and have a great sense of humour.'
Dave, UK

The Kite

Air

Even as the raven, the crow and the greedy kite
Do swarming flock where carrion corpse doth fall,
And tiring tear with beak and talons' might
Both skin and flesh to gorge their guts withal.
Anonymous, 1576

CHARACTERISTICS

Birds of the kite family are found all over the world, although in general their numbers are dropping. Having said this, the Red Kite is making a remarkable comeback in the UK, where introduced birds are adapting well. Its recovery has been so successful, in fact, that it now ranks as one of Britain's favourite birds.

Kites are powerful flyers and can cover large distances quickly. It is a large bird, with a wingspan of around 4–5 feet (120–150 cm), and it has a distinctive silhouette as it soars high in the sky.

The kite was once a common sight in London, particularly during Tudor times, when it was valued for its help in clearing up the filthy, garbage-strewn streets. As well as carrion, the kite will eat small rodents and insects. The nest of a kite, built primarily of sticks, will also sometimes contain scraps of clothing, paper bags and pieces of string, which the bird pilfers from what we consider to be rubbish.

The name of the kite is believed to come from the Greek word meaning 'to quarrel', reflecting the so-called argumentative nature of the bird. The kite as a sail-like object flown from a piece of cord is named after the bird.

ANCIENT GREECE

Since the kite was the harbinger of Spring when it returned to Greece from its winter migrations, the bird was greeted by bowing. Apparently some Greek peasants were so thrilled to see the bird that they would grovel in obeisance at the sight of the first bird, or would even turn somersaults! The arrival of the bird was a sign that it was warm enough for the sheep to be sheared.

Despite this, the bird was still seen as a thief, and there's an account of a kite even stealing a sliver of beef steak from the plate of a soldier as he was having his dinner on the verandah of a barrack room. Other stories relate that the kite was once a king, but his disreputable behaviour resulted in him being transformed into a bird.

Aristotle gives us an interesting, if slightly illogical piece of information; he mentions that the kite lays only two eggs but has three babies.

Kites were sacred to Apollo, who could change himself into a kite; and the flight patterns of these birds were of particular interest to the augurs, who associated the kite with the power of clairvoyance.

ANCIENT EGYPT

Reputedly, the first book of religious laws and customs was carried to Thebes by a kite, acting as a messenger of the Gods. In honour of the bird, the scribes would wear the feather of a kite in their hats.

THE FAR EAST

In China, there are similarities between the kite and the magpie of European literature. Both were seen as raucous birds, and both were supposed to be thieves, too. In Japan, though, the bird is sacred; a kite landed on the head of Japan's first emperor, Nihon-Gi, and showed him the way to victory. This meant that the effigy of a kite often accompanied the emperors.

INDIA

The Brahminy Kite is to be found not only in India but also as far south as Australia. As the name might suggest it was considered sacred to the God of the Brahmans, Vishnu.

Hebrew Belief

Although some people ate the kite, the Old Testament lists the kite as one of the 'unclean' birds, therefore sacred in some way and certainly not to be killed or eaten.

A Creation Myth from the Philippines

At a time when the world was made only of sky and water, a kite, flying between the two, was feeling a little bored, and when kites get bored they can become mischievous. So the kite decided to try to make the sky angry with the water. But the sky was wise to this game, and made lots of islands so that the bird might desist from its irritations. So the kite alighted on one of the islands, and thought it was nice to be able to rest awhile.

All of a sudden, a piece of cane landed just where the kite was sitting. Splitting it open, the kite found to his surprise that it contained a man and a woman …

The decline in the Red Kite population came about as cities started to develop sewerage systems and generally started getting cleaner; in 1777 they were happily breeding in the centre of London.

What Bird Would You Be?

'A bird of prey, so I could soar effortlessly through the sky … a kite perhaps … For all round fun, though, it would have to be a peregrine falcon, for the sheer thrill of the hurtle. For slate-grey enigmatic mastery of its medium, for its acuity and focus, it would have to be the peregrine … certainly for the day job. As hobby, could I be a hobby?'
Lou, UK

The Lark

Air

> Hail to thee, blithe Spirit!
> Bird thou never wert,
> That from Heaven, or near it,
> Pourest thy full heart
> In profuse strains of unpremeditated art.
>
> Higher still and higher
> From the earth thou springest
> Like a cloud of fire;
> The deep blue thou wingest
> And singing still dost soar, and soaring ever singest.
> **Percy Bysshe Shelley,** *To A Skylark*
>
> The lark now leaves his watr'y nest
> And, climbing, shakes his dewy wings.
> He takes the window for the east
> And to implore your light, he sings
> Awake, awake, the morn will never rise.
> **William D'Avenant,** *Song: The Lark*

CHARACTERISTICS

Larks are found throughout the Old World, but are especially common in Africa, where two-thirds of the species are found. They're small birds, not much more than five to nine inches (12–25 cm) in length, and their plumage is unobtrusive. Most larks are ground dwellers, living in open grassy heathland. Their nests are in the ground, too – simple cup shapes are scooped out of the ground by the bird. Both bird and nest are so well camouflaged that it's easy to miss them or even to step on them.

In order to protect its nest, the lark will often fly down to the ground some distance away from its nest, and will then cover the rest of the distance on foot. Its name in Old English, 'Laferce', means 'treason worker' and it is this habit which is the origin of the name (which has transmuted into 'laverock' in Scotland and some other parts of the British Isles). The lark will also draw people away from its nest by pretending to be injured and limping away from its cache of eggs, hoping to lead you with it.

The British are incredibly fond of the skylark and introduced it around the world at various times. Despite their affection for the bird, however, it used to be a delicacy – you may have heard of the grotesque dish, 'larks' tongues in aspic'. However, the bird is now protected and those days are gone, thank goodness.

The skylark in particular has been much written about. Tennyson, Shelley and Wordsworth are but a few of the poets inspired by the bird, and music has been written to extol the virtues of this lovely little creature who, according to Robert Graves in *The White Goddess*, is the bird of the Summer Solstice: 'At this season the Sun is at his highest point, and the Lark flies singing up to adore him.'

The scientific name of the lark comes from the Welsh words 'al', which means 'great', and 'awd', which translates as 'song'.

This is the skylark; these are his hours.
He has climbed yonder from his house in the flowers;
He stands by the gateway of dawn; he will bring
April in; he will rise up and sing.
Dafydd ap Gwilym, *The Skylark*

Ancient Greece

There's a peculiar little story about the lark, who is said to have been born before the earth itself. When her father died there was, consequently, nowhere for the unfortunate daughter to bury him except in her own head – this explains the crest of feathers on top of the bird's head!

A Weather Bird

Larks were observed carefully, since it was believed that if rain was on the way, the bird would drop straight down out of the sky when it decided to descend. Otherwise the lark will hover and glide, presumably making the most of the good weather.

SOMEWHERE BETWEEN HEAVEN AND EARTH

Symbolically, the lark exists somewhere between these two planes, and because of this is seen as an intermediary between the two worlds. The messages it can give us can be quite accurate, if only we can learn how to listen. There's an old saying from the North of England:

> If you want to know what the lark is saying, you must lie on your back in a field and simply listen.

What Bird Would You Be?

'I'd want to be a skylark – I love the way they twirl up into the sky, singing with delight ... I'd have to live where there were no human beings though, because they kill us with their chemicals and sometimes they crush our eggs and nests underfoot.'

Miel, France

The Oriole

Air

How falls it, oriole, thou hast come to fly
In tropic splendour through our Northern sky?
At some moment was it Nature's choice
To dower a scrap of sunset with a voice?
Edgar Fawcett, *To An Oriole*

CHARACTERISTICS

There are 28 species of oriole, but the one we'll be looking at is the Golden Oriole. Indeed, the English name for this bird comes from the Latin, 'aureolus', meaning 'golden'. There's also an archangel, Auriel, who is closely connected with this bird.

The Golden Oriole is considered by many to be one of the most beautiful birds in the world, with its delicate shape and yellow and black plumage. In the UK, the Golden Oriole is a relatively rare sight; although there are some breeding pairs in the south of the country, it's more likely to be an infrequent Summer visitor. It's more prevalent in North America, however, where it is held in great esteem, and the Baltimore Oriole is the state bird of Maryland. The oriole is a welcome sight, given that its appearance presages the coming of Summer.

Orioles live happily in Africa, Southern Asia and Eastern Australia. They are forest dwellers, living high in the tree-tops. These birds are not particularly gregarious, but will move about singly or in pairs.

Their nests are intricate affairs; the oriole is able to weave, and the nest is suspended hammock-like between the forks of a tree. Often, scraps of yarn or string or pieces of cloth will be used to construct the nest, as well as grasses and the like.

THE FAR EAST

The oriole has a lovely song, and therefore in China it represents music and happiness. The bird also has some sexual connotations, too, with several positions in the Chinese version of the Kama Sutra having reference to the bird; a 'floating oriole' is slang for a prostitute, and an 'oriole flower-hall' is a brothel! The bird is also a symbol of marriage, and of springtime.

ANCIENT GREECE

The oriole became involved in the myth of the Phoenix; there was a belief that the bird was born from fire. Aristotle described the oriole:

The oriole is entirely yellow. It is not seen in Winter, but is most in evidence during the period of the Summer Solstice … It is quick to learn, clever at getting a living …

NATIVE AMERICAN LORE

For Native American people, the oriole was an important symbol of the Sun, and is inextricably linked with yellow flowers, too, and in particular sunflowers. The feathers form an important part of rituals, particularly during the Winter Solstice, when the sunnier months are prayed for and anticipated. The word 'sikatsi' in the Pueblo language indicates any bird with yellow feathers, including the oriole; the word translates as 'yellowbird'. There's a Pueblo ceremony which sees the priest push four oriole feathers into a ball of snow, so that the snow should melt, and the water would symbolically fertilize the fields.

What Bird Would You Be?

'For birds, singing is a natural function of life. Same for me. I love the song of the blackbird in England, the song of the lark as illustrated in Ralph Vaughan Williams' 'Lark Ascending' (one of my favourite pieces) and the song of the Yellow Weaver bird in Africa. I think, ultimately, I would have to be an ornithological dimorphic mix of Blackbird and South African Yellow Weaver for their glorious song and discreet dress code: yellow/olive skin and a black dress singing songs as a natural expression of the present, that's me.'
Helen, Spain

The Seagull

> A white seagull on the breast of the sea.
> Surely as perfect in beauty is she
> As the white snow or the winter moon,
> A glove of the sea, gleaned from the sun.
> Proud and swift when she fishes and light
> Over the waves of the sea is her flight.
> O white, white bird, we will go, you and I,
> Your hand in my hand, the lily of the sea.
> **Dafydd ap Gwilym,** *The Seagull*

The name 'Gull' come from a Welsh word, 'Gwylan', which translates as 'wailing', and indeed the name is apt, since gulls do have a plaintive call. It seemed particularly apt to use a Welsh poet to illustrate this bird.

Characteristics

There are some 43 species of gull, found throughout the entire world; as well as living by the sea, gulls often find their way inland, since as long as there's plenty of water the bird will be happy. Despite the 'sea' in the name, the seagull isn't often found very far out to sea, but tends to stay closer to the shore; apart, that is, from the kittiwake, which travels farther afield. Kittiwakes ringed in the British Isles have been discovered in Newfoundland, for example.

As anyone who has seen seagulls at the shore or by a beach will know, the diet of the bird is extremely varied. In fact it will eat almost anything, from fish to ice cream cornets and snacks either discarded by people or stolen by the bird in a sudden raid; I'll never forget the look of astonishment on a little boy's face once as a seagull swooped down and deftly stole away his slice of pizza from out of his hands! The fact that gulls are unfussy eaters means that they can often be seen circling around garbage sites or dumps, and they are extremely useful when it comes to clearing away debris from beaches and the like.

In Temple Square in Salt Lake City, there's a Seagull Monument. In 1848, a plague of crickets was decimating the first crops planted by the Mormon settlers. Things were getting desperate when a huge flock of seagulls – literally thousands of them – appeared from the skies and devoured the insects. Notwithstanding the fact that the statue depicts a couple of eagles, it was erected as a tribute to the seagulls ...

Gulls are ground nesters; their nests are quite cumbersome and are comprised of scraps of seaweed and whatever other vegetation happens to be lying around.

WEATHER BIRDS

It used to be believed that if a seagull were spotted far inland, it was a sign of rain, or stormy weather at sea. It seems logical that the bird would choose to get away from the bad weather if at all possible.

DEAD SOULS AND WANDERING SPIRITS ...

In common with the albatross, the seagull was believed to carry the souls of dead sailors, and therefore the birds were considered an unlucky omen (unless they were swimming rather than flying). In the *Daily Sketch* newspaper in November 1954 there's an account of the Remembrance Day Service at the Cenotaph in London. A mother whose only son was killed in the war looked up at the seagulls flying in the overcast sky, and mentioned that 'David told me they had the spirits of dead seamen ... I like to think he was right.'

THE CELTIC WORLD

There's a Welsh story that tells of a flock of seagulls discovering a canoe with a tiny baby inside it. The baby was wrapped in a purple cloth and had obviously been taken good care of. The gulls picked up the baby and took it to their nest, high on a rocky outcrop. They made the infant comfortable by providing a bed of their own feathers, plucked from their breasts. They somehow managed to feed the baby with doe's milk.

But the baby was kidnapped by an old man, who took it back to his house. However, the doe told the gulls, who rescued their baby and brought him back to his nest. When the baby grew up, so the story goes, he was a very happy man indeed, presumably having led the carefree life of a bird in everything except the ability to fly.

Native American Lore

Taking the well-known fact that seagulls will audaciously steal food, there's a story from one of the Indian tribes about a giant who was cooking some fish over an open fire. The seagulls swooped down and stole the fish, just as they were cooked to perfection, from under the giant's nose. Understandably, this put the giant into such a rage that he caught the birds and threw them into the fire. This explains the black tips of the seagulls' wings …

As a boy scout on a trip to the Isles of Scilly myself and a fellow Owl (coincidence?) patrol member thought it fun to feed jam sandwiches to the seagulls. This was particularly appetizing to one seagull in particular who seemed to follow us around – we thought he was recognizable due to the jam on his beak. It was only later that I noticed all the gulls had a red stain on their beaks. So that's how the gulls got their red beak splodges (so legend has it!).

Mikey, France

What Bird Would You Be?

'I'd be a cross between a seagull and a raven – a seagull for its grace, its adaptability, its anonymity; a raven for its intelligence, its mystery, its conversational skills.'

Adam, Colorado

The Thrush

Air

At once a voice arose among
The bleak twigs overhead
In a full-hearted evensong
Of joy illimited;
An aged thrush, frail, gaunt and small
In blast-beruffled plume,
Had chosen thus to fling his soul
Upon the growing gloom.

So little cause for carolings
Of such ecstatic sound
Was written on terrestrial things
Afar or nigh around,
That I could think there trembled through
His happy good-night air
Some blessed hope, whereof he knew
And I was unaware.

Thomas Hardy, *The Darkling Thrush*

CHARACTERISTICS

The thrush family is large and encompasses many different birds. Aristotle described some of them thus:

> One is the mistle thrush. It feeds only on mistletoe and resin and is the least spotted and ... is about the size of a jay. The second is the song thrush. It possesses a shrill voice and is the size of a blackbird. The third is the smallest and is called by some the redwing.

The one thing all these thrushes have in common is their beautiful voices. The nightingale is part of the group, as is the bluebird and the robin. But the song thrush is so famed for its voice that it deserves some space all to itself.

Song thrushes are widespread, and wherever they live they're very welcome and often seem to be particularly unaffected by the close proximity of human beings. They are to be found in many parts of the world, even in New Zealand, to where they were introduced in the middle of the nineteenth century by the British.

Song thrushes will often use a stone to crack open the shells of the snails they're partial to, demonstrating the intelligence of the bird since it knows how to use tools. The nest of the song thrush is quite a tidy affair; it is a neat, bowl-shaped construction lined with mud, which strengthens it.

THE SONG

Like the nightingale, which is part of the same family, if you see the song thrush while it is singing it is hard to believe that such a small bird can produce such a big sound. Melodious, trilling, with repeated patterns and overtures, the song of the song thrush is sweet and memorable. Its singing improves with age, too, as mentioned in Thomas Hardy's poem above. The embellishments added are for the bird's own entertainment as much as anyone else and there's a palpable feeling of joy which comes from the bird; anyone who has heard it will testify to this, and it does tend to make some of our own concerns seem a little petty sometimes.

Birds often sing together, not only in duets or trios but also in quartets and quintets. They also revise and improve their songs.

As well as its own song, the song thrush is a powerful mimic and will borrow stanzas and refrains from other birds, such as the nightingale and the lapwing. It can also imitate telephones and car alarms!

THE MISTLE THRUSH

It feeds on naught but mistletoe and gum.
Aristotle

It's likely that the Mistle Thrush got its name because of its reputation for spreading the seeds of mistletoe – a sacred plant of the Druids – from one tree to another, therefore helping it to germinate.

Weatherlore

Some of the old names for the thrush reflect its important status as one of the weather birds. It was also called the Storm Cock or Storm Thrush.

If the Mistle Thrush starts to sing from the top of a tree into the wind, it is said to be welcoming rain. The bird is also happy to sing in bad weather, and doesn't seem to mind the rain at all. Because of this, the bird is said to be singing, 'Wet! Wet! Wet!'

What Bird Would You Be?

'A thrush, for sure ... When I was a child, my father came home late from work one night, and I was woken up to see what he'd brought home. There on the kitchen table was a cardboard box, and in the cardboard box was a bird's nest with two tiny baby thrushes inside, not old enough yet to fly.

'We put the nest in the saddlebag of a bike and kept them in the shed. We fed them mashed-up worms, which we fed them with a pipette, and water. They would raise their little yellow beaks eagerly and although we thought at first they were bound to die, they got stronger and stronger, and eventually they started flapping about.

'This was going to be risky – we now had to teach them how to fly. In for a penny, in for a pound, my father put the birds carefully on top of the edge of the shed roof, and after a moment's hesitation, off they went ... We were sad to see them go. But the next day they returned, back to where they'd taken off from the shed roof, and they came back every year after that.'

Georgina, Ireland

The Vulture

Air

Subtle is she and witty, for when she hath seized upon
tortoises and caught them up with her talons, she
throweth them down from aloft to break their shells.
And it was the fate of the poet Aeschylus to die by
such means. For when he was foretold by wizards
out of their learning that it was his destiny to die on
such a day by something falling on his head, he,
thinking to prevent that, got him forth that day into a
great open plain, far from house or tree, presuming on the
security of the clear and open sky. However, a vulture let fall a
tortoise, which hit him on the head, dashed out his brains and laid him
asleep forever.

Pliny the Elder

CHARACTERISTICS

The vulture is the ultimate example to mankind; it doesn't take anything,
but recycles what it is given: it's not built to kill. It's also a fact that this bird
is often misunderstood and much maligned, and it's to be hoped that some
of the following information may redress the balance in favour of this amazing bird.

The vulture has extremely week feet and its talons are very short,
making the bird unfit for tearing or grasping like other raptors in its family.
It has to rely on others to do the killing, or simply finds corpses that have
died a more natural death. Although the vulture is often viewed as being
quite a repugnant bird, because of its supposed habit of circling struggling
victims waiting for them to die, and then tearing their lifeless corpses to
pieces, a lot of this imagery seems to have been derived from cowboy
movies rather than any reality.

In the USA there are two types of vulture – the Black Vulture and the
Turkey Vulture. The Black Vulture has a white patch at the end of each wing
and is not really built to soar like the Turkey Vulture, but will rather be spotted

perching in trees. The Turkey Vulture, on the other hand, is a fantastic flyer, and very graceful when soaring at a height. They have a habit, beautiful if you should ever chance to see it, of congregating together at night and then spreading their wings to shake off the dew first thing in the morning, as though they were honouring the Sun.

Another powerful gift belonging to the vulture is its ability physically to see thermals, currents that allow the birds to be lifted into the air so that they can soar effortlessly. This ability is not dissimilar to the faculty for auric vision, the skill to be able to see the aura of a person, which is considered by us humans to be a 'psychic' skill. It is this talent that gives the bird magical powers for many people. The ability to ride the thermals means that the vulture can span long distances without having to expend too much energy – the condor, a member of this family, can cruise for 10 miles (16 km) without a single flap of its wings!

In the same way that vultures simply take what is given for food, they take what is given to enable flight, relying on the forces of nature to provide what it needs. If the vulture does need to change direction or make a move, it will give a powerful adjustment of its wings and will let nature's forces take over once again.

Vultures' eyesight is extremely sharp, and it is believed that they can pass messages to one another via their eyes. They can also spot food from several miles away. In addition to powerful vision, the vulture also has a strong sense of smell – the Turkey Vulture's being stronger than that of the Black Vulture.

As you might imagine, the vulture has a digestive system that is pretty unique within the animal kingdom. It is resistant to many strains of bacteria which other creatures fall foul of. The habit the vulture has of excreting on its own feet would appear to be peculiar but in fact there's a reason for this; excreta contains powerful antibacterial qualities and by doing this the bird ensures that its feet will be cleansed of any infections or germs lurking in the meat it has been eating. Additionally, the lack of feathers on the head of the vulture means that infection is less likely to occur via feathers as it dips its head inside the corpse it is eating in order to access entrails and the like.

EGYPT

In Ancient Egypt, the Goddess Isis is associated with the vulture, and there's a relief of her in this aspect. She is shown enclosed in the wings of a huge vulture, with the solar disc symbol behind her, and ready to suckle. This image personifies the birth process, and shows the association of the vulture with the maternal instinct.

There's another vulture Goddess, Nekhbet, or Nekht. One of Nekhbet's duties was to guard and protect the Queens of Egypt; therefore these royal ladies would wear headdresses in the shape of vulture heads.

Because as scavenger bird the vultures kept the streets clean, it was forbidden to harm them, and they were even referred to as 'Pharaoh's Pets'.

ANCIENT GREECE AND ROME

The incredible flying capability of the vulture, able to crest thermals and soar effortlessly, led the Greeks to believe that the bird was born from the wind. To the Greeks, the vulture symbolized the union of Heaven and Earth, good and evil, the combination of the spiritual and the material contained in one bird. They also believed that the vulture was a direct descendant of the Griffin.

The vulture was connected with Ares, the Greek God of War, probably because the birds would congregate on battlefields after the fighting. The vulture had magical powers, the powers of a sorcerer, and could transform death into new life. It was an essential part of the cycle of birth and death.

In both Greece and Rome the vulture was one of the most important symbols in augury. The bird was sacred to Apollo, and its appearance during auguries on the hills outside Rome determined the site of the city, as well as its founder: Romulus saw twelve of the birds, as opposed to his brother, Remus, who saw only six.

As in Egypt, the vulture was considered to be a symbol of the feminine, possibly because of its habit of eating corpses; this would imply that it could use other life to sustain itself. In addition, life and death were symbols of the Great Mother.

NATIVE AMERICAN LORE

The vulture feather was a powerful totem to the Pueblo Indians, who would of course use the feather to take on the characteristics of the bird. The characteristics they would want to empower themselves with would include the ability to 'come back to the self' after shape-shifting ceremonies. If the Indian had been in contact with the spirits of the dead, the energy of the vulture would help break that bond and restore the shaman to his own full consciousness.

For the Pueblo, the vulture was again a symbol of purification and renewal. Other tribes believed that the vulture was the helpmate of the Golden Eagle; his main task was to keep the Earth clean. In many South American Indian stories, the vulture is believed to be the first creature to be given fire, which he brought to mankind.

There's a tale about how the vulture ended up with a bald head from the Iroquois. Originally, all birds were naked; after a while they started to be embarrassed about this and decided that clothing of some kind would be good, with the preferred option being feathers. The Gods told them this was no problem, but they'd have to choose one of their number to go and collect the clothing, and the journey was likely to be a long one.

The birds chose the vulture for this important errand. Because the seeds and berries the vulture was accustomed to eating became scarce during the long journey, he was forced to eat whatever came his way, including carrion.

When he eventually arrived at the end of this long journey and found the clothes, the vulture understandably took the very best ones for himself. But the headdress he chose was so grand and immensely heavy that he was forced to remove it, and as a consequence he has been bald ever since!

The vulture was also thought of as a powerful, magical bird, able to contact the dead, recover the bodies of lost warriors and dispel evil. However, because of the bird's scavenging habits, the feathers were not used in prayer sticks although, as mentioned, they were used as 'grounding' tools after shape-shifting ceremonies.

AFRICA

In Africa, the Bambara tribe has a grade of initiates known as 'Vultures'. The initiate is scorched, and therefore cleansed, by the effects of his initiation, and then has access to the wisdom of the Gods. This process of initiation uses the vulture symbol as one of rebirth, and after the ceremony the candidate is believed to have transcended physical death and can transmute dirt, filth and decay into what we know as Philosopher's Gold, which he is able to understand the true value of.

Latin America

The vulture here is associated with water, and in the Mayan calendar it is in charge of the precious storms after the season of drought.

The story of the Great Flood is, of course, not restricted to Hebrew sources but occurs throughout the world. In Mexico, which has a similar deluge tale to the Noah's Ark story, the first bird to be sent from the vessel was the vulture. Another story goes that, because the vulture didn't return to the boat and chose to feed on carrion instead, the bird, which was formerly white, was turned black except for the tips of its wings.

India and Tibet

Because of its habits of renewing and recycling, the vulture is favoured amongst Buddhists, and indeed, the fifth Dalai Lama, Losang Gyatso, was believed to be able to shape-shift into the form of a white vulture. This magical vulture was then able to educate other vultures, especially those consuming human bodies at the Sky Burial sites; the bird would also bless these corpses by tapping them three times with its beak.

The Sky Burial

The sky burial is an ancient way of disposing of the dead. It is now not such a common practice as it once was and the description of such a burial is dramatic. The exposure of flesh for disposal in this way is known as excarnation.

The Zoroastrians or Parsees believed that a corpse would contaminate everything it touched, so it could not either be buried or thrown into the river, both customs prevalent in other traditions. Cremation was an option, but the traditional way to dispose of the dead was by the sky burial.

The corpse would be put into a tall hollow stone structure, the Dakhma. The Dakhma is designed in such a way that the carrion birds and vultures can devour the body in as hygienic and efficient a way as possible. The corpse remains hidden from view; the only opening is to the skies, to allow the birds ease of access.

In the Tibetan Buddhist tradition, the sky burial takes a more dramatic, visible turn. There's a description of the tradition by Niema Ash in her book

Flight of the Wind Horse; A Journey into Tibet, which tells the story fully. This is a ritual that is now rare, and the description is a valuable insight into something which is quite primal.

Niema takes a journey an hour or so out of town, to where there's a small stony outcrop. Men are sitting around joking and laughing and drinking tea. Close by is the altar

> where the Tibetans sit by a shallow gully strewn with bits of discarded clothing and hanks of hair … Rows of silent birds are perched on the ledges … vultures. Their colours blend so perfectly with the mountains that at first they are hard to distinguish.

Although Westerners are welcome, photographs are forbidden; if a camera is spotted the user is likely to be showered with stones. The time for the ceremony to begin is as the sun touches the altar stone.

There follows a graphic description of the deftly efficient cutting-up of the body of a young woman. When this is completed, the vultures start to circle closer until the presiding monk approaches the altar, prostrates himself, and prays; this is the signal for the 'vanguard' vultures to approach.

> At the signal, about a dozen vultures (the vanguard) leave their mountain perch and swoop on to the rock … The butcher throws bits of flesh as they gather round him. They are huge beautiful birds with white necks and legs, and speckled tan and white bodies … Some are so close that we can see their bright blue eyes.

The disposal of various parts of the body continues, and when this is done, another signal is given:

> Suddenly, hundreds of vultures fill the sky, hovering in a quivering cloud above our head, their wings beating a nervous fluttering sound, and descend on the rock, completely covering it … It is a bad omen if anything is left uneaten.

The custom of the sky burial is dying out now, the cost being prohibitive (at around a quarter of a year's salary).

In Buddhist philosophies, the vulture's habit of stripping flesh from bones is analogous to revealing truth. Lower personal delusions can be transformed, transmuted and consumed, hence the importance of such a ritual as the sky burial.

What Bird Would You Be?

'I'd be a vulture ... they are much misunderstood. Their flight is effortless because they have the wits to crest thermals; they take nothing from anyone, only what God gives them. They are beautiful, useful birds.'

Cedric, Jerusalem

The Woodpecker

Air

> His bill an auger is
> His head, a cap and frill
> He laboureth at every tree
> A worm his utmost goal.
> **Emily Dickinson,** *The Woodpecker*

> I once a King and chief
> Now am the tree bark's thief
> Ever 'twixt the trunk and leaf
> Chasing the prey.
> **William Morris,** *The Woodpecker*

CHARACTERISTICS

There are about 215 species of woodpeckers, found in all continents apart from Antarctica and Australasia.

In the USA, the Northern Flicker is a member of this family.

Although there are different types of the bird, the variety I'm going to concentrate on is the Green Woodpecker, a beautiful, colourful bird that has (as its name suggests) primarily green feathers, with a flash of yellow down its back and a distinctive red head.

Woodpeckers are adapted specially to live their virtually vertical lifestyle on the trunks and branches of trees; their legs are quite short, but the toes are long, with very sharp claws. The woodpecker's tail is particularly strong since the bird will use it for stability. Because of its habit of drilling holes into wood, the beak of the woodpecker is also long and sharp, and its neck muscles are especially strong in order to be able to pound into the surface of the tree. Another adaptation is the woodpecker's long tongue, which is necessary because of the bird's habit of feeding on the grubs and insects it finds in crevices in tree trunks and branches.

Woodpeckers don't really fly for long periods, and very few are migratory, although some will transfer to a warmer climate, but not necessarily on a regular basis. You wouldn't be able to set your clocks by this bird as you would be able to with, for example, the crane!

A Magical Bird

Wherever the woodpecker is found, man has seen it as a magical bird, gifted with the powers of prophesy, and so the woodpecker had an important part to play in divination and auguries. It's worth bearing in mind, too, that the woodpecker ranks as one of the most intelligent birds, and indeed, it has quite a knowing expression; this would have helped to associate it with magical powers.

The Rain Bird

There are numerous accounts of the woodpecker's ability to forecast the weather, and colloquial names for the bird testify to this fact. In Britain in Shropshire, the woodpecker is also known as the 'Rain Pie'; in France, it's the Pic de la Pluie or 'rain-woodpecker'; in Germany it's the Giessvogel, or 'pouring rain bird'; and in Sweden it's called the Ragnfagel, meaning 'Rainbird'. In most countries the woodpecker is said to be forecasting rain when it calls out loudest.

There's an explanation of this in the Bible, from Genesis, which is said to have taken place during the time of the Great Flood. God had commanded all the animals who had been on board the Ark to dig out channels and pits for rivers and lakes, once the waters had abated. All the creatures started to work hard to accomplish the task, except for the woodpecker, who simply sat on the top of the mast and laughed at their endeavours. As a punishment, the woodpecker was commanded that it should forever more have to dig holes in order to build its nest, and the bird would also have to cry out for raindrops whenever it was thirsty. Indeed, in France the 'yaffle' sound the bird makes is interpreted as 'pluie-pluie-pluie', literally, 'rain, rain, rain', so the woodpecker really does seem to be calling for the heavens to open!

Woodpeckers can peck 20 times per second.

There's also a tale from Germany about the woodpecker as the herald of water, which is similar to the deluge story. God had asked the birds to help dig a well, but the woodpecker, afraid to spoil his lovely feathers, refused; so God punished him by refusing to let him drink from ponds or pools. Instead, the bird must call for rain and catch raindrops as best he might.

BRITAIN AND EUROPE

The old name for the woodpecker in Britain is the 'yaffle', deriving from its loud call, which sounds a little like a laugh.

In some parts of Europe it is believed that ownership of the beak of a woodpecker will be sufficient to ensure that the owner will never be stung by a bee. Indeed the bird is called the 'bee eater' in some parts of Germany, because of its habit of eating bees and wasps it finds in the crevices of trees.

The woodpecker has a habit of digging about in the ground for ants and other juicy insects, and it's this action that has led the bird to become associated with fertility and the plough.

NORSE MYTHOLOGY

The woodpecker was the bird of Thor, the Norse God of thunder and lightning. Because the bird could pierce the things it struck at, like lightning, the association is very apposite.

Ancient Rome

There is a lot of evidence to support the importance of the woodpecker in Ancient Rome. The bird was dedicated to Mars, the God of war, and the bird also appeared on some Roman coinage – the image used is of two woodpeckers perched in a fig tree, with Romulus and Remus being fed by a wolf, since the woodpecker was popularly supposed to have helped in bringing food for the children. In another tale, an early king of the Italians, King Picus, was transformed into a woodpecker; the Latin name for the woodpecker is Picus, which is where the word 'pick' comes from. King Picus was a renowned seer, and his divinatory powers have been attributed to the bird, too.

In Roman auguries, the woodpecker was considered to be a lucky sign if it appeared on the right hand side of the sky.

Ancient Greece

The woodpecker is the bird of Zeus, and, as in Rome, it was considered to be a lucky omen, whether it was seen or just heard. Aristophanes, in his play *The Birds* reminds us of this association. The story goes that Zeus's mother, Rhea, hid her son away from his father Kronos, the God of time, who had an unfortunate predilection for eating up his children. The young Zeus survived on honey kindly brought to him by bees, but one day a man came and stole the honey; Zeus turned the man into a woodpecker. Aristophanes refers to this:

> 'You'd better keep your beaks well sharpened; I can't see Zeus handing over his sceptre to a woodpecker, especially if it's been making holes in his sacred oaks.'

Moreover, the God Pan is said to have been hatched from the egg of a woodpecker.

Native American Lore

The continuation of the bird's association with thunder and lightning continues. For example, the Pueblo associate the bird's drumming with the sound of thunder, which is the precursor to rain. Many Native Americans believed that the woodpecker had the skill to be able to avert lightning, and its feathers were used in rituals and ceremonies because of this power. Among some tribes it is the woodpecker who was believed to have brought fire to mankind.

The bright red feathers of the woodpecker were used as currency by Indians in California. If you've ever seen the colour of this bird you'd immediately understand why its feathers were valued in this way. And in Omaha, the tribes saw the bird as a protector of children because it keeps its own chicks in such a safe environment.

In Christianity

Unfortunately, in Christian symbolism the woodpecker is representative of the Devil and is said to undermine belief in the goodness of human nature. The origins of this are possibly because Zeus and Mars, not to mention Indra in Hindu mythology, would shape-shift into woodpeckers when they fancied having a little fun. In many stories the bird is cast in the role of villain, or people who have done some wrong are transformed into a woodpecker as part of their punishment.

Sometimes in Northern Europe the woodpecker is called the Gertrude Bird. In a story retold by the Brothers Grimm, an old woman, Gertrude, who refuses to feed Christ and St Peter, is turned into a woodpecker. Christ is said to have told her:

> 'Since thou hast grudged to give me aught, thy doom is that thou be a little bird, seek thy scanty sustenance twixt wood and bark, and only drink as oft as it shall rain.'

At this the poor old woman was transformed into a woodpecker, and escaped by flying up the chimney; the red cap and the sooty colour of the bird are all that remain of Gertrude's former appearance.

What Bird Would You Be?

'I'd probably be a woodpecker so I could talk to my old friend Jason ... We just moved into a new house up in Raleigh for me to record in ... there's a red-headed woodpecker that comes to a tree outside the studio window every day. I've named him Jason because I, being the kook that I am, think he's my old bass player, who died in 2003, far too early, coming to watch over my bass lines and encourage me.'
Tera, USA

The Cardinal

Fire

A day and then a week passed by:
The redbird hanging from the sill
Sang not; and all were wondering why
It was so still –
When one bright morning, loud and clear
Its whistle smote my drowsy ear,
Ten times repeated, till the sound
Filled every echoing niche around;
And all things earliest loved by me, –
The bird, the brook, the flower, the tree, –
Came back again, as thus I heard
The cardinal bird.
William Davis Gallagher, *The Cardinal Bird*

CHARACTERISTICS

Found in the warmer parts of Eastern North America and Mexico, the cardinal is a very popular little bird, about 8 inches (20 cm) long and coloured bright red. The birds prefer to live in woodland areas. The name of the bird comes from the red robes of the Cardinals of the Roman Catholic Church.

The cardinal mates for life and tends to stay in the same area; they are highly territorial, too, and will chase away any intruders. Since the cardinal is a lovely songbird as well as being very attractive, it used to be a popular pet and was kept in cages, and was known as the 'Virginia Nightingale'.

The popularity of the cardinal is indicated by it being the emblem bird of seven American states.

NATIVE AMERICAN LORE

Because of its colour, the bird represented the South and the Sun, and indeed is considered to be the Daughter of the Sun by the Cherokee. The Cherokee have a story about how the bird got its amazing colour.

One day in the forest, a raccoon and a wolf passed each other on a track, and as they passed, the raccoon made some insulting remarks to the wolf. Angered, the wolf started chasing the raccoon, who just laughed some more and ran very fast through the forest. Then the raccoon ran up a tree and stretched out smugly on a branch overlooking the water.

The wolf saw what he thought was the raccoon, and leaped at it, but it was only the reflection of himself in the water and consequently the wet wolf got even more angry. However, after a long swim to shore he'd calmed down a little, and was more tired than anything else, so settled down for a nap.

The raccoon saw this, and once the wolf was asleep, he came down from the tree and threw some mud from the river into the eyes of the sleeping wolf. When he awoke, the poor wolf was alarmed to find that he seemed to have been blinded, so he asked for help; a small, plain brown bird came up and removed the mud, and once more the wolf could see.

Because he was so grateful, the wolf showed the little bird the whereabouts of a small pool of a magical red colour. The bird jumped in and swam about happily, then asked his mate to join him. By this time nearly all the red had gone, so the lady cardinal had only a splash of red on her wings, crest and breast.

What Bird Would You Be?

'After much deliberation, I think I'd choose a cardinal. I remember that from when I was a child ... they always seemed to be around the yard. And I love red.'
Dorene, Michigan

The Eagle

Fire

> An eagle so caught in some bursting cloud
> On Caucasus, his thunder-baffled wings
> Entangled in the whirlwind, and his eyes
> Which gazed on the undazzling sun, now blinded
> By the white lightning, while the ponderous hail
> Beats on his struggling form, which sinks at length
> Prone, and the aerial ice clings over it.
> **Percy Bysshe Shelley,** *Prometheus Unbound*

> He grasps the crag with crooked hands;
> Close to the sun in lonely lands,
> Ringed with the azure world, he stands.

> The wrinkled sea beneath him crawls;
> He watches from the mountain walls,
> And like a thunderbolt he falls.
> **Alfred, Lord Tennyson,** *fragment*

The eagle is of course one of the most important birds, in terms of its meaning, symbolism and associations, in all the countries of the world. Its size, its appearance, and its dwelling places in high mountainous areas all add to its mystique. For many, the eagle is the 'King of the Birds' and the equal, in the bird world, of the Lion.

In general, think of all things big, and bright, and noble, and powerful, and spiritual, and grandiose – that's the eagle.

CHARACTERISTICS

Eagles, unfortunately, are not so prevalent anywhere in the world as they once were; this is largely due to their being hunted. Thank goodness, we are wiser today, but it's shocking to think that one group alone of 'sportsmen' in Texas were responsible for the deaths of 5,000 eagles in the 1940s. In recent years, loss of habitat has affected the numbers of this seminally important bird. Eagles prefer to live in high, remote places, building their huge nests on inaccessible crags and ledges. The nests are added to every year and can get to be quite cumbersome.

The eagle is a large, muscular and powerful bird; the adult Golden Eagle has a wingspan of approximately 6–7 feet (180–210 cm). When hunting, the eagle will glide at altitude over its hunting ground, scanning for possible prey. Once a potential catch has been spotted, the bird will fly away and furtively lose height. Then it will turn around, and, flying very swiftly just a few feet above the ground the eagle will pounce, and the prey animal will usually have no idea what hit it.

THE ORIGINS OF THE NAME

The word 'eagle' originally stems from the Latin, 'aquilus'. Even earlier origins of the name carry associations with the Sun, and light, and aquilus stems from the Hungarian, 'kvil', meaning 'light'. In Greek, 'aigle' means 'ray of light'. Following this pattern, the Greek for 'golden eagle', 'chrysaetos', has its roots in the word 'chrusos', which means 'gold', and 'aetos', which means 'eagle'.

EAGLE-EYED

The eagle's reputation for sure-sightedness is well deserved, and the word we use to describe this keen sightedness, 'acumen', derives from the Latin word for the bird, 'aquilus'. Their eyesight is infinitely superior to that of human beings, at least four times sharper. An eagle, soaring at a height of 1,000 feet (300 metres) over open terrain, is able to spot prey over an area of 3 square miles (7.5 square km).

A Latin bestiary of the twelfth century describes the prodigious eyesight of the eagle thus:

> When he is poised on the seas on motionless plume – not even visible to the human gaze – yet from such a height he can see the little fishes swimming, and, coming down like a thunderbolt, he can carry off his captured prey to the shore, on the wing.

The Bird of the Sun and Spirituality

Because the eagle flies so high, and is so powerful, it is the ultimate solar symbol of the bird world. The eagle is one of the very few creatures said to be able to look directly into the sun without harming its eyesight, and there's an anecdote related by Pliny about this very characteristic; the mother eagle would encourage her children 'to look straight against the Sun's beams'. Furthermore, he goes on to say,

> if any one of them to wink, or their eyes to water at the rays of the sun, she turns it with head forward out of the nest, as a bastard and not right, and none of hers.

The concept of the bird being able to stare directly into the Sun is symbolic of the mental enlightenment of mankind, and something that we should all aspire to; to be able to look directly into the face of 'the source'.

> Fearlessly the eagle looks the Sun in the face … as you can stare at the eternal brightness if your heart is pure.
> *Angelus Silesius*

This association with the eagle and the Sun is the same the world over; belief systems from the Arctic Shaman to the Zuni Indians equate the two.

THE SECRET LANGUAGE OF BIRDS

The Bird of Shamans

As well as being a key bird in American Indian shamanic practice, there's a Siberian tradition that makes an association between the eagle and the shaman, too. The Gods had sent the eagle to assist mankind during a time of great strife, at a time when evil spirits were spreading death and disease on earth. Although the Gods had sent the eagle as a messenger, man had forgotten how to understand what the bird was saying to them; therefore the Gods asked the eagle to show man the gift of shamanism. This the eagle accomplished by flying down and impregnating a woman; the child she gave birth to became the first shaman.

This story is reminiscent of the angel being sent down to the Virgin Mary, whose child, Jesus, could communicate directly with God, and brought this gift of communication to mankind.

Eagles and Angels

More than any other bird, the eagle is the closest thing you'll get to an angel, in terms at least of the traditional symbolism of both entities. In describing angels, there's a passage at the beginning of the book of Ezekiel, which goes:

> They four … had the face of an eagle … and their wings were stretched upward; two wings of every one were joined one to another, and two covered their bodies … whither the spirit was to go, they went.

As a messenger from the Gods, the eagle is the most visible and one of the most important emissaries, and it is essential that we manage to preserve this rare and beautiful bird.

The Eagle and the Serpent

The eagle is frequently depicted battling with a serpent, and snakes, symbolically, are seen as the enemy of the bird. This frequent imagery is representative of opposites – of the triumph of good over evil – with the eagle being emblematic of celestial goodness, spirituality and the power of light; conversely the serpent in this instance stands for all that is opposite to light: the powers of darkness, evil and underworld forces.

Nevertheless there is a balance here. Although as the opposite of the eagle the serpent would appear to have the raw end of the deal, together the two creatures represent the unity and wholeness of the cosmos, and the union of the material and the spiritual, intellect and instinct. If we are to be balanced individuals, it would seem that we have to embrace and balance these opposites within ourselves, too.

The Bird of Emperors and Empires

The eagle, because of its great power, has always been the symbol of emperors and empires. It was the imperial representative of the Caesars and also of Napoleon, and of course America's symbolic bird is the Bald Eagle, chosen in 1787. Everywhere in the world – Africa, Japan, Europe, China – the qualities of the bird have been 'borrowed' in order that its power might be shared. More sinisterly, the eagle was also the symbol of Hitler's Third Reich, showing how a powerful symbol can be twisted to reveal a darker side. The Nazis' imagery was borrowed directly from that of the Roman Empire, whose armies marched under a symbolic representation of a silver eagle, wings unfurled, grasping a thunderbolt in its talons as a symbol of the bird's universal association with the God of storms and lightning.

> Eagles are not really powerful. They are strong and independent – and not gregarious. Corruption in the context of power depends on social status; having control over other individuals. Eagles are solitary. They hunt, but do not normally fight. They nest in places where nobody can reach them, so they rarely even have to defend their nest.
>
> When they hunt they kill quickly. They do not play with their prey like cats, or tear it apart like dogs, or kill for fun like foxes – so they could not accurately be described as cruel. The eagle as a symbol has been misappropriated in many contexts (the Third Reich, Rome). This is normal – such totalitarian edifices do not use torture implements or guns or bombs in their iconography. Instead they take imagery that suggests bravery, nobility, strength and honour. It's all part of the deceit.
> *Andrew, UK*

The Symbol of America

As we've seen, the Bald Eagle has been the symbol of America for more than two centuries. At the time that it was chosen, it was believed that the bird was exclusive to the continent.

Apparently, apart from its symbolic meaning of freedom, the eagle was chosen because it was awoken from its sleep in the mountains by the noise of battle during the early revolutionary fights, and circled the fighting men, uttering loud shrieks, which the Patriots took as a sign of encouragement. The decision was initially a controversial one; it was believed generally that the Bald Eagle was a less 'noble' bird than the Golden Eagle, and Benjamin Franklin favoured another bird altogether. Indeed, this statesman wrote:

> I wish that the bald eagle had not been chosen as a symbol of our country, he is a bird of bad moral character … he is a rank coward … He is by no means a proper symbol for the brave and honest … of America … A turkey is in comparison a much more respectable bird.

Nevertheless, the Bald Eagle has been a popular symbol, appearing in all places and in many guises. Famously, its position on the presidential seal was altered by President Truman in 1946. The American Eagle symbol has the bird holding 13 arrows in one talon, and an olive branch in the other. Prior to Truman's intervention, the bird faced the arrows of war; when Truman revealed the newly designed emblem, he said:

> The new flag faces the eagle towards the staff … which is looking to the front all the time when you are on the march, and also has him looking at the olive branch for peace, instead of the arrows of war.

The Double-headed Eagle

Although not strictly a real creature, I thought it worth mentioning the emblem of the double-headed eagle, since it occurs frequently and has an interesting background.

The double-headed eagle symbol has quite a history attached to it. Believed to have originated with the Hittites, a powerful race from Asia Minor or Syria, the double-headed eagle is often known as the Eagle of

Lagash; Lagash was the ancient Sumerian city that was believed to have used it first, as its royal crest. The symbol was then used by the Turks, and then borrowed by Europeans. Despite this chequered past, the symbol is popular throughout the world, and, like the single-headed eagle, will often hold a serpent in its talons or, as the opposite to the Sun, it could be clutching the hare, which is a 'Moon' animal.

The double head of the eagle effectively doubles its strength and eagle-like qualities. It is omniscient, being able to look in two directions at once, and is a symbol of absolute power, appearing on several coats of arms and emblems of nations, including those of Imperial Austria and Russia. It is also frequently used as a Masonic symbol.

NATIVE AMERICAN LORE

The eagle is one of the most important birds in Native American tradition, as you might imagine, given the prominence of the bird everywhere else. The eagle is also strongly associated with the Thunderbird, which we looked at more closely in the chapter on birds in Native American belief systems (page 199).

For American Indians, the bird mediates between heaven and earth, the Great Spirit and mankind; it also represents daytime and light. The eagle was the keeper of the sun, moon, stars and fire; as a weather-bird, all the eagle needed to do was to shake its feathers and snow would start to fall.

The eyes of hawks and eagles are able to adjust in the same way as a telescope, enabling the bird to adapt its vision to investigate far-away objects.

There's a deluge story about the origins of the Native American peoples. When the waters rose, there was only one woman who escaped, and this she did by catching hold of the talon of her father, the eagle. She was deposited on a mountaintop and gave birth to twins, who became the ancestors of all Native Americans in the world today. As a result there are many dances in honour of this great bird, and the use of the eagle feather in either ritual items or ornamentation was reserved for the most important tribes people – the best warriors, for example.

The eagle feather is still a highly desirable item; as a totem object it carries all the power of the bird, and was the main feature in the incredibly beautiful feathered headdresses and war-bonnets of the tribes. The Cree Indians of the Plains believed that the mystical powers of the eagle could be shared by anyone who possessed a part of the bird. The

Pawnee have individual names for each of the 12 tail feathers of the eagle used in their headdresses. Indeed, the feather of the eagle is held in such high regard, especially since the bird is protected, that it is considered a felony for anyone to possess such an item unless he or she is a bona fide tribal member. We saw the implications of this earlier on in the book.

The Pueblo tribes have a very logical directional system; as well as North, South, East and West they include the Nadir (below) and the Zenith (above). The Pueblo believe that the eagle represented the zenith, and, accordingly, could fly so high that it was able to pass through the hole in the sky to the country where the sun lived, and from there it could observe all the other directions.

THE AZTECS

The Aztecs held that the eagle would feed upon the hearts of warriors who had been slain in battle or in sacrifice, and these warriors were immortalized as the 'people of the eagle'. Whereas the eagle is often portrayed as being the equivalent of the lion, in Aztec imagery the bird was equated with the jaguar. Reflecting this association, the throne of the Aztec emperor must have been an extraordinarily grand affair – the seat was covered in eagle feathers, while the back of it was made of jaguar skin.

The land on which Mexico City stands was actually discovered by a hunter-gatherer people, the Mexica, who founded the Aztec civilization. The Mexica had a firm belief in a certain ancient legend, that they would one day establish a great civilization in a swampy area, and the sign that they were in the right place would be that they would see a cactus, growing out of a rock, with an eagle perched upon the cactus.

Sure enough, when they arrived at Lake Texcoco, the priests of the Mexica announced that they had seen the sign, and accordingly work was started. The location proved to be perfect, given that the land was fertile and the abundance of water meant for effective transportation. The historical significance of the sign of the eagle is still observed, on the reverse side of the country's coins.

Possibly the most important eagle for the Aztecs was the Harpy Eagle. With a wingspan of seven feet (just over two metres) it is an awesome sight, although it is endangered – forestry clearances have done a lot of damage to the bird's habitat. It was called the 'Winged Wolf' and images of the bird are to be found everywhere – in the ruins of ancient buildings, on wall paintings, and on shields worn by the Princess of Tlascala, a Mexican princess who converted to Christianity during the conquest of her country by Cortez, since the bird, in common with eagles everywhere, was a symbol of royalty.

Ancient Rome

In Rome the eagle was dedicated to Jupiter, who among his other jobs was the bearer of storms and lightning. To avert such calamities, eagle feathers were 'planted' in fields.

When one of the Caesars died, it was customary to release an eagle during the cremation of the body to signify the ascent of the emperor's soul to the Heavens. The eagle was also one of the most important birds for the augurs, and more is explained about that in the chapter on augury (page 77).

The Greeks

The eagle was the bird of Zeus, who, like the Roman Jupiter, had had control of lightning and storms. The bird would often be depicted having lightning clutched in its talons, and in addition it was the only bird who lived on Mount Olympus. The eagle was also the bird of Pan. The eagle was depicted on some Greek coinage, on coins dating back to 400 BC from the city of Elis to be precise.

The Greeks held that two eagles, each setting out at the same time from opposite ends of the Earth, met each other and circled the spot at which the 'omphalos' (the 'navel', or the absolute spiritual centre of the world) was located, at Delphi.

The Legend of Ganymede

Ganymede, handsomest of mortals, whom the Gods caught up to pour out drink for Zeus and live amid mortals for his beauty's sake.
Homer, *The Iliad*

On Mount Olympus, the Gods were in need of a cup-bearer for Zeus. Zeus had a constant companion, an eagle, who would carry thunderbolts for the God. Zeus decided to send the eagle down to earth on a quest to find the most handsome youth possible to become his cup-bearer. Accordingly, off went the eagle on his mission, using his swift flight and keen eyesight.

Soon the eagle spotted Ganymede, who was, according to some stories, just a simple country boy, although in other accounts he was the son of the King of Troy. Whatever his parentage, he was stunningly handsome; the eagle gently lifted Ganymede up and carried him back to Zeus, who was delighted, and vowed to immortalize the eagle by finding a place for him amongst the stars. Ganymede was similarly immortalized, as the constellation Aquarius, the water-carrier.

As well as the constellation honouring Ganymede, the Eagle constellation, also known as The Bird of Zeus or The King of the Birds, has been known as such since at least 1200 BC.

Egypt

The eagle is the son of Horus. There are also strong associations between the eagle as the ultimate solar symbol, and the Phoenix; the eagle was rumoured never to grow old, but would fly into the Sun every few years to renew itself, much as the phoenix would immolate itself in order to be resurrected.

Milton puts it like this, in *Areopagitica*:

Methinks I see her as an eagle mewing her mighty youth, and kindling her undazzled eyes at the full midday beam.

The eagle was the symbol for the Nile, and in hieroglyphics was the symbol for the letter A; this important symbol was one of the keys to unlocking our current understanding of hieroglyphs through the translation of the Rosetta stone.

INDIA

In the myths of ancient Indian culture, the Vedas, the eagle is aligned with Garuda, who provided transportation for Vishnu. The Garuda is described as 'blazing like fire'. Coming back to the idea of the eagle as the enemy of and destroyer of serpents, the Garuda was also called 'nagari' – 'naga' meaning 'snake'. The contrast is a poetic representation of dark and light, good and evil, spirit and matter.

In addition, the eagle/garuda is the 'stormcloud' bird. The eagle was said to have delivered a sacred drink, called 'soma', down to mankind from the Heavens, and eagle feathers were a heroic symbol.

CELTIC LORE

At one time, on Mount Snowdon, in Wales, eagles were very prevalent. Indeed, the Welsh name for Snowdon, Caer Eryri, means 'abode of the eagles', 'eryr' meaning 'eagle'. When harsh weather is approaching, the Welsh will still say that 'eagles are breeding whirlwinds on Snowdon', although the birds are not nearly so prevalent there as they once were.

There are several places in the British Isles that are said to be the burial place of King Arthur, and Snowdon is one of them. The fact that there are rumours about several places is likely to act as surety that the secret remains intact, but if Snowdon truly is the place, then the grave will never be found in any case, since it is guarded by two Druids, who have shape-shifted into eagles in order that they might protect 'the once and future King'.

Lleu, the Welsh variant of the Irish God of the Sun, Lugh, is transformed into an eagle when his wife Blodeuwedd and her lover try to murder him. At the moment of being stabbed, he transforms into the bird and soars aloft, only to be transformed into a man again when he is struck by a magic wand by the magician Gwydion.

Elsewhere in the Welsh saga the *Mabinogion*, the eagle has an important part to play. It is one of the five sacred animals – the others being the stag, the salmon, the thrush and the owl.

Norse Myth

The eagle guarded Valhalla, which was the banqueting hall of Nordic Gods and heroes. The bird was seen as a God of the wind, sitting in the northern part of the sky; when his wings were spread wide the winds were said to come out from under them.

The eagle sits in the great ash tree, Yggdrasil, with its enemy/polarizing force the serpent lying below. This magical tree was sacred to Odin, who was also the God of thunder and lightning; and of course the eagle is his bird.

In some versions of the story of Yggdrasil, the eagle has another bird, a falcon, sitting on his beak.

Christianity

The eagle was the symbol of St John the Evangelist, and often appears on church lecterns. This could be due to the fact that it is the natural 'enemy' of the serpent (who is often the personification of evil in Christian belief systems because of the temptation in the Garden of Eden). The eagle's use on lecterns, though, is also symbolic of inspiration.

What Bird Would You Be?

'A tricky one ... I don't know why it took so long to come to mind. It was always flying off in the far distance, alone, just a little swooping speck in the sky. All I could tell was that it was black with a yellow beak and big wings, but not squawky like a crow or hopping round like a chuff. I had a black eagle badge when I was very young; I think that's what it is. Flying around the mountains, kind of intense, and observant, keeping itself to itself.'

Paul, Dharmsala

The Falcon

Fire

> Fair princess of the spacious air,
> Thou hast vouchsafed acquaintance here,
> With us are quartered below stairs,
> That can reach heav'n with nought but pray'rs;
> Who, when our activ'st wings we try
> Advance a foot into the sky;
>
> Bright heir t'th bird imperial
> From whose avenging pennons fall
> Thunder and lightning twisted spun;
> Brave cousin-german to the Sun,
> That didn't forsake thy throne and sphere,
> To be an humble pris'ner here;
> And for a perch of her soft hand,
> Resign the royal wood's command;
> **Richard Lovelace**, *The Falcon*

Throughout the world there are lots of different varieties of falcon, but for the purposes of this heading I've decided to concentrate mainly on the Peregrine Falcon (*Falco peregrinus*). Actually, I should tell you that the Peregrine in this instance has chosen me; I have been watching three of them just now at incredibly close range, and the flying ability of these birds is astonishing. I'm lucky enough to have the birds nesting near my house, on a vertical rocky outcrop, so their excited screech-like calls when they have caught prey is a regular sound in my life.

CHARACTERISTICS

There are between 38 and 43 species of true falcons in the world. One of the most exciting of these birds is the Peregrine, which is found in most of the countries of the world.

Possibly the defining feature of the Peregrine is its incredible speed and flying skill. It has been clocked at over two hundred miles an hour, the fastest creature on this planet, and if you are selected as peregrine prey then it's likely that you simply won't know what's hit you. Peregrines particularly like to chase pigeons, also fast flyers, and for several hours here I once watched a Peregrine attempting to bother a pigeon from off the top of a telegraph pole; the pigeon stayed as still as a statue in order to avoid being taken, until the Peregrine moved on to easier prey, and the pigeon was free to fly away. Peregrines hunt from several hundred feet up in the air, and will dive incredibly accurately from a great height; it's a thrilling sight.

The Peregrine is about 20 inches (50 cm) long with a long, narrow tail and elegant, pointed wingtips. One thing that falcons have in common with one another is that they do not build their own nests, preferring to occupy vacant nests left by other birds. Peregrines and Gyrfalcons will simply make their homes along ledges on cliffs, or will possibly occupy nests left behind by ravens. They will return to the same nesting sites year after year.

THE SPARROWHAWK

Smaller than the Peregrine, the Sparrowhawk is relatively common in the UK, and can often be seen hunting at the sides of roads.

FALCONRY

> Turning and turning in the widening gyre
> The falcon cannot hear the falconer;
> Things fall apart; the centre cannot hold;
> Mere anarchy is loosed upon the world,
> The blood-dimmed tide is loosed, and everywhere
> The ceremony of innocence is drowned;
> The best lack all conviction, while the worst
> Are full of passionate intensity.
> W. B. Yeats, *The Second Coming*

Birds have been used by man to help him hunt for hundreds of years. There was a 'hierarchy' of hunting birds, with the Peregrine as the most desirable hunter – unsurprising given its incredible speed and deadly accurate aim. Henry IV of France owned a Peregrine, which escaped; however, the bird had a name-tag on one of its legs so was easily identifiable as belonging to the King when it was found 12 days later in Malta, having covered 1,350 miles (over 2,000 km) in that time.

The largest of the hunting falcons is the Gyrfalcon; its natural habitat is in the Arctic, and the use of the bird was restricted to royalty. Smaller birds, such as the Hobby and the Merlin, were used by clergy and high-born ladies, but commoners were not allowed to hunt with birds at all. The hunting hierarchy of these birds was described in the 'Book of St Albans', of 1486:

An Eagle for an Emperor
A Gyrfalcon for a King
A Peregrine for a Prince
A Saker for a Knight
A Merlin for a Lady
A Goshawk for a Yeoman
A Sparrow Hawk for a Priest
A Musket for a Holy Water Clerk
A Kestrel for a Knave

There is a certain amount of jargon associated with falconry; a tiercel is the name for the male bird. The legs of the falcon are attached with bells and jesses, which are short silk or leather straps that enable the owner to keep a track of the bird while they're out hunting. Different coloured jesses were given the birds according to their rank, which was designated according to what other birds they had managed to kill. In the Far East, for example, the Goshawk was not allowed to wear purple jesses until it had successfully hunted the Manchurian Crane, which was a great deal larger than the Goshawk.

In Japan, falconry was considered a very noble art, and game preserves were maintained to ensure its future. The art has been kept alive for its cultural and historical value all over the world.

EGYPT

In Ancient Egypt, the very word for falcon, in the written language of the time, was that same as the word for God.

The falcon was the Prince of Birds, and, like the eagle, it was the personification of light and the Sun. Horus, of course, is the Falcon-headed God; specifically, he is depicted as having the body of a man and the head of a Peregrine. There is a particularly important Egyptian symbol, which is that of an eye with a specific curl underneath it, based on the markings on the cheek of a hawk. This is the Eye of Horus; it is 'the eye which sees everything' and also a symbol of fertility. Traditionally, the left eye of Horus was the Moon, and the right, the Sun.

The falcon was considered to be the Ba, or soul, of Horus. It was also the King of Hunting, and the personification of Ra, the Sun God, who sometimes appears with the head of the falcon, like Horus, with the solar disc behind his head. There were other falcon-headed Gods too, such as Month, the God of War, who is recognizable because of his crown of plumes.

In other instances, the falcon is a symbol of royalty, and will often be depicted hovering with outstretched wings over the heads of royal personages in Egyptian reliefs. The status of the falcon was such that at Saqqara, there's a catacomb, which was built specifically for mummified falcons; not just of one variety, but many different birds of prey were found there. The mummies of the pharaohs often had a falcon mask too, to show the status of the corpse.

THE GREEKS

As well as being the messenger of the God Apollo, the falcon has a close association with Circe, the sorceress. Indeed, her name means 'she-falcon'. The Goddess Thetis, the mother of Achilles, was also likened to this bird. The falcon was an important bird in auguries and divination; the *Iliad* relates an incident where the falcon had an important role to play, describing how

> there flew by a bird of omen on the right, a falcon, Apollo's swift messenger. And it plucked the pigeon which it held in its talons and scattered the feathers between the ship and Telemachus.

The action of the falcon was seen as a direct communication from Apollo that Odysseus would return home safely.

Celtic Lore

Regarded as the opposite of the hare, the falcon is the Sun to the hare's Moon, and is often depicted tearing a hare to pieces with its talons. In this instance the falcon signifies victory over lust, and the victory of light over darkness, male over female.

Peru

Again, the falcon represents the Sun. The Incas believed that each human being had a spiritual twin, which acted in much the same way as a guardian angel. This 'soul double' took the form of a falcon, and its name was Inti, which is the same as the Inca name for the Sun.

For Peruvians, the Gods of Creation were born from falcon's eggs and were birds before they took on the shape of humans. Some versions of the myth have the father of the Gods of Creation being the result of a union between a human mother and a bird who was a cross between an ostrich and a falcon, again, another instance of the Divine Spirit being represented by a winged creature.

Norse Mythology

The Norse God Odin was able to transform himself into a falcon when he wanted to visit Earth. And Freyja, the Goddess of Fertility, possessed a cloak of falcon feathers that enabled her to be able to fly. In one story, she lends this magical feathered cloak to Loki so that he can find and bring back the Goddess Idunn and her apples of eternal youth.

CHINA

In Chinese mythology the Falcon again is the symbol of the Sun. The bird is also associated with war, probably because of its skill in hunting.

OK, this is going to sound really strange, but it's true. We were out driving in the country, sort of looking for somewhere new to live, just sort of getting a feel for the area we were in. Then we saw a sparrow hawk flying along the hedge tops, and we took several odd turnings up country lanes to see where it was going to go next.

The bird led us up a track with a dead end at the top, then flew off. But it had led us to a small country cottage which had a home-made 'For Sale' sign outside ... We knocked on the door, saw the place – and moved in two months later. It really did seem as though the bird took us there; we'd never have found the place we're delighted to call home, on our own.

Izzy, UK

What Bird Would You Be?

'I am very drawn to hawks, always have been ... and especially more so since my running-up hills experiences here in LA ... also the kingfisher seems like a very good one for me, as I've always thought they were really amazing ... brightly coloured, hard to spot, like fish ... very like me!'

Jont, USA

The Hoopoe

Fire

Solitary wayfarer!
Minstrel winged of the green wild!
What dost thou delaying here,
Like a wood-bewildered child
Weeping to his far-flow troop,
Whoop! and plaintive whoop! and whoop!
George Darley, *Canto II*

CHARACTERISTICS

The hoopoe you might know is the variety with the beautiful crested plume on its head, and the inquisitive look. It has a long, thin, pointed beak, and its first two toes are fused together. Its name reflects its call, a soft, mellow sort of 'hoop-hoop' sound. It is this sound that gives the bird both its scientific Latin name and its common name.

These days, you might see them having dust-baths in the outskirts of Tel Aviv, although they can be seen throughout Southern Europe and Asia, and further south into Africa. Occasionally the hoopoe will be spotted in the British Isles – about a hundred every year make it to the southern shores of the country.

As the poem above points out, hoopoes don't really travel in flocks – two or three together is the most you are most likely to see. They like to nest in the cavities of trees, and lay a clutch of between four and six pale blue eggs. They are pretty appalling nest-keepers, it has to be said, since they never seem to have time to clear out any debris. The female also has a pungent smell which emanates from her preen gland, which is believed to have a protective effect similar to that of a skunk. This could be the reason that they are listed in the Bible as an 'unclean' bird; that is, not to be eaten.

There's a story that God offered each bird a particular grain to eat. To the hoopoe he offered millet; the bird didn't want it. Then he offered barley, but the hoopoe didn't fancy that either. So God told the hoopoe that he might as well eat his own droppings. This isn't true; however, the hoopoe will excavate for grubs and insects that might be tucked away in dung. Otherwise, this is an attractive and noticeable bird!

If the hoopoe is ever threatened, for example by a bird of prey, it flattens itself against the ground, spreading its tail and wings and therefore making itself pretty much impossible to catch. The hoopoe can run swiftly when necessary and tends to feed on the ground.

The Magical Hoopoe

The hoopoe is featured on the walls of tombs in Crete and Egypt, and has long been associated with magic and the supernatural. As a bird who carries messages from the 'other place' the hoopoe seems to be second-to-none. According to the Qur'an it was the hoopoe who, as part of King Solomon's army, carried back to his master the news of the Queen of Sheba.

> I have gained the knowledge that thou knowest not … I have come to thee from Sheba; I have found a woman reigning over them gifted with everything.

And then there's Aristophanes' play *The Birds*, which is about two men who wish to encourage the birds to make their own city in the sky. The hoopoe is the guide, and is described as a 'messenger from an invisible world'; the birds' king, Tereus, was once a man (clearly Aristophanes is referring to the punishment that Tereus received for his seduction of Philomela, which you can read more about on page 183).

Unfortunately for the hoopoe, it was commonly believed that its entrails also contained magical properties; as well as helping with vision and memory, they were renowned for their properties as an aphrodisiac. The bird's innards, dried and worn around the neck, served as a protection against the evil eye and were believed to be able to counteract spells. Its blood and its heart were used in various folk medicines, and indeed the blood of the hoopoe is said to be a powerful agent if spells are written with it.

Personally, I'd debate the efficacy of the hoopoe as a bird of good luck, since these practices were obviously of no luck to the bird whatsoever …

The hoopoe is also one of the birds reputed to be able to forecast the weather, particularly storms, and with very good reason. It has been discovered relatively recently that the bird is able to detect minute electrical charges in the atmosphere, called piezoelectric charges, which can herald either a storm or an earthquake up to ten hours before the event.

THE EGYPTIANS

The Egyptians believed that the hoopoe was the bird of gratitude. This is because they were supposed to take care of their ageing parents by preening them and licking their eyes if their vision was failing.

ARAB LORE

There was a belief among the Arabs that the hoopoe was a doctor and could cure just about any kind of sickness. The bird was also accorded the powers of being able to divine water. This may have come about since the bird never seems to drink. The hoopoe was the only bird who had the capability to tell King Solomon the whereabouts of essential underground springs, a testament again to the bird's divinatory powers.

PERSIA

The hoopoe makes a major appearance in Persian literature and folklore. One legend has is that the hoopoe used to be a woman who was disturbed by her father-in-law while she was combing her hair. In her alarm she leapt up, turned into a bird, and flew away – this explains the tufted crest on top of the bird's head.

In *The Conference of the Birds* by the twelfth-century Sufi poet Farid Ud-Din Attar, the birds want to get together to find their King, the Simurgh. The work is allegorical, giving the author the means to be able to inform the reader about the tenets of Sufism, for which he was later killed. The hoopoe has an essential role in the book as the leader of the birds, and their spokesperson:

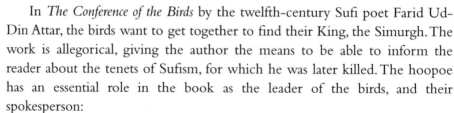

The Hoopoe fluttered forward; on his breast
There shone a symbol of the Spirit's Way
And on his head Truth's crown, a feathered spray.
Discerning, righteous and intelligent.
He spoke; 'My purposes are heaven sent;
I keep God's secrets, mundane and divine,
In proof of which behold the holy sign
Bismillah, etched forever on my beak.'

WHY THE HOOPOE CRIES 'OOP! OOP!'

Finally, there's a story from the Brothers Grimm as to how the hoopoe and the bittern came to have their distinctive cries.

The bittern and the hoopoe used to be shepherds. The bittern chose to keep his flocks on extremely rich meadowland, full of wildflowers, so the sheep, stuffed full of too many good things to eat (and no doubt suffering from bad indigestion), became difficult and unruly. The hoopoe, on the other hand, kept his flocks high up on windswept barren hills, where the grass wasn't very nutritious, so as a result the sheep were weak and unhealthy.

When it was time to gather the flocks together, those belonging to the bittern were too high-spirited and ran away from him. The bittern called, time and again, 'Come, sheep, come', but by then it was too late, and the animals took no notice. The sheep belonging to the hoopoe, however, were so weak that they could barely stand, and the hoopoe kept urging them, 'Up, up, up!' but again this was of no use at all.

And that's why the bittern's call sounds like 'come, sheep, come', and the call of the hoopoe is 'up, up, up!'

What Bird Would You Be?

'I would choose to be a hoopoe because they are my favourite bird, mainly because their Latin name is "oopooperepops" ... try saying it!'
Rose, London

The Hummingbird

Fire

I can imagine, in some otherworld
Primeval-dumb, far back
In that most awful stillness, that only gasped and hummed,
Humming-birds raced down the avenues.

Before anything had a soul,
While life was a heave of Matter, half inanimate,
This little bit chipped off in brilliance
And went whizzing through the slow, vast, succulent stems.

I believe there were no flowers, then
In the world where the humming-bird flashed ahead of creation.
I believe he pierced the slow vegetable veins with his long beak.

Probably he was big
As mosses, and little lizards, they say were once big.
Probably he was a jabbing, terrifying monster.

We look at him through the wrong end of the long telescope of
      Time,
Luckily for us.
D.H. Lawrence, *Birds, Beasts and Flowers*

CHARACTERISTICS

The Bee Hummingbird of Cuba lives exclusively in the Americas, and even the largest of these birds is relatively small; the Giant Hummingbird of the Andes is 8 inches (20 cm) long, whereas the smallest, the Cuban Bee Hummer, is just 2 inches (5 cm) long and weighs less than two grams (well under a quarter of an ounce).

Hummingbirds are incredibly beautiful, with iridescent feathers in all the colours of the rainbow. They are so lovely that a century ago millions of the birds were used as jewellery; the skins were exported from South America to Europe where they would be used on hats, or were fashioned into brooches, and the like. Thank goodness, this trade has now stopped, although the existing skins have provided some sort of a record of the different types of hummingbird.

Relationship to Flowers

The hummingbird has a relationship, almost unique in the bird kingdom, with flowers, since this tiny bird feeds virtually exclusively on nectar, and is able to extract massive amounts of energy from the sugars found in this substance. The hummingbird also helps to pollinate flowers.

How The Hummingbird Got Its Name

It's simple; its wings move incredibly quickly (beating between 50 and 75 times every second) as it flies or gathers nectar, and so makes a humming sound. In fact this small bird can fly incredibly quickly and incredibly long distances; although laboratory reports state that it's impossible for the Ruby-throated Hummingbird to fly 500 miles in one go, since its body cannot store enough energy for this journey, the bird is unaware of the report and manages to do so nevertheless.

The hummingbird is the most prodigious flyer. It can hover, move vertically or horizontally, and even backwards. The bird can flap its wings faster than any other bird on the planet.

The hummingbird has other names too. In Brazil it is the Colibri, or the 'passaro beja-flor', which translates into the lovely name 'flower-kisser sparrow'; and in the Caribbean it's appropriately called the 'Zoom Zoom'.

Most of the mythology and stories about the hummingbird come, not surprisingly given the bird's distribution, from the Americas.

The Hummingbird – Messenger Between the Worlds

The belief that hummingbirds were carriers of messages between 'this' world and the Otherworld is widespread, and in accordance with what we know about beliefs about birds from all over the world. With the hummingbird in particular, because of its extraordinary iridescent beauty and swift movements, we can see how this would be especially prevalent.

The Nazca Lines

On the Nazca Plains in Peru, artists living centuries ago carved out various shapes and patterns that are indecipherable from the ground, but which when viewed from the air come together in recognizable pictures. They also carved out a giant hummingbird, which can only be seen in its full glory when the viewer is about a thousand feet up in the air. It is ancient art like this that gives us a glimpse of just how sacred the hummingbird was to these ancient peoples, having a place in legend as one of the creators of the world.

The Andes

The hummingbird loses a significant amount of heat at night in order to conserve energy (indeed, the bird goes into a sort of hibernation every night, with its temperature dropping to not much more than that of the surrounding air, around about 65 degrees). Because of this, the bird can often appear to be dead if it is seen at night; but in the morning, and in the heat of the sunlight, it is of course alive and well. In the Andes, this means that the bird has become a symbol of resurrection.

The Aztecs

As with birds in many other cultures, the Aztecs believed that hummingbirds were souls of departed human beings; in particular, they were said to carry the spirits of warriors who had been nobly killed in battle, who, immediately after death, would circle the sun for four years and would then transform into hummingbirds, feeding on the flowers in a heavenly garden. At night the birds would turn back into soldiers and would do battle with the powers of darkness. Aztecs also believed that the heat of the Sun came about because of the hummingbird.

One of the more epic myths about the hummingbird concerns a great warrior, Huitzil. His full name was 'Huitzilpochtli', which translates as 'the hummingbird from the left'. The 'left' here refers to the otherworldly realms, running parallel with the known universe. The warrior's mother conceived him from a ball of brightly coloured feathers that fell from the sky one day. When Huitzil was killed in battle, his body disappeared and a hummingbird whirled up from the spot where he'd fallen.

Aztec veneration of the hummingbird was profound. The cloaks of the shamans would be decorated with the feathers of the bird, and wands would also use the feathers as decoration and as a tool of communication.

The Taino Tribe of Jatibonicu

The hummingbird is sacred to the Taino Indians of the Caribbean because of its role as a pollinator, and therefore as a bearer of new life. They believe that the birds were once flies that the Sun Father transformed into birds. The bird is also known as the 'Guaracacigaba' or the 'Guacariga', which means, appropriately, 'Rays of the Sun'.

The Taino had a legend that tells of a girl and a boy from rival tribes, who fell in love. Their love was highly frowned upon by the elders since, like the families of Romeo and Juliet, the two tribes were bitter enemies. So that they could escape the criticism and be together, the boy turned into a hummingbird and the girl turned into a flower.

In the Longhouse, a sacred space belonging to the Jatibonicu, are stone 'cemis' or totems, and the main, central totem depicts a hummingbird – the bee hummingbird, or Guani, to be precise.

The Tukano Indians

The Tukano are from Columbia, and again the hummingbird plays a central part in their mythology. It's a fertility symbol; the bird is actually believed to have sexual intercourse with flowers and to fertilize them in this way.

Mexico

In Mexico, the hummingbird is firmly attached to the mysteries of love and romance, and the bird, worn as a talisman, would bring these elusive qualities to the wearer, although this doesn't seem like such a lucky thing for the bird itself. However, the superstition has survived and carried on; even today the heart of a hummingbird, dried and ground to a fine powder, is a primary ingredient of a love potion.

Mayan Legends

There are lots of links between the hummingbird and the Sun throughout American Indian mythology. The Mayans believed that the hummingbird was the actual sun, in disguise as a bird, since he is in love with a beautiful woman – the moon.

The Mayans also have a legend that explains just how the hummingbird got its extraordinary colouring: the bird was simply constructed from the remaindered feathers of all the other birds in the world.

Mojave

The Mojave have a story about how light came to their people. Prior to this happy event, the world was dark and everyone lived underground. But the hummingbird was sent on a mission to look for light. He found a chink in the roof of the underground world, and flew up through it and therefore brought the people the route to sunshine.

The Hummingbird and Tobacco

The relevance of tobacco to Native Americans, and indeed to shamans from all over the world, has many reasons, including that fact that rising smoke sends messages to the heavens. Given that birds do the same job, there are many associations between birds and this herb, but particularly with the hummingbird.

Both the Cherokee peoples and the Arawak tribe of the Caribbean have legends connecting the hummingbird with tobacco. The Arawak, who are unfortunately now extinct, called the hummingbird the Doctor Bird. In the Cherokee story, a shaman transformed himself into a hummingbird so that he could find the lost tobacco plant. The Arawak have the hummingbird being sent on a mission, perched on the back of a crane, to gather some of the preciously guarded tobacco seeds.

According to the Pueblo Indians, the hummingbird got smoke from the caterpillar, who was the guardian of the tobacco plant, and gave this gift to the shaman.

The Hummingbird and Rain

The Pueblo use hummingbird feathers as part of their rain-bringing rituals. They also have hummingbird dances; and in a poignant ritual for stillborn babies, prayer sticks with hummingbird feathers are held aloft to the sunrise on the Winter Solstice in the belief that this will speed along the rebirth of the spirit.

A Cochti Legend

The Cochti have a story about the hummingbird's connection to rain, too. The people lost their faith in the Great Mother, who became very angry, and took away their rain for four years. The only creature that didn't seem to suffer under this regime was the hummingbird, so the people started to pay attention to its habits. It was discovered by the shaman that the bird had access to secret passages and routes into the Underworld, where he would go to collect nectar and honey. The reason this door had remained open to the bird was because he had never lost his faith in the Great Mother; this fact inspired the Cochti to believe in Her again too, whereupon the fertility of their land was restored.

THE HOPI AND ZUNI INDIANS

Both tribes have legends telling how the hummingbird could ask the Gods to send rain to the human world when it was needed. Hummingbirds are a popular emblem on water jars because of this story. The hummingbird also features prominently in rain-dances.

To illustrate the connection with rain even further, there's a Hopi tale about a pair of children, a brother and sister, who are left alone during a time of famine while their parents go in search of food and water. Although both children are starving, the little girl's elder brother fashions a toy hummingbird to distract her. The girl threw the toy into the air, whereupon it came to life, a real bird, and started to bring them a little bit of corn to eat every day. Eventually the little hummingbird went to appeal to the Gods to send rain so that the people wouldn't starve any more.

What Bird Would You Be?

'That's a tricky question ... still, thinking about it, I guess I'd have to say a hummingbird. They seem to eat lots of honey, and it most be lovely dipping your head into flowers all day long! And I'm Brazilian!'

Lupa, Sao Paolo

The Macaw

Fire

CHARACTERISTICS

Although opinions vary, there are about 350 different species in the parrot family, of which 17 are macaws. They share some characteristics, such as their bright colours and vocal abilities. Their natural habitat is the tropical rain forests from South America to Mexico, although they can be seen in cages all over the world. As pets, macaws have a high value, which has resulted in some illegal trafficking.

They nest on the tops of high cliffs or very steep escarpments.

NATIVE AMERICAN LORE

As you might imagine, the feathers of the macaw are highly prized items for both ritual and decorative use among many tribes. The feathers were used on masks, on prayer sticks, and as hair ornamentation. Like the parrot, the bird was a symbol of the Sun, although it's also considered by the Pueblo to be a 'child of the cloud'.

Because the birds are not indigenous to North America, they would be collected from more southerly areas at the same time as salt was collected. There's archaeological evidence of macaw bones in Native American villages from AD 1100.

The macaw was believed to be able to escort the souls of the dead to the Otherworld, and the members of the Bororo tribe believe that the cycle of reincarnation which man must undergo includes spending some time as a macaw.

The Mayans

The Mayans also believed the macaw to be a bird of the Sun, partly because of its long, fire-red feathers. The symbol of the bird was used to depict the six Cosmic Suns.

The Origins of Two Bird Tribes

There's a Zuni legend about how the Macaw People and the Raven People came to be …

Once, there was a shaman, named Yanauluha. Yanauluha was a wise man, and owned something not at all dissimilar to a magic wand. This wand was decorated with feathers, which blew about in the wind, and shells, which would tinkle as he walked along. Whenever people saw Yanauluha they'd want to ask him many questions, about all sorts of things.

One day a crowd had, as usual, gathered around him, and Yanauluha thought he'd show them something interesting. So he struck his wand upon a rock, and immediately he did so, four eggs appeared; two were red, and two were blue.

'These eggs,' said Tanauluha, 'contain the seeds of all living things. You must all of you choose which you will worship. From two of these eggs, the blue ones, will hatch creatures with beautiful feathers, and the creatures will be coloured in all the shades of Summer. Wherever these creatures go, you will go too, and it will always be summertime.

'But from the other two eggs, the red ones, will come evil creatures, white and piebald, with no colours. Whoever follows these creatures will always have to work hard in order to survive. Now, which do you choose?'

Of course, faced with such a choice, anyone in their right minds would choose the blue eggs. The blue eggs were immediately carried off by the strongest people, who took them into some sand dunes to see what would hatch out.

Soon, the chicks appeared. Even without their full feathers they appeared to be all the colours of the rainbow, so the people were glad, and fed the birds with all the favoured delicacies that they themselves preferred. However, when the first true feathers came, the birds proved to be black, with the occasional white banding – they were ravens, who flew away laughing, pleased at having played such a good trick; baby ravens do indeed appear to be rainbow-coloured, but grow up to look like very different birds

But there were a few people who had waited to see what would happen to the red eggs. They were fortunate, because the red eggs contained the chicks of the macaw, and sure enough, the followers of the macaw always lived in the summertime.

This is why the Raven People of the Zuni are known as the Winter people; there are lots of them, and they're very strong. The Macaw People of the Zuni are known as the Summer People; there are fewer of them, but they are thought to be more considered and deliberate about everything they do.

What Bird Would You Be?

'I'd be an eagle ... the reasons for eagle are sharp, long-distant views, can fly and sail the winds, strong bonds with partner, doesn't take any nonsense ... and builds its nest in hard-to-reach typographies.'

Brigs, Austria

The Mockingbird

Fire

> Not that he intends
> to be seen
> no not that

But instead
from the lonely cliff of his heart
an untame song becomes
a generous valve within the cherry branches
Whether the chipmunk looks up
from her rocky grove
or I
with bucket and sweet greed
pause
in picking
the red globes
It doesn't matter

The song itself
The only audience
The song
Jeffery Beam, *Mockingbird*

CHARACTERISTICS

The mockingbird, as you might imagine from its name, is a great mimic, and also a good singer. Native to America, they are active, inquisitive, funny and aggressive birds who live close to the ground, grubbing for insects. They are also fond of berries. Its popularity in the USA is proven in that it's the bird symbol of five American states: Texas, Mississippi, Arkansas, Tennessee and Florida. Indeed, in the Texan legislature's resolution on the matter it is stated that the mockingbird is 'a fighter for the protection of his home, falling, if need be, in its defense, like any true Texan'. This refers to another trait of the bird; it is also not afraid to vigorously defend its territory and will often attack cats and other intruders if it feels that it is necessary.

Mockingbirds can often be heard singing and chattering at all hours of day and night, usually from a high, exposed place – this bird is certainly not shy or retiring! Its ability to mimic is infamous, and it will soon build up a repertoire of car alarms, bells and buzzers, as well as being able to accurately copy the songs and calls of just about any bird under the sun; they can even copy the songs of imported European nightingales so closely that even with sophisticated sound equipment, experts find it difficult to distinguish between them.

Like the European nightingale, the appearance of the mockingbird belies its amazing vocal talents; it's quite a small, plain, brown bird. But the shyness of the nightingale is not shared by the mockingbird. It will often sing as it flies along – an unusual habit in any bird.

Native American Lore

The Choctaw's name for the mockingbird is 'Hushi Balbaha', which translates as 'the bird which speaks a foreign language'.

Seen as a bird of wisdom by the Hopi Indians, because of its uncanny ability for speech, the mockingbird was believed to have taught these people their ritual songs from the time of their 'Fourfold Underworld', when everyone spoke one of the four branches of the Pueblo language. The bird could both learn and teach, and could relay messages about everything that was going on in the kingdom of animals, so, as you might imagine, it was a valued bird.

In addition, there's a great deal of sympathetic magic based around the bird because of these associations. Some believed that the egg of the mockingbird would prevent stuttering; similarly, if a child was slow to talk then an effective cure was to take corn from the nest of a mockingbird and, after soaking it and grinding it, feed it to the infant. There also used to be a tradition among the Zuni of feeding the tongue of a mockingbird to a child in the hope that this would help in the learning of other languages.

The Mockingbird in Mayan Legend

There's a lovely story about how the mockingbird became the greatest singer. The Mayan word for the mockingbird is X-Chol-Col-Chek by the way!

The story is an analogy about natural aptitude and the determination to follow your dreams. Anyway, apparently the mockingbird's family was very poor, and could only afford to buy very threadbare and plain clothes. However, X-Col (let's shorten the name) seemed to have some aptitude for singing and longed to take proper lessons, but simply couldn't afford them.

The mockingbird was lucky to get work with a wealthy family of cardinal birds, at a time when the blackbird, Dr Xcau, a famous singing teacher, arrived in the area. The father of the family of cardinals decided that it would be a good idea for his daughter to take lessons from the blackbird.

X-Col, our little mockingbird girl, heard about this, and decided to hide in the woods whenever the lessons were taking place, in order to see what she could learn. However, the young cardinal seemed to have neither the aptitude to learn nor the ability to sing, so the blackbird soon despaired of his pupil and decided to simply up-sticks and leave.

The young cardinal was afraid to tell her parents that the lessons had ended, and was terribly worried because a recital had been arranged, and she just knew that she wasn't going to make a good impression. One day, however, the young cardinal heard X-Col singing, and immediately realized that there was a way to save the day. Accordingly, the woodpecker was asked to bore a hole in a nearby tree, the idea being that X-Col could hide in the cavity and sing, while the young cardinal mimed along to the song.

All seemed to be going well. The recital took place, the cardinal appeared to have the most exquisite voice, and the audience was enjoying every minute. However, the father of the cardinal had seen the mockingbird climbing into the hole … After his daughter had taken her bows, the father asked for silence, and invited X-Col to come out of the hole and not to be shy; she should sing for everyone in full view and not hide away.

At first X-Col was timid, but soon got into her stride. The audience could not believe at first that such a dowdy bird could produce such an exquisite song.

And the cardinal never did learn to sing!

What Bird Would You Be?

'I'd be a mockingbird … It's not a "gorgeous" bird by any means, not showy in its feathered self but well-groomed, dressed like a jazz-age crooner. It doesn't require an audience but it always receives one because the charm of its song is surround sound – rising up, circling and filling the air. Such a complete bird for it must be an efficient feeder, too, if it can spend so much of its day singing. I like that about it. Supreme in its craft, and yet economical, skilled and practical in its daily life.

'Perhaps the mockingbird is the Buddha of birds – teaching meditation through song, and right action and deed in its living.'
Jeffrey, USA

The Parrot

Fire

Never get up till the Sun gets up
Or the mists will give you a cold
And a parrot whose lungs have once been touched
Will never grow to live old
Never eat plums that are not quite ripe
For perhaps they will give you a pain;
And never dispute what the hornbill says
Or you'll never dispute again!
Never despise the power of speech
Learn every word as it comes
For this is the pride of the parrot race
That it speaks in a thousand tongues.
Never stay up when the Sun goes down
But sleep in your own home bed
And if you've been good,
As a parrot should,
You'll dream that your tail is red.
Mother Parrot's Advice To Her Children, **African poem translated**
by A.K. Nyabongo

CHARACTERISTICS

There are 315 different kinds of parrots, from the minute Pygmy Parrot from
Papua New Guinea, at just three and a half inches long (9 cm), to the large
birds from the Amazon jungles, whose tails alone can reach up to 40 inches
(100 cm) long. While they have never been domesticated to the point that
other birds have (for example, the pigeon family), parrots, nevertheless, have
been kept as pets for a very long time indeed; proof of this is found in the
mentions of the talking ability of the African Grey in early Greek and
Roman writings.

Parrots are very appealing birds; they're beautiful, affectionate, and appear to
be able to imitate many human traits. They're also very cute! The mimicking

only happens when parrots are kept in captivity, and they tend to learn better as young birds, copying just about any sound they might hear on a regular basis. In the wild, parrots communicate with one another via a series of shrill squaws and yells.

Parrot Fashion?

When we say 'parrot fashion', we often mean that something is being repeated with no particular understanding of what has been said, that there is something mindless about the process. However, there's evidence to support the theory that some parrots are able to use words in an intelligent and deliberate manner; you can read more about this in the chapter entitled 'Bird Brain?' (page 26); it is enough to mention here that Dr Irene Pepperberg famously possessed a parrot, called Alex, who could use over a hundred words correctly, and could count up to six … perhaps it is about time some of our ideas about the intelligence of birds was readdressed?

King George V of England would certainly have agreed with this. He owned a parrot named Charlotte, who would apparently read official documents with him while perched on his shoulder, occasionally saying 'What about it?' When the King, a keen sailor, was ill, Charlotte asked constantly, 'Where's the Captain?' Once he was better and Charlotte was allowed to see him again, she delightedly exclaimed; 'Bless my buttons, bless my buttons, all is well!'

The Far East

The parrot originated in South China, and is mentioned as being a talking bird in ancient manuscripts. The bird is often accompanied by Kuan-Yin, who was the Goddess of Compassion. The bird's origins in this part of the world explains the image we have of the sailor and his pet parrot, which would have been collected as a trophy on long voyages.

EGYPT

Parrots were carried at Pharaoh Ptolemy's procession at Alexandria, having arrived from India and Persia.

THE ROMANS

Allegedly, Julius Caesar was much enamoured of a parrot, given to him as a gift, which had been taught to utter the following rather sycophantic phrase:

> I, a parrot, am willing to learn the names of others from you. This I learnt by myself to say – 'Hail Caesar!'

Chocolate can be fatally poisonous to parrots.

ANCIENT GREECE

The parrot arrived in Greece from India, and Aristotle made the following comment about its powers of mimicry:

> The Indian bird, the parrot, which they call the bird with the human voice ... becomes even more insolent after drinking wine.

This refers to the fact that, if befuddled by alcohol, the parrot will repeat a series of completely random words and phrases – not unlike its human owner! Dionysius commented that 'Parrots take their mimicry to the point of actually mastering our language.'

AMERICAN INDIAN TRADITION

For the Pueblo people, the parrot is associated with the gathering of salt. The bird is a symbol of the Sun, not surprising when you consider their incredible coloured feathers, and these feathers were a valuable part of certain rituals. Parrots could also give blessings, and the birds were also used in trading, being considered to be a very expensive status symbol. There is even a Parrot tribe in the Pueblo Indian tradition.

INDIA

The parrot is considered a sacred bird by the Brahmans, and was never eaten, despite its large population. The bird is dedicated to Kama, the God of Love. This is because people in love often unconsciously imitate one another's body language and speech patterns. Consequently, the birds are emblems of marriage in Northern India (another reason the bird has sacred status), with parrot images being hung in the places where weddings take place.

The parrot is also meant to be the bird of oracles, and can herald rain. Parrots have a special place in Indian myths and legends, and are considered to be very special birds, holding knowledge of the four Vedas, and as well as being messengers of love, they are teachers of archery and dance.

There's a traditional series of folk tales, originally written in Sanskrit, called *Tales of a Parrot*, which is a 'chain' of stories in a similar fashion to *The Arabian Nights*. In the tales, a parrot relates 70 stories to stop a woman from taking the wrong path. The tale was later translated into Persian.

There's a story in which the parrot is chosen as King of the Birds over the owl; although the owl is a fantastic nightwatchman, the parrot wins the argument that it's more important to be able to see what's going on in the daytime!

Allegedly, the Maharaja of Tanager had a parrot who reached the grand old age of 115, and who, as well as being driven everywhere in a Rolls Royce, also possessed his own international passport!

ZEN BUDDHISM

I don't know about you, but I get a nauseous reaction when I see birds in cages. Apparently the Zen Buddhist Bodhidharma had the same reaction. There's a lovely story about how a parrot escaped to freedom.

The Bodhidharma met a parrot sitting in a cage, and stopped besides it to commiserate. The bird recognized the Bodhidharma, and said:

Mind from the West,
Mind from the West,
Do me a favour and teach me a way
To escape from this cage.

The Bodhidharma bent down to the parrot, and whispered in his ear:

Put out both legs
Close both eyes
This is the way
To escape from the cage!

The parrot thought about this for a moment and couldn't quite work it out. Nevertheless he decided to follow the instructions. Accordingly, when the owner of the parrot returned and saw the bird with stiff legs and closed eyes, he assumed the bird was dead. So he opened the cage and lifted the bird out … and of course the parrot grabbed its chance as soon as it was able and flew away.

A salutary reminder that sometimes we just have to follow the instructions from the Divine, however they come to us, without trying to analyse the meaning or content.

What Bird Would You Be?

'I think I'd be a toucan. Black with splashes of colour, partial to warmer climates (and beautiful locations), quite loud (big beak), obvious association with the Irish beer. And toucans are better than one.'

Jan, UK

The Peacock (Indian Peafowl)

Fire

> The peacock wedded to the world
> Of all her gorgeous plumage vain,
> With glowing banners wide unfurled,
> Sweeps slowly by in proud distain;
> But in her heart a torment lies,
> That dims the lustre of those eyes;
> She turns away her glance – but no,
> Her hideous feet appear below!
> And fatal echoes, deep and loud,
> Her secret mind's dark caverns stir;
> She knows, though beautiful and proud,
> That Paradise is not for her.
> For, when in Eden's blissful spot
> Lost Eblis tempted man, she dared
> To join the treach'rous angel's plot
> And thus his crime and sentence shared.
> Her frightful claws remind her well
> Of how she sinned and how she fell.
> **Azz' Eddin Elmocadessi,** *The Peacock*

CHARACTERISTICS

The peacock is universally accepted as one of the most spectacular and beautiful birds on the planet. Originally from South West India and Sri Lanka, they are now to be found just about everywhere. A member of the pheasant family, the Phoenicians first brought the peacock to Egypt and Syria, from whence it made its way across Europe. The peacock is the national symbol of India, and is a sacred bird there, particularly in Northern India. It is often associated with the phoenix.

The peacock is a polygamous bird, having four or five 'wives', who will lay their eggs in a hidden nest, a shallow hole lined with leaves. Peacocks are meant to be the world's most aggressive birds. They are often to be seen as a decoration, strutting around the grounds of stately homes and the like. Because of their aggressive natures, they make extremely good 'guard dogs'. Bearing in mind that the tail's 'arc' can have a spread of up to 90 inches (over 2 metres), you can imagine what this must look like as the feathers shimmer in the sunshine.

Although we seem to be willing to associate the peacock with vanity and pride, in fact the bird is a symbol of the Sun. If you've ever seen a peacock with its tail feathers unfurled in all their glory, this analogy is easily understandable. As you might imagine, because of its magnificent appearance, the peacock is associated with many deities.

PEACOCK FEATHERS

The tail feathers of the peacock are not true feathers but in fact they are 'covers' for the actual feathers, which are the much shorter quills that come into action to hold the longer, display feathers aloft. The 'eyes' on the feathers are called 'ocelli'. The male bird will have between 100 and 175 of these 'eyes' and the whole is an important part of his courtship display, given that the female will choose the male with the largest number. The iridescence of the peacock feather is only possible because of a particular adaptation, whereby the feather filaments are flattened, and do not contain the barbs which connect the feathers of flight together.

In the UK, Italy and other parts of Europe, peacock feathers are often considered to be very unlucky, probably because of the eyes on the tail being taken as the 'evil eye'. To bring one into the home is meant to signify disaster, and similarly, to take a peacock feather into a theatre would signify bad luck for the production. For myself, I have peacock feathers all over the house, and have never had any problem – although I was told in India that the feathers should always be placed close to something red!

Having mentioned that Italians are particularly superstitious about peacock feathers, nevertheless the Pope, during his Easter procession, carries a 'flabetti', which is a fan comprised of ostrich feathers tipped with peacock feathers. The peacock feathers represent the all-seeing eyes of the Church, and we might imagine that the ostrich feathers signify truth and justice.

In Asia, peacock feathers are considered to be an essential good luck token.

The Peacock's Cry

Contrary to its gorgeous appearance, the cry of the peacock is quite shrill and alarming. Its voice is said to give a warning of rain to come:

> When the peacock loudly bawls
> Soon we'll have both rain and squalls.
> *Anon*

It can also act as a warning that there may be intruders about.

There's a story that the reason for the peacock's cry, out of sync with its appearance, is because every time he sees his feet he realizes how ugly they are. This could be because the partridge beat the peacock in a dancing competition, and the penalty for the peacock was that they had to swap feet.

> The bird of Juno glories in his plumes: Pride makes the fowl to prune
> his feathers so.
> His spotted train, fetched from old Argus' head,
> With golden rays like to the brightest sun,
> Inserteth self-love in a silly bird,
> Till midst his hot and glorious fumes,
> He spies his feet and then lets fall his plumes.
> **Robert Greene,** *Verses Under A Peacock Portrayed In Her Left Hand*

Transformation of Poisons

The Latin name for the peacock is 'pavo', meaning 'purity', and this provides a pointer to another aspect of this bird; namely, its supposed ability to neutralize poisons. The colours in the peacock's tail symbolize these transformed poisons, which the peacock is said to ingest when it devours serpents and snakes. It could be this belief that gave rise to the fiction that peacock meat is poisonous – it isn't.

In the Hindu tradition, it's said that at the time of Creation, a poisonous substance poured out of a Sea of Milk. Luckily, the peacock was there to absorb the negative effects of the toxins. In the Punjab, smoked peacock feathers were used to heal snake bites. Additionally, in Tibetan medicine, the peacock is said to be able to neutralize the effects of a particularly deadly poison, Black Aconite, or Wolfbane, and the bird is able to use it as nourishment.

INDIA

The peacock has angel's feathers, a devil's voice, and the walk of a thief.
Hindu saying

For over 4,000 years peacocks have graced Indian temples, where they are venerated for their snake-eating ability and the good luck which they were believed to bring. The peacocks are still protected by law, so they can congregate safely around villages and shrines. However, in some parts of India they are hunted as a delicacy. Like other birds, the peacock is believed to be able to prophesy the weather, in particular, rain, which is foretold by the cry of the bird.

In Northern India, peacock feathers are burned to ward off disease and to cure snake bites – harking back to the powers of the peacock to be able to kill and eat snakes without suffering any ill consequences.

As well as being the national emblem of India, the peacock has many beliefs attached to it. Murugan, who was identified with Skanda, the son of Shiva, would ride a peacock, as would Skanda-Kartitikeya (the God of War), Brahma and Lakshmi. The Goddess of Music, poetry and wisdom, Sarasvati, also rides on a peacock. Lakshmi, Goddess of Abundance, has the peacock as her sacred bird since both she and the bird represent fertility. The bird is also sometimes seen being ridden by Kama, the God of Love – this represents impatient desire, or lust.

In *The Golden Bough*, J.G. Frazer tells us that

The Bhils in Central India worship the peacock as their totem and make offerings of grain to it; yet members of the clan believe that were they even to set foot on the tracks of a peacock they would afterwards suffer from some disease, and if a woman sees a peacock she must veil her face and look away.

CHINA

The peacock in China is also known as 'the pimp', because one look from the bird is meant to be able to make a woman pregnant! It's likely that the same belief was held in India, hence the need for ladies to look away from the bird as described above. The peacock feather was an attribute of the Goddess Kuan-Yin.

During the time of the Tang dynasty, in the eighth century AD, peacocks were paid to the state as tribute, since the feathers were in demand by the authorities. They were used not only for imperial processions but to designate rank; they were also used as a reward for good service and to show imperial favour.

The reason for the use of the feather in this way comes from a story about a general of the Chin dynasty who was fleeing capture and ran into a forest full of peacocks. He hid behind a tree, and when his enemies arrived in the forest the birds were so quiet they assumed that no one was there. The general escaped, and consequently the peacock was honoured in recognition for its help by keeping quiet.

ANCIENT GREECE

In Ancient Greece, the peacock was the bird of Hera, who was given the bird by the God Pan, who originally owned it. Hera was the Queen of the Sky, and the peacock is sacred to her, its tail feathers resembling the stars in the 'vault of heaven'. There was a peacock zoo in Athens, in the fifth century BC, and there were severe punishments for harming the bird in any way.

There's a story about how the peacock got the 'eyes' in its tail: Zeus fell in love with a mortal girl, Io, but Hera, his wife, was insanely jealous and became suspicious. So Zeus, to throw his wife off the scent, turned Io into a heifer (temporarily, it is to be hoped). Hera still had her suspicions, so she asked the hundred-eyed giant Argus to keep watch. However, Zeus had Argus killed, and Hera, whose sacred bird was the peacock, had Argus's eyes put into the tail of the peacock in memory of him.

The peacock is also the emblem of the Greek bird-God, Phaon.

The Romans

The Roman naturalist Pliny tells us that magicians said that the names of the Sun and Moon were written on an amethyst, and that if this amethyst were tied to the neck with peacock feathers and swallow feathers, then this would act as an effective talisman against the workings of sorcerers and witches. Also, being sacred to Juno, the peacock featured on Roman coins.

The Egyptians

The peacock was a sun symbol in Egypt, connected to the worship of Amon Ra, who was the Sun God. Not surprisingly, it was also linked to Horus, the hawk-headed God, who was said the have 'all-seeing eyes'. The peacock was held second only to the ibis among birds.

There's a very similar story to the Greek myth about how the peacock inherited all the eyes in its tail. Apparently, Argos, who was a traitor to Osiris, locked Osiris' wife away during an absence of Osiris, and declared that he was King. Argos had spies everywhere so was able to track the movements of Osiris. However, Osiris learned of this, and as a punishment turned Argos into a peacock and gave the tail of the bird all the eyes of the unfortunate victim's former spies.

Islamic Lore

Muslims believe that the peacock symbolizes the Sun and Moon, and when the tail is displayed, the bird symbolizes the entire universe.

Sufi mystics believed that the Great Spirit originated as a peacock. It caught sight of its reflection and was so overawed with its own beauty that it broke out in sweat. The drops of sweat dripped from the bird, and where they fell other living creatures were born.

The Yezidis and the Peacock Angel

Yezidism is possibly one of the more unusual religions on Earth. The word 'Yezidi' is derived from the name for 'Angel'. It remains unacknowledged as a religion by the Islamic world, although it has many followers among the Kurds. The belief system exists throughout Northern Iraq, Georgia, Armenia, Iran, Turkey and Syria, and used to be considered the main religion of the Kurds scattered across these areas. There's no official sacred text, but the tradition is oral – remember what we said about the world prior to the written word?

Central to Yezidism is the image of the peacock. The peacock is called 'Melek Taus', or 'Eblis' (see the poem at the beginning of this section), which means the 'Peacock Angel'; in the West this Peacock Angel equates with Lucifer. In the Christian tradition, the very mention of Lucifer can be enough to make people nervous. But the Yezidis have a different take on the matter, which is well worth considering since it encourages us to think where certain beliefs may have come from, and to learn about the viewpoints of others can only increase our understanding and tolerance.

The Yezidis do not consider that Lucifer is a 'fallen angel' or the enemy of God, but instead that he is the chief Archangel and the creator of the material world, which was made from a broken pearl. The Peacock Angel was the messenger of God. There's an Islamic story that relates how, when God cast Adam and Eve from the Garden of Eden, he cast out the peacock also.

The Peacock Throne

It seems only right to include some details about the famous Peacock Throne, which originally belonged to the Indian Moghul ruler, Shah Jahan. Named after the peacock because of its opulent splendour, the throne was originally one of seven. Its measurements were said to have been six feet by four feet (roughly two metres by one metre); it was constructed of marble, and was covered in gold and then encrusted with jewels. There were diamonds, 108 rubies of between 100 and 200 carats, and 116 emeralds of between 30 and 60 carats. There was also a jewelled peacock on the throne, made of sapphires, one extremely large ruby, and a 50-carat pearl. Later, the throne was taken to Persia.

Juno and the Peacock

Finally, there's a lovely story from Aesop's Fables about Juno and the Peacock, which is a salutary reminder that we should be happy with what we have …

The peacock, being sacred to Juno, thought that he would ask the Goddess for a favour.

'Why is it that the nightingale, who is really not much to look at, should make everyone so utterly delighted with his song, whereas I only have to open my beak to become a complete laughing stock? It just doesn't seem fair somehow.'

Juno replied, 'But you're so beautiful to look at! You far excel the nightingale in size. You're the most splendid-looking creature – you shine like the rainbow! I can't see that there's a problem.'

'But, Juno,' complained the peacock. 'What's the point of being beautiful, if I can't sing? I'm a bird! We're meant to be able to sing!'

'Peacock,' said Juno, more sternly. 'The lot of every creature has been assigned by the Fates. You have beauty. The eagle was given strength. The nightingale has the lovely voice you envy. The raven and the crow carry favourable or unfavourable auguries. They are all content with what has been given to them, and you should be, too.'

It is not only fine feathers that makes for a fine bird.
Proverb

I'd just broken up with a lover in fact, someone whom I'd thought was more than that. I'd kidded myself about lots of things and although I guess he'd been straightforward, I'd made the big mistake of trying to change him. I was feeling like a fool, like I'd wasted two years from passing my expectations on to this man and deliberately not seeing the true story.

I took a shortcut through a park and stopped to watch the peacocks, when one of them unfurled his tail. Looking at this beautiful, beautiful sight, this radiant bird, I realized that although I'd been a fool, there had been a beauty in the relationship which I'd failed to grasp and that I should be proud, and that the whole experience was a lesson for me, and I should regard it as a privilege. The sight of the peacock was a real turning point in my consciousness.
Anonymous

What Bird Would You Be?

'I'd want to be a peacock ... it's the feathers, something about being able to flaunt those beautiful feathers and the mad, theatrical elegance of them.'
Ptolemy, London

The Robin

Fire

A robin red breast in a cage
Puts all Heaven in a rage.
William Blake, *Auguries of Innocence*

Art thou the bird whom man loves best
The pious bird with the scarlet breast
Our little English robin?
William Wordsworth, *The Redbreast*

CHARACTERISTICS

Although the American Robin is much larger than the European Robin, species of the robin exist pretty much all over the world, having even been introduced into Australia by the British. Wherever it is found, the red-breasted bird is regarded with a huge amount of affection. The first thing you'll usually notice about the robin, as with all members of the thrush family, is that its song is loud and lovely and very noticeable, and it has an almost human chattering quality as well as a more musical sound.

Robins are very protective about their 'patch', and their song is used as a territorial warning. If there's a new robin 'on the block' then a battle will ensue in the form of song, as the robins puff themselves up to their fullest size in order to stake their claim. The bird who loses the contest will alter his song very slightly, literally 'changing his tune' in order to back down.

Among garden birds, robins can be remarkably tame; on a cold winter's day the robin can often seem to be the only bird around, and its red breast is a cheering sight. The robin will often hang around close to any gardening activity in case any tasty worms might be turned up from the soil. Although the robin will migrate, if there are enough food supplies it will stay through the bad weather and is a welcome sight in a bird-bereft winter landscape.

Robins can also get a little drunk from eating too many over-ripe soft fruits, such as cherries!

Myths and Legends

The robin seems to have more myths and legends associated with it in the British Isles than anywhere else, which is quite fitting given that it is the national bird emblem of the country. The little bird has never been trapped or used for meat to the same extent that it has in mainland Europe, and most of the stories associated with the robin have it as a benevolent friend of mankind.

The robin is often associated with the wren, and it used to be supposed that the robin was the husband of the smaller bird. Both have legends in which they are responsible for bringing fire to mankind, which is one explanation for the robin's red colouring.

Interestingly, when I was asking for bird anecdotes, I had more stories of the robin being associated with lost loved ones, and therefore providing comfort as some sort of evidence of survival after death, than for any other bird. A couple of these tales are related at the end of this section.

The Robin and Fire

Unsurprisingly because of its red breast, there are many associations with the bird and fire. The old Anglo-Saxon name for the bird was the 'ruddock', which means 'red' or 'ruddy'. The bird is of course often known as the Redbreast, or Robin Redbreast.

On Guernsey, off the main coast of the UK, it was believed that there was no fire at all until it was brought by the robin. However, it is not only

Baby robins eat 14 feet [over 4 metres] of earthworms every day.

in the UK that the bird is associated with the bringing of fire. There's an Australian Aborigine myth that the robin was sent by man to steal fire from the terrifying Red Crested Cockatoo, who had wanted the element all to himself. The courageous robin got too close to the actual fire he was stealing and accordingly was scorched; in addition, in his haste to get away with the magical fire stick, the robin caused an almighty conflagration, leaving behind a smoking black waste; but once again here's a story of the robin as the friend of mankind.

DON'T HARM A ROBIN!

There are numerous grisly outcomes for anyone doing harm to this little bird.

In Ireland, if you killed a robin, a large lump would form on your hand. In parts of the UK there's still a superstition that the taking of a robin's nest will result in all the crockery of the thief's family being smashed. In Scotland, the supernatural punishment for the same deed would be a sudden attack of epilepsy. The punishment for harming a robin is also meted out to cats – if a cat should kill a robin, then the cat will lose one of its own limbs.

NORSE MYTHOLOGY

The robin is sacred to Thor, the Norse lightning-God. If the nest, or indeed the bird itself, were hurt or damaged in any way, then the perpetrator of the crime would be struck dead by lightning. Alternatively – a slightly lesser punishment, admittedly – the culprit's cows would produce milk tainted by blood.

CHRISTIANITY

The robin, in the Christian world, is a symbol of death and resurrection, probably because of its appearance in the winter months.

The robin is a popular image on the front of Christmas cards; however, it's a lesser-known fact that the bird was once more closely associated with

Easter. There's another story that explains how the robin got its red breast. When Christ was hanging on the cross, the robin pulled out a spike from the crown of thorns, and in so doing injured himself – hence the red stain.

There's a sixteenth-century reference to this story:

> Bearing His cross, while Christ passed forth forlorn
> His God-like forehead by the mock crown torn,
> A little bird took from that crown one thorn
> To soothe the dear Redeemer's throbbing head.
> **John Hoskyns**

There's another story that corroborates the robin's status as a symbol of death and resurrection. The founder of Glasgow, in Scotland, was a sixth-century bishop who was later accorded saintly stature, Kentigern. When Kentigern was a boy, he was the favoured pupil of his teacher. Some of the other boys killed a robin and tried to blame Kentigern in order to discredit him. But Kentigern somehow magically restored the life of the robin, and even today there's a robin on the city's coat of arms.

CELTIC LORE

One of the only places where the robin is found as an omen of calamity (apart from having one fly into the house, which is generally regarded as a no-no and can portend a death in the family) is in certain sections of Celtic lore, and, in particular, in Wales. Coal miners are understandably superstitious because of the dangerous nature of their job, and there's an account in the *South Wales Weekly News* of 1901 of an explosion at the Llanbradach colliery:

> There is a pathetic and melancholy interest in the mention of a 'bird of ill-omen' in connection with the Llanbradach explosion. It is reported that several days before the explosion a robin redbreast was seen in the pump-house underground, where it had made its home. It was declared by some of the more superstitious of the miners that this was an ill omen of coming disaster, for a similar bird had been noticed in the Seghenydd Mine just before the explosion there.

However, in other parts of Celtic mythology the robin was said to try and quench the fires of Hell on a daily basis by carrying what little water it could in its tiny beak – again, an explanation for the scorched red breast.

Native American Lore

The robin, as in other parts of the world, represents good fortune to many Native American tribes. The Naskapi explain that the red breast of the robin is there because the bird was once a woman; her violent husband pushed her into a fire and after her death she returned as the bird. The Iroquois people plant cherry trees in order to attract the bird, and in addition many chiefs have assumed his name: 'Jis-go-ga'. Similar to traditions across Europe, to steal the egg of a robin would mean terrible things happening to the thief.

The Babes in the Wood

> No burial these pretty babes
> Of any man receives
> Till Robin Redbreast piously
> Did cover them with leaves.
> *The Ballad of the Babes in the Wood*

This old fairy story, about two children who get lost in the wood, uses as its central motif the idea that robins would cover a dead or sleeping human body with leaves. According to Robert Yarrington, writing in 1601:

> No burial this pretty pair of man receives
> Till Robin Redbreast piously did cover them with leaves.

The Bird of Reincarnation?

I was devastated after the death of my Father and every day I longed for some sort of a sign that he was still with me. I visited mediums and clairvoyants and got plenty of evidence that he *had* been here, but I worried that this could just be some sort of telepathy.

Then I visited a lady, a medium, who asked if there was a robin in my garden, that the bird was a messenger from my father. I was insistent that there were no robins in my garden, not that I'd particularly noticed despite being a keen gardener. I realized on the way home that it was time to stop looking for any evidence that my Father was still around – that he really was gone. In amongst the sadness was a sense of relief.

> 'One bush cannot harbour two Robin Redbreasts.'
> *Proverb*

Then when I got home, I went out into the garden and saw, for the first time there, a robin. It stayed around three days then disappeared. I felt as though, in having the message from the medium, and in seeing the bird, that I had let him go somehow, and could start to look forward again.

Trini, Germany

My husband John's mother was really ill in hospital, she was an old lady and she'd had a good life, but it was upsetting to see her in bed wired up to so many machines, it wasn't her at all or what she would have wanted I think. We were routinely making visits to the hospital every day after picking my 2-year old, Sophie, up from nursery – seeing the baby cheered Mum up no end. One morning on the way to the car Sophie saw a robin in the garden, pointed at it directly, and said 'Grandma! Grandma!' We said no, Sophie, it's a little robin redbreast, took her to nursery, and came home to a message to call the hospital … John's Mum had died that morning. We were really spooked for a while but then it seemed like a nice thing.

Siobhan, Ireland

What Bird Would You Be?

'A robin, because when I'm gardening they come by and watch me, and I believe that they are my grandmother and grandfather come from Heaven to check up on me.'
Jo, UK

The Rooster

Fire

> Father of lights! What sunny seed,
> What glance of day hast thou confined
> Into this bird? To all the breed
> This busy ray thou hast assigned;
> Their magnetism works all night,
> And dreams of paradise and light.
>
> Their eyes watch for the morning hue,
> Their little grain expelling night
> So shines and sings, as if it knew
> The path unto the house of light.
> It seems their candle, howe'er done,
> Was tinned and lighted at the sun.
> **Henry Vaughan,** *Cock-Crowing*

CHARACTERISTICS

The domestic chicken is descended from a wild species, Red Junglefowl, found in parts of Southern Asia. There are now an estimated eight billion individual chickens in the world, easily outnumbering the human population and making the domestic chicken the world's commonest bird. Initially the reason for their widespread distribution around the world was probably for use in the 'sport' of cock fighting rather than for their use as providers of eggs and meat; these more useful qualities would have come later.

The rooster would be easy to overlook as a bird of mystic significance, given that we are so used to seeing it in other guises; nevertheless there's a rich history of magical lore surrounding this very beautiful bird. It is the ultimate masculine bird symbol; it signifies the sun, power, pugnacity, sexual prowess (no accident that a slang word for the penis is the 'cock') and strength. In Hungary, the rooster often takes the lead in wedding processions, or is carried by the groom, as both a symbol of fertility and of the Sun.

> At cock's crowning the robber leaves his wiles, the morning star himself wakes up and shines upon the sky. At his singing the frightened sailor lays aside his cares and the tempest often moderates, waking up from last night's storm.
>
> *The Book of Beasts,* twelfth-century Latin bestiary

THE COCK'S CROW AND CHRISTIANITY

Although the rooster can be seen as a blustering, arrogant bird because of the way it struts about and crows loudly, seeming to proclaim its superiority to all and sundry, this same habit gives the bird its association with the sun in many cultures. The actual crowing also has a poignancy within the Christian religion; the cock crowed when Christ was born; it crowed again when St Peter denied Christ; and its crow will be the final warning of the Day of Judgment.

Many churches have a cockerel on their weather vanes. This is to remind the congregation of the time when the cock crowed three times when Christ was denied, and is a warning against doing the same.

ANCIENT GREECE AND ROME

In both Greece and Rome, the rooster was the bird of the war gods; obviously the rooster is a fiercely competitive bird and has a proud appearance so this association is entirely fitting. Aristophanes called the rooster 'the terrible bird, the chicken of Ares' – Ares being the God of War.

Because of the cock's habit of greeting the sunrise – or perhaps, it has been said, of the sunrise greeting the cock – in Ancient Greece he was the bird of Apollo, the Sun God. The rooster's red comb is another aspect of the solar force, depicting the rising sun.

In Crete, there was a cock-God, called Velchanos, who was later assimilated into Zeus.

Pythagoras stated that cocks should be cherished, because of their ties to the Sun and the coming of the light, and therefore should not be sacrificed as was often the practice. Despite this, the bird was the sacrificial bird of Asclepius, the God of Healing and the son of Apollo. The cock was also the bird of Mercury, since the bird called men to their business and banished the evils lurking in the dark hours of the night.

Roosters are banned from entering bakeries in Massachusetts.

Pliny, the Roman naturalist, had a recipe for a stew containing the meat of the cockerel, which was supposed to give the eater the qualities of the bird, namely, courage and vigour. The stew would apparently also give protection against wild animals. In more recent times in Britain a beer was brewed called Cock Ale, a peculiar concoction no doubt, which also contained a residue of a broth containing the bird; again it was meant to confer courage and vitality on the drinker, a little like chicken soup is still prescribed for invalids. In ancient Greece (and in other cultures), the bird was said to prevent disease; this belief could also explain the supposed efficacy of chicken soup!

Another curious Roman recipe is described in *The Book of Beasts*, where, we are told, 'their limbs … are eaten mixed with liquid gold'. Although what the point of such a concoction could be is not described, we can guess that the Romans could have been combining the powers of the bird with longevity; gold was believed by alchemists to be a constituent in the Elixir of Life.

JAPAN AND CHINA

In Japan, the crowing cock wakes Ameratsu, the Goddess of the Sun, from the cave in which she dwells during the hours of the night. Because of their association with the coming of light, the birds are often to be seen in and around Shinto temples; indeed, cockerels are bred especially for this purpose. In China, the cockerel is a happy omen, and the ideogram for its name reflects this, having the same meaning as 'good omen'. As in other cultures, in China the bird symbolizes the coming of the light and is often painted on doors as a symbol of good luck.

The Cock was the bird of Attis, an Oriental Sun-God, who, like Christ, died and was resurrected.

The Rooster is one of the 12 signs of the zodiac in Chinese astrology, and its attributes include a sense of humour and enthusiasm.

Tibetan Buddhism

Because of its association with lust and pride, the cockerel is not a favourable bird in Tibetan Buddhism, and forms one of a trio of 'three poisons' in the Wheel of Life. It stands alongside the serpent and the pig as a reminder not to become attached to material things and not to be greedy.

Norse Mythology

The cockerel sat in the topmost branches of the magical ash tree Yggdrasil, and would warn the Gods of the approach of their enemy, the Giants. The rooster is also the bird that crows to awaken the heroes of Valhalla for the final battle.

> 'It is not the hen which cackles most that lays the most eggs.'
> *Proverb*

Teutonic Myth

In Ancient Germany, the cockerel was one of the creatures that could guide the souls of the departed from this world to the next. The bird was often sacrificed as a part of ancient funeral rites in order that the spirit of the bird would be able to help the human spirit find its way into the next world.

The Qur'an

According to the Qur'an, there are seven heavens; in the first heaven resides a giant cockerel whose job it is to awaken all creatures with the exception of mankind. When the cock ceases to crow, beware, for the end of the World is at hand.

Voodoo Rites

I have it on good authority from an acquaintance, who used to be involved in certain voodoo ceremonies, that many of the practices involved the ritual slaughter of a chicken, preferably black. I am also reliably informed that not a single one of the 'spells' witnessed while he was a part of the group actually 'worked' in the way intended. Leave the bird alone!

Africa

There's an African legend associating the rooster with secrecy. This myth belongs in particular to the Fulani peoples, and the nature of the secret is defined by the behaviour and appearance of the bird. In another part of Africa, the supposed foreknowledge of the dawn by the rooster has the bird labelled as practising witchcraft.

Weather Lore

If hens fly up to a raised part of the ground and start to preen their feathers, it's said to be a sign of rain in the UK.

What Bird Would You Be?

'I wouldn't be anything fancy with brilliant feathers or an alluring song. I'm not a performer or a fashion slave ... I'd be a nuthatch. Small, nippy and beautifully made, no wonder it's a favourite of bird carvers. The nuthatch is a bit aggressive (yes, I admit it) but a delight to watch all the same.'
Judy, UK

THE SECRET LANGUAGE OF BIRDS

The Swallow and the House Martin

Fire

O Swallow, Swallow, flying, flying South,
Fly to her, and fall upon her gilded eaves,
And tell her, tell her what I tell to thee.

O tell her, Swallow, thou that knowest each,
That bright and fierce and fickle is the South,
And dark and true and tender is the North.

O Swallow, Swallow, if I could follow, and light
Upon her lattice, I would pipe and trill,
And cheep and twitter twenty million loves.
Alfred, Lord Tennyson, from *The Princess*

CHARACTERISTICS

The Ancients didn't really differentiate the swallow from the martin, and what's good enough for them is good enough for us.

The only places in the world that don't benefit from the beautiful swallow are New Zealand, the Arctic Circle, and a few small islands. The flight of the swallow is the most gorgeous thing to see, and these birds really are deft in the air, swooping and circling, and you easily get the sense of the 'extra dimension' by watching these birds, especially on a warm Summer's evening when they come out to feed on the gnats and midges brought out by the setting Sun.

That the coming of the swallow is regarded universally as a sign of spring has its basis in solid fact. They are migratory birds, and their movements usually coincide with a temperature of 48 degrees hitting the currents which they travel by. There are always outriders – birds who forge ahead a couple of weeks earlier than the rest, and who often suffer because of late frosts – again, another old saying proving itself true: 'One swallow doesn't make a Summer.'

The house I live in has martins nesting on every side now except for the East gable, which is overshadowed by trees, and according to the bird diary

I've kept for 11 years, they return without fail between April 25th and 30th every year, which is probably a little later than other parts of the UK because I'm so high up and the air is cooler. Both swallows and martins will return every year to the same nesting sites; both construct cup-shaped structures from mud collected in a series of busy swoops.

At the height of the nesting season, when the House Martins are kept moving all day from dawn until dusk feeding their young, I have noticed that the parents don't just feed their own young. Instead there's a sort of communal effort going on, and they'll fly along the nests looking to see who's hungry.

How the Swallow Got its Name

There are quite a few stories concerning Christ and swallows, including an explanation of how the bird came by its name. There's a Scandinavian myth relating how the birds hovered above the cross, crying 'Svala! Svala!' which means 'Console! Console!'

The old French name for the swallow, Hirondelle, from the Latin Hirundinarium, came about because of the bird's habit of eating on the wing.

Swallow Medicine

Because the swallow has a fast chattering speech and sounds as though it stutters, a broth made of swallows was said to be able to cure this affliction in people – a case of sympathetic magic. There was also a cure for epilepsy that involved 100 swallows, white wine and an ounce of castor oil – thank goodness for modern medicine!

Migration Myths

As with many of the migratory birds, there was a great deal of speculation about what, precisely, happened to swallows when they disappeared for the Winter. The Greek philosopher Aristotle believed that they hibernated in holes. And there was a book, published in 1703 by a writer called Morton, which stated that they went to the moon!

Weather Lore

Pretty much all over the world, swallows and martins flying low were said to presage rain. This is feasible, because insects fly lower during stormy weather, and therefore the birds would have to fly lower down to catch them.

The Swallow – A Firebird

In Asia and Eastern Europe, the swallow features in myths and legends as one of the birds responsible for bringing fire to mankind, in much the same way as the robin and the wren in Western European tales. In one account of the story, the devil is said to have thrown a firebrand at the bird, which resulted in its forked tale and reddish markings. In another account of how the swallow acquired this distinctive tail, we see the bird fetching fire from the Heavens when its tail accidentally catches fire.

Snow geese make long journeys and have to fly fast; therefore they need to conserve fuel. The V-formation assists in this, helping to streamline the group of birds; the geese will also feed intensively for several days before starting an arduous journey.

The Swallow's Magic Stone

In common with some other birds, there's a common belief – written about by illustrious scholars such as Albertus Magnus and Pliny – that the swallow has a stone inside its belly just before the full moon in August. If you could get hold of this stone, it was a guaranteed cure against epilepsy. Alternatively, it was said to be able to cure blindness.

China

In China, the swallow is seen as a symbol of good luck, and many buildings have special shelves built into them to allow the swallows to construct their nests more easily. To take the eggs of the swallow is considered very unlucky, and on the day that the first swallows of summer arrived, an offering would be made to the household Gods to ensure that the women of the home would be fertile.

There also used to be a prophecy that a swallow would give birth to the Shang Dynasty. Accordingly, the ancestress of the family swallowed an egg of the bird, which resulted in her pregnancy.

In the same way that I have observed the punctual nature of the housemartins and swallows arriving here, the Chinese were similarly impressed with the time-keeping abilities of the bird. Their arrival generally heralded the Spring Equinox, and there were tales of 'miraculous' pregnancies in girls who ate swallow's eggs. Confucius himself was said to have been the product of such a peculiar liaison, which accounts for the epithet of 'Swallow's Son' that is sometimes applied to him.

There are similar migration myths applied to swallows in China as there are in the West – it was believed that they hid in water and transmogrified into a shell for the Winter months.

Peking used to be known as the Swallow City.

> 'The interested friend is a swallow on the roof.'
> *Proverb*

THE ROMANS

Swallows were used as messengers of a practical kind in Ancient Rome. Before the chariot races, the mother swallows would be taken from their nests and the silk threads in the colours of the chariot teams would be tied to their legs. The bird bearing the colour of the winner would be released when the race was over, and so everyone back home would know who the winner was. In a variation on this theme, the organizers of the gambling associated with the races would dip a swallow in the colour of the winning team to announce the results.

As in many cultures, to have a swallow building a nest on your house was considered to be a lucky thing, but if the nest was abandoned then the luck would disappear as quickly as the bird had left its home, given that the bird was sacred to the household Gods, or Penates.

EGYPTIAN LORE

The Goddess Isis was said to change into a swallow at night, and would fly around Osiris's coffin, singing mournful songs, until the Sun arrived back the next morning.

Islamic Lore

Apparently when Mecca was being besieged by a Christian army, the swallows saved the forces of Muhammad by dropping stones on their enemies.

The swallow is called the Bird of Paradise, and, contrary to other beliefs about the bird, the Persians thought that the bird signified the separation of friends and neighbours, and represented loneliness, migration and separation – all facets of the bird's habit of leaving everything behind, seemingly, to go far away.

Africa

Because the swallow rarely touches the ground, the Bambara of Mali have it as representing all that is pure and good. It is also a manifestation of the God Faro, who is master of the waters. The blood of victims sacrificed to Faro would be carried up to him in Heaven, and then the blood would fall in the form of enriching rain.

Celtic Lore

There's a Celtic legend about the swallow, whose name is Fand. Fand was the wife of the sea-god Mananaan, but she fell in love with Cúchulain, who spent just a month with her before abandoning her. Fand returned to her husband and Cúchulain's wife took him back.

Native American Mythology

The swallow apparently brought fire to the Earth by stealing a little bit of the sun, and carrying the burning flames on its tail feathers. This story explains the swallow's sharp, forked tail. In the same tradition as the Chinese who built shelves to enable the swallows to roost more easily, some Indian tribes hung up hollow gourds so that the birds would be encouraged to take up residence close by.

A Whistling
woman, a crowing hen:
Bird Superstitions

There are so many superstitions associated with birds; perhaps they are a relic of our time before language, when birds were seen as the interface between the two worlds and hence bringers of messages from the Gods; perhaps because of their ability to move in another dimension. Some have a certain logic, for example, black-coloured birds are often associated with evil, or many gannets flying over the sea will indicate a good catch of fish, but many are downright strange and seem to have no logic at all, the reason for the superstition being lost in the mists of time – for example, a duck laying a dun-coloured egg being an omen of bad luck, or a stick from the nest of a kite as a cure for a headache.

Some people seem to have an irrational fear of birds, such as this 21-year-old friend of mine:

> It's just the way they flap … it frightens me. And my granny told me that you should never throw the hairs from your hairbrush where birds might get them and use them in their nests, otherwise you'll get headaches!

There are some archetypal beliefs to do with any kind of bird; for example, the notion that a bird in close proximity to the home could mean a death, or the arrival of an important message. Another warning of death is a bird at the window of a house, or worse still, entering it. Personally, I have evidence that the opposite can be true, but we have to understand that many of these beliefs may have been skewed over the centuries and all we are left with is a vestige of the original meaning.

470

For some unknown reason, if bird droppings hit you, it's said to be lucky:

> I was working in a card shop in London and carrying racks of postcards
> to display outside. As I was struggling with the heavy rack some pigeon
> poo hit me squarely in the eye. It smelled disgusting. A passerby said
> 'Oh! That's so lucky!' Didn't seem so lucky at the time!

Perhaps the belief that this is a lucky omen is to make the victim feel better.

If we think rationally about many of these superstitions, it's not surprising
that, for example, crows and ravens were seen as harbingers of death; their
spooky appearance and the fact that as carrion birds they would have
been present on battlefields would be enough to give rise to
this particular superstition. But running counter to this is
the intelligence and adaptability of these birds. The owl
seems to be particularly unfortunate in carrying news of
all kinds of doom, but it is also symbolic of wisdom!
Birds with nocturnal habits or with dark colouring,
unfortunately, are often seen as a bad omen, however, it is
important to understand the superstitions are not the same
as signs or auguries.

Bearing this in mind, and remembering to use a large pinch of
salt, enjoy the following A to Z of just a few superstitions concerning birds!

ALBATROSS

The albatross is said to carry the souls of dead mariners. Samuel Taylor
Coleridge's poem 'The Rime of The Ancient Mariner' reflects many beliefs
concerned with this huge bird:

> And I had done a hellish thing
> And it would work 'em woe
> For all averred, I had killed the bird
> That made the breeze to blow.

To see this bird flying around a ship would presage stormy weather. To kill an
albatross will mean that the killer will be dogged by bad luck for the rest of
his days. Strangely, however, the feet of albatrosses would be used as tobacco
pouches, so who knows what horrible fate awaited those who might have
killed the albatross for its feet?!

BLACKBIRD

To see two blackbirds together is regarded as lucky, since blackbirds are very territorial. If a blackbird nests on your roof, it's also a happy thing to happen.

In Celtic folklore, the song of a blackbird is said to lull the listener into a sleep or trance which will take the listener into the 'other world'. Blackbirds are said to hold the souls of the damned in purgatory until Judgment Day; the telltale sign is a blackbird with a shrill or harsh voice, so beware! If the call of the bird sounds unusually shrill, these tortured souls are crying out for water.

BUZZARD

A buzzard feather placed over the door of your cabin (if you're a Native American Indian) or your house (if not) will keep out witches for sure. No witches anymore? Personally I still keep one over the door, because you never know …

CARDINAL

A cardinal flying towards you means good luck. If it's flying away, however, it signifies the opposite.

CHICKADEE

According to the Cherokee, the chickadee is the bringer of truth. It works alongside the tufted titmouse, which is said to bring lies. Don't get them mixed up!

COCK

A cock used to be buried in the foundations of a new building to protect it from evil. They also used to be buried at the junction of three streams to avert evil or to cure disease.

In the Outer Hebrides, a cock crowing at midnight was a sign of impending news. If you could catch the cock and found that it had cold legs, then this would presage a death; if warm, the coming news would be more favourable.

CROW

There's an old rhyme about the crow, which is similar to the better-known one about magpies:

One means anger
Two means mirth
Three a wedding
Four a birth
Five is heaven
Six is hell
But seven is
The devil's own self

In the USA and also in Britain, to 'eat crow' means to be humbled.

CUCKOO

The call of the cuckoo is a happy event, heralding as it does the arrival of Spring and warmer days to come. However, do be careful; it's a good omen to see a cuckoo after breakfast, but not before. In fact it's also important to bear in mind your personal circumstances when you hear the first cuckoo of spring:

And now take this advice from me,
Let money in your pockets be,
When first you do the cuckoo hear,
If you'd have money all the year.
From *Poor Robin's Almanac* of 1763

CURLEW

Sailors believe that the cry of a curlew is a call from a dead friend. The call of the curlew is also meant to be a warning of harsh weather and/or the death of someone you know.

In Scotland it is associated with a long-beaked goblin, which is said to carry off evil-doers at night.

Dove

To kill a dove is regarded as very unlucky in India, where the bird is believed to contain the soul of a lover.

Miners believe it is unlucky to go down a mineshaft if a dove is seen nearby, and, similarly, a dove circling a house portends a death.

In Europe, in order to discover who she was going to marry, a girl was meant to take nine steps forwards and nine steps backwards when she heard the first dove of Spring. This ritual was meant to result in the hair of the intended being found in the girl's shoe! However, if you make a wish on the first dove you see in the year, then your wish will definitely come true.

Duck

If a duck lays dun-coloured eggs, they and the unfortunate duck should be destroyed as soon as possible or bad luck will follow. And hanging a duck upside down will ensure that any negative energies will fall away from it.

Gannet

Plenty of gannets signifies a good fishing catch – unsurprisingly, given the birds' predilection for fish!

Goose

The colour of the breastbone of the goose can be used to predict the weather for the coming winter, with a dark-coloured bone signifying harsh weather and a lighter-coloured bone, milder weather.

Grouse

If you're a pregnant Cherokee squaw, you'd be advised against eating the meat of this bird – they have such a large brood the same thing could happen to you!

HAWK

If a hawk's cry is heard during a journey, one must be aware of the situations around one and beware of being thrown off balance.

HEN

There's a spooky old English rhyme:

> A whistling woman and a crowing hen
> Brings the Devil from his den.

Was whistling considered not to be a very feminine thing to do?

HEN HARRIER

If the hen harrier is missing from its usual place, then watch out – there's an evil spirit close by!

HUMMINGBIRD

In New Zealand, a hummingbird entering a house is a sure sign of a death to follow.

In Native American Indian lore, these birds signify permanence and eternity and are a good sign, whether indoors or out.

JAY

Jays are said to bring mischief, and to eat a jay would mean that your spouse would die.

KINGFISHER

The kingfisher is generally regarded as a very propitious bird. Carrying a feather – if you should be lucky enough to get hold of one – will protect you from negative energies and act as a good luck charm, and will also bring good health.

To see a kingfisher sitting on eggs means no storms at sea, while hanging a dead kingfisher from a ship would enable the direction of the wind to be predicted.

KITE

A stick from the nest of the kite will cure your headache … unfortunately you have to find the nest first though.

MAGPIE

Because the magpie did not wear full mourning at the crucifixion of Christ, it is said to carry a drop of the devil's blood hidden under its tongue. Some believe that the magpie is actually the devil in disguise. However, if you address the bird by saying 'Good Morning, Mr Magpie' then you can let Satan know that you're on to him.

To avert the evil entities which seem to hang around the magpie you'll need to take off your hat and cross your fingers.

MARTIN

The martin is said to bring good fortune to any house where it nests and rears its young.

MOCKINGBIRD

People living in the Okefenokee Swamp area in the USA believe that eating a mockingbird egg can cure stuttering.

NIGHTJAR

The nightjar is said to bear the soul of an unbaptized infant; to hear its call is not a favourable sign.

Osprey

If for any reason an Osprey is shot, then all the mackerel and herring will disappear with it.

Owl

The poor owl! The list of accusations against this beautiful creature is endless. Partly due to its nocturnal nature and its eerie looks, with its flat, human-like features and huge, knowing eyes, the owl seems to be either a harbinger of doom, or wisdom, all over the world.

Just about anywhere, to see an owl during the day is unlucky and to have an owl flying around a house is also unlucky. To have an owl alight on a house is a sign of death, and should an owl brush against a window it also means a death. For Apaches, to dream of the owl meant that death was on its way.

In Wales, to hear an owl hooting means someone has just lost their virginity, while in France, if an owl hoots within earshot of a pregnant woman the baby will be a girl. Cree Indians believe the cry of the owl is a call to the spirit world.

Cherokees believed they could consult owls on matters of sickness and punishment. In Africa the bird is associated with witchcraft and sorcery, especially amongst the Zulus. They're also meant to bring illness to children. Among the Bantu people too, the owl is seen as the familiar of wizards. In Madagascar owls and witches are said to dance together on the graves of the dead. Zuni and Keres Pueblo Indians believe the owl is the spirit of a departed person in disguise.

In Britain, nailing an owl to a barn door was said to keep away evil and lightning.

Parrot

Native Americans believed that parrots could carry prayers and bestow blessings. However, in India the parrot is seen as an agent of deception. There's also a belief that you don't choose a parrot, but the parrot chooses you!

Partridge

Apparently, to sleep on a bed of partridge wings will speed an easy death. However, St Jerome and St Augustine were both in agreement that the Devil could take the form of a partridge.

Peacock

The tail feathers of a peacock are held to be unlucky because they contain the evil eye, said to be the eye of Lilith, the she-demon. However, in India, the feathers are said to be lucky if placed alongside the colour red, or tied with a red ribbon. In Northern India, peacock feathers are burnt to ward off disease, and are said to be able to cure snake bites.

In European folklore, the scream of a peacock was said to portend evil. It was a Christian belief that a peacock's blood could dispel evil spirits – the peacock was said to have the power of resurrection, like the phoenix. Alchemists believed that peacock feathers could contribute towards turning base metals into gold.

Pigeon

The blood of pigeons was considered an efficacious cure for a fever. Apparently, Samuel Pepys tried this remedy …

It was considered very unlucky to use pigeon feathers in mattresses; if this happened, the sleeper would die a painful death.

Plover

To hear the cry of the plover would herald a death of someone you know. This is possibly because the birds were said to carry the souls of Jewish people who died at the same moment as Christ.

Ring Ousel

In County Wicklow in Ireland, where there used to be a large population of ring ousels, it is important to pay special attention to their singing. Should they hesitate in their song and then produce an unusually loud shrill whistle, it's time to go inside, lock the doors, draw the curtains and turn out the lights. This shrill cry is a call to the fairy folk, who will come from miles around and dance until dawn in the moonlit mountain hollows.

Robin

It is regarded as extremely unlucky to kill a robin. In Yorkshire, England, it is believed that if you own cows and kill a robin, the milk will be blood coloured. Whatever you do to a robin will be done back to you – for example, you break an egg something of yours will be broken too. A robin coming into a house presages a death.

You should make a wish on the first robin of Spring; if it flies away, however, then there will be no luck for the following year.

Seagull

If there are lots of seagulls wheeling about over the water, this is a good omen for fishermen – and an entirely logical one too! However, three seagulls directly overheard is a warning of an imminent death.

Sparrow

To kill a sparrow or have one fly into the house is unlucky and in general portends a death.

If sparrows are chirping merrily, rain is imminent.

Stork

The stork is said to deliver babies. If a stork builds a nest on your roof, it's a very good sign indeed and means good fortune and the promise of love, directly from Venus herself.

Swallow

In Scotland, it is believed that the swallow has the blood of the devil in its veins. In Germany, if a woman treads on swallows eggs she will become barren, and in France, if one lands on your shoulder, then death is present.

Farmers believe that to kill a swallow will result in a poor milk yield, and if the nest is disturbed then the harvest will also be a poor one. Conversely, a swallow nest on your roof means you are protected from fire, lightning and storms.

To see swallows fighting amongst themselves is a bad omen.

The birds are reputed to carry two stones in their bodies; a red one to cure insanity and a black one to bring luck.

Swan

If wives are worried about a straying husband, then to sew the feather of a swan into his pillow should ensure that he remains faithful.

Three swans together is a sign of something terrible about to happen.

Thrush

If a great number of thrushes are seen feeding upon hawthorn bushes, then apparently the winter will be harsh.

If the nest of the thrush seems to be unusually high, this is also a bad sign; it means that the fairies are distressed. Usually these smaller winged creatures build their homes lower down among the grasses so that they can hear the thrushes singing.

Vulture

A flapping vulture was meant to portend rain, whereas a soaring one would bring the sun.

If you saw the shadow of a vulture but not the bird, this was an ill omen and meant a coming death.

Water Ousels

If these birds appear in an unusual place and in unusually large numbers, then there should be plenty of freshwater fish available for fishermen. However, the downside is that the birds bring with them a warning of disease.

Wheatear

In Scotland and Northern England these birds were sign of bad luck … In Orkney their eggs were said to be incubated by toads.

THE SECRET LANGUAGE OF BIRDS

WHIPOORWHIL

If the whipoorwhil landed on a roof, it would presage a death for someone inside the house. The bird is also reputed to try to snatch the soul as it leaves the body.

WREN

In France, if a child touches the nest of a wren, then the unfortunate child will suffer from pimples.

And anyone, anywhere, harming a wren will suffer a terrible fate.

AND FINALLY . . .

On St Valentine's Day, February 14th, birds can bring messages about love, particularly to girls. If the bird the young lady sees is a goldfinch, then the girl will marry a wealthy man, whereas a blue bird signifies poverty. See a blackbird and you'll marry a clergyman. A robin means you'll marry a sailor, and a woodpecker means you'll die an old maid!

Birds as Symbols:
An at-a-glance guide

Birds as symbols have been with us since time immemorial. Often, we see how cultures and religions that would appear to be at odds with each other on the surface agree as to the nature of various birds, and their symbolic meanings.

In general, then, there are archetypal symbols that reoccur throughout the world, carrying the same meanings wherever they are seen. For example, fantastic mythological birds often represent the celestial and spiritual realms. Wherever you find a story with a bird giving a message to the hero, this is said to represent the Gods speaking through the birds to aid in the particular quest being undertaken.

The symbol of a bird resting on top of a pillar signifies the union of spirit and matter and is also often a representation of the Sun God. The analogy seems obvious when you start to think about it. Indeed, many of the meanings and symbols associated with birds can be interpreted simply by knowing a little bit about the nature and habits of the bird in question. One of the most obvious is the albatross, which signifies tireless flight and distant oceans – not difficult to analyse why!

Here's a brief summary of what birds mean in general in different cultures. There is an alphabetical list that follows in which I've investigated the different symbolic meanings attached to birds around the world. You'll find that some of the symbols and their meanings are looked at in more depth in the section on different birds (pages 237–469).

In **Buddhism**, birds are a symbol of the Buddha, and are considered to be a lucky sign.

In **Celtic** belief, birds can symbolize either divinity and goodness, or the opposite – magical power which could be said to be malevolent.

In **China**, birds are a symbol of good luck, and particularly auspicious are the cock, the crane and the peacock.

In **Christianity**, the bird in general represents the transcendence of the soul, although unfortunately for any black-coloured birds there are accusations of evil, and many tenets of the Christian faith have these unlucky birds down as belonging to Satan.

In **Hinduism**, the bird symbolizes transcendence and intelligence, and in the Holy Scriptures of the Rig Veda is written 'He who understands has wings'.

In **Islam**, birds represent the souls of the faithful.

In the **Japanese** Shinto religion, birds signify the creative principle.

The **Maori** people see birds as divine, all-seeing and all-wise.

In **Scandinavia** the bird represents the spirit free from the body, and wisdom.

In **Taoist** philosophies, the bird represents the Sun, and also Heaven, Earth and man.

Here is an alphabetical list of some birds and their symbols. You may choose to add your own meanings, too.

ALBATROSS

In general, the albatross signifies tireless flight and distant oceans.

BALTIMORE ORIOLE

Harmony and equilibrium (American Indian)

BLACKBIRD

The Devil; sin; temptation of the flesh (Christian)

BUSTARD

Because the bustard often has two or three hens with him as he runs along the ground, in Africa he's a symbol of the polygamous family. Other symbols include:

The union of souls and fertility (Africa)
The return of a soul to whence it came (Africa)
The questing human soul (Africa)

COCK

In general the cock is a symbol of the Sun, probably due to its strident dawn cries! Not surprisingly, the bird also represents the dawn, and the masculine/yang element, courage, vigilance and supremacy. A black cock is meant to be an agent of Satan.

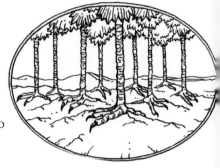

Watchfulness and vigilance; the banishment of darkness
(Christian)
Carnal passion, pride; attachment to material things (Tibetan Buddhist)
The Gods of the Underworld (Celtic)
The yang (male) principle; a good omen; the fighting spirit (Chinese)
Vigilance and foresight (Egyptian)
Vigilance and argumentativeness (Greek/Roman)
Fertility (Hebrew)
Royalty (Iranian)
Sacred to the Sun God (Mithraic, Pueblo Indian)
Courage (Japanese)
Anger and frustrated desire (Europe)
Secrecy and witchcraft (Africa)

CRANE

The crane is a messenger of the Gods; it's also symbolic of an ability of being able to enter into higher states of consciousness.

Vigilance and loyalty (Christian)
Reincarnation (Buddhist)
A herald of death or war (Celtic)
Intermediary between Heaven and Earth; happiness; longevity; prosperity
(Chinese/Japanese)
Spring and light (Greek/Roman)
Faithfulness (Chinese)
Immortality (Taoist)
Treachery (India)
Self-knowledge, self-awareness (Africa)
The Messenger (Germany)

CROW

As one of the 'black' birds, there is some ambivalence about the crow; it seems to be either very good or very bad, depending on where you come from.

Thievery (Hindu)
Creator of the World (Native American)
If black, malice; if red, the Sun (Chinese)
Solitude, the Devil (Christian)
Two crows symbolize a happy marriage (Egyptian)
Carrion, or a corpse (Hebrew)
Ill-omen or misfortune (Japanese)

CUCKOO

Depending on where you are in the world when you first hear it, the cuckoo can represent either Spring or Summer, and is a harbinger of better times to come.

King of the Birds (Tibetan)
Marriage (Greek)
Unrequited love (Japanese)
Royalty (Phoenician)
Jealousy and laziness (France)
Justice (Siberia)
The human soul before and after incarnation (Hindu)

DOVE

The dove is an important archetypical bird. Ask anyone around the planet what she represents and probably the first thing anyone will say will be 'peace'. However, the dove is also representative of passing from one world to another; it is sacred to the Mother figure in all religions and as such depicts maternity and femininity. The dove also means gentleness and innocence. Because of all these reasons, the dove could also be said to be representative of the sublimation of erotic desires.

The Holy Spirit; also, a white dove represents a 'saved soul' (Christian)
Longevity, faithfulness, piety (Chinese)

Innocence (Egyptian)
Love, and the renewal of life (Greek/Roman)
Purity, simplicity, meekness (Hebrew)
Virginity (Islam)
Longevity, deference (Japanese)
Rebirth (Plains Indians)

DUCK

For some reason, the duck can often represent chatter and deceit, and because it is often seen floating on the water, this can indicate superficiality.

The connection between the water and the sky (American Indian)
Faithfulness and a happy marriage, beauty; the duck and the drake together
    are yin and yang energies (Chinese/Japanese)
Immortality (Hebrew)
Faultless guides (Plains Indians)

EAGLE

Another of the great archetypical birds, the eagle is an extremely powerful symbol. It represents the Sun, inspiration, victory, authority, pride and strength, among other attributes. The eagle appears on the insignia of the USA and was, of course, a symbol of Nazi Germany and the Roman Empire.

New life, resurrection, generosity, spiritual endeavour (Christian)
The Sky God and the Sun God (Egyptian)
Power and Nobility (universal)
God (Aborigine)
The Universal Spirit, daytime (American Indian)
Celestial power (Aztec)
A vehicle of Buddha (Buddhism)
The Sun; male energy; warriors, courage, wisdom (Chinese)
The Sun; victory (Greek)
Renewal (Hebrew)
The Sun (Hindu)
The Sun; dignity; courage, victory, intelligence (Roman)
Wisdom (Scandinavian)

FALCON

Sharing many of the attributes of the eagle, the falcon is an emblem of victory and of aspiration, of rising through the spiritual planes. It also represents freedom from bondage. In Ancient Egypt the Falcon was the personification of light, and was considered to be the prince of the birds.

Evil thoughts and deeds (the wild falcon); conversion (domesticated falcon)
    (Christian)
Victory over lust (Celtic)
The Sun; also war (Chinese)
The Sun; superiority and conquest (Egyptian)

GOLDFINCH

Christ's Passion (Christian)

GOOSE

The goose is another powerful symbol, and is often interchangeable with the swan. It is a solar representation, and also is a symbol of the wind and the breath.

Providence and vigilance (Christian)
Purity (Asian)
Loyalty; watchfulness; war; fertility (Roman)
War (Celtic)
Yang (the masculine principle), inspiration, swiftness, good news (Chinese)
Creator of the World, Love (Egyptian)
Love, vigilance, good housewifery; also war (Greek)
The creative principle; freedom, spirituality, learning (Hindu)
Autumn; messages from Heaven (Japanese)

Hawk

Again, the hawk shares many of the same qualities as the eagle and the falcon. A hawk is meant to be able to fly directly up at the sun and gaze at it unflinchingly.

The Sky God; the soul; inspiration (Egyptian)
A messenger of the Gods (Aztec)
A messenger (Roman/Greek)
A messenger (Hindu)
Light (Iranian)
The Sun God (Mithraic)

Hen

In general, the hen is a symbol of the feminine, yin principle, signifying maternal care and procreation. However, the black hen can often be an aspect of the Devil.

The solicitude of Christ (Christian)
The conductor of souls (Bantu)

Heron

The heron shares much of the symbolism of the crane, particularly in China and Japan. In addition to these qualities the heron also indicates quietness and watchfulness.

The rising Sun; transformation; the heron is a representation of Benu, who
    holds these qualities (Egyptian)
A white heron and a black crow together are symbolic of yin and yang in
    Chinese and Japanese symbolism.

Hoopoe

Gratitude, the truth (Arabic)
Inspiration (Hindu)

Ibis

The soul; the morning; aspiration; perseverance (Egyptian)

Kingfisher

Calm; beauty; dignity; speed (Chinese)
Calm seas and a promise of spring (Greek)

Kite

Clairvoyance (Greek)

Lark

The lark, because of its habit of flying upwards very rapidly from the ground while singing, is a symbolic mediator between Heaven and Earth.

Humility (Christian)

Macaw

The Sun; fire (Mayan, Native American)

Magpie

Universally, the magpie is regarded as a thief and a gossip.

Good fortune (Chinese)
The devil; vanity (Christian)
God (Sioux)

Nightingale

Joy and love (Universal)

ORIOLE

Marriage; the coming of Spring (Chinese)

OSTRICH

Truth and justice (Universal)
Air and space (Egyptian)
Light and water (Dogon)

OWL

There's some ambivalence about the owl, in that it is, of course, a nocturnal bird, and in general anything associated with the night is believed to be 'dark'. However, the owl is also universally regarded as a symbol of wisdom.

Satan, solitude (Christian)
Wisdom, darkness (Greek/Roman)
Wisdom, divination (American Indian)
Death, night, coldness (Egyptian)
Blindness (Hebrew)
Death, a bad omen (Japanese)
Night, death (Mexican)

PARROT

Because of the parrot's ability to mimic sounds, it can be a symbol of unintelligent repetition and imitation.

Love (Hindu)
A warning to unfaithful wives (Chinese)
Love; rain-bringing (Native American)

PARTRIDGE

Fecundity (Universal)
Theft; the Devil; also the Church; truth (Christian)

PEACOCK

Another of the great archetypical birds, the peacock is a glorious bird, but for some the appearance of the 'eyes' on its tail are regarded as a bad omen. It represents love, immortality and longevity, and is a symbol of the sky and the stars. It is also a symbol of the Sun.

Immortality, resurrection, vanity, pride (Christian)
Compassion, watchfulness (Buddhist)
Dignity and beauty (Chinese)
The stars, the Sun (Greek)
Love; impatient desire (Hindu)
Duality; royalty (Iranian)
Light (Islamic)
Royalty (Roman)

PELICAN

The pelican is depicted in history and art as feeding its young from its own blood; therefore it has become associated with sacrifice, and charity.

Atonement for sins (Christian)

PHEASANT

The male principle (yang); virtue, light, good fortune and prosperity
    (Chinese)
Motherly love and protection (Japanese)

Phoenix

Although I decided to include only 'real' birds in this section, the phoenix is the exception to the rule. Universally, the phoenix is a symbol for resurrection, immortality and rebirth by fire, royalty, nobility and gentleness.

Resurrection (Christian)
The Sun; resurrection; happiness (Aztec)
Yin and Yang; also a bridal symbol (Chinese)
Resurrection; the Sun; Heliopolis (Egyptian)
The Sun; truth; faithfulness and obedience (Japanese)

Pigeon

In general the pigeon is a symbol of love, particularly two pigeons together; there are other aspects to this bird, though.

Lasciviousness; but also longevity, springtime, and fidelity (Chinese)
Reincarnation (Hindu)

Quail

The quail is generally held to be a symbol of good luck, and is associated with the Spring; it's also often taken as a symbol of lasciviousness.

Summer, courage, military zeal (Chinese)
Spring, renewal (Greek)
Spring (Hindu)
Courage; victory in battle (Roman)
The Sun and the springtime (Russian)
Satanic powers; sorcery (Witchcraft)

Raven

Another of the great archetypal birds, the raven has some ambivalence. It is symbolic of prophecy, magical powers, and is either a symbol of the Sun or of the evil Gods of the Underworld. It is also associated with the 'trickster', probably because of its extreme intelligence and cunning.

Deceit, the Devil (Christian)
The Master of Life; the Trickster (Native American)
Good luck (Tibetan Buddhism)
War and battle (Norse, Old English)
Power (Chinese)
Destruction, malevolence (Egyptian)
Longevity; the Sun (Greek)
Impurity; deceit (Hebrew)
The Sun (Mithraic)

Bedouins, and other peoples for that matter, have a firm belief that small birds are sometimes transported on the backs of bigger birds.

ROBIN

Death and resurrection (Christian)

SPARROW

The incarnation and resurrection; lowliness and insignificance (Christian)
Loyalty (Japanese)

SPARROWHAWK

Autumn, the season of hunting, and retirement (Chinese)
The Sun (Egyptian, Greek and Roman)

STORK

The stork is a bird of the Sun, but because she also fishes in the water she has a lunar aspect too and is connected with the waters of creation. She symbolizes the coming of Spring so is representative of hope and new life. Many of the associations with the crane are the same for the stork.

Mother Earth; new life; springtime (Universal)
Vigilance; piety and chastity; the Annunciation (Christian)
Longevity; contented old age; the dignified recluse (Chinese)
Filial piety (Egyptian)
Archetypal woman, the mother, the nourisher (Greek)
Piety and filial devotion (Roman)

Swallow

The swallow appears at the changing of the seasons, from winter into spring or from spring into summer and is thus a universal symbol of hope and good fortune.

Advantageous change; danger; success (Chinese)
The incarnation and resurrection (Christian)
Unfaithfulness; domesticity (Japanese)
Fertility and renewal (Celtic)
Purity (Bambara of Mali)

Swan

Because the swan has domain over water as well as air, and probably also because of her great beauty, the swan is considered to be the Bird of Light and is associated with the dawning of the Sun. Its whiteness is considered emblematic of purity and integrity. The swan is also symbolic of poetry and music.

The Sun; love, purity, magic and the angelic realms (Celtic)
The Yang principle; grace, nobility, valour (Chinese)
Purity and grace, martyrdom (Christian)
Amorousness (Greek)
Perfect union; breath and spirit (Hindu)

Turkey

Thunder and rain (Toltec)
Male virility and female fertility (American Indian)

Vulture

In general, the vulture has some ambivalence, as might be imagined. It signifies the feminine principle, shelter, protection and motherliness, but also, because it consumes the flesh of rotting carcasses, has connotations of greed and destruction. However, because of its scavenging nature, the vulture also symbolizes purification.

The Mother Goddess, purification and good works (Egyptian)
Death (Mayan)

Wagtail

Love, and magical potions (Greek)

Woodpecker

Universally the woodpecker means magical power and sorcery.

Heresy, the Devil (Christian)
War (American Indian)
Security (Pawnee Indian)

Wren

The world over, the tiny wren is considered to be the King of the Birds. It can represent the Spirit but also in some cases it can symbolize a witch, becoming a less benevolent creature.

I hope this quick guide proves useful – you may find it helps with augury.

Birds of the Gods:

Divinities and their birds

This is a simple list, which may help in your own understanding of the nature of both the birds and of the Gods and Goddesses around the world. It's useful to think of the latter as extrapolations of human energies, which can help us better understand aspects of our own personalities.

I decided to present this section as a chart; however, some of the birds here are dealt with in greater detail elsewhere in the book.

The relationships between the birds and the Gods may well help you when you come to establish a pattern for your own auguries, bearing in mind that the Romans used to divide the sky into sections, each of which was dedicated to a particular deity. You may well decide to follow this method, or you might choose to watch the birds and then let them tell you where they're coming from, metaphorically speaking, because of the associations they carry with them. More information about this and other aspects of auguries can be found in the chapter entitled 'Of Ravens and Rainbows: The Modern Augur' (page 60).

For a brief description of just who these deities are, see the key at the end of this section.

The Birds

Cormorant
Mananaan

Crane
Apollo
Jorojin
Kali
Midir
Pwyll

Crow
Amaterasu
Apollo
Athena
Badb
Hera
Macha
Nemain

Cuckoo
Freyja
Kama
Zeus

Diver
Glooksap

Dove
Sacred to all mothers
    and 'Queens of
    Heaven'
Adonis
Anahita
Aphrodite
Astarte
Atargatis
Athena

Bacchus
Hachiman
Ishtar
Nantosuelta
Nirutti
Sophia
Venus
Yama

Duck
Isis
Luonnotar
Sequanna

Eagle
Asshur
Buddha
Horus
Indra
Jupiter
Kee-Zos En
Kinich Ahau
Lugh
Ninurta
Odin
Tannus
Taranis
Vishnu
Zeus

Falcon
Frigg
Horus
Loki
WekWek

Goose
Bau
Epona
Gengen Wer
Horus
Isis
Mars
Osiris

Hawk
Ahura Mazda
Horus
Indra
Kebhsenuf
Khonsu
Ptah
Sokar

Hen
Cerridwen

Heron
Osiris

Hummingbird
Huitzilpochtli
Quetzalcoatl

Ibis
Aah
Hermes
Isis
Mercury
Thoth

Linnet
Frigg

Lyrebird
Baiame
Nungeena

Magpie
Bacchus
Dionysus
Skadi

Nightingale
Zeus

Ostrich
Ma'at
Tiamat

Owl
Ah Puch
Arianrhod
Athena
Blodeuwedd
Cailleach
Demeter
Gwynn
Hecate
Kutan Kor
Lakshmi
Lei Gong
Lilith
Minerva
Varahi
Yama

Parrot
Bullai-Bullai
Kuan-Yin

Partridge
Aphrodite

Peacock
Brahma
Hera
Juno
Kama
Kuan-Yin
Kujaku
Lakshmi
Phaon
Sarasvati
Si Wang Mu
Skanda Tammuz

Pheasant
Li

Pigeon
Aphrodite
Yama

Quail
Asteria
Leto

Raven
Asclepius
Apollo
Athena
Badb
Bran
Epona
Kronos
Kurkil
Lugh
Macha
Mari
Mictlantecuhtli
Mithras
Morrigan
Nantosuelta

Nemain
Nergal
Odin
Yama
Yetl

Robin
Jupiter
Thor

Rooster
Abraxas
Mercury
Priapus

Sparrow
Aphrodite
Venus

Stork
Hera
Juno

Swallow
Aphrodite
Faro
Isis
Nina
Venus

Swan
Aengus
Aphrodite
Apollo
Artemis
Berchta
Brahma
Brighit
Clio
Cygnus

Erato	Mertseger	Thoth
Freyja	Mut	Triptolemus
Kara	Nekht	
Kunnawara	Nekhbet	**Wren**
Sarasvati	Saturn	Jupiter
Turan		Taliesin
Zeus		Taranis
	Woodpecker	Thor
	Ares	
Vulture	Ishtar	**Wryneck**
Apollo	Jupiter	Aphrodite
Isis	Mars	Philyra
Kronos	Silvanus	
Mars	Thor	

The Deities

But who *are* all these Gods and Goddesses? The following is a very simplified explanation of what all these deities represent.

Aah Egyptian Moon God

Abraxas Persian Sun God; a supreme deity

Adonis Greek Corn God

Aengus Celtic God of Poetry who turned into a swan

Asclepius Greek God of healing and medicine

Ah Puch Mayan God of Death

Ahura Mazda Zoroastrian God of the Universe

Amaterasu Shinto Sun Goddess

Anahita Persian Goddess of Water

Aphrodite Greek Goddess of Love

Apollo Greek God of the Sun

Ares Greek God of War and agriculture

Arianrhod Celtic Moon Goddess

Artemis Greek Goddess of Hunting and childbirth

Asshur Assyrian Storm God

Astarte Sumero-Semitic Great Mother Goddess

Asteria Greek Goddess of Oracles and falling stars

Atargatis Syrian Goddess; half-woman, half-fish

Athena Greek Goddess of Wisdom

Baiame Aboriginal Sky God and 'father of all things'

Bau Sumerian Goddess of Dogs

Bacchus Roman God of Wine and intoxication

Badb Celtic Goddess of Fertility, war wisdom and inspiration

Berchta German Goddess of Winter and witchcraft

Blodeuwedd Celtic Goddess of Flowers who was turned into an owl

Buddha The Enlightened One

Bullai–Bullai Aborigine Parrot Goddess

Brahma Indian God; The Creator

Bran Celtic God of Music and prophecy

Brighit Celtic Goddess of Fertility, poetry, healing and the home

Cailleach Celtic Goddess of the Sun, Moon and Sky; also controls the Seasons.

Cerridwen Celtic Goddess of Wisdom

Clio Greek Goddess; one of the Muses

Cygnus Son of Apollo who was turned into a swan

Demeter Greek Earth Goddess

Dionysus Greek God of Wine, sex, and intoxication

Epona Celtic Horse Goddess

Erato Greek Goddess; one of the Muses

Faro African Goddess of Water

Freyja Norse Goddess of Fertility, magic and love

Frigg Norse Goddess and love and fertility

Gengen Wer Egyptian Goose God

Glooksap Algunquin culture-hero

Gwynn Celtic God of the Underworld

Hachiman Japanese God of War

Hecate Greek Goddess of Secret Wisdom, change and darkness

Hera Greek Queen of the Gods

Hermes Greek God of Communication, wisdom and the magical arts

Horus Egyptian Falcon-headed Sky God

Huitzilpochtli Aztec Warrior God who took the form of a Hummingbird

Indra Hindu Supreme Ruler of the Gods

Ishtar Mesopotamian Goddess of Fertility and war

Isis Egyptian Goddess of Love

Jorojin Japanese God of Wine and fortune

Juno Roman Queen of the Gods

Jupiter Roman God of the Skies

Kali Hindu Mother Goddess; creator/destroyer

Kama Indian God of Love

Kara Norse Goddess who was a swan maiden and a valkyrie

Kebhsenuf Egyptian Falcon-headed God

Kee-Zos En Abenaki (Native American Indian) God of the Sun

Khonsu Egyptian God of Time, the Moon and knowledge

Kinich Ahau Mayan God of Sun and time

Kronos Greek God of Time

Kuan-Yin Chinese Goddess of Compassion

Kujaku Japanese Rain God

Kunnawara Australian Aboriginal Goddess; mother of all females; the Black Swan

Kurkil Mongol Creator God

Kutan Kor Ainu God of Villages

Lakshmi Hindu Goddess of Abundance

Lei Gong Chinese God of Thunder

Leto Greek Goddess of the Moon

Li Chinese Sun/Fire Goddess

Lilith First wife of Adam, latterly cast as a demoness

Loki Norse God of Fire and magic; the trickster

Lugh Celtic Sun God

Luonnotar Finnish Goddess; daughter of nature

Ma'at Egyptian Goddess of Truth and justice

Macha Irish Mother Goddess and Warrior Queen

Mananaan Celtic God of Magic, travel and the sea; the ultimate shape-shifter

Mari Middle Eastern Goddess of the Sea and the Moon

Mars Roman God of war

Mercury Roman God of Communication

Mertseger Egyptian Goddess; Guardian of the Valley of the Kings

Michtlantecuhtli Aztec God of Death

Midhir Celtic God of the Underworld

Minerva Roman Goddess of Wisdom

Mithras Saviour-God of the mysterious Mithraic cult

Morrigan Celtic Goddess of War who can shape-shift into a raven

Mut Egyptian Goddess; Mother of the Pharaohs

Nantosuelta Gaulish River Goddess

Nekht Egyptian Goddess; Mother of Re

Nekhbet Egyptian Vulture Goddess, guardian of Upper Egypt and the Pharaoh

Nemain Celtic Goddess of Fury

Nergal Mesopotamian God of the Underworld

Nina Sumero-Semitic Goddess; The Great Mother

Ninurta Sumerian God of Rain, the plough and the earth

Nirutti Indian Goddess of the South West

Nungeena Australian Aboriginal Mother Goddess

South African sunbirds pollinate flowers by carrying the pollen on their tongues.

Odin Norse God of War, death, poetry and wisdom

Osiris Egyptian God of the Underworld

Phaon Greek bird-God

Philyra Greek Goddess of writing, paper, healing and perfume

Priapus Greek God of Fertility

Ptah Egyptian God of Creation, craftsmen and rebirth

Pwyll Celtic King of the Otherworld

Quetzalcoatl Aztec Feathered Serpent God

Sarasvati Hindu Goddess of Knowledge, music and the creative arts

Saturn Roman God of the Harvest

Sequanna Gaulish Goddess of the River Seine

Silvanus Roman God of Forests and fields

Si Wang Mu Chinese Goddess; keeper of the peaches of immortality

Skadi Scandinavian Goddess of Winter

Skanda Indian Warrior God; 'warrior of the army of light'

Sokar Egyptian God and guardian of the tombs

Sophia Hebrew Goddess of Wisdom

Taliesin Celtic poet and prophet, son of Cerridwen

Tammuz Sumerian God of Vegetation

Tannus Gaulish God of the Sun

Taranis Celtic God of Thunder and the seasons

Thor Norse God of Thunder

Thoth Egyptian God of Truth, wisdom, time and communication, among other things

Tiamat Babylonian Mother Goddess

Triptolemus Greek God; the first priest of Demeter

Tulingersak Canadian Arctic Inuit; Father Raven and Sky God

Turan Etruscan God of Love

Varahi Hindu Goddess of Death

Venus Roman Goddess of Love

Vishnu Hindu God; Preserver of the Universe

WekWek Native American (Tuleyone) Falcon God

Yama Hindu God of the Dead

Yetl Tlingit Raven God

Zeus Supreme God of the Greeks

Birds in our World today

Birds are very much barometers of environmental change, and although they have been around on this planet for considerably longer than mankind, it's a pretty shocking fact to realize that since 1600 – just over 400 years ago – over 100 *species* of birds have become extinct. The rate of extinction seems to be getting worse, too; of the 10,000 or so species of birds we have in the world today, just over 1,000 of them are believed to be threatened. The majority of the threats to the lives of these birds are, unfortunately, man-made. There are only 11 species that are threatened in other ways.

I don't want to make this final chapter into a 'doom and gloom' lecture about how awful human beings are, by any means. However, it might be useful to see just which species are missing, never to return, and to take a look at why these birds aren't with us any more, in an attempt to understand how important it is that we make every effort to arrest the declining population of our remaining birds.

It's been a difficult chapter to compile, since the fortunes of birds change all the time; however, you will be able to get up-to-date information from the respective bird organizations and charities listed on page 515.

Under Threat Right Now

It is probably impossible to saw just which birds are most at risk; however, some species of parrots are often specified since it is believed that there may be less than ten of each bird left in the wild. Otherwise, two of the major concerns for environmentalists around the world include the vulture and the albatross.

THE INDIAN VULTURE

The Indian Vulture finds itself in an alarming degree of risk; numbers have dwindled by a massive 95 per cent from what they were just 10 years ago. The effect of the loss of these birds is having profound consequences.

In 1991, the *Indian Express* ran a story saying that the Parsee Council had had to install solar reflectors in their Dakhmas (the towers used for the sky burial rituals described more fully in the section about the vulture, page 397), since the decomposition of corpses was taking too long because there were not so many vultures as there had been. They were also building an aviary for vultures close by.

> The much-maligned bird of prey, which is a self-appointed scavenger, is meeting an unnatural death due to ignorance and unawareness among people about their significance in our environment since they provide some protection from viruses which are contained in decomposed bodies.

The article goes on to say:

> The vulture breed is on the verge of extinction in India and studies about vultures pointed out the fact that the use of pesticides and chemicals in the tanning process was proving fatal for our vultures. According to scientists, 'Chemicals used in the tanning process to get the skins of animals, remained viable in the flesh of the animals. After the skin recovery, the flesh of the animals is given to vultures and this results in the vultures' death.'

It seems ironic that the vulture, despite having a bellyful of powerful anti-bacterial agents that can withstand the very worst kinds of contagion evident within rotting carcasses, is being killed outright by man-made chemicals.

THE ALBATROSS

Among the largest flying birds in the world, Albatrosses are suffering huge losses because of an illegal fishing practice, called long line fishing. The fishing boats involved in this practice leave a mass of bait in their wake, pieces of squid and the like. Naturally the albatross is attracted to the bait; the albatross is hooked and dies a horrible death, speared violently, then dragged down 2,000 feet under the surface of the sea and drowned.

One hundred thousand albatrosses are killed in this way every year.

Things are made even more difficult for the bird when you take into account the fact that they lay only one egg, and the incubation period is 70 days. If one or both of its parents are killed, the chick will die of starvation.

Nineteen of the 21 species of albatross face extinction because of long line fishing; the birds are dying because of our greed.

Our Past Unawareness – The Bad News

Many bird species died out because of early settlers on certain islands, and their need to survive. There was also a lot of ignorance about the fragility of some birds, and unawareness about the value of the creatures on this planet. Eggs have been plundered, birds have been killed as meat and for their plumage, which was used either decoratively or usefully in mattresses, bedding and the like.

You may remember that, in the chapter about mythological birds, we had a look at the origins of the giant birds seen in Madagascar, and you'll remember the stories about the more recent sightings of a giant bird in America, which could have given rise to the myth of the thunderbird. I really hope that these sightings were accurate – it would be wonderful to think that, somewhere in the world, these giant birds have managed to find a safe haven. Well, in Madagascar, the Elephant Bird, which seems to have had to go away to hide as the island became deforested, was probably dying out before traders from Europe arrived, but the plundering of their eggs as souvenirs was certainly the final nail in the coffin.

ISLAND BIRDS

Island birds seem to be particularly under threat. The bird population in New Zealand has suffered dreadfully. New Zealand did not originally have many indigenous mammals; the island was populated almost exclusively with birds, many of them flightless as might be expected from a relatively small island a significant distance away from any large land mass. Because of the lack of mammals the birds didn't really need to be 'on guard' against predators, and some lost their ability to fly altogether, and nested on the ground. One large flightless bird in particular, the Moa, is believed to have been extinct before many Europeans arrived, having been wiped out by the first people to find the island, the Polynesians, who arrived there in 800 BC. The birds were easy to catch and made good meat. As more Polynesians took up residence, of course they needed timber for dwellings, and the birds started to lose their natural habitat. Add to the equation the arrival of Europeans several hundred years later who brought animals with them, many domesticated or for farming, but including many 'stowaways' such as rats, and the fate of many of the indigenous New Zealand birds was sealed.

There's another New Zealand bird, the Haast's Eagle, which is believed to have been extinct by around about AD 1400. This was another giant bird, with records showing a wingspan of up to eight and a half feet (2.6 metres), and it is again believed to have disappeared because its natural habitat was lost when humans started settling on the island.

There are more specific records of when some birds died out. The Great Auk, for example, was a large bird, standing two and a half feet (over half a metre) high. Although the bird lived out to sea and was an incredibly strong swimmer, it laid its eggs on shore, at which point it was vulnerable and easy to catch. The final pair of Great Auks were killed on July 3rd, 1844, in Iceland, with the mortal remains of the birds being used to stuff mattresses … let's hope the hunters had a very bad night's sleep.

THE DODO

Probably one of the most famous of the extinct birds, the Dodo, immortalized in Lewis Carroll's *Alice's Adventures in Wonderland*, was indigenous to Mauritius, in the Indian Ocean. The phrase 'dead as a dodo' is still used to signal the conclusive ending of something. Flightless, the Dodo was a member of the pigeon family, and the island it lived on is remote, so much so that it wasn't even discovered until the start of the sixteenth century. A hundred years later more sailors were arriving, and, because of its flightless nature, the Dodo was easy prey; they would be clubbed to death. The last of these birds was killed in 1681, less than two hundred years after the first man set foot on the island.

THE PASSENGER PIGEON

Another member of the pigeon family that is now extinct is the Passenger Pigeon. It was once thought to be one of the most abundant of birds, and the skies would be almost black with them in the plains of Central America. One particular flock was estimated to have contained two thousand million birds and took three days to fly over a certain point. The birds started disappearing just a hundred years ago and now they are extinct. We don't know precisely why they have disappeared, however, it could be that as the forests were brought into cultivation and their habitats dwindled, the birds lost many of their natural dwelling places. Because the birds had been so abundant for so long, and almost taken for granted, no one noticed the decline until it was far too late, and the last bird, called Martha, died in a zoo in Cincinnati in 1914.

The Tooth Billed Pigeon of Samoa used to be a ground-nester, but when cats were introduced to the island the bird was wise enough to alter its habits; it now nests high up in the trees.

Awareness – Some Success Stories

We can't do anything about the bird life that we've lost. But, hopefully, we can learn from our past mistakes and work to reverse the trend, and ensure that no more of our birds are rendered extinct by our actions, whether direct or otherwise. Fortunately, by the middle of the twentieth century we started to realize what was happening to many of the birds and animals on the planet, and much has been done, by all nations of the world, collectively, to conserve what we have left.

The Ne Ne

For example, the Ne Ne, a variety of goose that lived in Hawaii, had dwindled down to just 35. However, after an intense breeding programme led by a collective of bird-lovers and ornithologists, including Sir Peter Scott, the Ne Ne has survived and pairs bred in captivity have been successfully released back into the wild.

The Kakapo

New Zealand, as we've mentioned, has been one of the hardest-hit areas in terms of dwindling bird species and population. The good news is that measures are being taken to keep what's left. The Kakapo, which is a giant flightless parrot, had been believed to be extinct by 1960, but then a few were discovered in a remote spot on South Island. The five which were trapped and taken for study and breeding unfortunately were all male, and the whole operation was extremely difficult and costly since the only way to access the birds was by helicopter, so rough was the terrain which they were inhabiting. All was not going well. Then, another small colony was discovered on a small island off the South Coast of South Island, and the operation started again; cats then managed to find the spot and it looked as though the Kakapo was doomed to extinction. The team responsible was given permission to capture all the birds, which numbered 61, but yet again they proved all to be males.

Breeding conditions had been found to be extremely difficult, and by 1993 only 19 females were left. However, despite all the setbacks and difficulties, it seems as though the fortunes of this bird might be turning around.

The Whooping Crane

In the USA, one of the great success stories is that of the Whooping Crane, which stands five feet (1.5 metres) tall and is, of course, fair game for hunters. Because of this, by 1945 there were believed to be only 16 of the birds left, and desperate measures were taken to make the hunters able to identify the whooper from other cranes. A programme was started whereby the eggs of the birds were 'fostered' by other birds, in this instance Sandhill Cranes. This seemed to be fine until the young birds grew up thinking that they were Sandhill Cranes too, and refused to mate with their own species.

Incubators were then brought into action, and an ingenious method of getting the baby bird to recognize its own kind now takes place. Once the chick hatches, the head of a whooper appears and drops food into its mouth. The 'parent', however, is actually a puppet, operated by one of the rearing team. For the first two weeks of its life the only moving thing that the chick sees is this surrogate – and that's not all: once the birds are released from the incubation chambers they meet humans dressed in whooping crane costumes!

There's one more sticky part of the equation, though: how to release the birds back into the wild, which obviously means that they need to be taught how to fly. A farmer in the area has rigged up a small microlite plane, painted white with black markers on the edges of its wings. The whoopers form part of a flock, along with Sandhill Cranes, with the small aircraft being the 'leader' of the birds, taking them back on their migratory route towards New Mexico.

The Bald Ibis

Recently there was an incredibly exciting discovery for ornithologists working in the ancient Roman city of Palmyra. There a bird was discovered called the Bald Ibis, which was believed to have been extinct for 70 years.

In a newly established conservation area in a Bedouin region, called Al Tilila, about 185 miles (300 km) from Damascus, a scientist called Gianluca Serra was cataloguing the diverse variety of birds and animals in the reserve. The Bald Ibis had been declared officially extinct in 1991, but a local hunter approached Gianluca and suggested that the data was wrong. Working with the local Bedouin community, a team set out to comb the huge area to try to find signs of the bird, and after several months, moving from camp to camp and winning the trust of the people, the bird was rediscovered, having taken up residency on a stony cliff about 30 miles (50 km) from Palmyra.

There are still many mysteries surrounding the bird, such as its migratory route; but the fact that the bird is still alive and well (although its existence is fragile) is a sign of hope.

In the UK there are more stories of success in keeping birds safe:

The White Tailed Eagle

The White Tailed Eagle, also known as the Sea Eagle, had been gone from British skies for nearly 70 years. The bird is an incredible sight, having an eight-foot (2.4-metre) wingspan, and was a target for egg collectors and keepers. Because of this it had died out in its home territory prior to the First World War. However, the bird still lived in Norway and has reappeared in Scotland thanks to a reintroduction scheme, which started in 1985.

The Dartford Warbler

The Dartford Warbler had been reduced to just 10 or so nesting pairs, its population having been hit hard in a severe winter in the early 1960s. However, its population is now at a healthier 2,000 breeding pairs; this is all made possible by heathland management, care and attention.

The Peregrine Falcon

The Peregrine Falcon, which is said to be the ultimate flying machine (speeds in excess of 220 miles per hour have been recorded), had its numbers dwindle massively during the Second World War when many were shot because they were believed to kill racing pigeons, and of course pigeons were being used during the war effort. The Peregrine's fortunes declined even further with the advent of intensive farming methods, which involved the use of heavy pesticides and insecticides that poisoned the birds. Once a particularly bad culprit, DDT, was banned the numbers started to climb again, until the bird population levels in the UK are now at a healthier 1,400 pairs.

The Bittern

The Bittern, a marsh bird, was reduced in numbers down to just 11 males in 1997, because drainage schemes were damaging their traditional reed bed habitats. But the decline was arrested before it was too late, and although it is still a rare bird, its numbers have increased to 42.

The Avocet

Whereas the Peregrine population declined because of the Second World War, the Avocet is a bird that actually benefited from it. Having almost disappeared from the English coastline of East Anglia for about a hundred years, this bird returned in the 1940s when sea defences, built to protect Britain from Hitler's armies, provided a toehold and some refuge for the birds, which now number approximately 980 breeding pairs.

The Cirl Bunting

The Cirl Bunting is one of the UK's most threatened birds. In 1989 there were believed to be only 118 pairs left. Today, the numbers are on the increase and there are nearly 700 pairs.

Cetti's Warbler

Cetti's Warbler is a Mediterranean bird that arrived in the UK relatively recently. There are now 550 pairs nesting in the country, although it suffers badly in harsh winters because it doesn't migrate.

Eggs and Feathers

Egg hunting still occurs, with eggs or chicks from rare birds or birds of prey being highly sought after by professional hunters, who can gain financial reward by stealing the eggs or the young birds.

Feathers have, of course, been used in various ways for thousands of years. But now it's believed that the national bird of India, the peacock, may be endangered. Although the bird was classified as a Schedule One species in the Wildlife Protection Act of 1972, the tail feathers were exempted, and the exemption clause in the Act even goes so far as to say '… tail feathers of the Peacock and the animal articles or trophies made therefrom'. Trading in feathers was also permitted, with the assumption being that this wouldn't affect the peacock population, and that any such feathers would simply be those shed from the tails of the bird. Unfortunately, this isn't the case.

In the USA, the trend for using feather ornaments in millinery and the like had a devastating effect on wild birds. It was estimated that, by 1900, two hundred *million* birds a year were being killed for their feathers. In 1884, *Forest and Stream* magazine, in an editorial, warned that 'the destruction of American wild birds for millinery purposes has assumed stupendous proportions'.

Some good came out of this though; the American Ornithological Union and the Audubon Society were founded to protect the birds and stop their slaughter for feathers.

THE RIGHTS OF THE FIRST PEOPLE

The eagle feather, so much a part of Native American tradition, has hefty fines attached to its possession. In a famous case, in 1995 a woman from Illinois made a dreamcatcher for Hillary Clinton, which contained an eagle feather. Her home was raided by the US Fish and Wildlife Service, but they believed her explanation that she'd found the feather in a zoo. She was lucky – illegal possession of an eagle feather carries a $100,000 penalty, or up to a year in jail.

However, a company shipping caviar into Baltimore-Washington International Airport wasn't so lucky. Among the consignment cases was a very elaborate Sioux war bonnet headdress, containing beads, ribbons and 33 Golden Eagle feathers. The bonnet had been 'bought' by a Special Service agent working undercover in Montana. It transpired that the bonnet had been bought from a woman who had inherited it from her father, who had been a banker handling cattle and land transactions for members of the Standing Rock Sioux tribe in the 1920s. The daughter said that her father had been given the headdress as a gift.

The caviar company was fined a massive $10.4 million dollars, after other charges were taken into account. What happened to the headdress? It was returned to the tribe; the agent from the US Fish and Wildlife Service saying,

> The Service has long recognized the importance of eagles to Native Americans and we work closely with the tribes on these and other wildlife enforcement issues … Our work to prevent profiteering in eagle items and feathers has restored a sacred headdress to the Standing Rock Sioux and demonstrated our commitment to stop illegal wildlife trafficking.

What Can We Do?

What can we do to ensure that our bird populations are not harmed? It is too easy to take the birds we see for granted, especially the small garden birds. However, even the House Sparrow, once one of the commonest birds, is dwindling; in the UK, in 1950 there were 9.5 million of these humble little birds. In 1970 there were 12 million. Now their population has declined by 62 per cent and is being flagged as of major concern to wildlife and bird organizations. But why? The infuriating thing is that no one seems to know for sure why these birds are dying. A likely reason is almost certainly to do with the shortage of insect food to feed the young in the crucial early days of life. Other possible causes are lead-free and leaded petrol, cats and mobile-phone masts.

If we want to protect our birds, we have to look to our immediate environment to start making a difference. We can make sure that nesting boxes are sited in the right direction, and we can make sure that birds are given food and water in the colder months of the year.

CATS, REFLECTIONS AND RIBBONS

In the USA, it's said that the major causes of fatalities amongst birds are cats, and the birds crashing into shiny surfaces. With cats, there's a problem, although we can make sure that our cats have collars with bells, but I learned a good tip from my friend Swan Storm, a Native American writer. She's very conscious of the wildlife around her, and when I visited her at a lodge that had huge glass windows on all sides, I noticed that she had hung coloured ribbons all the way around the building in front of the windows, to break the reflections for the birds so they wouldn't hurt themselves.

Chemicals – Leave Them On The Shelf!

Chemicals and pesticides are a big problem, too. In our desperation to have manicured lawns and gardens, we use all kinds of noxious substances, which are not only totally unnecessary but positively harmful to birds. Slug pellets, for example, have been a major contributory factor in the decline of the song thrush; the slugs eat the pellets, the birds eat the poisoned slugs, and then the bird ingests the poison. I mentioned this to someone recently whose garden was awash with the little blue pellets. The response was that the pellets were doing no harm since there were no song thrushes, anyway …

Wouldn't it be better to stop using these toxins and encourage the song thrushes simply to do the job for us?

Starlings line their nests with herbs that boost their immune systems.

Although manicured gardens can look lovely, it's worth letting some of the land 'do its own thing' so that butterflies, insects and the birds can continue to co-exist with us. They don't care how clipped your lawn is, but they certainly do like a few thistles and long grasses left lying around, and if it all gets out of hand you could tell the neighbours it's a wildlife refuge!

We sometimes need to take the time to stand and stare, to lie in the long grass and look up at the sky; sometimes we need to stop thinking we can be in control of this planet, and remember that we are a part of the whole – integrated, not separated. I suspect that if you are reading this book then you are already aware of this.

It is never too late to do something to make the world a better place for our birds. As human beings, it is our responsibility to husband the planet for all creatures.

Birds, by their quickness and intelligence and their alertness in acting upon every thought, are a ready instrument for the use of God, who can prompt their movements, their cries and songs, their pauses and wind-like flights, thus bidding some men check and others pursue to the end their course of action or ambitions. It is on this account that Euripides calls birds in general 'Heralds of God' while Socrates speaks of making himself 'a fellow servant with swans'.
Plutarch

Bird organizations around the World

UK

British Trust for Ornithology
www.bto.org.
The Nunnery
Thetford
Norfolk
IP24 2PU

Royal Society for the Protection of
    Birds (14 offices around the UK)
www.rspb.org.uk
The Lodge
Sandy
Bedfordshire
SG19 2DL

Wildfowl and Wetlands Trust
www.wwt.org.
Slimbridge
Gloucester
GL2 7BT

Wildlife Trusts
www.wildlifetrusts.org.
The Kiln
Waterside
Mather Road
Newark
Nottinghamshire
NG24 1WT

USA and Canada

American Bird Conservancy
www.abcbirds.org.
PO Box 249
The Plains
VA 20198

American Birding Association
www.americanbirding.org.
4945 North 30th Street
Suite 200
Colorado Springs
CO 80919

American Ornithologists' Union
www.aou.org
Suite 402
1313 Dolley Madison Blvd
McLean
VA 22101

Audubon Society (over 500 chapters
around the USA)
www.audubon.org
700 Broadway
New York
NY 10003

Society of Canadian Ornithologists
www.sco-soc.ca
8541 Esplanade
Montreal
Canada H2P 2S1

Australia

Birds Australia
www.birdsaustralia.com.au
415B Riverdale Road
Hawthorn East
Victoria 3123

International

Birdlife International (6 offices and
numerous associates around the
world)
www.birdlife.org
Wellbrook Court
Girton Road
Cambridge
CB3 0NA
UK

The Nature Conservancy (5 offices
around the world)
www.nature.org
4245 North Fairfax Drive
Suite 100
Arlington
VA 22203-1606
USA

Further Reading:
A Selected bibliography

Larousse Encyclopaedia of Mythology (Readers Union/Paul Hamlyn 1961)

The Penguin Dictionary of Symbols (Penguin, 1969)

Auguries and Omens, Yvonne Aburrow (Capall Bann, 1994)

Animal Speak, Ted Andrews (Llewellyn Publications, 2000)

Paulo Coelho: Confessions of a Pilgrim, Juan Arias (HarperCollins, 2001)

The Birds and Other Plays, Aristophanes (Penguin Classics, 1978)

History of Animals, Aristotle (Bohn, 1862)

The Folklore of Birds, Edward A. Armstrong (Collins, 1958)

Flight of the Wind Horse, Niema Ash, (Rider and Co, 1990)

The Life of Birds, David Attenborough (BBC Books, 1998)

Illusions, Richard Bach (Pan, 1978)

The Human Nature of Birds, Theodore Xenophon Barber (St Martin's Press, 1993)

Psychic Animals, Dennis Bardens (Barnes and Noble, 1996)

Birds and Beasts of Ancient Latin America, Elizabeth P. Benson, (University Press of Florida, 1997)

The Secret Garden, Frances Hodgson Burnett (Penguin, 1911)

The Arabian Nights, translated by Richard Burton (Routledge and Sons, 1877)

Arab Folktales, Inea Bushnaq (American University in Cairo Press, 1986)

The Hero With A Thousand Faces, Joseph Campbell (HarperCollins, 1993)

The Alchemist, Paulo Coelho (HarperCollins, 1999)

An Illustrated Encyclopaedia of Symbols, J.C. Cooper (Thames and Hudson, 1982)

Sacred Feathers, Maril Crabtree (Adams Media Corporation, 2002)

Shamanism; Archaic Techniques of Ecstasy, Mircea Eliade (Penguin, 1989)

Beyond Painting And Other Writings By The Artist And His Friends, Max Ernst (Wittenborn, Schultz, 1948)

The Conference of the Birds, Farid Ud-din Attar (Penguin Classics, 1984)

On Divination and Synchronicity, Marie-Louise Von France (Inner City Books, 1980)

The Golden Bough, J.G. Frazer (Macmillan and Co, 1957)

Les Demeures Philosophales/ The Dwellings of the Philosophers, Jean-Julien Fulcanelli (Archive Press and Communications, 1994)

Le Mystere des Cathedrals, Jean-Julien Fulcanelli, (Archive Press and Communications, 1999)

The Druid Animal Oracle, Philip and Stephanie Carr-Gomm (Simon and Schuster, 1994)

The Birth of Western Civilisation, edited by Michael Grant (Thames and Hudson, 1964)

The White Goddess, Robert Graves (Faber and Faber, 1960)

All The Birds Of The Air, Francesca Greenoak (Book Club Associates, 1979)

The Mabinogion, translated by Lady Charlotte Guest (Dover Publications, 1997)

The Language of the Birds, edited by David M. Guss (North Point Press, 1985)

The Gift of Birds, edited by L. Habegger and A.G. Carlson (Travellers' Tales, 1999)

Bird Lore, C. E. Hare (Country Life Ltd, 1952)

The Ornithology of Shakespeare, James Edmund Harting (Gresham Books, 1978)

Ravens in Winter, Bernd Heinrich (Vintage, 1990)

The Fowles of Heaven, Harrison Hoeniger (University of Austin at Texas, 1972)

The Odyssey, Homer

Birds in Legend Fable and Folklore, Ernest Ingersoll (Longmans, Green and Co., 1923)

The Origins of Consciousness in the Breakdown of the Bicameral Mind, Julian Jaynes (Houghton Mifflin, 1976)

Hunting The Wren, Elizabeth Atwood Lawrence (University of Tennessee Press, 1997)

The Cult of the Green Bird, Antony Clare Lees (Scotforth Books, 2002)

The Gods and Symbols of Ancient Egypt, Manfred Lurker (Thames and Hudson, 1974)

The Folklore of Birds, Laura C. Martin (Globe Pequet Press, 1993)

The Penguin Book of Bird Poetry, edited by Peggy Munsterberg (Penguin, 1984)

Birds in Greek Life and Myth, J. Pollard (Thames and Hudson, 1997)

Birds of the World, Austin Singer (The Reprint Society, 1963)

A Little Bird Told Me So, Eleanor H. Stickney (Rutledge Books, 1997)

The Secret History, Donna Tartt (Penguin, 1992)

Religion and the Decline of Magic, Keith Thomas (Weidenfeld and Nicolson, 1971)

Pueblo Birds and Myths, Hamilton A. Tyler (University of Oklahoma Press, 1979)

The Book of Beasts, T.H. White (Readers Union/Jonathan Cape, 1956)

The Nature of the Divine

Although this book purports to be about birds and their language and messages, what this book is really about is discovering the nature of the Divine.

As human beings we have invented all kinds of barriers and distractions to keep us rooted firmly in the part of the world which appears to be material. However, I hope this book will help towards a greater understanding of how to recognize these restraints for what they are, and to 'let go' of some of the ideas and concepts left over from a time when we needed tangible explanations for just about everything. I'd like to see if we can get back to the state before words were needed quite so much and when we 'knew', without having to ask, both the question and the answer.

Our development as creatures of Earth has been extraordinary; we are capable, and intelligent, and inventive, but I feel that we need to re-awaken the skills and talents that belonged to such peoples as the Native American Indians, the Druids and the Ancients. We know now that they may not have been right about everything, but if we can combine the latent powers of our intuition with the knowledge acquired from generations of education, philosophy, music, physics and the arts, then we could truly start to fly, to be at one, in our minds, with the birds of the air … then we could really start to explore profound vistas of new knowledge and understanding.

And speaking of the Heavenly …

I've had an extraordinary amount of help, from both birds and people, especially in my initial investigations. So a big thanks to all the following divine beings!

A big thank you to the birds who helped with my research.

Albatross
Mark Craig
Alan Ward
Emma Holton-Craig
Adrian Bossey
Paul Bailey
Simone Johnson

Bird of Paradise
Debbie Lamb

Blackbird
Penny Holton
Wilsey Mockett
Helen Shepperd
Alex Layzell
Joggs Camfield
Ross
Nathan Jones
Chris Turtell
Sian Morgan

Bluebird
Mia Crowhurst
Sarah Coursey

Bluetit
Izzy Heath

Buzzard
Ben Fuest
Ben David
Matthew Regan
Robert Whiting
Herbie Hancox

Canada Goose
Angi Thomas
Suzi Nashimura

Cassowary
Andy Imogene

Cockatoo
Colin Johnson
 (Sulphur
 Crested)
Mark Moore

Condor
Adrian Seary
Natasha Seary
Rachel James
Spike Lion
Jonathan Sumpton
Zak Lewis-Smith
Natalia Dorey
Susan Green
Silke Svensen
Tory Blacker
Naomi Guinness
Carly Carlton
Polly Jensen

Crow
Jill Pliskin
Drew McConnell
Mick Jones

Cuckoo
Steffan Schneider
Arthur Layzell

Curlew
Elizabeth Daniel

Dove
Mike Alway
Gill Evans
Marina Rendle

Margaret Davies
Bill Price
Catherine Maggs
Graziana Luca
Pierre Schmidt
Susan Williams
Stephanie Dorling
Marsha Engel
Pat Layzell

Duck
Vivien Goldman
David McAlmont

Dunnock
Simon

Eagle
Andrew Catlin
Reuben Fuest
 (Golden)
Volente Lloyd
Paul Khera (Black)
Philip Carr-Gomm
Tim Bricheno
 (Snow)
Tony Layzell
Finlay Cowan
Martin Heath
Jayme Tovey
 (Golden)
Toby Hollowell
Robert Plant
Lisa Johnson
Pritty Patel
Reavis Daniel Moore
Michaelis Mitikaides
Brandon McWhorter
Bobs Littlechild
Doug Browning

Emu
Bob Brimson

Flamingo
Netty Turner
Kas Armstrong
Rhodri Viney
Cerys Regan

Flycatcher
Davina Hogg

Gannet
Alexis Williams

Goose
Sarah Coursey
Sarah Christie (Pink-
 footed)
Yoshi Horito
Blake Stedman

Goshawk
Finlay Cowan

Greenfinch
Stanley Green Finch

Guinea Fowl
Marina Rendle

Hawk
Jont Whittington
Jon Naramine
Martin Jones
David Melbye
Boubacar Saye
Jonathan Sumpton
Clara Jones
Melissa Wilson

Doug Browning
Matilda Wright
Peter Strang
Douglas Evans
Cleve Jones
Steve Alberti

Heron
Jean Jacques Smoothie

Hobby
Luke Sutherland

Hoopoe
Rose Pomeroy
Caroline Danby

Hummingbird
Jeanne McKenzie
Beryl Nozedar
Chris Tine
Stephanie Carr-
    Gomm
Lupa Mabuse
Wendy Stefanelli
Corey Matthews
Fabrice Eckhardt
Marie Frieda
Inez Capaldi
Natalia Ferucci
Artemis Cooper
Lucy Fuest

Jackdaw
Brychan Llyr
David Handford

Kestrel
Chris Limb
Tex Tiger Alice

Kingfisher
Jont Whittington
Lucy Fuest
Lyndall Fernie

Kite
Gavin Hogg
Mia Crowhurst

Loon
Dave from Detroit

Lory
Charlie Budden

Magpie
Peter Doherty
Mike Davies
Lee Turtell
Lynn Regan

Merlin
Sarah Wills
David Vanetta
Dikka

Mynah Bird
David Little

Nightingale
Simon Edwards
Linda Halls
Landsley Ware

Nightjar
Mark Ferelli

Nuthatch
Judy Roland

Osprey
Bob Sharples

Owl
Louise Brimson
Alison Fuest
Bernie Plain
Rosie Whiting
Andrew Harrison
Dan Tovey
Helen Price
Mog Yoshihara
Gillian Davis
Kate Smoothie
Mariella Morgan
Lily Featherstone
Cathy Marchant
Siobhan Brown
Danny Hagan

Parakeet
Lars Jensen

Parrot
Priscilla Miller

Partridge
Marina Rendle

Peacock
Elizabeth Daniel
Vanessa Sanders
Bronwen Stanzler
Robert Harlow
Ptolemy Mann

Penguin
Eilir Whiting
David Chubb
Tallis

Peregrine Falcon
Jonathan Morgan
Michaelis Mitikaides
Mark Watts
Volker Bertelman
Chris Lewis
B.D. Foxmoor
Dylan Fowler

Phoenix
Sophie Carr-Gomm
John Crowhurst
Lou Smith

Pigeon
Sian Coggins
Patrick Walden

Puffin
Cassie Rendle
Ursula Brimson

Quail
Cassie Rendle

Raven
Theo Chalmers
Ashley Mcavoy
Marina Rendle
Derrick Coyle
Teco Fuchs
Leonie Petriades
Jon Spong
Gareth Greenaway
Josias Damasceno
Jimmy Page
Josh Levendis
Twinkle McRoy
Steve Featherstone
William Wainwright

Tom Ingraham

Red Kite
Sam Whiting

Red-Tailed Hawk
Phil O'Sulluvian

Robin
Robin Wealleans
Joseph Fuest
Rhiannon Davies
Robert Fuest
Jo Feldman
Deby Crowhurst
Robin Baker
Rachel Mari Kimber
Lydia Durkan
Steven Cook
Trevor Nozedar

Seagull
Ioanna Anastassiou
James Kelly
Fox Longbow
Neil Arthur
Robin Wealleans
Adam Fuest
Olly Maggs
Katie Whiting
Sam Taylor
Joshua Hogg
Matthew Green
Becca Drury

Lloyd George
John Guilfoyle

Simurgh
Oscar Van Gelden

Siskin
Guy Davies

Skylark
Melangell Jones
Chris Bradshaw

Song Thrush
Jill Stevens
Cassie Rendle
Carol Williams

Sparrow
Robert Tepoel
Mark Fellis

Starling
Alan G. Jones
Dan McAlister
Fleur O'Malley

Swallow
Carla Edgley
Paul Edgley
Izzy Edgley
Alison Wilson
Tim Jibson
Paula Gardiner

Swan
Swan Storm
Mee
Susannah Renwick
Marina Rendle
Leana Zuniga
Yolante Tsiabokolou
Kristina Lyon
Joy Browning
Meenakshi Devi
    Bhavanani
Sarah Muckerjee
Jane Fuest
Dora Keegan
Selena Moore
Stacey Moon
Amy Genevieve
    Swan Marchant
Kalavathi Devi

Swift
Janette Swift
Joe Stafford
Jo Bartlett
Gilly Fuest

Thunderbird
Dion Fischer

Toucan
Jan Cotgrove

Vulture
Antony Littlechild

Adam Ficek
Cedric Bezinque
Sam Maggs

Whipoorwill
Janette Beckman

Woodpecker
Sheila Osborne
Terry Woolmer
Laura Inglese
Mairead O'Leary
Phillipe La Plante
Bryn Espinoza
Brian Flynn
Maurice Dickson
Lili Mae Smith
Harriet Fuest

Wren
Charlie Carr-Gomm
Caroline Danby
Alan Cooper
Tim Borrill
Sarah Gregory
Tanya
Margaret Regan
Libby Richards
Megan Hazlitt
Carla Ryan
Vita Pollock

Yellow Weaver
Helen Shepperd

Special thanks must go to several total strangers, who have given their time, knowledge and advice to ensure that I've got my facts right. These include:

Dr Frannie Berdan, California State University
Dr Richard Thomas, Birdlife International, UK

Ian Peters and all at the Royal Society for the Protection of Birds, UK
   (www.rspb.org)
Professor Erich D. Jarvis, Duke University Medical Center, Durham, North
   Carolina
Pat Durham, National Eagle Repository, US Fish and Wildlife Service,
   Colorado
Caroline Ingraham, ISAAP, IIAEA (Ingraham Institute of Aromatic Extracts
   for Animals). Caroline is currently the only person in the world using
   aromatic oils to treat dangerous big cats – special thanks for the invaluable
   information about the vomeronasal organ in birds (www.ingraham.co.uk)

Alan Sandstrom
Dr Louis Lefebvre, McGill University, Montreal
Michael Szabo and all at the New Zealand Royal Forest and Bird Protection
   Society
Jean-Claude and Roxanne Flornoy, Sainte Suzanne, France (www.letarot.com)
Dennis William Hauck, Master Alchemist, Flamel College, and Andrea
   Zuckavich (www.alchemylab.org)
Derrick Coyle, Ravenmaster of the Great Tower of London, and Natasha
   Woollard, PR Manager at the Tower of London.
Stephen Moss

Thanks to the following poets who kindly allowed me to use some of their
work:

Jeffery Beam, USA (Mockingbird): Jeffery was born in North Carolina and is
the poetry editor of the print and online journal *Oyster Boy Review*, which
any sentient being should subscribe to immediately. Jeffery is also a botanical
librarian at UNC Chapel Hill. His award-winning works of poetry include
Visions of Dame Kind (Jargon Society, 1995), *An Elizabethan Bestiary Retold*
(Horse and Buggy, 1997) and *The Fountain* (NC Wesleyan College Press,
1992). His new and selected spoken-word CD collection, *What We Have Lost*,
was a 2003 Audio Publishers Association Award Finalist. Among several
current projects Jeffery is working on a libretto for an opera based on the
Persephone Myth. You can read more of his poetry at his website:
www.unc.edu-jeffbeam/index.html.

Tom Berman, Israel (Stork): Tom is Emeritus Research Professor at the
Kinneret Limnological Lab at Migdal in Israel. He has lived at the Kibbutz
Amiad in the Upper Galilee, Israel, for more than 50 years. He's a scientist
specializing in aquatic microbiology – hence the association with the Sea of

Galilee. He's Editor in Chief of the annual *Voices Israel Anthology*, and I highly recommend you get on to Amazon to buy his gorgeous book, *Shards, A Handful Of Verse*. It's published by the Writers Club Press.

Nancy Carlson Ness, USA (Swan): Nancy Ness lives in Cape Cod, Massachusetts, and is never far away from the ocean, which she loves. Poetry is an absolutely essential part of her psyche – she reads it, writes it and teaches it. She also has a special relationship with one of Ernest Hemingway's cats, but don't tell anyone. You can read more of her work at her website: www.netpoets.net.

Sarah Coursey, UK (Swan): Sarah was born in 1976 in Southampton, New York. She studied literature, history and film studies at Mount Holyoke College and has since lived as what she describes as an 'urban nomad' in search of treasure and inspiration, her travels taking her to the outposts of New York, Rome, Munich and London. On good days, she says modestly, she fancies herself a writer.

Jont, USA (Hawk/Kingfisher hybrid): Among other things, Jont is a poet, songwriter and performer, and organizer (since 1977) of the free event, 'Unlit', a nomadic hybrid of a party and a gig celebrating the invisible connection between the audience and the performer. He was told that the definition of healing is being present and loving, and he was very thankful he'd heard that. For more, go to www.jontmusic.net.

Elene Kurtesz, Hungary (her bird is a secret): Elene was born in 1977, in Los Angeles, but moved back to the home of her ancestors in 1991. She lives in a cabin in the forests, essentially alone apart from her mynah bird and several cats, who, she says, share an uneasy living arrangement. Elene's cabin has no electricity, running water or other modern conveniences except for her laptop (which she charges from a solar panel), and a bread-making machine, an unwanted gift she uses to store bird seed in. She feels that, rather than living at the edge of civilization, she has found her space in the centre of it. She is a qualified medical herbalist, astrologer and psychic. She has no website but can be contacted through me.

Thank you to my mother, Jeanne McKenzie, who had the patience to teach me how to read.

Thanks to Caroline Danby, for invaluable additional research and to Theo Chalmers, for help and encouragement. And thanks to Ysanne Spevack for the contact and some timely swan information.

A colossal thank you to Finlay Cowan, who worked tirelessly to produce the illustrations inside this book, well into the dawn hours, accompanied occasionally by an owl on the window ledge; thanks are also due to Janette Swift and Tyler Swift Cowan.

I need to thank many people for straightforward inspiration and enlightenment: *Namas te* to all my friends at the Ananda Ashram, Pondicherry, but especially to Amma, Meenakshi Devi Bhavanani and Dr Ananda Balayogi Bhavanani, both a source of constant inspiration; and to all members of Rishiculture around the world.

Thanks to Matthew Bellamy, Chris Wolstenholme and Dominic Howard of Muse (Swan, Eagle, Raven), without whom this book may well have never been written.

Thanks to Tim Borrill for the loan of some fantastic old books, which smell amazing, and to Chris Bradshaw for turning me on to Dafydd ap Gwilym.

To Hyemeyohsts Storm, Swan Storm, Fox Longbow and Jade.

To Philip, Stephanie, Sophie and Charlie Carr-Gomm and all at the Order of Bards, Ovates and Druids (www.druidry.org).

At HarperCollins, thanks to:

Wanda Whiteley (Robin/Kingfisher hybrid)
Jacqui Caulton (Raven)
Laura Scaramella (Eagle)
Nathalie Revel (Owl/Crane hybrid)
Anne Cox (Male Zebra Finch)
Gail Simpson (Penguin)
Katy Carrington and Sarah Christie (both secret birds)
Simon Gerratt (Eagle)

A specially huge thanks to Charlotte Ridings (Woodpecker) who undertook the editing of this book.

Thanks to Bran, Branwen, Hugin, Munin, Gwylum, Gundulf, Baldric, George and Hardy, and to all the other noble ravens of the Great Tower of London. Thanks for all your hard work, and the hard work of your predecessors, repelling invaders from the green shores of Albion.

Special thanks to Jont, and a timely kingfisher, and to Paul, and a timely raven, and to Adam, and a timely ghost.

Adele Nozedar

Index

Conley, Pamela 327
conservation 503–14
cormorant 353
    divinities 497
Corvid family 24–5, 70, 98,
    247, 290, 331
    see also crow; jackdaw; jay;
    magpie; raven
Coues, Elliott 181
Coyle, Derrick 330, 331, 333
Crabtree, Maril 134
crane 361–6
    and the alphabet 5–6, 362,
    365
    Celtic tradition 147, 365–6,
    484
    divinities 497
    symbolism 484
creation myths 22–3
    ancient Greece 126
    egg in 126–7
    Philippines 50, 381
    Yokut 300–1
Cree Indians 320, 412–13,
    477
Creek Indians 274
crow 289–96
    alchemical meditation
    225–6, 232–3, 235
    alchemical symbolism
    222
    in augury 62, 63, 145, 291
    Celtic tradition 145, 147–8,
    293
    divinities 497
    Egyptian hieroglyphics 176
    feathers 137
    intelligence 24–5
    language 26, 291
    Native American tradition
    200–1, 293–4, 485
    Pancha Pakshi Shastra 84
    superstitions 473
    symbolism 485
    in tasseography 59
    Yokut creation myth 300–1
Cu bird 37
Cúchulain 336, 469
cuckoo 9, 72, 160
    divinities 497
    New Zealand 159–60
    superstitions 473
    symbolism 485
Cukulcan 188
Cupid 371
curlew 146
    superstitions 473

Daedalus 262
Dartford warbler 510
Demeter 182, 500
Devil/Satan 245, 248, 262,
    292, 297–8, 377, 403, 476,
    477, 483
Diomedas 358
Dionysius 443
Dionysus 250, 377, 500
diver see loon
divination 2–3, 55–9
    Celtic tradition 144–5
divinities 496–502
    bird relationships 497–9
Djuwe 166
Dodo 506–7
Dogon people 126, 259, 490
double-headed eagle 411–12
dove 13, 181, 240–6
    African messenger 175
    divinities 66, 137, 497
    gift of language 188
    Native American tradition
    204, 243
    Old Testament 11–12, 241
    superstitions 474
    symbolism 485–6
    in tasseography 59
    Virgo 89–91
dreamcatchers 138
dreams 57–8, 71, 81
    shamanistic 215–16
Druids 62, 80, 146, 391, 416
    blackbird 285–6
    'Crane Knowledge' 365–6
    raven 336
    swan-feather cloaks 130,
    144, 354
    wren 145, 149, 150, 280,
    281
duck 296–302
    divinities 497
    superstitions 474
    symbolism 486
    in tasseography 59
    weather lore 2, 293
    Yokut creation myth 300–1
Durham, Pat 197

eagle 72, 406–17
    in alchemy 222
    in augury 63, 65, 77
    divinities 497
    Egyptian hieroglyphics 176
    Leo 85, 117–19
    and Mexico City 77,
    189–90, 413

Native American tradition
    130, 137, 195–6, 412–13,
    486, 512–13
    in shamanism 208, 212, 214
    symbolism 486
    tool use 27
    vision 30, 407–8
    Yokut creation myth 300–1
earth element birds 238–84
    astrology 85–94
Easter Island 358
eggs 125–8
    hunting 512
    'lightning eggs' 173
    ostrich 126, 256–7, 258
Egypt, ancient 176–9
    Ba 34
    Benu 35
    bird symbolism 484, 485,
    486, 487, 488, 489, 490,
    492, 493, 495
    Cosmic Egg 127
    crane 364
    dove 242, 486
    duck 299
    eagle 415, 486
    falcon 177–8, 421, 487
    goose 370, 487
    heron 304, 488
    hoopoe 426
    kite 380
    ostrich 178, 258, 490
    owl 323, 490
    parrot 443
    peacock 451
    Phoenix period 45
    raven 339, 493
    Sphinx 178–9
    stork 346, 493
    swallow 468
    vulture 178, 394–5, 495
    wren 282
Eider Duck 297
Elephant Bird 48–9, 505
Eliade, Mircea 207, 213, 214,
    216
Elf Owl 317
England 281, 324, 325, 352,
    475, 479, 480
Eriu 80
Ernst, Max 216–17
Erui 145
Eskimos 332, 378
Etach 145
Etruscans 58, 258
Europe 263, 285, 334, 447,
    474, 484

crane 366
crow 292
magpie 259
peacock 447, 478
woodpecker 401, 403
extinct birds 505–7
    New Zealand 154–6, 506
Eye of Horus 421

faerie realms 253–4, 337
falcon 418–23
    ancient Egypt, 177–8, 421,
    487
    divinities 497
    symbolism 487
falconry 419–20
familiars 212
Fancha 251
fantail 158–9
Faro 469, 500
Feathered Serpent 188
feathers 129–38
    dove 243
    Druid cloaks 130, 144, 354
    eagle 130, 137, 195–6,
    412–13, 512–13
    Eider Duck 297
    goose 132, 368
    heron 303
    ostrich 130, 131, 178, 257,
    258
    peacock 131, 169, 447, 478,
    512
    Peruvian feather work 191
    in shamanism 14–15, 130,
    214–15
    trade 131, 512–13
    turkey 202, 275
    wren legend 283
Feng Huang 37
fire dimension 7, 187–8
fire element birds 404–69
    astrology 113–22
First World War 19, 20
flamingo 308
flight 210–11
flightless birds 153–6
Flornoy, Jean-Claude 13
Fokulon 250
France 81, 248, 279, 281, 290,
    292, 300, 366, 400, 401,
    479, 481, 485
    wagtail 276
Francis of Assisi 16
Franklin, Benjamin 273, 411
Freyja 15, 130, 373, 422, 500
Fulani people 464

THE SECRET LANGUAGE OF BIRDS

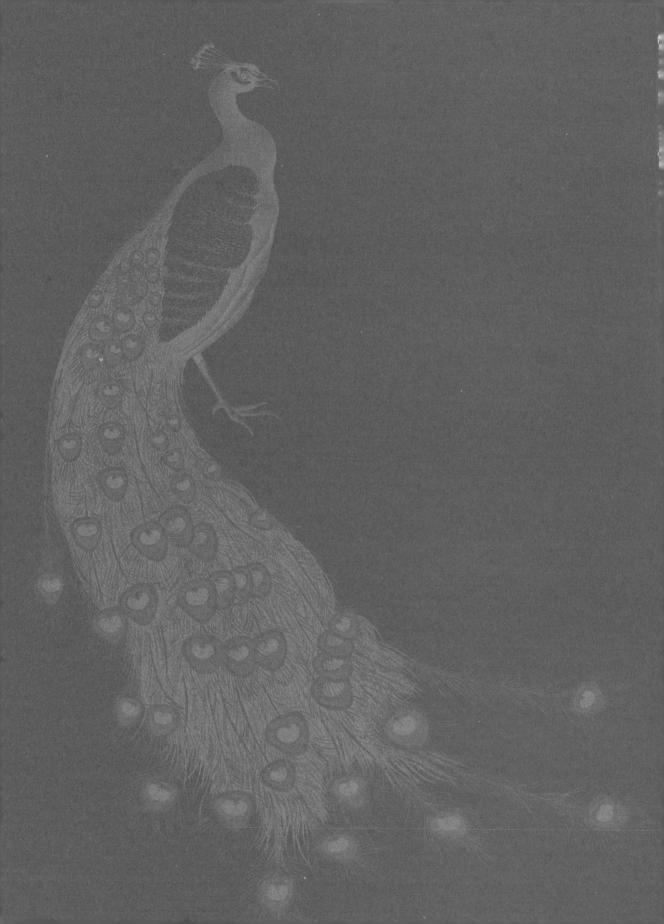